WINGS
Like Eagles

WINGS
Like Eagles

*The Story of Soaring
in the United States*

Paul A. Schweizer

SMITHSONIAN INSTITUTION PRESS

WASHINGTON and LONDON

First paperback edition 1989

Library of Congress Cataloging-in-Publication Data

Schweizer, Paul A., 1913–
   Wings like eagles : the story of soaring in the United States /
Paul A. Schweizer.
   Includes index.
   ISBN 0-87474-828-3.   ISBN 0-87474-803-8 (pbk.)
   1. Gliding and soaring—United States—History.   I. Title.
TL760.4.U6S37 1988
   629.132′31′09—dc19   87–28850
ISBN 0-87474-828-3   CIP

   ∞ The paper used in this publication meets the
minimum requirements of the American National Standard
for Performance of Paper for Printed Library Materials Z39. 48—1984.

   Edited by Venka V. Macintyre

   *Cover illustration: The Schweizer Sprite flies over Harris Hill,
with the National Soaring Museum and glider hangars below.*

10 9 8 7 6 5 4 3 2
97 96 95 94 93 92 91 90 89

Contents

Preface

The first national soaring contest was held in 1930 and the Soaring Society of America (SSA) was formed in 1932, but it was not until 50 years later that the history of soaring in the United States attracted much attention. In fact, there was no such history except for the brief review that Capt. Ralph S. Barnaby (USN Ret.) wrote in 1965 for the *American Soaring Handbook* (which was expanded in 1974 by Victor Saudek). Barnaby's overview was necessarily brief, however, because only a limited number of pages were allocated to each subject in the American Soaring Handbook Series. A more complete history needed to be written while those who were involved in motorless flight during the late 1920s and 1930s were still around and could help both in gathering the facts and in confirming information that was on hand.

No one, as far as I knew, was working on such a history. Since I had accumulated extensive files during the more than fifty years of my involvement with the soaring movement, I decided to go ahead and write one. This book is the result of that decision. In putting it together I have made use of these files, as well as the SSA files and the archives of the National Soaring Museum (NSM).

This history covers the development of gliding and soaring in the United States and automatically includes the history of the Soaring Society of America, since the two are inex-

tricably woven together. The period I am covering is principally the 50 years from 1932, when the SSA was formed, to 1982, when the SSA celebrated its 50th anniversary. I have tried to write this history from a national point of view, but in order to keep the book a reasonable length I have had to limit the discussions to the most significant events that occurred and to the people involved. This has proven to be a frustrating experience for I would have liked to include many other events and the people involved. There are a lot more details that can be told, and I hope that others will do this and help to record and preserve all the history of soaring in the United States.

I have used sidebars to present information that is not part of the formal history but that will add to the understanding of a particular event or situation. I have also used this device to cover some of the experiences and viewpoints of the Schweizers in order to help to explain the situation at a particular time and to give the reader another viewpoint.

In gathering historical information from those who were involved in the early days, one quickly learns that some people have difficulty remembering the precise details. Soaring is such a fascinating sport that it often induces daydreaming, and thus in looking back one may confuse the daydreams with the facts. Whenever this seemed a possibility, I carefully checked that particular source against other available information before using it.

In writing this book, I have had the help of many people, in and out of soaring, who not only located information and photographs, but also assisted me in other ways. I want to thank them all for their generous support. I also want to thank various members of the Schweizer family for their help with various aspects of the project, and particularly my wife, Virginia. She played an important part in gathering material and information and in typing the seemingly endless revised versions of the manuscript. She has participated in soaring since 1940, being active in competition and training in the 1940s and 1950s, and in the promotion of soaring since that time. Her comments have been invaluable.

For quick reference, I have provided a yearly fact sheet in the back of the book listing the main event of the year, along with the awards given each year and the names of the SSA officers and directors. A list of the abbreviations used is also provided.

Chapter 1

The Beginning of Motorless Flight

Introduction

The history of soaring is in part the story of man's creation of motorless planes and their evolution from the primitive gliders of the early days to the sophisticated sailplanes of today. It is also the story of the progress in flying them, from the erratic flights that were first measured in seconds and feet, to the present soaring records that are measured in high speeds, great heights, and distances approaching a thousand miles!

The history includes the activity of many dedicated people whose efforts through the years have advanced both the sport and the science of motorless flight. These are the people who have not only enjoyed its challenge, but who have derived from soaring an inner satisfaction that goes beyond the usual zeal for a sport. To some it is like being involved in a "cause." At times the beauty, the thrill, and the challenge infuse the participant with a sense of spiritual strength. I hope that the title of the book, which was taken from a passage in Isaiah, conveys to the reader something of this feeling, which is akin to mounting up with "wings like eagles."

Lloyd Licher, who was executive director of the Soaring Society of America for many years, touched on this feeling in his article in the May 1982 golden anniversary issue of *Soaring:*

I have always believed that the Soaring Society of America was much more than some employees, an office, a magazine, some members and a Board of Directors. What it really is relates to the members and their collective and individual senses of what it means to belong to a group of like-minded enthusiasts. Elected representatives may tend to give it guidance and direction, and a staff may effect their biddings, but in the end it is within the individual member that the essence of the Society resides. One doesn't join SSA as much as he joins an idea, the concept of flying free, wheeling and soaring aloft in a way that only certain birds and fellow enthusiasts may experience, either directly or vicariously.

One of the first questions that the uninitiated ask is how to tell the difference between gliders and sailplanes, and gliding and soaring. They wonder which terms to use. Those involved in motorless flight add to the confusion by using these terms almost interchangeably. The reason for this dates back to the early days, when motorless aircraft were very crude and inefficient and soaring techniques had not yet been developed. Thus most flights consisted of gradual descents to the ground. The downward flight was called "gliding" and the craft used was called a "glider."

In England, the term "gliding" is still used to refer to all motorless flight activity, whereas in the United States we try to use the words "sailplane" and "soaring" to cover all motorless flight activities. This practice began when the Soaring Society of America was formed and it wanted to differentiate between its "soaring" and the "gliding" of the National Glider Association.

As motorless flight developed, designers made their gliders more efficient and controllable so that when they were flown in areas where updrafts occurred, flights could be extended and greater heights could be reached. The term "sailplane" refers to these advanced motorless craft and "soaring" to these upward flights. When sailplanes can no longer find upward air currents to sustain them, they are said to "glide" back to earth.

As soaring techniques improved, knowledge of meteorology increased and sensitive instruments became available. Soon it became possible to soar in any glider, or airplane for that matter, if the upcurrents were strong enough. As a result, the distinction between the two sets of terms became less important.

The reason that both terms are still used is that the government agency in charge of aviation in the 1930s, the Bureau of Air Commerce (now called Federal Aviation Administration), introduced the terms "gliders" and "gliding" in its regulations. Because the bureau was mainly concerned with the basic requirements and regulations for the pilot and the craft rather than the soaring phase, both sets of terms came into use.

This book follows the development of motorless flight beginning with Orville Wright's soaring flight of 1911, through the changes up to 1982. It covers only briefly the accomplishments of the pioneers before the Wrights, since their history has often been told. Like other forms of flight, however, soaring owes much to these pioneers. They strived hard to achieve flight.

One of the first of these pioneers was Leonardo da Vinci, who in the 15th century designed a number of flying machines, but unfortunately based them on the impractical wing-flapping principle. If he had gone further with his aeronautical designs, he might very well have produced a fixed-wing glider. Adequate material existed at that time and da Vinci had the ingenuity and skill so that a fixed-wing glider could have been built and flown. Soaring might have followed, for by watching the soaring birds, da Vinci could have learned how to soar with the aid of upward moving air in its various forms—the lift from the wind deflected from natural slopes, such as those that gulls find along cliffs; the rising air from the solar heating of the earth, which supports the flight of hawks and buzzards, for example; or the wave action from the winds that blow over ridges or ocean waves and that aquatic birds use to sustain flight. If da Vinci had been successful, one can only speculate how far soaring might have progressed in the 400 years between his time and 1903, when technology produced an engine that made powered flight possible.

During the 19th century, Sir George Cayley, Percy Pilcher, Prof. John J. Montgomery, and many others added to man's knowledge of flight through their continuing efforts to fly. Of this early group, Otto Lilienthal used the most scientific approach to the problem. Although his progress in achieving stability and control was slow, he made many gliding flights. Unfortunately, on August 9, 1896, he lost control of his glider and "nosedived" into the ground. His injuries proved to be fatal.

For the Wright Brothers, the quest for flight had started as curiosity, but soon became a consuming passion. They worked as a scientific team and were thorough in their approach to flying. Furthermore, they had the insight to identify the precise problems that needed to be solved if man was to fly, something that previous designers had not been able to do. They carefully studied the designs and experiments of other pioneers and followed Lilienthal's progress, in particular, with great interest. They were shocked when he was killed, but rather than being discouraged by this accident, they resolved to meet the challenge of flight head on. They were convinced that a system could be developed to improve the stability and controllability of gliders in flight.

The Wrights had many contacts with Octave Chanute, the famous structural engineer who was also trying to design a flyable glider. He gave them useful advice on how to design their first glider, which was based on a biplane design similar to the one that Chanute and his assistant Augustus Herring had developed.

The Wrights also asked Chanute for advice on the best place to fly their gliders. They wanted a site with steady winds of 15 miles an hour or more. Chanute suggested the coastal region of the Carolinas. When the Wrights contacted the U.S. Weather Bureau, it referred them to the weather station at Kitty Hawk, which had the favorable wind conditions they were looking for. Thus, they settled on Kitty Hawk as the site for their tests. Unknown to them at the time, the site had other advantages that would also greatly improve their chances of success.

For one thing, the soft sand dunes provided gentle slopes that permitted them to extend their glider flights and ease their landings. In addition, the combination of the slope of the dunes and the steady strong winds provided an upward thrust that enabled them to prolong their glider flights.

Kitty Hawk's greatest advantage was its location at sea level and its cooler temperature. This gave a low-density altitude, which was a favorable factor in their glider tests and of major importance in achieving their first powered flight. As Harry Combs points out in his book *Kill Devil Hill*, the density altitude during the first powered flight at Kitty Hawk on December 17, 1903, differed greatly from that during the unsuccessful tests of the Wright Flyer II at Simms Station near Dayton, Ohio, the following May. The 34-degree temperature at Kitty Hawk on December 17, 1903, gave a density altitude of *minus* 1,800 feet, whereas the 81-degree temperature at Simms Station, which is at 815 feet above sea level, gave a density altitude of *plus* 2,900 feet. This difference in density altitude of 4,700 feet between the two flights helps to explain the good results at Kitty Hawk and poor results at Simms Station.

Another factor that contributed to the Wrights' success was the great number of flights that they made. Capt. Ralph S. Barnaby (USN Ret), an authority on the Wrights and an experienced airplane and soaring pilot, points out that the Wrights had made over 1,000 flights. Barnaby suggests that some of the other pioneers may have had "flyable" designs (even though they may not have been fully controllable), but they lacked the experience to fly their gliders successfully. For example, in 1903 Charles Manley, who had no flying experience at all, made an unsuccessful attempt to fly the Langley Airdrome, whereas only a few years later Glen Curtiss and Gink Doherty, a Curtiss test pilot, proved that the Langley could fly. Even if the Langley had not had any structural problems during Manley's test, it is doubtful that he could have flown it, although it was claimed that design modifications were responsible for the success of Curtiss and Doherty.

The most important innovation of the Wrights was their combined use of wing warping and a movable vertical rudder on their 1902 glider, which enabled them to achieve, for the first time, three-axis control, which refers to the ability to completely control an aircraft in roll, pitch, and yaw. They learned how to fly with this type of control during the summer of 1902 and by the fall they were ready to design and build their first powered plane. Within a little more than a year, on December 17, 1903, they were able to make their world-famous first powered flights.

Once the Wrights had completed their first powered flight, their interest and that of most people in the aviation world turned away from gliders to powered flying. Nonetheless, a few persisted in their efforts to fly without engines since gliders were simple to build and cost less than powered craft. As Ralph S. Barnaby notes in the *American Soaring Handbook*,

> As a result of the publicity generated by the successful airplane demonstrations of the Wrights in 1908 and 1909, and their acknowledgment of the contribution of gliding to the solution of human flight, there was a slight flurry of gliding enthusiasm in the United States during the 1910–1915 period. Newspapers, popular science magazines and the like, all carried articles with plans on "How to Build a

Glider." The designs followed one general pattern—a "hang-type" glider of biplane configuration, following closely the Chanute structural pattern, modernized by the Wright developments. At least one of the early reputable airplane companies, the Witteman Brothers on Staten Island NY, built a production version of such a glider and it was in one of these gliders that a number of our soaring pioneers, such as Ralph Barnaby, Russell Holderman and Percy Pierce, got some of their flying experience.

Some of this gliding activity was carried out at a few of the New England colleges. In 1910, for example, a collegiate meet was held in Squantum, Massachusetts, in which Edward Warner, a Harvard student, won first prize in the "body-controlled class." Similar activity was under way in Germany, where a group from Darmstadt University flew rather primitive gliders at the Wasserkuppe, in the Rhoen Mountain Range, from 1907 to 1914, when the war began.

The most noteworthy activity in the United States occurred in October 1911 when Orville Wright and British flight pioneer Alec Ogilvie took Glider no. 5 to Kitty Hawk ostensibly to conduct experiments with an automatic stabilizing device that the Wrights hoped to use on their airplanes. This expedition was to have a significant impact on motorless flight.

The First Soaring Flight

On October 24, 1911, winds of 40 miles per hour swept against the North Carolina sand dunes at Kitty Hawk and were deflected upward. A motorless aircraft, the Wright Glider no. 5, maneuvered quietly above the dunes, sometimes hovering almost motionless in the sky. Its flight contin-

ued for 9 minutes 45 seconds, when a lull in the wind forced it down on the soft sand. The pilot, Orville Wright, had just made the first sustained soaring flight. The significance of the flight was not immediately recognized—it marked the beginning of the soaring movement in the world. Moreover, this flight became the first soaring duration record.

The Wright Glider no. 5 was built from parts and components of Wright airplanes that were under construction at that time. There were no drawings, and it was, apparently, what is now called "a quick and dirty" project. The early test flights at Kitty Hawk showed that a number of changes had to be made. These included a 4½-foot aft ex-tension of the fuselage, which had to be compensated for by adding a for-ward boom that carried a sandbag as a bob-weight. A number of vertical rud-ders of different sizes were tried, as well as a vertical vane mounted for-ward of the pilot that they hoped would prevent sideslipping.

Orville and Ogilvie made many flights during their stay at Kitty Hawk, the longest being Orville's world re-cord flight of 9 minutes and 45 sec-onds, on October 24, 1911. On this flight he reached a height of more than 50 feet above the hilltop.

One wonders whether Orville's interest in motorless flight was more than scientific. Or was he also at-tracted by the sporting side of soaring?

Orville Wright soars the Wright Glider no. 5 over the sand dunes of Kitty Hawk for 9 minutes and 45 seconds on October 24, 1911, the world's first sustained soar-ing flight. He established a world duration record for motorless flight that was not broken until August 29, 1921.

(Library of Congress)

Ralph S. Barnaby does not believe that this was the case. He argues that the Wrights looked upon soaring as a means of proving a theory, and that the record Orville set at Kitty Hawk was the logical result of using an improved glider and a better flying technique, and of having the right wind conditions. This theory is supported by Orville's report on that day's flying, in which he made no special mention of their record soaring flights.

However, Orville's continued interest in soaring was reflected in a letter he wrote eight years later, on December 4, 1919, to Lawrence L. Driggs:

> Our early experiments at Kitty Hawk were conducted for the purpose of developing a method of maintaining equilibrium in the air and *also to learn something about soaring flight*. At Kitty Hawk we had the opportunity of witnessing daily the soaring flights of the buzzards, fish & chicken hawks, and eagles. Attempts to imitate their flights without a motor have not been very successful, although in 1902 and 1903 we made a dozen or more flights in which we remained in the air for more than a minute with no, or scarcely any descent; and in 1911 Mr. Alec Ogilvie and I *continued* the soaring experiments at Kitty Hawk and succeeded in making a number of flights of more than five minutes duration (the longest of which was nine & three-quarters minutes) without loss of any height at all. In many cases we landed at a higher point than the one from which we started. I see no reason why flights of several hours duration cannot be made without use of a motor. But, of course, these flights must be made in rising trends of air—a condition required by all birds for soaring flight.

Another clue to the Wrights' motive is given by Victor Saudek, who had been a member of the Carnegie Tech Glider Club and was in charge of barographs at some early national soaring contests. In June of 1939, Saudek, who had just graduated from Carnegie Tech, was hitchhiking his way from Pittsburgh to Frankfort, Michigan, to take a job with the Frankfort Sailplane Corp. Saudek wanted to meet Orville Wright and so went to Frankfort by way of Dayton, Ohio. He was fortunate in being able to meet Orville, who by then was 68 years old, but in good health. Saudek remembered his firm handshake, which he said was like "cracking the whip." Saudek talked with Orville about soaring:

> In answer to my question of why he had returned to Kitty Hawk to fly gliders in 1911 when his powered airplane had been successful since 1903, his reply was, as closely as I can recall it: "We have given several answers to different people to that question; that it was to experiment with stability and controls. But, you know and we knew then that it was more fun to fly gliders than to fly powered airplanes."
>
> The question comes up: Was Mr. Wright being condescending when he gave that answer? I think not. He gave me no reason to think that at the time, though it was an answer very suited to the occasion of my imminent employment at the Frankfort Sailplane Corp.

A similar view of the purpose of the trip to Kitty Hawk was expressed by Horace Wright, a nephew of the Wright Brothers, who had been taken along by his uncle and his father, Lorin. Horace was only 10 years old at the time. When I asked him in October 1985 about the reason for Orville's trip to Kitty Hawk, he said that it was for fun. Although Horace was eighty-four when I interviewed him, his other comments regarding the trip checked with known facts and he seemed to have a clear recollection of the trip.

If one takes into account these various comments and a footnote in Orville's diary noting that "the experiments were concluded without any tests of the automatic stabilizer having been made," a case can be made that soaring was one of the reasons for the expedition to Kitty Hawk, that Orville was probably the first soaring enthusiast, and that this famous flight marked the beginning of the soaring movement in the world.

Regardless of what Orville's motives were, he demonstrated the possibilities of soaring. The world record that he set stood for almost 10 years before it was broken by Dr. Wolfgang Klemperer in Germany. It was not until 1929, almost 18 years later, that an American was able to beat Orville's national record.

The 1911 flying expedition was the last one that the Wrights made to Kitty Hawk. It is now remembered most for the world record soaring flight.

Development of Motorless Flight

After World War I aviation activity in the United States was increasingly taken up with the design and construction of powered aircraft. The rapid expansion of military aviation during the war had shown that airplanes had great commercial possibilities. As a result, glider activity received little attention in the United States following the war. In Germany, however, gliding soon started again since the restrictions with the Treaty of Versailles that prohibited the Germans from building powered airplanes did not apply to gliders. Therefore gliding gave them the opportunity to continue to be active in flying, which had a strong following not only among the country's engineers, scientists, and technical people, but also among influential Germans, who thought it was important to keep Germany involved in aviation.

As early as 1919 glider enthusiasts gathered for an informal get-together on the Wasserkuppe, the mountain in central Germany where the Darmstadt group had carried out its early glider experiments. The smooth slopes were excellent for gliding and, as would soon be discovered, also ideal for soaring.

In 1920 Oskar Ursinus, a civil engineer and publisher of *Flugsport* magazine, invited Germans experimenting with gliders to participate in a competition at the Wasserkuppe. Twenty-four gliders were entered, many of primitive design and construction. The outstanding glider was the Schwarze Teufel, designed and built at Aachen University by a graduate student, Wolfgang Klemperer, and a group of fellow students. Klemperer set two records for the meet, a distance of 1,830 meters and a duration of 2 minutes 23 seconds. The Schwarze Teufel incorporated a number of new ideas—an enclosed fuselage, a thick cantilever wing, and a double-skid landing gear.

The first competition aroused such enthusiasm that a second one was held in 1921. Twice as many gliders were entered, and this time Klemperer and his group brought a new glider called the Blaue Maus, an improved version of the Schwarze Teufel. On August 20 Klemperer made a 13-minute flight that beat Orville Wright's record and won the first "C" award in the world. The "A" and "B" awards were given for gliding proficiency, while the "C" award was given for a soaring flight lasting 5 minutes or more.

Another new glider at the meet was the *Vampyr*, designed and built by

the Hanover Technical Group and flown by A. Martens, one of the students. Some of its features were to become standard elements of sailplane design for some time to come.

Later in the meet, Martens beat Klemperer's record with a flight of 15 minutes, and before the meet was over Harth, flying his crude "broomstick" glider, increased the duration record to 21 minutes.

Three National Meets in 1922

Not to be outdone by the success of the German Soaring Meets of 1920 and 1921, the French and the British held their own competitions in 1922. The French meet was held in August at Combegrasse, 22 kilometers from Clermont-Ferrand in central France. The English meet was held in October at Itford, near Brighton. Meanwhile, the Germans held yet another contest, which also took place in August and thus overlapped with the French meet. Eddie Allen, who later became famous as a Boeing test pilot, attended all three meets and wrote a comprehensive report on these competitions for the Massachusetts Institute of Technology (MIT).

Allen was a test pilot for the U.S. Army's aviation division and the National Advisory Committee for Aeronautics (NACA), but was doing graduate work at MIT at that time. He was a member of the Aeronautical Engineering Society (AES), a student organization that had first experimented with gliders in 1910. The members were much impressed with the reports of the soaring flights made by Klemperer, Martens, and Harth that summer in Germany. Since technical universities were playing an important role in the soaring activity in Germany, the AES

members encouraged MIT to become involved. In addition, the AES sponsored a glider design contest and were able to attract a total of seven entries. Impressed with the winning design of Eddie Allen and Otto Koppen, the AES then proceeded to raise about $200 and asked the society members to donate 100 hours of labor each week so that they could build the Allen-Koppen glider.

The glider was completed in May and was tested at Hog Island near Ipswich, Massachusetts. Although the group had problems with the landing gear, the glider flew quite well. After these successful glider flights, Prof. Edward Warner, advisor to the AES group, encouraged them to enter the meet in France. Thus, the alumni of MIT immediately began raising funds to make the trip possible, while the AES members concentrated on the modifications to their glider. They used a new airfoil shape and added full-span ailerons, which could also be used as flaps.

The French Meet

Twenty-five gliders were entered in the meet, but only the AES glider had been flown before. Most of the gliders were designed for lightness and low sinking speed and their performance was relatively poor in comparison with that of the German gliders that had flown the year before at the Wasserkuppe. Allen put the gliders into four categories: (1) those designed for soaring, (2) powerplanes (of that period) with engines removed, (3) hang gliders, and (4) freaks of all kinds (the product of nontechnical inventors).

The AES glider flew fairly well, but was damaged in a strong gusty

Dr. Wolfgang B. Klemperer flying the Blue Mouse over the Wasserkuppe in 1921. He broke Orville Wright's record and earned the first "C" award.

(Keystone View Co., National Soaring Museum Collection)

The MIT glider flying in Clermont-Ferrand, France, in 1922. This was the first American entry into an international glider contest. The fuselage was later covered with fabric to improve the glider's performance.
(Keystone View Co., NSM Collection)

(slender) wings, and smoother wing contours, which they achieved by covering the leading edges with plywood.

Allen had not done much flying during the contest so he stayed on after the meet. He made a last effort to fly before leaving, but the conditions were too windy with gusts. Allen lost control of the AES glider and cracked it up. That experience convinced him that the relatively heavier and more controllable features of the German gliders should be used on future U.S. designs.

wind. Although it was quickly rebuilt and improved, there was not enough time to make a sufficient number of flights to raise the glider's standings. The winner would be the glider that had the greatest total time. Because the AES group had rebuilt their glider extensively, it was considered to be a new glider and the previous flights could not be added to the total time.

Two French pilots—M. Bossoutrot and Paulhan—flying Farman gliders (airplanes without engines) won first and second place. Bossoutrot had a total of 48 minutes. The best single flight lasted only about 3 minutes.

The German Meet

The AES group then went to the Wasserkuppe for the German meet, which was already under way by the time they arrived. The performances during this meet and in the following weeks were outstanding. In the period of a week, an improved version of the Vampyr raised the soaring duration record to 1 hour, then 2 hours, and then 3 hours and 10 minutes. The German designers were making good progress in improving performance by using new airfoil shapes, high aspect ratio

The English Meet

Allen attended the English meet as an observer. It was sponsored by the Royal Aero Club and the Daily Mail newspaper and was held on a ridge in Itford near Lewes in the South Downs region, which was chosen by a survey team that had earlier been sent to the Wasserkuppe to study soaring and soaring sites. The ridge was free of trees, was 5 miles long and about 250 feet high, and could be used with either a north or south wind.

Of the nine gliders that were entered, only six had previously been flown. Some of the entries were from Germany and France. The winner was Manyrolle of France, who flew a tandem-wing design similar to the Langley airplane. Soaring conditions were excellent and he set a world duration record of 3 hours 20 minutes. This flight beat the record that F. H. Hentzen had set at the Wasserkuppe only a few weeks earlier.

Although the meet was well publicized in the *Daily Mail* and the performances were outstanding for that time, the English soaring movement surprisingly failed to get started until seven years after this event.

In a detailed report on the three meets submitted to MIT, Allen concluded that designers needed to strive for more efficient design and better control rather than light weight.

German Motorless
Flight Grows

While the rest of the aviation world was busy improving the airplane, the Germans were refining their motorless craft and soon moved far ahead of the rest of the world.

In the United States, however, little had happened since Orville's 1911 flight, except for the MIT involvment in 1922. Regretably, MIT subsequently lost interest in glider development.

Chapter 2

The Gliding Period,
1928–1931

The Evans Glider Club of America, 1928–1929

In 1927 aviation in the United States suddenly and dramatically captured public attention when Charles Lindbergh made his famous transatlantic flight. The excitement of his flight plus those of Richard E. Byrd, Clarence Chamberlain, and others stimulated many in the country to become "air-minded." Even though few could get into flying because of its high cost, there was a growing awareness that aviation would soon be changing everyone's lives.

With the growing interest in aviation, the newspapers and magazines were more receptive to news about flying. Press reports from Germany told of the rapid progress of gliding and soaring there, and many in this country hoped to see gliding make similar strides here. However, it was difficult for anyone to get started then. There were no gliding schools, and no production gliders were available until early in 1929. Those interested had to build their own so-called primary from plans, usually of the German Zoegling type, that were very sketchy. It is not surprising that many homebuilders had problems working with these plans.

Nonetheless, interest in motorless flight continued to increase and, if anything, the problems of getting

Flying caught the fancy of many teenagers but there was little that they could do except read about it. American Boy Magazine ran a series of "how to" articles on building small model airplanes that gave them a chance to become "involved" in aviation. In addition, the Airplane Model League of America encouraged young people to start model clubs throughout the nation. One such club was the Mercury Model Airplane Club, formed by a group of youngsters in Peekskill, New York. Model building increased the club members' interest in flying and encouraged them to follow developments in aviation.

started led enthusiasts to band together and eventually to form a national glider organization, at the instigation of the Aviation Bureau of the Detroit Board of Commerce.

The chairman of the Aviation Bureau was Edward S. Evans, a prominent Detroit businessman, financier, and an ardent supporter of aviation development. He was on the board of directors of several aircraft companies and he saw motorless flight as a logical way to promote aviation and to create a pool of pilots who would eventually buy and fly airplanes.

In the spring of 1928, Evans sent his two sons, Edward Jr. and Robert, who were attending school in Switzerland, to the Wasserkuppe to learn about gliding and soaring. When they returned home in the early summer and reported their experiences to their father, he decided it was time to get a glider program started in the United

A typical gliding scene in the 1928–32 period. The Detroit Gull, built by Gliders, Inc. of Orion, Michigan, is shown being launched by shock-cord, with members of the Airplane Model League of America watching.

(NSM Collection)

States. Under his encouragement, Gliders, Inc., was founded in Orion, Michigan, for the purpose of building the Detroit Gull primary glider. To stimulate interest in record flying, Evans put up a prize of $2,500 for the first soaring flight over 10 hours in duration.

The Aviation Bureau, spurred on by Evans, investigated the possibility of forming a national association, but was told that the Detroit Board of Commerce had no funds to contribute to the venture. Thereupon Evans decided to provide the financial support himself, and in August of 1928 he organized the Evans Glider Club of America. He engaged Don Walker, who had been active in Chamber of Commerce work, to act as general manager. Walker immediately started to get the organization functioning by signing up interested individuals and clubs around the United States as members.

Soaring at Cape Cod

In 1928 Evans also learned that J. C. Penney, Jr., the son of the founder of

the J. C. Penney stores, was providing the funds for the American Motorless Aviation Corp. (AMAC) glider school, which was about to conduct its first trials from the sand dunes of Cape Cod, Massachusetts. This location was a logical choice as AMAC's German pilots had gained experience in soaring the up-winds along the sand dunes at Rossitten (now Rybachiy) on the eastern shore of the Baltic Sea.

At Cape Cod, three takeoff sites were chosen for the school: one facing the west (Corn Hill in Truro) and two facing the ocean (Highland Light on the northeast shore and South Wellfleet in the center of Cape Cod).

The group's first goal was to make some outstanding flights in order to attract favorable publicity for their school. Peter Hesselbach, AMAC's chief pilot, made the first flight on July 29, 1928, launching from the dunes at Highland Light in the Darmstadt I. He stayed up 57 minutes, exceeding Orville Wright's record by more than five times. Three days later, taking off from Corn Hill, he stayed up over 4 hours. This outstanding flight was given good press coverage and made the front page of the *New York Times*.

That fall in Detroit, J. C. Penney, Jr., and Evans met for the first time and Penney promptly unfolded his grand plan: He wanted the Evans Glider Club of America to drop the name Evans and become a national organization dedicated to promoting motorless flight; a second organization would operate the Cape Cod glider school, and a third group, Gliders Inc., would produce and sell the gliders at a profit—to meet the demands created by the other two groups. It was clear that Penney was out to make a business of motorless flight. He wanted to set up a headquarters with hangars and dormitories where a profit-making school similar to the Rhoen-Rossitten Gesselschaft soaring school in Germany could be operated. Evans responded that the purpose of the Evans Glider Club of America was to promote gliding, not to make money. Evans and Penney failed to agree on the plan, and soon after Penney severed his association with AMAC and his name disappeared from the gliding scene.

The National Glider Association

Although Evans disapproved of Penney's overall plan, he did agree that the name of the Evans Glider Club of America should be changed. Thus in January 1929 it became the National Glider Association (NGA). Evans felt that the movement had too much potential to be in the hands of one individual and that it needed the financial support of others if it was to grow and fulfill its mission.

The organizational meeting of the NGA took place at the Statler Hotel in Detroit on February 6, 1929. Evans and the twelve other men present agreed that the NGA would be a nonprofit or-

The story of the flight that ran in the New York Times *made quite an impression on the members of the Mercury Model Airplane Club. The appeal of motorless flight and the lower cost of gliders gave them some hope that flying might possibly become available to them in the near future. However, they quickly realized that accidents could happen, for a few weeks later, they read in the papers that an automatic tail-release mechanism used for shock-cord launching had malfunctioned and caused Hesselbach to hit a flagpole with the Darmstadt I. Hesselbach was not hurt, but the sailplane suffered extensive damage. The metal fittings, control surfaces, and some of the other parts were later used to build Jack O'Meara's "Chanute" sailplane.*

ganization and elected the following officers: president, Edward S. Evans; first vice-president, Prof. Alexander Klemin, New York University; second vice-president, Maj. Tom Lanphier; secretary, Capt. Eddie Rickenbacker; and treasurer, Robert O. Lord.

Thirty-two directors were appointed. The list looked like a "who's who" of the aviation industry. Unfortunately, few of these directors ever attended meetings or were active in the association's affairs.

The overall aim of the NGA was to get as many people as possible involved in gliding. A goal of 200,000 was suggested by Evans, who pointed out that this was the number of people reported to be active in motorless flight in Germany. (The actual number was considerably less.) The consensus was that gliding could best be done by using low-priced primary gliders with shock-cord launching. In order to finance its program, the NGA launched a fund-raising campaign, the goal of which was to raise $20,000 in 1929 and $30,000 for each year thereafter.

The NGA also decided to sponsor a national gliding conference to attract public attention, which they believed would help expand the NGA. This

National Geographic's soaring article was read with enthusiasm by the members of the Mercury Model Club. This comprehensive article included many pictures of sailplanes and provided details of their construction. From this and other information, Ernest Schweizer, one of the club members, designed a primary glider. Although he was only a senior in high school, he recognized the importance of running a rudimentary stress analysis of the most important parts of the glider and did so.

Shortly thereafter the model club became a glider club, and the members had to buy a $5.00 share in order to be a part of the glider project. Some of the model club members were unable to raise the money for their share and drifted off into other activities, leaving Ernest Schweizer and his brothers, Paul A. and William, to carry the main load. (Of the Mercury Club's initial members, three—Atlee Hauck, Ernie Whidden, and Robert Yellott—later joined Schweizer Aircraft Corporation in Elmira, New York, and became valued permanent employees.)

In order to help raise the $100 needed for material and a used shock-cord, the Schweizers saved their bus fare by walking the 2 miles to and from school. They were not allowed to hitchhike or to have bicycles, which "Papa" Schweizer considered too dangerous.

conference was held in Detroit on April 8, 1929, and approximately 60 people attended, coming from many parts of the United States. The discussions covered various aspects of gliding, but the main topic was how to make drawings available to NGA members so they could construct primary gliders. The conference was followed by a meeting of the NGA Board of Directors.

The Geographic *Article*

In June 1929 motorless flight received a boost when an article entitled "On the Wings of the Wind" appeared in that month's issue of *National Geographic* magazine. It covered the gliding and soaring movement in Germany and brought motorless flight to the attention of many Americans throughout the country.

The First "C" in the United States

Another important event that year was AMAC's training session. Once again, it operated its school at Cape Cod using South Wellfleet as its base. Ralph Barnaby attended the Cape Cod school in August for two weeks, during which he made a record flight:

> On August 18th the Prüfling was disassembled, carted over to Corn Hill, where it was reassembled and I was launched from Corn Hill for my "B" flight of one minute 5 seconds. In the meanwhile the "Professor," a soaring plane, had been assembled for me to use for my "C" Certificate attempt. As this glider had not been flown since its arrival from Germany, Herr Knott decided to make a check flight on it before I flew it. On his launch he zoomed up too steeply, stalled and did one turn of a spin before hitting on the beach below. That was that! When it developed that Knott's only serious injury was to his pride, I elected to try for my "C" Certificate in the Prufling, and was duly launched. As the lift was good, I cruised up and down the ridge, getting 30 to 50 feet above the brow. When the necessary 5 minutes had been completed, I was enjoying it so much that I decided to keep going. It was then that I recalled Orville Wright's 1911 soaring flight of 9 minutes 45 seconds, and decided "Why not"! With 15 minutes under my belt, I finally heeded Herr Knott's pleading and landed.

Cape Cod was the center of soaring activity in the East in 1929 and a number of aviation writers visited the school there. R. E. Dowd described his visit in the September 1929 issue of *Aero Digest*, noting that "the whole development of the sport and its great service to aviation as a step toward power plane piloting, demands several good soaring centers and schools for advance study and further teaching of sailplane instructors who can return to the individual club and community and be responsible for activities there." As can be seen from this comment, gliding was still considered a way of developing interest in flying power-planes. Nonetheless, many others found soaring to be the main attraction of motorless flight, as Dowd's closing remarks in the same article clearly indicate: "Without soaring the American sailplane sport and business would be like the young lady who was dressed up but had no place to go."

Ralph S. Barnaby soaring along the sand dunes at Cape Cod, Massachusetts, in the Pruffling glider in August 1929 when he broke Orville Wright's duration record and earned the first "C" soaring award in the United States.

(NSM Collection)

National Glider Association Meeting

In its continuing effort to popularize gliding, the NGA that summer "zeroed in" on the premier annual aviation event in the country, the Cleveland Air Races. Don Walker and Louis Ross, aviation editor of the *Cleveland News* and organizer of the Cleveland Glider Club, were able to arrange glider activities for the last week in August during the 1929 races. These activities included the Second National Glider Conference, the NGA board of directors' meeting, and a glider contest.

Don Walker pointed out at the board meeting, that it had been one year since the Evans Glider Club of America was founded and that during that time, owing to the generous support of Edward S. Evans, the organization had been able to get up on its feet and had secured exclusive recognition from the National Aeronautical Association. He noted that clubs had been established across the United States

and that "interest was increasing by leaps and bounds, but that it was becoming more difficult to handle the situation properly with the funds available."

The technical phase of gliding was covered by Klemperer, who spoke on the development of standard plans for a primary training glider. He, too, remarked on the lack of funds, which he said was hampering the work of his committee.

Appropriately, the balance of the meeting was devoted to NGA finances. It was reported that the Wright Aeronautical Corp., Anthony Fokker, and Frederick Crawford of Detroit, among others, had joined Evans as founders of the NGA and were assisting him in finding additional financial backers.

Second National Glider Conference

In outlining the NGA program, Evans emphasized the fact that experimental work had been completed, except in the advanced technical field, and that "the association now knew exactly what to do and how to do it—and as rapidly as the funds were made available would carry on a program with the goal of organizing a glider club in every hamlet, town, and city in the USA, and the training of a million glider pilots to the third class license requirements." He also stated that in

Dr. Klemperer in the Akron Condor with (left to right) Dr. Frank Gross the designer, and Jack Sperry and H. E. Sperry of the Baker McMillan Co., the builders. With this sailplane Klemperer set a distance record of 15.75 miles near Uniontown, Pennsylvania, in the fall of 1929. Note how the shock-cord is attached to the Condor's nose hook.

(NSM Collection)

his judgment the aircraft industry should "provide the association $100,000 a year for this purpose."

The glider contest that followed included four events. The first three were for primary gliders with shock-cord and auto tow launching, with the best duration being 1 minute 14 seconds. The fourth event was called "The Famous Motored Pilots' Derby." All pilots used the taper-wing Franklin secondary glider from which the Franklin PS2 Utility was later developed. The tow cable could be up to 600 feet in length, and duration was to count 50 percent and distance from the spot 50 percent.

Capt. Frank Hawk won this event with a flight of 1 minute 45 seconds and a landing distance of 14.25 yards from the spot. Major Reed Landis, Lady Mary Heath, and Amelia Earhart finished next, in that order. Earhart's flight ended in a crash landing when she was confused by some power traffic. Her time was 21 seconds and her distance 233 yards from the spot. Earl Southee later said that although she was uninjured, she had "hurt" her pride and never got into a glider again!

At the end of the air races, Dr. Klemperer attempted a blimp tow from Akron to the Cleveland Air Races in the newly completed *Akron Condor* sailplane. The *Condor* was a high-performance sailplane designed by Dr. Frank Gross and built by the Baker-McMillan Co. of Akron. Gross based the *Condor* design on his experience with the Darmstadt I, which he had helped design. Unfortunately, turbulent air caused an early release, and although Klemperer tried to reach the Cleveland airport by soaring, he had to land short. Since Klemperer, in extending his flight, had soared longer than anyone at the contest, he was given the top prize for what the contest officials called "his victorious failure."

Stock Market Crash

Not long after these events the stock market crashed, and its devastating effects extended beyond businesses to the American public. This was not the best time to be promoting gliding, but Don Walker kept at it. On November 23 the NGA sponsored the Detroit Glider Carnival, which included a conference, NGA Board of Directors' meeting, and some flight demonstrations. Dr. Klemperer made a flight in the *Akron Condor* in which a month earlier he had made a 15¾-mile flight at Uniontown, Pennsylvania, that had set a U.S. distance record. Although there were no outstanding performances at the carnival, the 30,000 spectators led Walker to hope that motorless flight was becoming more popular.

At the NGA Board of Directors' meeting, Evans was elected honorary president and William B. Mayo, who was president of the Ford Airplane Co., was elected president of the

NGA. The other officers were Dr. W. Klemperer, first vice-president; George Lewis, of NACA, second vice-president; Eddie Rickenbacker, secretary; and Robert Lord, treasurer. It is not clear why Evans no longer wanted to be the head of the association; perhaps he, like many other businessmen at that time, was feeling the impact of the stock market crash on his business and personal finances.

The board approved a financial goal of $100,000 a year for three consecutive years and suggested that plans be made for a dinner in New York City on December 5, at which time the "entire matter would be placed before a select group of leaders of the aircraft industries for action." No dinner meeting was held, however, probably because of the aircraft industry's increasing financial problems. At the NGA meeting, citations for distinguished service were awarded to Ralph S. Barnaby, Hawley Bowlus, Dr. Wolfgang Klemperer, Wallace Franklin, and Milton Stoughton, all active *soaring* pilots who continued their soaring activity for many years.

Glider Development around the United States

Although Hawley Bowlus was not active in NGA affairs, he was at the center of gliding activity on the West Coast. The news of soaring in Germany had renewed his interest and in 1928 he started his 16th glider, often referred to as the Paperwing. He made the ribs of wood and butcher paper and was reported to have used a stiff cardboard paper made by Zellerback for the leading edge. It was first flown early in 1929, but it took Bowlus nine months of gliding that included three crashes and rebuilding sessions before he was able to make a soaring flight.

The Mercury Club's primary was being built in the Schweizer barn. Construction of the metal parts and wooden ribs was under way and they had to be hidden away when completed. The Schweizer brothers' big concern was whether "Papa" would let them fly the glider when they had finished it! He commuted to his Carnegie Hall Restaurant in New York City during the week, so he was not likely to go into the barn except on weekends. When they reached the point where things were getting too big to hide, they decided to pin everything together so it would look impressive. They hoped he would see how much work they had done and would not have the heart to stop them. Their plan worked! When he saw the assembled framework of the glider, he asked what it was and, when told, he walked away, resigned to the fact that this was what his boys and their friends wanted to do. He later referred to gliding as "the coming thing" when asked about his sons' involvement in gliding.

On October 5 he made a 14-minute flight that won him the second American "C" award and he became the first American to exceed the Wright record in an American-designed and built sailplane. During the following two months he raised the record to almost nine hours.

Within a few months, a number of established aircraft manufacturers, looking for work to replace their dwindling airplane sales, started producing primary gliders. Waco, Cessna, Alexander-Eaglerock, and Northrup were some of the aircraft manufacturers who were turning out primary gliders in production quantities and selling them at very low prices. For example, a ready-to-fly Waco primary sold for $385. Among the many new companies that were formed to manufacture primary gliders and to sell kits and plans were Associated Gliders; Gliders, Inc.; Mead; Leonard and Evans. Franklin and Baker-McMillan built utility gliders, Bowlus and Haller both built high-performance sailplanes in limited quantities, and the Peel Gliderboat Co. built a two-place water glider.

Bowlus also built primary gliders and he used them and an Evans primary glider for training. He attached wheels to these gliders so they could be auto-towed and returned to the starting point without having someone hold the wing tip or making the student leave the seat. This made it practical to train from flat fields and airports and was a big improvement over the shock-cord methods. A shock-cord launching required a long slope for a 15- to 30-second flight as well as a lengthy retrieve in order to get the glider back to the top of the slope. In the Bowlus School the students first mastered the primary and then made the transition to Bowlus high-performance sailplanes.

Early in 1930, three events brought gliding some favorable publicity: the Lindberghs' soar, Barnaby's flight from a dirigible, and Frank Hawks's transcontinental flight. These events received good coverage in the newspapers and they caught the public's imagination.

The Lindberghs' Soar

Charles Lindbergh was checked out by Bowlus and made his first soaring flight on January 19, 1930, in no. 18 Model A, an improved version of the Paperwing, and earned "C" award no. 9. Anne Lindbergh was checked out in an Evans primary named *Tilly* and then flew no. 18 for "C" no. 10. They were on their honeymoon and much in the news, so soaring received a lot of favorable publicity.

Barnaby's Flight from a Dirigible

Barnaby's flight from a dirigible on January 31, 1930, was the result of Adm. William A. Moffet's efforts to stir up more publicity and support for the Navy's airship program. The tests were made to demonstrate that a glider worked better than a parachute when an officer had to be landed to get assistance to moor the dirigible and there was no established mooring mast nearby. The glider was capable of reaching an airport or town some distance away. Barnaby's flight from the Los Angeles was in the same Prüfling in which he had made his record flight at Cape Cod. That flight was duplicated a few months later over Washington, D.C., by Comdr. T. G. W. Settle. However, the Navy's plans changed and in place of gliders the authorities decided to use small airplanes that could attach themselves to the dirigible and later be released.

Transcontinental Tow

Frank Hawks's transcontinental flight that began in April 1930 showed that it was possible to tow a glider by airplane for a long distance. The *Eaglet* was a new Franklin glider developed for this purpose. It had a span of 50 feet and was one of the first gliders with an enclosed cabin. It was towed the 2,800 miles by a *Waco Ten* biplane.

Texaco sponsored the flight and handled the publicity. Gliding was demonstrated to thousands of people as Hawks made many stops on his way across the country. He unexpectedly showed them a soaring flight when he was approaching the Syracuse, New York, airport for a landing and unknowingly flew into a large thermal and was carried up to cloud base. A very large crowd was present when he landed at the end of the flight on the big meadow in Van Cortland Park in New York City.

Bayside Glider Contest

The NGA encouraged glider clubs to conduct contests around the country in order to help publicize the sport. One such contest was held at the Bayside Golf Course, Long Island, New York, on May 12, 1930. Bowlus, Barnaby, and Hawks were among those competing. This turned out to be a memorable event, as Ralph Barnaby later recalled: "It was the first time I had met Hawley, and he was my closest competitor. I believe he would have bettered my 36 second duration flight, except for an unusual incident. While he was in flight he heard a loud 'bang' and he landed immediately. Inspection showed a hole in the side of the fuselage, and a golf ball was found rolling around inside."

The biggest attraction of motorless flight was soaring, which had to be expanded if the movement was to grow. Soaring was done in only a few areas and few sailplanes were available. As a result, people had few opportunities to see any soaring, and glider pilots received little encouragement to keep going. However, they did get some encouragement now and then. For example, on April 29–30 Jack Barstow made a flight of 15 hours in a Bowlus Paperwing over Point Loma and beat Ferdinand Shultz's world record flight. This won Barstow the Evans $2500 prize for the first soaring flight of 10 hours in the United States. Unfortunately, it did not become an official world record since he had failed to carry along a recording barograph.

NGA's Financial Problems

As 1930 dawned, the NGA found itself bogged down by financial troubles. Not only were funds harder to obtain from businessmen and wealthy individuals, but many glider enthusiasts were unable to pay the $1 NGA membership fee. It is hard for anyone who did not live through that period to realize how bad things were. Walker put an appeal in the June 3 NGA Bulletin encouraging members to sign up "sustaining patrons" and "founders" and indicating that the NGA would split the receipts. Walker said that the NGA could be self-supporting if it had 50,000 members at the $1 membership rate. The problem was that Evans, NGA's principal backer, had announced a few months earlier that "regretfully, but firmly, . . . it has to be someone else's turn." In an article in the August 1939 issue of National

Top: Charles Lindbergh in a "paperwing" Bowlus in southern California getting ready for a shock-cord launching. He was successful in soaring and earned "C", the ninth such award in U.S. Pacific and Atlantic.

(NSM Collection)

Comdr. T. G. W. Settle makes the second launching from the dirigible *Los Angeles*. On Barnaby's first launch, he said that the most exciting part of the launching was climbing down from the dirigible into the cockpit of the glider.

(U.S. Navy, NSM Collection)

Frank Hawks and Duke Jern-
igan with the Franklin "Eaglet" and the Waco tow plane
that made the 2,800-mile
transcontinental airplane
tow.
(Underwood and Underwood,
NSM Collection)

Glider magazine, he noted that in 1930 there were 2,500 members and 60 clubs in the NGA and again stated that if the NGA could be adequately financed, it could turn out one million pilots a year.

The Discovery of Elmira, New York, 1930–1931

To broaden its appeal, the NGA proposed to run a national soaring contest in 1930 and asked Klemperer to make a survey of potential soaring sites for

The enthusiasm of the members of the Mercury Club was high in June 1930 when they successfully flew their primary glider. The Peek-skill Evening Star ran the story with the headline LOCAL LIND-BERGHS SAVE BUS MONEY TO BUILD GLIDER. *It was launched by shock-cord from a nearby hayfield. At first it was easy to convince enough neighborhood kids to pull the shock-cord, but once the novelty wore off and their prospects of flying dwindled, the volunteers drifted away and launching became a problem. Then they hit upon the idea of having a Model A Ford pull the shock-cord. Auto shock-cord made it possible to achieve greater heights and longer flights. The members flew the primaries all that summer. The time of their flights was measured in seconds, and the total flying time that summer was much less than an hour.*

this event. After studying maps of the Northeast in the hopes of locating a ridge suitable for soaring, Klemperer selected the Elmira sites because he was impressed with the ridges that faced many wind directions and the wide valleys of the New York State Fingerlakes region. In the early spring of 1930 he "diverted" a business trip to Washington, D.C., by going from Akron, Ohio, to Washington via Syracuse, Binghamton, and Elmira, New York. In Syracuse he met Martin Schempp, a German pilot, who was living there with his brother. Schempp took him to meet Warren Eaton in Norwich. Eaton and Jack Sperry of the Baker-McMillan Co. had been flying "buddies" during World War I and Sperry had no doubt told Klemperer to make this stop.

Eaton gave him a tour of his glider operation and the surrounding country and then flew him to Bingh-amton, where he visited the Chenango Valley area. Another plane then flew him to Elmira, where Sherman Voor-hees, a local aviation booster, took him on a tour of the Elmira area. Klemperer was greatly impressed with the many ridges there, which would make it possible to soar in almost any wind direction; he also noted that the wide valley and large hayfields would provide good landing fields. In the evening Klemperer met with members of the Elmira Association of Commerce to discuss the possibility of holding the national contest there. After the meeting Klemperer sent a wire to the NGA office saying, as he later recalled, "after all I had seen I unhesitatingly recommended Elmira for the first Soaring Contest." He then took the Pennsylvania Railroad Sleeper to Washington D.C. for his Monday morning appointment.

Elmira, the Queen City of the Sourthern Tier, as it was known at that time, is located in Chemung County, one of the seven New York counties whose southern boundaries lie along the forty-second parallel. Elmira was a typical upstate community with elm tree–canopied streets, many churches, and a small town atmosphere. It was an industrial city that made products such as Remington Rand typewriters, American La France and Ward La France fire engines, Morrow coaster brakes, and Thatcher milk bottles. It had cultural assets, too. Mark Twain married Olivia Langdon of Elmira and became one of the city's leading citizens. He wrote a number of his most popular books at his octagon study on East Ridge. Elmira College, the first women's college to grant degrees equal to men's, brought students from all over the East. Thomas K. Beecher, the noted preacher and brother of Henry Ward Beecher and Harriet Beecher Stowe, had been the minister of the Park Congregational Church and a source of controversy. It was an active city and open to new ideas.

Moreover, Elmira was looking for something to spark its economy. The Elmira Association of Commerce saw motorless flight as one way of accomplishing this, and so the city aggressively sought the contest. The NGA Bulletin of June 3 announced that, providing sufficient financing could be secured, the first National Gliding and Soaring Contest would be held at Elmira New York, on September 13–29, 1930.

Jack O'Meara, a 27-year-old test pilot for the Baker-McMillan Company, followed Klemperer's suggestion that the Elmira ridges be given a try. While on a demonstration tour in the East, he was in Elmira the morning of July 2 and noticed that a northwest wind was blowing. He contacted Sherman Voorhees who arranged for the use of a field as a takeoff site.

Barney Wiggin, the famous soaring meteorologist, was asked during an interview in 1985 to look back over 50 years at the weather maps of July 2 to see what the weather was like on that eventful day. He reported:

> The weather maps show a summer cold front moving across Western New York on July 1st and east of Elmira on the 2nd, continuing on eastward. It marked the leading edge of cooler, unstable Canadian—or technically—polar continental air which, with diurnal heating would produce quite active thermals and probably cumulus clouds. Surface winds would be brisk (15–20 mph) northwesterly, ideal for ridge lift.

It was an ideal day for ridge soaring. Voorhees and some volunteers drove to the airport to meet O'Meara and his 19-year-old crewman, Willis Sperry, a brother of Jack Sperry, who was vice-president of Baker-McMillan. O'Meara had a disassembled Baker-McMillan Cadet II glider on a trailer hitched to his model A Ford coupe. A caravan was formed, and they drove to the Walsh Farm on top of South

J. K. Jack O'Meara and the Baker-McMillan Cadet on South Mountain getting ready for the first soaring flight in the Elmira area on July 2, 1930.

(NSM Loomis Collection)

Mountain, which overlooked the city of Elmira to the north.

When the Cadet was assembled, they prepared to shock-cord launch O'Meara, a technique that Klemperer had developed in the early 1920s. A shock-cord launch was somewhat similar to releasing a slingshot. The shock-cord, a ¾-inch diameter cord made up of a large number of small rubber strands encased in a woven cotton covering, was about 150 feet long and was laid out in the form of a V with a steel ring secured to its apex. O'Meara arranged the eager volunteers on each side of the shock-cord and put two men at the back of the glider to hold the rope attached to the tail. O'Meara climbed aboard and a volunteer placed the shock-cord ring on the open hook on the nose of the glider. On O'Meara's command of "ready," the wings were leveled. He then shouted "walkout," and the launching crew started to stretch out the shock-cord. After 10 strides, he yelled "run," and the crew responded. When the cord was stretched out a sufficient amount, he told the tail holders to "let go." The glider quickly accelerated, took off, and then zoomed over the heads of the launching crew. It headed out over the ridge, the shock-cord ring dropping from the nose hook when the tension was released. The fresh northwest winds deflecting against the South Mountain ridge carried O'Meara

upward. This sight was greeted by cheers from the launching crew below, who were witnessing soaring for the first time.

O'Meara worked his way along the ridge, steadily gaining height. When he got to the east end, where the ridge was lower, he turned back and retraced his path to the other end, then turned back again. His flight path formed a series of figure 8's as he steadily gained height. He did this for over an hour, before the wind weakened and he slowly lost height and gently glided down to a landing at Caton Avenue Airport in the valley below. His time was 1 hour 34 minutes, which was an outstanding flight for that time. It was his first soaring flight and earned him a "C" award. O'Meara made two soaring flights on the following day and sent back optimistic reports to the NGA about the soaring conditions at Elmira.

Bob McDowell, an Elmira attorney often told this story of the first soaring flight in Elmira:

One sunny July I happened to be in the office of Sherman Voorhees in the Realty Building in downtown Elmira NY when the phone rang. After Voorhees had talked for a few minutes he turned to me and said, "Hey Bob, do you want to help launch a glider?" I said, "What in the hell is a glider?" Voorhees gave a quick explanation saying that a pilot named O'Meara from Akron OH wanted to try to soar a glider and they needed man-power to launch him with the special shock-cord that he had brought along. I agreed to help. So, we went to Caton Avenue Airport where we met O'Meara. We proceeded to a field on top of South Mountain. . . . There were about 15 of us. When the glider was assembled in the high corner of the field, O'Meara attached the shock-cord and 6 of us were put on each side of the shock-cord "V". We were told to start running and I soon was about ready to drop from running so fast. I looked around and there was no glider in sight—when I looked up there it was, overhead, shooting out over the face of the hill.

McDowell was responsible in 1939 for getting the Schweizers to move their company to the Elmira area. He helped them form Schweizer Aircraft Corporation and became its secretary. He also became a strong supporter of soaring.

First National, 1930

O'Meara's flights excited the members of the NGA. These were a far cry from the short glider flights, measured in seconds, that members were used to. As a result, the NGA decided to go ahead with the first national contest and, after negotiating with the Elmira Association of Commerce Aviation Committee, it changed the dates to September 21–October 5 to give people more time to prepare for the contest.

A special Elmira group called the Minute Men took on the responsibility of organizing the contest. A number of other launching sites were chosen, one for each wind direction. The contest headquarters was to be based at the Caton Avenue Airport, where the pilots were to meet each morning. The contest director would choose the site for the day depending on the wind direction, and the pilot and his crew would take trailer and sailplane to the site for assembly and then takeoff. Louis Ross, who had conducted the glider contest at the Cleveland Air Races, was contest director and Don Walker was contest manager.

A total of 14 sailplanes and utility gliders were entered in the contest.

Albert Hastings, in his Franklin PS-2 utility, made the best duration flight, at 7 hours 43 minutes, and was awarded the duration trophy. Gus Haller flew 21.1 miles for the best distance, and Warren Eaton made the best altitude gain of 2,400 feet. Wolf Hirth, the famous German pilot, had actually flown the greatest distance, but his flight could not be counted since he was not a U.S. citizen.

Hirth's flight was in the *Musterle*, from South Mountain to Apalachin, New York, a small town 33 miles to the east and later the site of a famous Mafia-FBI encounter. This flight was made in a cloudless sky using, for the first time, the spiraling technique for flying thermals. This was a significant flight because it was the first time "blue thermals" had been used and was the start of the thermal soaring technique that freed soaring from the hills and made it possible for soaring to be done almost anywhere.

The FAI certificate of Al Hastings, which was signed by Orville Wright. Hastings won the first and second National Soaring Contests in a Franklin Utility.

(NSM Collection)

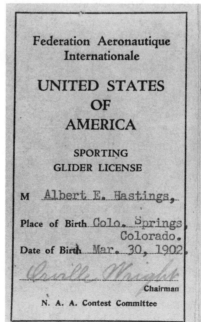

Federation Aeronautique Internationale

UNITED STATES OF AMERICA

SPORTING GLIDER LICENSE

M Albert E. Hastings,

Place of Birth Colo. Springs, Colorado.

Date of Birth Mar. 30, 1902.

Orville Wright
Chairman
N. A. A. Contest Committee

Sporting License No. 22
Class A License No. 39
Class B License No. 15
F. A. I. Certificate No. 6
Date Issued August 5, 1931.
Issued by N.A.A.
Type of Glider

Albert E. Hastings
Signature of Licensee

Up to that time, the deflection currents found along the windward side of a ridge or mountain were the main source of rising air that made soaring possible. Pilots would often run into "lift" in other areas away from the ridges, but would fly through them since they had no way of knowing where the lift was. Instruments are now used to locate these "thermals." It was not until many years later that Wolf Hirth, on a visit to Elmira, admitted to a group of soaring pilots that on that flight he had secretly used one of the first rate-of-climb indicators (or variometers, as they are also called) to locate the thermal lift. At that time only he and Robert Kronfeld, the two top soaring pilots in the world, had rate-of-climb indicators!

Al Hastings was the winner of the contest and was presented the Evans Trophy by Bob Evans, whose father, Edward, had donated the $5,000 silver trophy to the National Glider Association in 1928. It was to be awarded at each national contest to the national champion until someone won it three times.

Although there were some operating problems, the contest was considered a resounding success. It showed what soaring was all about. The Franklin and Baker-McMillan Cadet demonstrated that excellent soaring flights could be made with utility gliders. Many government and aviation figures were present, and the event was given the publicity it needed. Consequently, everyone was eager to have another national contest in 1931.

After the contest Don Walker began to concentrate on finding new members and obtaining more contributions to keep the NGA going. He was working against serious odds, particularly because of the bad publicity soaring had received as a result of numerous accidents involving inexperienced individuals who had tried to glide without proper instruction. This had happened in hundreds of primary gliders that were scattered all over the country. Even powered pilots had many accidents because they did not take the time to learn how gliding differed from powered flying.

Commenting on this problem, an editorial printed in the March 1937 issue of *Soaring* stated that "airplane pilots were not properly checked out and that more than 50% of gliders built in the USA during 1929 and 1930 were smashed when in the hands of these competent airplane pilots." These accidents and the continuing effect of the depression seriously hampered the growth of the NGA.

Nonetheless, an effort was made to meet the need for gliding and soaring schools, and several were eventually established. One of these was started by Gus Haller, who had attended the soaring school at the Wasserkuppe. In the fall of 1931 he opened the Haller School of Flight at the Pittsburgh-Greensburg Airport. He featured glider training and used both auto-tow and shock-cord launchings. He also offered instruction in soaring flight. It was Haller's great ambition to make Pittsburgh the American Wasserkuppe.

Another training school was started by Hawley Bowlus and Wolf Hirth. Bowlus had brought two of his sailplanes to compete in the First National, where he met Hirth for the first time. They discussed the possibility of setting up several schools together, and immediately after the Nationals forged ahead with the idea. They formed the Bowlus-Hirth Soaring Schools, with a base in New York City. The early training was done at the North Beach Airport on Long Island.

They had planned to have a permanent soaring site on Mt. Peter near Warwick, New York, 50 miles from the center of New York City. Although they did make a number of soaring flights there, it never became a permanent site.

At North Beach they used the Franklin utility with a two-wheel gear similar to the one Bowlus had successfully used on his primary *Tilly.* Although the name of the school implied that one would be instructed by Bowlus and Hirth, the "classes" were given by a teenager named Emil Lehecka, who became national champion in 1938.

In order to publicize both the school and motorless flight, O'Meara and Hirth made a number of flights over New York City. The first of these occurred on February 12, 1931, when O'Meara was aero-towed over the city and then released to soar over the skyscrapers. Exactly a month later Hirth made his famous ridge soaring flight along Riverside Drive just south of the George Washington Bridge, which was under construction at that time. Before he was allowed to fly from the small park along this busy thoroughfare, the police insisted that he agree to be signaled down if a traffic tie-up should develop. Hirth was successfully launched by shock-cord in the *Musterle* and rapidly gained height with the brisk west wind. As might be expected, the sight of the sailplane soaring above Riverside Drive at heights up to 1,500 feet caused an immense traffic jam, and the police signaled Hirth down. He was able to make a successful landing in the small park along the drive, but he had asked Emil Lehecka to wait at the edge of the Hudson River with a life preserver, just in case.

Although the Bowlus-Hirth School

Hawley Bowlus in a "paper-wing" Bowlus at the second National Soaring Contest. Although this ship normally had a cantilever wing, it had a set of wing struts as additional support.

(E. Mehlhose)

received much publicity and made many promotional flights, it was not successful. Hirth backed out of the partnership when he was called back to Germany in March 1931 to run the national glider school at Hornberg. The school disbanded and Bowlus went back to California.

A few months later Al Hastings started a school at the Caton Avenue Airport in Elmira, New York, using a Standard Franklin glider and auto tow. One of his first students was Floyd Sweet, a local youth, who, with a group of high school friends, had built a primary and had flown it in the spring of 1930.

Warren Eaton opened still another soaring school, Norwich Flying Service, Inc., at his airport at Norwich, New York. The glider courses that Eaton offered cost $40 for a noncommercial license and $60 for a commercial license.

A while later the *New York Times*

ran a story about some members of Philadelphia society taking a keen interest in the courses at a glider school operated at Wings Field. Lewin Barringer was the instructor and used a primary glider with auto tow. It was reported that he was experienced in transitioning glider students to power, with considerably less dual time required for soloing.

Second National, 1931

In the spring of 1931 Don Walker wrote Warren Eaton to say that the organization's financial problems were steadily getting worse. He could no longer afford to keep his secretary and the NGA was several months behind in its rent. The overall debt was approaching $2,000, much of which consisted of his own unpaid salary. Although the NGA had 50 member clubs, there just was not enough income to keep the NGA going without extra financial support. He mentioned the possibility of getting support from a new organization, the American Glider League, that was being formed in the New York City area and that was supposed to have good financial backing.

Walker also mentioned that he was working on plans for the second national contest and that several areas seemed interested in holding it. Gus Haller, who was pushing his site near Pittsburgh, had even persuaded Wolf Hirth to look it over before returning to Germany. Hirth reported that it had good potential. However, financial commitments were slow in coming from Haller's backers.

Meanwhile, Bill Purcell and the Bowlus-Hirth group in New York City were promoting the site at Warwick, New York. They claimed to have sup-

port totaling $19,000, of which $15,000 was for prizes. This site was recommended by Bowlus and Hirth, but when Warren Eaton flew over the area in his airplane on his way to New York, he found that it did not have enough good landing fields for the large number of inexperienced soaring pilots who would be flying at the Second National Soaring Contest. Purcell was also having trouble putting a firm proposal together.

Elmira, which had lost about $1,200 on the first contest, came up with a $2,500 guarantee for 1931. At that time, Walker considered it way out of line compared with the other proposals. A half-hearted proposal was also submitted by Dansville, New York. It was backed by Bernard McFadden, a publisher who owned a health farm in the area.

As summer approached, there were still no firm commitments from either Haller or Purcell, and so the contest was awarded to Elmira. This delay meant that the contest had to be run in August.

Twenty-six sailplanes (18 utilities, 3 secondaries, and 5 sailplanes) and 36 pilots showed up for the Second National. This was a substantial increase over the previous year and confimed that interest in soaring was on the rise. The winner of the contest was again Al Hastings, who flew a Franklin PS-2. The best distance flight was 15 miles and best altitude gain 3,130 feet, both made by Martin Schempp in the Schloss-Mainberg. Hastings also turned in the best duration flight, 7 hours 30 minutes.

Demise of the NGA

During the Second National it was apparent that the National Glider Association was running "out of steam." The soaring pilots were not happy with the way the meet was being conducted, and the three serious accidents that occurred raised questions about glider safety. Some people were also concerned about the future of the NGA and wondered whether soaring contests would continue if the NGA folded.

When the Second Nationals ended, Don Walker returned to Detroit to write up the meet for what was to be the last NGA Bulletin, the July-August issue. When he saw that little support was forthcoming from the Detroit area, he proposed that the NGA move its headquarters to Elmira, where it could be run at a much lower cost. He also suggested that a drive for more members be conducted, with a goal of 10,000 new members at $5 each. An Elmira group was willing to pledge $3,000 toward the project. Walker proposed a three-month trial program with the Elmira group guaranteeing him a salary of $300 per month. There is no record of any further developments on this matter. Soon after, Walker left the NGA for another position.

In the September 1944 issue of *Gliding*, Edward S. Evans blamed "circumstances" for the dissolution of the National Glider Association in October of 1931. Surely one reason that the NGA fell so short of its goal was the stock market crash of 1929 and the disastrous economic conditions that followed. There just was not enough "big money" around to support the NGA as Evans had envisioned, and few people were financially able to participate in gliding. Even if "times" had been normal, Evans's projections were unrealistic, particularly his goal of matching the number of glider pilots active in Germany. The NGA

The Second National Soaring Contest was given more publicity than the First and it attracted more soaring enthusiasts from distant places. Many aspiring soaring pilots came to see what soaring was all about and to rub elbows with the soaring pilots. Howie Burr and a friend came from Schenectady, New York, and were able to crew for Ralph Barnaby.

Five members of the Mercury Club, including the three Schweizers, drove from Peekskill to attend the contest. On their way to the airport late that afternoon they passed an ambulance with siren screaming coming from the Caton Avenue Airport. They later learned that Capt. Thomas Phillips had gone under the wires instead of over them on his landing approach, and the pull-up took the wings off his Bowlus sailplane. He broke both his legs in the crash. Phillips's sailplane had been stored in Panama, while he was stationed there, and the heat and humidity had taken their toll.

The following morning at the airport they saw Fritz Germershausen in a Baker-McMillan Cadet II transition from shock-cord launching to auto tow, take off, and climb at a steep angle. Release occurred at an altitude of about 600 feet. The Cadet stalled and spun in, crashing right in front of them. Both the pilot's legs were broken. Later in the meet Maj. William Purcell "spun in" in his Franklin glider on East Ridge and received serious injuries.

These three accidents made a lasting impression on the Schweizers and emphasized the need for strength, stability, and pilot protection in glider design.

membership total of 2,500 was a far cry from his projected figures. Another significant factor was that the NGA had treated gliding as a first step to power flying rather than an introduction to the sport of soaring.

In evaluating Evans's contribution, we can readily see that he was responsible for assembling those interested in gliding into an organization. He also gave considerable financial support to the fledgling organization. However, Evans approached gliding and soaring as a promoter rather than as an enthusiast. He was not an active glider pilot and seldom had any direct association with those who were involved in gliding and soaring. He had set high goals for the NGA, but backed away when they were not achieved. Nonetheless, he felt that he had made a great contribution to gliding and soaring, as he explained in an article that appeared in the August 1944 issue of *Gliding:* "If I am correctly called the father of organized gliding and soaring, of whose paternity I was accused of on the floor of Congress, then I certainly take pride in the way my family has grown and prospered, thanks mainly to the devoted efforts of many men besides myself."

Don Walker is the forgotten man. As general manager, he had to run the NGA with little help. He continued to work on the Second National with no assurance that he would be paid. He was a dedicated person who worked hard doing his job, but, unfortunately, the NGA had become a lost cause. He received little credit for his efforts in helping to make the first two national contests possible, which marked the beginning of competition soaring in the United States.

Although the main purpose of the National Glider Association was to develop thousands of pilots as potential buyers of airplanes, its principal contribution was to provide an arena for competitive soaring in the two national contests it sponsored. These events demonstrated that soaring was the real attraction of motorless flight. It provided the challenge and excitement around which the movement would eventually grow.

Chapter 3

The U.S. Soaring Movement Starts, 1932–1936

Formation of the Soaring Society of America, 1932

The idea of creating a new organization to carry on the national soaring contests and to feature *soaring* rather than *gliding* got its start during the Second National Soaring Contest in 1931. There was a growing concern about whether the NGA could survive and a number of soaring pilots discussed the possibility of forming a new organization that could conduct the Nationals in 1932.

Arthur L. "Larry" Lawrence was the chief motivator in this move. He had learned to fly at Cape Cod and had competed in the first two Nationals, leading the very active Providence R.I. Soaring Club. He was a good organizer and eager to get things done and vigorously promoted soaring in New England.

In December he wrote Warren Eaton that he had sounded out Malcolm Wilson, of the Elmira Association of Commerce, as to how the people of Elmira felt about having the Third National Soaring Contest there. He said that they were interested but that finances were a problem. Lawrence suggested that an association of "C" soaring pilots be set up to help the Elmira committee hold another contest.

Eaton replied that he was not optimistic about the coming year and did not figure much could be done until business conditions improved. He said

that he had talked with E. P. "Ed" Warner, former assistant secretary of the Navy, NGA board member and editor of *Aviation* magazine, and thought that Warner would support such an effort. Although not an active pilot, Warner had flown in the 1910 Collegiate Glider Meet and had been the advisor of the MIT group that had gone to France.

Eaton mentioned that a West Coast organization wanted to stage a meet in conjunction with the 1932 Olympics in Los Angeles. He suggested to Lawrence that a get-together be held in New York early in January to discuss the overall soaring situation. He ended the letter by saying that "this coming year I am going to en-

Warren Eaton, first SSA president, in his Franklin glider at an early national meet.

(NSM Loomis Collection)

The Founders Gallery at the National Soaring Museum shows the 15 founders of the SSA. These sketches were done by Gerald C. Pomeroy for the 50th anniversary of the founding of the SSA. Top, left to right: E. Southee, R. S. Barnaby, W. E. Eaton, R. E. Franklin, C. Gale, E. W. Cleveland, A. L. Haller, and S. P. Voorhees. Bottom: W. K. Klemperer, F. K. Iszard, W. Enyart, R. Holderman, A. L. Lawrence, E. P. Warner, and A. Hastings.

(Tony Fusare)

deavor to cut down on both time and money expended in gliding." Little did he know what lay ahead.

The first informal meeting of the group was held in New York City in the McGraw-Hill Building on February 20, 1932, in Warner's office. Those present were Eaton, August C. "Gus" Haller, Lawrence, Franklin Iszard, Jacob Fassett III (all of whom had competed in the national meets), plus William Enyart of the NAA, Warner, and Charles H. Gale (Warner's assistant editor).

All agreed that a new organization was needed to conduct the national soaring contests. In working out the details, someone proposed that the organization be called the American Soaring Society, but this name was quickly discarded when an observant founder noticed that the acronym it formed would not be too flattering. The organization was thus called the American Soaring Association.

The founding group looked to Warren Eaton to take the lead, for he was a successful business executive of the Norwich Pharmaceutics Company in Norwich, New York, and an enthusiastic soaring pilot who had flown in both Nationals. His flying career had started in World War I and continued long after. He was well liked and a logical candidate for president.

Warner, the senior aviation person there, was proposed as chairman of the board, since his presence was de-

sired for prestige purposes. Haller was named vice-president, Lawrence secretary, and Charles Gale editor. Seven of those attending became directors, and Warren Eaton wrote to 10 other people who were proposed for directors to see if they would accept the directorship. Included were 6 who had been involved in previous Nationals (Ralph Barnaby, R. E. Franklin, Al Hastings, Russel Holderman, Klemperer, Sherman Voorhees) and four others who had shown interest in the soaring movement (Earl Southee of the Curtiss-Wright Co.; E. W. "Pop" Cleveland, a prominent figure in aviation; Robert Walker, assistant to William Mayo, former president of NGA; and Cy Caldwell, assistant editor and well-known writer for *Aero Digest*).

The 14 directors on the certificate of incorporation were Ralph S. Barnaby, E. W. Cleveland, Warren Eaton, William Enyart, R. E. Franklin, Charles Gale, A. C. Haller, Albert Hastings, Russell Holderman, Franklin K. Iszard, A. L. Lawrence, Earl Southee, Sherman P. Voorhees, and E. P. Warner.

Eaton's files show that Klemperer did not answer Eaton's letter until May 7, because he had been in Europe recuperating from an illness. Although the letter said he would be glad to help, it did not state that he would accept a directorship. However, at the top of the letter Eaton had penciled, "Add his name to our directors." It

was too late to be included in the list of directors on the incorporation papers, but he became the 15th director.

The directors decided that, at the start, it would be unwise to attempt to do anything more than hold a national contest. They agreed to consider the matter of a permanent national association in the autumn. A letter was sent to all known soaring enthusiasts appealing for support of the ASA and asking them to send in a dollar for the six issues of the planned bulletin. Haller wrote to Eaton on February 23 to say that he had just learned that there was already an American Soaring Association, which had been formed by O'Meara. Haller suggested that the name be changed to the Soaring Society of America. Eaton, Southee, Haller, Gale, and Lawrence then met in Providence, R.I., on April 16 and 17 to work on the rules for the contest and to discuss the need for a new name. Those present agreed that the name should be changed to the Soaring Society of America. A few days later Eaton wrote Warner about the Providence meeting and said that he had second thoughts about the new name. He had tried it out on a number of friends, including his brother Melvin, whose response was that it would be confused with the Sewing Society of America.

When news about the formation of the ASA was released, Don Walker wrote Sherman Voorhees of Elmira an irate letter. He had seen the story on the ASA in a Detroit newspaper and objected to the suggestion that the new organization was the NGA's successor, since neither he nor Bill Mayo had been consulted about such plans. Both had hopes that the NGA would be the basis for any new association and that this would allow the NGA's debts to be paid.

Voorhees sent a copy of the letter to Eaton, who replied that the new organization was only interested in running the soaring contest and therefore did not feel any responsibility to the defunct NGA.

At the first formal directors' meeting in New York City on March 7 the name was officially changed to the Soaring Society of America (SSA). The SSA was incorporated as a nonprofit organization in the state of Delaware on May 11, 1932, at a cost of $50.

In the early years the SSA operated on a low budget and had no employees. Eaton took care of business matters and Gale edited the mimeographed Bulletin. At the start Eaton spent most of his time preparing for the 1932 Nationals. The SSA membership assumed that Eaton was able to give substantial financial support.

A letter to Gus Haller dated March 22, 1932, however, indicated that Eaton had financial problems, too. Haller had written Eaton about buying stock in the Haller-Hirth Sailplane Company. In his reply Eaton said: "It would be absolutely impossible for me to purchase any stock in your corporation at this time. – Only last week a bank with whom I have some loans notified me that they would appreciate my taking up my notes. Fortunately, I am able to do so but it has changed my entire outlook on things. – Frankly, Gus, I do not like the way

Jack O'Meara, the 1932 national champion, and his glider, named the Chanute, which was rebuilt from the Darmstadt I that Hesselbach flew so successfully at Cape Cod in 1928. The trailer for the Chanute advertised the Lustig Sky Train that would fly in 1934.

(NSM Loomis Collection)

things look at present. – I appreciate very much the opportunity to join with you but do not feel at this time I am in position to do anything."

The Eaton Period, 1932–1934

Once the SSA was formed, its first project was to work out plans for the Third National Soaring Contest, which was to be held in Elmira, New York, from July 11 to 24. It was to be strictly a sporting affair since the effects of the depression were still being felt and it was difficult to get financial support. Expenses were to be kept at a minimum and all prizes were to be in the form of trophies. Entry fees were $5 for each glider and $2 for each contestant. (The cost of staying at Elmira's YMCA at that time was $3.00 a week for a double room; breakfast was 10¢ and up, dinner 50¢—or less. At the Mark Twain Hotel, a room with twin beds and bath was $2.50 per person per day.) Pilot meetings were to be held at 7 a.m. at the Caton Avenue Airport with attendance taken by the officials. There was to be no flying after 5:30 p.m.

Information on the meet was outlined in Soaring Bulletin no. 3. Wire-braced gliders were permitted if approved by the technical committee. There were to be two classes, utility and sailplane, and two types of pilots, junior and senior. A senior pilot was one who had earned his "C" license prior to Janaury 1, 1932. Prizes were to be given for distance, duration, and altitude. Warren Eaton was chairman of the contest and Earl Southee was the referee.

In the spring, when the plans for the Third National Soaring Contest were well under way, a series of letters between Eaton and Mayo and Evans of NGA discussed the possibility

of awarding the Evans Trophy at the 1932 National. Evans finally agreed to do this. In the correspondence they also talked about whether the SSA might take over the defunct NGA. Eaton said that the SSA would consider it, but only if the organization did not have to take over any of NGA's debts. The only assets that the NGA had were its membership lists, files, and whatever "goodwill" that remained, all of which were of questionable value to the SSA. Eaton proposed that Mayo and Walker come to the Nationals to discuss the matter.

Third National, 1932

Six sailplanes, 10 utility gliders, and 45 pilots entered the contest. Jack K. O'Meara in his Chanute, which he had rebuilt from the Darmstadt I, came in first with the best distance of the meet, a 66.6-mile flight to Tunkhannock, Pennsylvania; O'Meara also made the best duration flight, at 8:18 hours. Stan Smith won the junior pilot trophy with a total of 13:08 hours flying time.

At the end of the contest, Bulletin no. 6 reported: "A gratifying record of safety, many outstanding performances, a great volume of soaring activity and a fine spirit of cooperation. The worst accident involved a mere bloody nose! Pilots went further and higher than at any previous National Meet, setting at least two new American marks. . . . It was conducted purely as a sporting event for the sake of furthering soaring flight in this country without any commercial entanglements of any sort and with no affiliation with any other organizations."

A noteworthy improvement at this meet was the weather reports provided by a group of meteorologists from MIT, led by Dr. K. O. Lange. They brought various equipment for taking soundings every morning, which made it possible to give much improved weather briefings.

Little information is available for the period between the end of the 1932 contest and the Fourth National Soaring Contest held in 1933. Bulletin no. 6, which covered the contest, was the last one in 1932. The next issue was dated June 19, 1933. It appears that in the intervening 10 months there was no communication between the SSA and its members. This was not unexpected since the SSA had been set up specifically to conduct the national contest and initially it did not plan to do much else. However, it gradually became involved in many related matters, such as contacting the Department of Commerce about glider regulations; dealing with NAA matters relating to awards, records, and the FAI; answering inquiries from the public; and publishing a bulletin to keep the membership informed. Recognizing that it would have to take on these responsibilities, the SSA gradually broadened its activities to cover all phases of motorless flight.

During this time some of the officers and directors changed. Klemperer became vice-president in place of Haller, and K. O. Lange and Martin Schempp replaced Hastings and Cleveland.

As often happens with a volunteer organization, one person ends up doing most of the work. In this case it was Warren Eaton. He was the one mainly responsible for preparing and operating the Third National Soaring Contest. During the spring of 1932 he must have spent most of his time on SSA activities. His files show that in April, May, and June he had written more than a hundred letters in connection with the contest and the SSA. He made frequent trips to Elmira from Norwich to work with the people of Elmira in planning the meet. At the same time he was demonstrating soaring to others and practicing for the Nationals at the nearby Norwich airport.

In the spring of 1933 the SSA put out its first brochure, which explained the purpose of the SSA and its objectives, and provided details on membership. The leaflet also announced that the SSA was to operate a soaring camp in Elmira before the contest. The SSA saw the need for such a school since no others seemed to be operating at that time. It was to be operated by Lawrence, with Eaton acting as general manager of the school and the contest. Haller was to take care of the advanced flying. Fourteen students attended.

Fourth National, 1933

Several sailplanes, 15 utilities, and 72 pilots were entered in the Fourth National, which ran from July 10 to 23, 1933. The poor weather limited the flying to 99 flights, which totaled 54 hours of flying time. The time when flying was not possible was filled with lectures and discussions. Stan Smith, of the University of Michigan Glider Club, won the contest flying a Franklin Utility.

Richard C. (Dick) du Pont, a young aviation enthusiast of the famous du Pont family, had combined with Bowlus to develop single- and two-place sailplanes called the Bowlus-du Pont Albatross, which appeared at the National for the first time. On the two-place Albatross's first flight there, Dick took his father (A. Felix) for his

A view from site no. 6 on the Rhodes Farm showing Dick duPont and his Albatross and a Franklin soaring over the Big Flats Valley.

(NSM Loomis Collection)

first sailplane flight. They were launched by shock-cord from the steep slope of Hill 6, but were unable to take off and so crashed into the trees. Fortunately, neither one was injured. A short while later Dick took off in his single-place Albatross and came within 500 feet of O'Meara's altitude record. Larry Lawrence wrote the following about this incident:

> I am sure that it had been properly test-flown from an airport and probably airplane-towed. It was set up for launching on our down-sloping field with the trees at its end. No one noticed that the bottom of the vertical stabilizer and rudder only cleared the ground by inches. As one of the contest officials, I was standing by to watch the shock-cord launch, with extra manpower on each strand of the shock-cord V, the 2-place was launched, with Richard at the controls and his father, A. Felix du Pont, as the

passenger. Well, you guessed it—with full elevator for the take-off, the bottom of the vertical stabilizer just dragged on the ground. The sailplane was catapulted down the slope and disappeared into the trees. Fearing the worst, I raced to our headquarters building and phoned the hospital for an ambulance and doctor. To my relief, when I returned to the launching scene, there were Richard and his father emerging from the woods, the latter with his pence-nez glasses clamped to the bridge of his nose, looking calm and as though nothing had happened.

There were several firsts at the Nationals. Warren Eaton made the first glider airmail flight by flying 16 pounds of mail to the airport in the valley. Gus Scheurer, of the New Jersey Albatross Glider Club, gave the first winch launching with the club's winch.

All flights in that contest but one were made from Hill 6 on the Rhodes farm, located on the west end of the Harris Hill Ridge. Tom Rhodes, his wife Irene, their children Frank and Barbara, plus neighbors, were congenial hosts, and the Rhodes dining room became the main eating place during the Nationals. Seats at the large oval table seemed to be filled all the time. One could get as much as one wanted for 50¢. Some of the Rhodes family slept in the woodshed to allow more room for boarders. Pilots and crew were allowed to camp in the orchard. The Rhodes farm, a New York State Century Farm, is now run by Tom's son Frank and his wife Mavis. It is used occasionally for an emergency landing place for sailplanes that miss Harris Hill.

Directors' Meeting, 1933

At a directors' meeting held the last Friday of the contest Dick du Pont and Hawley Bowlus were elected directors, and Sherman Voorhees resigned from the board. The bylaws were amended to provide for two vice-presidents, and Dick du Pont was elected second vice-president.

Shortly after the contest, the SSA joined ISTUS, the international organization, which linked together the national soaring groups of countries active in soaring. This enabled the SSA to issue Jack O'Meara the first "D" in the United States, later called the Silver "C" badge, for which he had qualified during the 1933 national contest. Dr. Karl O. Lange was appointed to act as official ISTUS representative of the SSA.

First Shenandoah Expedition

In September, du Pont organized an expedition to the Blue Ridge Moun-

tains to attempt to set a distance record along the ridges. Du Pont brought his Albatross I, Gus Haller and Emerson Mehlhose brought a Haller-Hawk, and Rudy Setz a Franklin Utility. Rudy and Walter Setz had started their gliding activity in the Philadelphia area and flew with Barringer at Wings Field. In 1932 Rudy, the older brother, had signed up for a course at the Haller-Hirth School near Pittsburgh. When he got there, he flew so well they made him an instructor. He later went to California with Martin Schempp to help build the Bowlus-du Pont Albatross. When he returned East, du Pont loaned him his Franklin Utility to fly at the Big Meadows contest.

Emerson Mehlhose was enrolled in the Haller School at the same time

Top: Hans Groenhoff, noted photographer, taking a picture of Gus Haller in the Schloss-Mainberg with Vic Saudek holding the wing tip. Later in the contest Haller had to parachute from this sailplane when its wing failed.

(E. Mehlhose)

Four SSA directors at an early National. Left to right: Edward Warner, editor of *Aviation* magazine; Bill Enyart, NAA executive director; Earl Southee, contest director; and K. O. Lange of MIT, chief of meteorological services.

(NSM Loomis Collection)

O'Meara's U.S. record by the necessary 5 percent. The next day du Pont made a 122-mile flight from Waynsboro, Virginia, to Frederick, Maryland, for a new national record. In a formal report on the expedition, Larry Lawrence, expedition director, predicted possible ridge flights up to 600 miles in the future. Although the prediction seemed visionary at that time, this distance was exceeded in the 1970s by Karl Striedieck, Jim Smiley, Bill Holbrook, L. Roy McMaster, and later by many others.

After this event, the Franklin Setz had flown was used to instruct Dick du Pont's sister in Wilmington. One day, Rudy put on a parachute to do some aerobatics in the Franklin and while he was attempting to do an outside loop, the Franklin's struts collapsed. Rudy "bailed out" but was killed when his parachute did not open in time.

Directors' Meetings

The next meeting of the directors coincided with a meeting of the American Society of Mechanical Engineers in New York City, at which Barnaby and Haller gave talks about soaring. The SSA directors discussed the possibility of hiring a salaried general manager. In addition, they proposed that regional contests be encouraged since there was also interest in soaring at Big Meadows, Virginia. Hawley Bowlus and Martin Schempp suggested that a Pacific Coast division of SSA be established. At that time, Schempp was helping Bowlus on the Albatross project.

At the annual directors' meeting in New York on February 10, 1934, the decision was made to hire Earl Southee as the first general manager of the SSA, starting on April 1 of that

Emerson Mehlhose and his Haller Hawk sailplane, in which he made some outstanding flights in the Blue Ridge Mountains.
(NSM Loomis Collection)

as Rudy Setz. Mehlhose had learned to fly a few years earlier with Jack Laister at the Theodore Roosevelt High School in Wyandotte, Michigan, where they had built a Zoegling-type primary glider. Haller, Schempp, Setz, and Mehlhose decided to search for a new site, but finally chose the ridge in Uniontown, Pennsylvania, that Klemperer had used in 1929 to make his distance record. Mehlhose made a 2-hour 15-minute flight in the Haller Hawk. While they were there, Dr. Klemperer arrived with his new bride, Mia, for a weekend and they celebrated with a dinner at the Summit Hotel, which had been the headquarters for Klemperer's 1929 expedition.

On the third day of the Shenandoah expedition, Mehlhose made a 70-mile flight, which did not quite break year. Subsequently, all SSA activity was moved to Southee's home in Elmira and the organization's official address became Box 222, Elmira, New York. Southee also took over editorship of the Bulletin from Charles Gale, as well as the task of running the 1934 National Soaring Contest.

A New Permanent Site

The Fifth National Soaring Contest was the first to be held from Harris Hill field. The hill became known as Bud's Hill, since Franklin "Bud" Iszard, one of the founders of the SSA, had taken the lead in locating a permanent soaring site.

The previous National had shown that launching with shock-cord from one site did not provide enough soaring for a good contest. Also, people were beginning to recognize the potential of winch and airplane tow. Iszard therefore led a group of Elmirans in search of a permanent site where the new methods of launching could be used. They picked a site east of the Rhodes farm. The Chemung Board of Supervisors purchased land from the Rhodes family and two other farmers. Bill McGrath, general manager of the Eclipse Co., asked his chief engineer Maurice Whitney to have a layout made, which Frank Christian, a glider pilot in the engineering department, completed. Site development followed, although there were no permanent buildings there for the first few years.

Fifth National, 1934

The Fifth National was officially opened by Col. Carroll Cone of the Bureau of Aeronautics. Ben Badenoch of the MIT club made the first launching as a tribute to Hank Harris, who had made the first soaring flight from the site a few weeks earlier in a try for his duration leg of the Silver "C." This turned out to be his last soaring flight. On June 15, at the auxiliary airport in the Big Flats Valley, he was riding in the 1917 Hudson touring car used as a tow car by the MIT group. Harris was sitting next to Jim Kendrick, who was at the wheel, and was facing backward watching the glider on tow, which was the MIT club's procedure for the instructor. However, the glider was late in releasing, and the tow car had to make a sharp turn to avoid hitting the fence at the end of the field. The wooden wheels of the car broke and the tow car flipped over, killing Hank Harris and breaking Jim Kendrick's shoulder.

Because of Harris's great interest in soaring, his continuous help to the MIT club, and the fact that he had made the first flight from the new takeoff site and had helped fly the weather ship at the previous national contest, there was a wave of feeling among the soaring group that the field should be called Harris Hill. Although the building and flying field were formally named the Warren E. Eaton Motorless Flight Facilities in 1937, the name Harris Hill caught on and has been used ever since.

Six sailplanes, 24 utililty gliders and 63 pilots entered the Fifth National. The most outstanding performance of the contest was Dick du Pont's world record flight of 158 miles to Basking Ridge, New Jersey, in the Albatross II. Of all the records, this is the most sought after. For the first time, a U.S. pilot had exceeded the world distance record, and it was done in an American-designed and built sailplane. It spoke well for the progress of soaring in the United States.

It did not take long, however, for

The pilots of the Lustig Sky Train. Left to right: Stan Smith, glider no. 2, R. E. Franklin, glider 3; J. K. O'Meara, glider 1; and Ellwood Keim, tow pilot.
(International News, NSM Collection)

off at a different city. He convinced the sponsor, Elias Lustig, owner of the Adams Hat Stores, that glider trains had commercial possibilities.

O'Meara used three Franklin gliders to carry mail from New York to Philadelphia, Baltimore, and Washington, D.C., and back. The train took off from Floyd Bennett Field in New York on August 2, 1934. When it arrived over Philadelphia, the last glider on the line, flown by Prof. R. E. Franklin, cut loose and landed at the airport and delivered the mail to the postmaster. Bad weather made it necessary for the train to stop at Philadelphia for the night. The next day Stan Smith landed at Baltimore and O'Meara at Washington to complete the mail deliveries. A day later the tow plane picked up each glider for the return trip to New York. Although the Lustig Sky Train had attracted a great deal of publicity, nothing further was done with the idea.

the record to be broken. At the 15th Wasserkuppe Contest a month later, German pilots were eager to win the record back, and before the contest was over four pilots had exceeded du Pont's record: Dittmar made 233 miles; Hirth, 218; Weigmeyer, 195; and Hoffman 192. It would be 18 years before it would be won again by an American.

Du Pont also set a national altitude record of 6,224 feet and won the contest. Lewin Barringer, also flying on Albatross, finished second. Eaton took delivery of a mahogany Albatross II, which he named the *Falcon*. The contest was successful and attracted many spectators and important visitors.

The Lustig Sky Train

J. K. O'Meara did not fly in the Fifth National since he was promoting a sky train, a towplane towing three gliders, in tandem, with each glider dropping

Eaton Plan Presented to Congress

Eaton, having been relieved by Southee of the day-to-day responsibilities of running the SSA, was now able to spend more time on promoting soaring. On October 22 he presented SSA's case to the Federal Aviation Commission:

The future value of the motorless flight movement lies first in the training of air pilots and subsequently in scientific research. Being less expensive than the usual course in flying, glider training offers a reasonable solution to the problem of satisfying the youthful craving to fly. Through courses in schools, in sport flying clubs, in the reserves at college, and in the Army and Navy, flyers may be economically trained in large numbers. We believe that a student is best trained by first mastering the simplest rudiments of plane control and gradually passing to each succeeding phase, as by recommended method of glider training. Without the added responsibility of concern for the operation of the engine, he can concentrate entirely on the technique of real flying.

The SSA recommended the following program:

I   Soaring activity should be encouraged by just and wise regulations passed upon by those thoroughly conversant with the problems of motorless flying rather than hampered by rulings which do not tend to make it safer but only retard its normal growth.

1. The Bureau of Air Commerce to employ a soaring pilot who is also an aeronautical engineer to supervise glider activities.

2. The present Bureau of Air Commerce regulations to be revised with the advice of the above supervisor aided by the manufacturers.

3. Twenty-five hours of certified soaring to be credited toward the fifty hours required for a private pilot's license, any flight of over one-hour duration to count.

4. Eligible local men to be recommended by the S.S.A. to act as advisors to inspectors subject to the approval of the Bureau of Air Commerce.

II Motorless flying should be promoted by the establishment of glider training schools and the development of soaring sites.

5. Courses in gliding at Annapolis and at West Point to be offered in order to discover at small expense the degree of a student's natural aptitude for flying before admission to the course for a naval or army aviator.

6. Required courses in motorless flying at naval and army air stations.

7. Reserve Officers Training Camps and Civil Military Training Camps to include glider training.

8. Establishment of soaring sites through National & State Park Commissions.

III Scientific phases of motorless flying could advantageously receive aid.

9. The N.A.C.A. to be invited to cooperate on design, construction, etc. and to have several different types of gliders with which to experiment.

10. The Bureau of Standards to cooperate on developing instruments to be used in soaring.

11. A National Research Institute for Motorless Flight to be established by the U.S. Government, more especially to do experimental work in meteorology and to find and prove new soaring sites.

IV Motorless flying should be endorsed by the Federal Aviation Commission as a valuable aid in the constructive program of aeronautical development in the United States.

Thus, in less than three years the SSA had changed from a group that was interested only in seeing the national soaring contests continued to one proposing a broad program for gliding and soaring.

The Loss of Warren Eaton

The November 1 Bulletin announced that, owing to the lack of financial support, the position of general manager had to be discontinued. This meant that all of Southee's duties had to be taken over by Eaton.

Nonetheless, Eaton continued his promotional work, and later in November he took a group that included Southee, E. Paul du Pont (a cousin of Dick du Pont), and Harold Bowen (Eaton's pilot) south to promote soaring and to start a soaring school in Florida. They had a tow plane and two Franklin gliders. On December 1, shortly after a double-tow takeoff from Miami Municipal Airport with Southee and du Pont in the tow plane and Bowen in the other Franklin, Eaton unexpectedly hit the turbulence of the tow plane slipstream. His specially designed removable cockpit fairing came loose and hit him in the eye and incapacitated him. Although he had released his safety belt and had fallen clear, he failed to pull the parachute ring and fell to his death.

Eaton's death was a severe blow to his family, friends, and the SSA. He had been the mainstay and stabilizing

element of the organization throughout the two and a half years of its existence. Eaton had been a very private
person so that no one knew just how
much financial support he had given
the SSA. However, it was there when
it was needed. He must have felt that
the SSA had to learn to operate on its
own, as was demonstrated when he
let Southee go, even at great inconvenience to himself. Soaring people
looked to him for leadership and he
gave it in his firm but pleasant way.
He recognized that soaring needed
more exposure, and the accident occurred during one of his efforts to
demonstrate soaring in a new area.

A special directors' meeting was
held in Norwich, New York, in December with Mrs. Warren Eaton acting
as chairperson. Present were Gale,
Southee, Lange, and Dick du Pont.
The consensus was that the directors
of the SSA should carry on, since they
felt that this was what Warren would
have wanted them to do, and so they
voted to hold the annual directors'
meeting in January, at which time they
would elect a new president and make
plans for the future. In the meantime,
Southee would run the SSA and put
together the Bulletin.

The Barnaby Period, 1935–1936

Ralph S. Barnaby was elected president at the next directors' meeting on
February 1–3, 1935. He was the logical
choice for he had been active in motorless flight for many years and he
had the time to spend on such a position. He also agreed to take over the
editorship of the Bulletin and to handle all other SSA functions, except
those specifically connected with the
national contests.

At the same meeting, R. C.

du Pont was elected vice-president and
Lewin Barringer, secretary-treasurer. In
addition, five new directors were
elected, including Lewin Barringer,
Don Hamilton, William McGrath,
C. B. Milliken, and Art Schultz. This
brought the number of directors to 19.
A board of 20 directors was authorized, but one spot was kept open for a
possible special appointment.

Elmira was named the site of the
Sixth National Soaring Contest. The
Elmira group said they would match
up to $1,000 any money raised by SSA
as a prize fund for the coming nationals. A life membership category was
set up at $50.

The first membership meeting to
be held at a time other than during the
Nationals took place Saturday evening
with 55 persons present. Barnaby reported on the SSA activities planned
for 1935 and on the U.S. Navy's glider
program.

The Navy had announced that
they would use five Franklin gliders in
a training program to determine its
aviation students' aptitude for flying.
The starting classes at Pensacola, Florida, were divided into two groups.
The first group was given the normal
power course. The second group was
given a glider course before taking the
power plane course. At the completion
of the glider course the students were
evaluated by their instructors as to
how they would do in the power
course. At the end of the power
course their performance as a pilot
was compared with their forecast performance, to see whether it was possible to predict how they would do in
the power course. The overall aim was
to reduce the cost of training by using
a glider course to weed out those who
obviously would not qualify for the
power rating. It was also felt that the
experience of glider training would in-

crease their motivation for flying. This system turned out to be effective, but was never adopted as standard practice, probably because of the resistance to change that is often present in the military.

When Barnaby returned to Pensacola, he found himself swamped with work, but was able to use his Navy secretary for SSA matters and got his mother to help to mail out the Bulletin. In the first issue he put out (vol. 4, no. 2, dated February 1), Ralph wrote a tribute to Eaton. In the March issue he reported on the Federal Aviation Commission's report:

> These recommendations are the result of our late President Warren E. Eaton's efforts. While the fate of the Commission's report seems to be somewhat uncertain, in that it is felt that the President's [Roosevelt] message transmitting it to Congress did not give it unqualified backing, there is no doubt but that the recommendations regarding gliding are good, and carrying them out lies within the province and power of existing government departments.

One part of the official FAC report referred specifically to soaring and its rapid spread in recent years:

> Half a dozen countries now have active gliding associations and schools, and in at least four, Germany, Russia, France and Great Britain, government support is given. The Germans have long spent considerable sums of money on gliding, $82,000 being allowed in the German budget for 1933, and the British government has just decided to give direct assistance, to the extent of $25,000 per year for the next five years.
> Gliding and soaring have struggled along in the United States without government support or interest, and under the handicap of various waves of ridiculous exaggerated promotion. They now seem to have been put upon a reasonable orderly footing, at least to the extent that it is apparent what can and cannot be done with gliders. It appears to us from what we can learn, that they possess no miraculous properties, but that they have a certain interest as instruments of research and of study of atmospheric conditions. They seem to have marked possibilities in simplifying the training of pilots and eliminating some of the unfit before they get to the expensive stage of taking instruction on powered aircraft, and we are further informed by certain expert pilots that they have found gliding most helpful to their own technique and consider it a very useful phase of a post-graduate course for the really finished flier. Despite the precedent of most of Europe, we propose no direct governmental assistance here. We question its justification, and even if we thought it justified, we have seen no sound way of administering and controlling the expenditure. We do, however, suggest that the government departments concerned with aeronautics should take a considerably more active interest in gliding than in the past.

The Bureau of Air Commerce took an active interest in helping the SSA. Col. Cone, the administrator, planned to be at the Sixth National to look further into the possibility of having a glider specialist assigned to the bureau.

Sixth National, 1935

The Sixth National Soaring Contest held from June 29 to July 14, 1935, had the largest number of participants up to that time, with 31 sailplanes and 96 pilots entered. The best distance flight of 120 miles was made by du Pont who won the championship for the second year in a row. J. K. O'Meara

(NSM Loomis Collection)

The Contest pilots at the 1935 National. *Bottom row, left to right:* Prat Jones, Bud Southerland, Chet Decker, Earl Southee, Larry Lawrence, Ralph Barnaby, Allaire duPont, Dick duPont, Percy Pierce, Russ Holderman, Dorothy Holderman, Don Hamilton, and Emerson Mehlhose; *second row,* Dick Randolph, Cleveland Hyde, Emil Lehecka (?), Floyd Sweet, Nelson Shapter, Udo Fisher (?), Charlie Tubbs, Dr. Klemperer, and Bernard Wade; *third row,* Jack Laister, Milt Stoughton, Art Ramer, Joe A. Oberg (?), Youston Sekella, Rudy Thoren, Leon Kubinsky, Bud Iszard, James Kendrick (?), Julius Schliemann, Richard Koegler, George Stead, Henry Runkel, and R. E. Franklin; *fourth row,* Stan Smith, Al Santilli, Harold Bowen, Dana Darling, William H. Cook (?), Ben W. Badenoch, George Casey, Hank Whitman (?), and William Bye.

was second and Chester Decker third. Allaire du Pont, Richard's wife, set a women's record with a 5-hour 31-minute flight in the new du Pont Utility.

At their annual meeting on July 7, the directors agreed to sponsor another expedition to Big Meadows. Klemperer was authorized to proceed with developing a point-award system for scoring the next national contest, and a spring soaring expedition to the Ellenville, New York, site was also approved. In addition, the fee for club (or group) membership was set at $6, which would entitle a group to receive six issues of the Bulletin, all sent to one address. Larry Lawrence was appointed to head a committee that was to collect data on sailplane design and to make a formal application to the federal government for financial assistance to carry this out. Schultz was appointed to investigate the possibility of the SSA sponsoring a meet at Sleeping Bear near Traverse City, Michigan.

The directors elected Dr. Klem-

perer as a second vice-president and Earl Southee to replace Barringer as secretary-treasurer.

Barringer had resigned as secretary-treasurer since he had accepted a position as head of the aviation department of an archaeological expedition to Persia. On April 3 he had made an outstanding ridge flight in the Albatross II from Ellenville, New York, to Harrisburg, Pennsylvania, a distance of 155.4 miles, just short of du Pont's national record.

Membership Meetings

July 11 and 12, were not soarable so flying was canceled and membership meetings were held on both days. At those meetings a number of pilots said they were unhappy with the SSA because its officers and directors were self-appointed and the membership had no voice.

The founders of SSA had originally drawn the officers and Board of

Directors from the small group of active soaring pilots and a few other persons who were interested in seeing soaring grow. Because of the many problems of getting SSA going, this method of choosing officers and directors had continued.

Now, however, the members demanded a change. Barnaby later noted: "After much hullabaloo at Elmira about the management of the society being in the hands of a closed corporation of self-appointees, and the demand for representative gov't, arrangements were made for an election of directors for 1936 by direct popular vote of the membership." In the August Bulletin Barnaby commented on this matter and the fact that SSA members could not agree on who to recommend to the Bureau of Air Commerce for the glider specialist position:

> The Soaring Society missed one of its greatest opportunities to aid gliding and soaring in this country. As the result of the effort of our late President, Warren E. Eaton, and the directors of the Society, Colonel A. Cone of the Bureau of Air Commerce came to Elmira all set to appoint a man to handle the glider affairs in the Bureau, as the first step in a program of revising into a more logical and practical form the rules and regulations covering this branch of aviation. What happened? Let me quote Colonel Cone's letter:
>
> "I was also surprised and somewhat concerned to find that there are several factions in the soaring group with divergent ideas and although each faction is interested in the Department of Commerce employing a competent man to guide us in the writing of gliding and soaring regulations and in the general sponsorship of the development of soaring and gliding, no two factions seem to be able to agree as to whom in their group

would be the best qualified to fill the position—but when I found so much friction and division of opinion as to who would be fitted for the job, about five different men having been recommended by various groups, I decided that perhaps it would be better to defer any action until some later date."

If the Soaring Society is going to be worth its salt, it must maintain a reputation and position which will make it be looked to as the authority on gliding and soaring matters, and as the representative in this country of those who are connected with this branch of aviation. In order to do this, it is necessary that it have officers and directors who have the confidence and support of its membership. As discussed at length later in this issue, there will be a general election of directors. Members, it is up to you!

The du Pont Utility

In du Pont's view, a new utility was needed to replace the Franklin and Cadet, which were no longer in production. He engaged Heath McDowell and Stan Smith to design, engineer, and build what was to become known as the du Pont Utility. Ted Bellak was also hired to work on the project. The ship was first flown in June 1935 and soon after it was taken to the Nationals, where it showed that it had good soaring performance.

When du Pont saw the problems and cost of putting a utility into production, not to mention its uncertain sales, his interest must have cooled off. McDowell and Smith's employment ended in June when the ship left for the Nationals. However, Bellak stayed on as du Pont's handyman, and in December of 1935 the du Pont Utility was offered as a kit.

The 100th Silver "C"

Reports from Germany announced their 100th Silver "C" award. Great Britain was next in order with six and the United States was tied with Hungary at three each. The U.S. Silver "Cs" were held by Jack O'Meara, Richard du Pont and Lewin Barringer, in that order.

The First SSA Election

In the first SSA election by the membership all but two of the previous directors were reelected. (Art Schultz and Clark B. Milliken, who had only been on the board for one year, were not reelected.) This vindicated the officers and directors who had been accused of operating a "closed corporation." Four new directors were elected at that time: J. K. O'Meara, Stan Smith, Mrs. Eaton, and Youston Sekella.

The total number of SSA members on September 1, 1935, was 197. The 113 members who voted in the election represented only 57 percent of the membership. Although this low percentage greatly disturbed Barnaby, it seems good when compared with more recent experience. For example, the average return for the 1980 SSA election was only 15 percent. However, when a copy of Barnaby's 1935 editorial was reprinted in the July 1981 *Soaring,* the election participation that fall increased to 26 percent, the highest it has been in many years.

Directors' Meeting

The 1936 annual directors' meeting was held in New York from January 31 to February 1. Barnaby was reelected president, Southee and K. O. Lange were elected vice-presidents, Don Hamilton secretary, and R. C. du Pont treasurer. When Enyart of NAA offered several pages of space in each issue of the NAA magazine for SSA news and comments, the offer was accepted. Elmira was chosen as the site for the Nationals and changes in the rules were discussed. Over 100 members attended a membership meeting on Saturday—this was approximately half of the SSA membership.

Soaring around the United States

Soaring activity in the Northwest started in the early 1930s through the efforts of Charles McAllister, who had a flying service in Yakima, Washington, and Cloyd Artman, a high school student of Oroville. McAllister had built a 50-foot Darmstadt-type sailplane and on June 16, 1933, made an 8-hour flight.

Cloyd Artman, who had started from scratch, completed a primary and taught himself to fly above the bluffs along the Snake River. He was the main booster of soaring in the Northwest and traveled around the state trying out different sites. In the summer of 1933 he made a $13\frac{1}{2}$-hour flight in a primary. In 1936 he helped organize the First Northwest Soaring Meet, which was held at Wenatchee. At that time Artman was attending the Washington State College, where he formed an aerial club. They built a two-seater, but in April 1937 Artman and his passenger Frank See were killed because of a structural failure of the wing.

Other reports in the Bulletin from around the United States showed that soaring was growing. Speed Westphal, a southern California pilot, told about his first flight in the new BG-1, Gus Briegleb's first design, a small single-place utility. Speed clipped a tree on his second flight in the BG-1, so Gus had to take it back for repair before he could fly it. Ed Knight wrote about making auto tows to an altitude of 2,400 feet from the frozen Maumee River near Toledo, Ohio. Chet Decker and his group reported on flying from the ice on Greenwood Lake near Warwick, New York, and soaring along the slopes of Mt. Peter.

Seventh National, 1936

The Seventh National Soaring Contest was the next big event in 1936. Soaring flights were made on 14 of the 16 days. Chet Decker was the winner, with du Pont close behind. Henry Wightman finished fourth after an outstanding 135-mile flight to Middletown, New York, in the du Pont Utility.

Five more pilots (Stan Smith, Emil A. Lehecka, Chet Decker, Emerson Mehlhose, and Henry Wightman) completed their Silver "C" awards to bring the U.S. total up to eight. Again, the majority of the ships entered were utilities and secondaries. New ships were the Buxton Transporter, a two-place sailplane designed and built by Jay Buxton and flown by Red Slatter. Two Gull-wing Franklins were entered by Bob Auburn and Bill Placek.

An H-17 and a Wolf that du Pont had ordered from Germany arrived in time for the 1936 Nationals; du Pont made his first flight in the H-17 by winch tow, and he was not impressed. The Wolf was much more satisfactory, and du Pont was able to finish second to Decker, who was flying du Pont's old Albatross I, a much higher performance sailplane. Although there were somewhat fewer pilots and soaring craft than in the previous years, a record number of miles were flown across country.

Ernie and Paul Schweizer attended this meeting and they were impressed with the number of soaring enthusiasts present. In the fall of 1935 they had decided to manufacture sailplanes, and they were pleased to see the interest in soaring growing in spite of the depressed economic conditions. They had graduated as aeronautical engineers from the Guggenheim School of Aeronautics of New York University (NYU) during a period when aviation was at a very low point and few aeronautical engineering jobs were available in the industry. They felt there was a future in designing and building sailplanes and they were convinced that all-metal construction was the way to go. In 1938 the Schweizer Metal Aircraft Company was formed as a partnership. They worked part-time in their father's restaurant, Bonnie Brook, which he had started in Peekskill, New York, after closing the restaurant in Carnegie Hall. The two Schweizers developed their sailplane business in the barn behind the restaurant. Brother Bill Schweizer helped when he was home from Syracuse University._

The original H-17s, which were made in Austria, weighed only 145 pounds, whereas the German-built H-17s weighed over 220 pounds. The German authorities required that the structure be "beefed up"—the controls be mass balanced—and a wheel added. However, the H-17's small size (32-foot span and 100-square-foot wing

Cloyd Artman launches his primary glider from a novel greased launching track at Oroville, Washington.
(NSM Collection)

Top: Chet Decker with the Albatross I at the 1936 National with four members of the North Jersey Soaring Association. Left to right: Warren Merboth, Ken Findesen, Felix Chardon, unkown member, and Carl Schaub.

(NSM Loomis Collection)

A group of officials at the 1936 National. Left to right: SSA directors, Charlie Gale, Dr. Karl Lange, and Larry Lawrence; Jack Sommers of the CAA; SSA director and Elmira businessman Franklin "Bud" Iszard; and Youston Sekella of the Elmira Glider Club.

(NSM Loomis Collection)

area) and the increased weight created an adverse "scale effect." This, plus the much higher wing loading than du Pont was used to, must have surprised him. He released from tow in a partly stalled condition and was only able to complete a tight 360-degree turn back to Harris Hill. He walked away in disgust, convinced that this was not the ship to replace the slow-flying utilities.

Directors' Meeting, 1936

Barnaby was not present for the Seventh National and so did not chair the two directors' meetings that were held

during that time. At the meeting of June 25, du Pont presented an ambitious plan for expanding the activities of the SSA. This plan was received enthusiastically, for the directors realized du Pont had the means to underwrite such a program. At a second meeting held on July 2, an Executive Committee was appointed for the first time. It consisted of R. C. du Pont (chairman), W. Enyart, Mrs. Eaton, A. L. Lawrence, and C. Gale. Their mission was to develop and implement the expansion plan. The committee also was authorized to act for the Board of Directors.

It was obvious that the directors expected du Pont to become the next president and by appointing him chairman of the Executive Committee hoped that he would be able to get his program going by the time Barnaby completed his term at the end of the year.

The directors voted to hold the 1937 national contest at Elmira from June 26 to July 10 and decided to make it an international contest for the members of the ISTUS.

Mrs. Eaton announced a donation of $1,500 to encourage the design and construction of sailplanes. She also gave $500 each to the SSA and the EAC for the advancement of soaring.

Another action of the directors was to create a new group membership classification. The Detroit Glider Council became the first group member. Soon after they were joined by the Northern California Soaring Association and the Purdue University Glider Club.

In September du Pont went to Germany to study the soaring movement there and to determine whether the European sailplane industry could fill the sailplane needs of this country. He was interested in the Schempp-

Hirth line of sailplanes, the Göeppin-gen I Wolf, and the new Minimoa, a high-performance sailplane.

With du Pont and the Executive Committee taking over the operation of the SSA, Barnaby spent most of his time bringing the Bulletin up to date. Vol. 5, no. 12, dated December 1936, was the last one published.

Barnaby's Two Years

During Barnaby's two-year period as president the SSA evolved from a soci-ety run by a small closed group to a bona fide membership organization. Barnaby had to cope with a number of problems in this transition, and as he did not have Eaton's financial means, SSA's financial problems grew worse. With less than 300 members and the cost of membership at only $2.00, the actual total income for 1936 was $548. Barnaby said that at one time he had bought an extra life membership in or-der to have enough money for the postage. In his "Ave et Vale" editorial, Barnaby said that his tenure as presi-dent was without doubt one of the most exasperating, tiresome, and end-less jobs in the world, but nonetheless one of the most interesting.

Chapter 4

The du Pont Era,
1937–1939

Soaring Gets an Angel, 1937

Dick du Pont was elected president at the 1937 annual meeting held in New York City in January. However, he had already taken over the previous July when the directors elected him chairman of the executive committee. Du Pont believed that if the SSA had a general manager to run the organization and edit *Soaring* magazine, the membership would grow and attract advertisers, and thus could soon be self-supporting.

This had also been the hope of Evans for the NGA when he hired Walker in 1928, and of the SSA directors when they hired Southee in 1934. Unfortunately, neither of these had worked out because financial support was impossible to obtain during the Depression. However, with du Pont willing to underwrite the program for at least a couple of years, there was optimism that it would be successful.

Du Pont had organized his program in five executive meetings before the annual directors' meeting in January. The first meeting was held in New York City on September 26, 1936. It was proposed that the SSA have a permanent executive office, preferably in one of the larger eastern cities. The committee favored such an arrangement, but postponed their decision on a location to the next meeting. Plans for a pamphlet describing soaring and

the SSA, its aims, and programs were discussed and a draft was to be prepared. The question of a more elaborate monthly publication was also discussed, and all agreed that an illustrated printed magazine similar to the British *Sailplane and Gliding* would be highly desirable.

Du Pont suggested that since the United States was not producing sailplanes, the SSA should invite Sport-Flugzeugbau Göeppingen to distribute their sailplanes and equipment in the United States and Canada for a two-year period. The SSA would then distribute these gliders to its members at no profit to itself. A proposal to this effect was sent to each director with a statement that unless a majority of objections were registered before October 11 the contract would become effective on that date.

The second meeting of the Executive Committee was held on October 11 at Ellenville, New York, the takeoff site that Barringer had used for his ridge flights. At that meeting the committee further discussed the new plans for SSA and decided to encourage model builders to move up to motorless flight by holding a model contest in connection with the Nationals.

At the next meeting of the Executive Committee in New York City on October 26, du Pont reported on the results of his discussions with the Bureau of Air Commerce concerning a reciprocal agreement between the United States and Germany on the licensing of sailplanes. This was needed in order to license the Schemp-Hirth sailplanes that would be imported to the United States.

The committee also voted that the SSA publish a magazine to be known as *Soaring* for a three-month trial period. R. du Pont would serve as editorial director pending the appointment of a general manager for the SSA.

At the committee's fourth meeting on November 17, du Pont recommended that the SSA's charter be changed so that it could be classified as an educational institution and contributions could be tax-exempt.

A number of important developments took place at the fifth executive committee meeting on December 19 that would be acted upon at the annual directors' meeting: (1) the procedure for electing SSA directors was changed to a staggered arrangement, as suggested by Dr. Klemperer; (2) the SSA was made a tax-deductible organization (in a letter to Barnaby, du Pont mentioned that his overall program for the SSA and *Soaring* was contingent upon getting the tax-deductible features); and (3) an editor-in-chief was selected for the glider construction manual.

Soaring *Magazine*

The first issue of *Soaring* appeared in early January of 1937. The SSA members were delighted to see this "slick" magazine, which was a pleasant change from the old mimeographed bulletins. In order to encourage membership, this issue was distributed free to 10,000 prospects, who were offered a one-year membership for $1 along with a free one-year subscription to *Soaring*.

Du Pont's first editorial showed that gliders were playing an important part in the military preparedness programs of some European countries. In it he explained the need for creating airmindedness among the young and proposed that this be accomplished by having them progress from model gliders and airplane building to glider flying, and then later into powerplanes. Du Pont lamented the fact that the United States had no such system and expressed the hope that soaring could help more people become familiar with flying. Included in this first issue was an eight-page insert entitled "Soaring in America," which gave the history of motorless flight and showed what contributions soaring could make to American aviation.

Annual Meeting

The dates of January 29 to 31 were chosen for the 1937 annual meeting so that those attending the SSA meeting could also attend the Institute of Aeronautical Science meeting and the aviation show that were held during the same period. The directors also elected R. S. Barnaby vice-president, W. Klemperer vice-president, A. L. Lawrence secretary, P. Pierce treasurer, and K. O. Lange chairman of the contest board. In addition, they approved a change in the charter making the SSA an educational institute for the promotion of gliding and soaring.

The bylaws were amended to provide for a board of directors of not more than 20 members with 6 directors elected each year for a three-year term and 2 directors-at-large for a term of one year. Before this, all directors were elected at one time for a one-year term, and since their terms all expired at the same time there was no assurance of any continuity in the board of directors.

When it was announced that Germany planned to have an international meet in 1937, the board decided to postpone the SSA plans for an international meet until 1938.

An open meeting for SSA members and other interested persons was held Saturday afternoon and evening, with approximately 150 present. Barnaby presented a report on the directors' meeting and introduced the new directors and officers. He then introduced Lewin Barringer, who spoke about his experience as the pilot for an archaeological expedition to Persia on which his soaring experience had enabled him to reach his destination in a desolate region, in spite of unexpected headwinds. A paper by Art Schultz was read and talks were given by R. E. Franklin and Larry Lawrence. The evening program included an explanation by Milton Stoughton of the proposed Bureau of Air Commerce glider regulations. A discussion was held regarding Mrs. Eaton's $1,500 glider design prize and general approval was given for the contest rules. Dr. K. O. Lange spoke on the plans for the 1937 contest.

Lewin Barringer with his Minimoa at the 1937 National. His jacket was modeled after the type that being worn in Europe and included soaring badges and club insignias. He encouraged other pilots to adopt this custom.

(NSM Loomis Collection)

Barringer Appointed

At a special executive committee meeting on February 20, Barringer was elected general manager of the SSA and editor of *Soaring*. This was to be effective April 1 and was contingent on the receipt of a $5,000 pledge by du Pont to guarantee a manager's salary for two years. Du Pont noted that it was imperative to have someone to handle the routine inquiries as well as edit the magazine. He proposed the following plan.

The manager's salary would be $1,800 a year for two years beginning on April 1. Fifty percent of magazine subscription receipts would constitute additional salary until it totaled $2,400. After subscriptions reached 1,000, the bonus would be reduced as the subscriptions grew. In addition he would receive 10 percent of the advertising receipts and donations that were received through his efforts. Expenditures by the manager to increase membership and advertising would first have to be approved by the president, the Executive Committee, or the directors.

Barringer's appointment and the opening of the new executive office in Philadelphia was announced in the April issue of *Soaring*.

The next executive committee meeting was held on March 13 in New York City. It covered the plans for a formal agreement between the NAA and SSA. On being appointed general manager, Barringer resigned as director and was replaced by Milton Stoughton.

The March issue of the British *Sailplane and Gliding* magazine conveyed the good wishes of the British

Richard C. (Dick) duPont by his Minimoa sailplane in which he won the national championship in 1937.

(NSM Loomis Collection)

position of the representative body in the United States for motorless flight and guarantees to the Society control of the National Soaring Contest and any international or regional contest organized by the SSA."

Bill Enyart presented the agreement and the executive committee recommended that the SSA directors accept the agreement with the understanding that SSA members would include $2.00 for membership in the NAA.

Eighth National, 1937

The new administration building, hangar, and cabins were officially dedicated at the Eighth National Soaring Contest, which had a record number of entries—54 sailplanes and 147 pilots. Most impressive were the cross-country miles flown, which were almost double the miles flown in the 1936 contest and seven times those of 1935.

Three foreign competitors, Peter Riedel of Germany and Jonas Pyragius and Bronius Oskinis of Lithuania, were entered. Riedel's sailplane, a Senior Sperber from Germany, attracted much attention because of the swastika on its tail, a required element of the German certification insignia. Riedel finished far ahead, demonstrating the superiority of a tight spiraling technique over the shallow turns of the other competitors, but he could not be named champion. Dick du Pont received that honor flying a new Minimoa; Chet Decker was second in an Albatross; and Emil A. Lehecka in a Rhonsperber and Harland Ross in the RS-1 tied for third place.

For the first time, aero-tow was used for contest takeoffs of the high-performance sailplanes. The large number of utility gliders without gov-

Glider Association to the SSA. In a friendly manner, it took the United States to task for overstressing the practical advantages of gliding. Barringer's response appeared in the May editorial of *Soaring:* "It's often necessary to lay emphasis on the useful side when trying to convince those practical men of business to whom we must go for support, and there is no denying that flight training, aircraft design, and meteorology knowledge are useful adjuncts quite aside from its appeal as a superb sport."

An executive meeting was held in New York on May 15. All members were present and guests were R. E. Franklin, Milt Stoughton, Percy Pierce, and Barringer. The meeting covered policy for the prize money for the national contest and the status of the two manuals that were under way. Stoughton hoped to have his *Glider Construction Manual* ready for the Bureau of Air Commerce by June 15th, and Lawrence expected to have his *Glider Operation Manual* by June 1. The minutes of this meeting noted: "The most important business completed at the meeting was the adoption of a plan of joint cooperation between the Soaring Society and the National Aeronautic Association, which secured for the Society the

ernment aero-towing permits had to stay on the ground when the winds were not in the right direction for winch launching. The August 1937 *Soaring* stated,

> It showed a marked step ahead for the movement and opened our eyes for the first time to the need for Regional contests and acceptance of entries of qualified pilots only, in future National contests. . . . For the first time since 1932 a perfect safety record was marred by accident. There were 4 crashes resulting from stalls. It's very fortunate that the most serious injury was that of broken legs. The most disastrous, from an equipment point of view, resulted in serious damage to three high performance sailplanes. As a result of these accidents it was painfully brought home to us that our present license requirements were inadequate and that from a safety point of view we must require a knowledge of stalls and spins and recovery therefrom for anyone qualified for a commercial glider pilots license.

Eaton Design Contest

One of the special events of the Eighth National was the Eaton design contest. Any new American utility or sailplane

that had not flown at the previous National was eligible. Drawings and stress analysis had to be presented with the entry and it was Mrs. Eaton's hope that drawings and kits of the winning designs would be available to individuals and clubs, and that the designs would eventually be approved for licensing by the Bureau of Air Commerce. The winners of this contest were as follows: Arthur B. Schultz, ABC Sailplane, first ($700); Harland Ross, RS-1 Sailplane, second ($500); and Ernest and Paul Schweizer, SGU 1-6 Utility, third ($300).

The ABC Sailplane design by Art Schultz was a good intermediate sailplane but rather complex for the average homebuilder. The RS-1 design by Harland Ross was a real step ahead in high-performance sailplane design. It was the first of the clean, higher-wing loading sailplanes designed for high cross-country flying speed that are so popular today. The Schweizer 1-6 was an attempt to meet the requirements for a popular utility sailplane. It was the first all-metal glider ever built in the world and it had a "pod-and-boom" fuselage that was intended to make it simpler and cheaper to construct.

None of the three winning designs was an easy-to-build home construction

Above, left: Peter Riedel alongside his Senior Sperber sailplane at the 1937 national championship, at which he was the unofficial winner. At that time he was employed as an airline pilot in South America.

(NSM Loomis Collection)

Arthur Schultz and his ABC sailplane, which won the Eaton design contest.

(NSM Loomis Collection)

After 1932, the responsibility for carrying out the national contest was divided between the glider committee of the Elmira Association of Commerce, which provided the facilities and the finances, and the SSA Contest Board, which operated the competition phase of the contest.

The Contest Board felt that Elmira benefited from the contests and so had no qualms about asking the Elmira group to supply finances and service. However, the Elmira people felt that they were doing more than their share, particularly since it was through their efforts that the administration building, hangar, and cabins had been added to Harris Hill. As a result, relations between the two groups were often strained.

At a luncheon at the Iszard Tea Room in downtown Elmira during the Eighth National, Don Hamilton (an SSA Director), Eddie Mooers (a local soaring booster), and Franklin Iszard (one of the founders of SSA), proposed that a nonprofit corporation made up of board members from both groups be created to run the contests.

Top, right: Harland Ross and Harvey Stephens with their RS-1 sailplane, which won second place in the Eaton design contest.

(NSM Loomis Collection)

Top, left: Ernie Schweizer with the SGU1-6 Utility sailplane. The first all-metal glider built, it placed third in the Eaton design competition.

(NSM Loomis Collection)

The "Pterodactyl" of the Altosaurus Soaring Club of North Conway, New Hampshire, was the second SGU1-7 built and the first glider sold by SAC.

(Margaret Noyes, NSM Collection)

sailplane that Mrs. Eaton was trying to encourage. The contest did bring forth many design concepts, among which the Schweizer's 1-7 set the design philosophy for many of their popular sailplanes that were to follow. Only two 1-7s were built, and the second one was sold to a group of Harvard skiers from the Schussverien Ski Club in North Conway New Hampshire, who, led by Eliot Noyes, formed the Altosaurus Soaring Club (the 1-7 had the likeness of a pterodactyl, the ancient flying reptile, painted on each side of the fuselage). The club members, all experienced skiers, taught themselves to fly using auto and winch tow. This same 1-7 was still flying in California in 1984. The basic design configuration was later expanded into the 2-22 and then the 2-33.

The matter was discussed informally during the national contest and it was agreed that the Elmira group should proceed with the formation of such an organization.

At a meeting of the SSA executive board at Mrs. Warren Eaton's summer home in Osterville, Massachusetts, on August 7, the new corporation and what the SSA should expect from it were the main topics of discussion. One of the things SSA wanted to see was the establishment of a soaring school in the Elmira area.

The new corporation was formed at a meeting in Elmira on August 24, 1937, and was named the Elmira Area Soaring Corporation (EASC). Richard C. du Pont was elected its first president and the directors were du Pont, Mrs. W. Eaton, Dr. K. O. Lange, and Lewin Barringer from the SSA, and J. Arthur Mann, Wm. L. McGrath, Oscar Monrad, Melvin Reynolds, and Youston Sekella from the Elmira area. The meeting dealt primarily with organizational matters and the possibility of holding an international contest at Harris Hill in 1938. Du Pont wanted to explain the SSA's attitude toward corporations of this type but did not have an opportunity to do so. He therefore wrote an open letter to the directors of the EASC in the October 1937 issue of *Soaring* explaining that the SSA would be interested in joining such a relationship with other soaring centers in the United States, but emphasized that the SSA was not obligated to choose Harris Hill for its contests. He noted that soaring could be carried on almost everywhere as long as there were facilities to launch sailplanes and sufficient places to land. At the same time, he noted that "with the construction work that has already been done there, there is little question that it is the finest equipped soaring site in the

When the 1-6 was entered in the 1937 National, the Schweizers had limited soaring experience and so were looking for an experienced pilot to fly it in the contest. Jack O'Meara was at the National without a sailplane to fly but proudly carried around the latest Kollsman rate-of-climb. The Schweizers offered him the 1-6, but he was looking for a higher-performance sailplane that would be more in keeping with his status as a top pilot. O'Meara, on seeing the 1-6 for the first time, told the Schweizers that Hawley Bowlus was also building a new "pod-and-boom" type of sailplane. It became the Baby Albatross that first flew the following year.

United States. It would seem to me that, with the already going Aviation Ground School and the present facilities on Harris Hill, an effort should be made by this corporation to hold Elmira in the position of a National soaring center. In order to do this, I would suggest that attempts be made to carry out the Soaring Society's recommendations for improvements.—Firstly, the acquisition of the airport (for training), and secondly, the construction of a spacious hangar." These requirements were met the following year with the addition of a two-story hangar and the operation of a glider school by the EASC at the American Airlines auxiliary field in Big Flats, New York.

SSA Appeal

The first indication that du Pont's plan was not working out financially appeared in Barringer's article entitled "Appeal," in the November *Soaring*. He said that the membership had grown from 300 at the beginning of the year to just under 1,100 members. Although he felt this was a sizable increase, he said that the membership had to at least double that in order to be self-supporting. He also mentioned that it had been necessary to go back to the $2.00 associate membership as in former years and that a new active membership at $4.00 a year had been created that included NAA membership. He referred to du Pont's open letter, which had noted the SSA budget for 1937 was $14,000, with $5,000 for the magazine, $3,000 for the manager's salary, and $6,000 for prize money for the Eighth National Soaring Contest. He said that $8,000 for the first two items was guaranteed for 1938, but no mention was made of a contest prize fund, or what support there would be for 1939. He also noted that "this Appeal is to each member of the SSA to do his part in helping to get new members."

Barringer's Second Year, 1938

On the first anniversary of *Soaring* magazine, Barringer's editorial expressed an optimistic view. He was gratified that the membership had increased by 400 percent in the past year, and he hoped it would continue to grow in spite of the necessity of increasing the membership and subscription rates.

Barringer felt that the new glider pilot requirements as published in the January issue were acceptable to the bureau and should soon be in effect. He also mentioned that there were a few cases in which glider pilots had been prohibited from flying unlicensed gliders on a federal airway, but that the bureau now permitted this if the glider flights stayed below a certain altitude. He announced that, as a service to the readers, he had begun a monthly column on sailplanes and another column on soaring centers.

First National Gliding and Soaring Conference

The first National Gliding and Soaring Conference was held in conjunction with the annual meeting in Washington, D.C., on February 11 and 12. The two-day session was well organized, and some distinguished guests attended the luncheon: Gen. H. H. Arnold, assistant chief of the U.S. Army Air Corps; Dr. George Lewis, director of the NACA; Richard Boutell of the Bureau of Air Commerce; Capt. Richardson of the Bureau of Aeronautics of the Navy; and Paul Garber of the Smithsonian Institution. Du Pont, Barringer, and Lange reported on SSA plans and the progress that had been made. A total of 76 persons attended the luncheon, an impressive number for that time.

After the luncheon, Lewin Barringer made a sailplane demonstration flight for the Washington guests at Boling Field. The low ceiling prevented aero towing so Barringer made several auto tows in a Wolf sailplane. Later in the afternoon a session on design and construction was led by Dr. Eastman Jacobs and Fred Weick of the NACA. The closing event was a tour of the aeronautic exhibits at the Smithsonian Institution conducted by Paul Garber, director of the Aeronautics Department.

Not much time was available for general discussion during the conference, but some of the delegates complained about the distribution of prize money at the Nationals. Barringer replied in the March editorial that he did not think they would have felt that way if they had heard the treasurer's report, which showed that the budget for the last year was more than ten times the amount received from the membership. The main business was the election of the officers, who remained the same, except that Charles Gale replaced Ralph S. Barnaby as vice-president, and Mrs. W. E. Eaton was elected treasurer to replace Percy

Pierce. The group also discussed Mrs. Eaton's plans for the Warren E. Eaton Memorial Trophy, which was to be the primary soaring trophy in the United States.

Record Attempts

Two events in the spring of 1938 foreshadowed the future of U.S. distance and altitude soaring. At that time the U.S. distance record was 158 miles and the U.S. altitude record was 6,233 feet, both of which had been set in 1934. Thereafter the world record had steadily increased and in the spring of 1938 stood at 405 miles for distance, which was held by the Russians, and 14,189 feet for altitude, which was held by the Germans.

Barringer was anxious for the American records to be increased and he felt that this could be done over the flatlands of the Southwest. He encouraged other pilots to join him in an expedition to investigate the possibility of level-country soaring in that area and to increase the U.S. records. Because the Wichita Falls, Texas, Chamber of Commerce had put up $500 toward the expense of the expedition, they used this city for their base. The original hope was that Harland Ross's R-2 sailplane, which was being built in Wichita Falls for the SSA, would be ready for Barringer to fly.

Barringer learned that the R-2, later called the *Ibis*, would not be ready in time, so he borrowed Dick du Pont's Minimoa and the du Pont winch for the expedition. Unfortunately, no other pilots were able to go, so Barringer left for Texas in early April with Peter Bonotaux and Ken Findesen as crew members. Ted Bellak was winch driver and used the versatile du Pont winch to tow the Minimoa

A group of Hudson Valley Soaring Club members attended this first conference. It was their first trip to the national capital and they were impressed by it and also the famous people at the conference. They particularly enjoyed the Smithsonian tour led by Paul Garber. At that time there were two sailplanes on display—Frank Hawks's Franklin Eaglet *and Warren Eaton's mahogany Bowlus-du Pont.*

Another young enthusiast who attended this convention was Vic Saudek who was attending Carnegie Tech. He had car trouble driving to Washington and had to use most of his funds to get there by train. He spent a cold night sleeping in a parked car near the Lafayette Hotel so he could attend the meetings the next day.

The Schweizers came back from the first conference infused with a feeling that the soaring movement was moving ahead and their manufacturing efforts might succeed.

and trailer to Texas. Dr. Karl O. Lange was the meteorologist.

They spent almost a month at Wichita Falls and in spite of the generally poor weather they did have some good days. On April 19 Barringer set a new national distance and goal flight record when he flew 212 miles from a winch tow start to a landing at Tulsa, Oklahoma. This was a significant increase over the previous record and was made by using thermals over the flat country of the Southwest.

In May of that year John Robinson made an altitude flight to 10,400 feet over the desert in California. This would have beaten the existing U.S. record by 4,000 feet, but the flight was made without a barograph and so was not official. The following year Robinson made a number of official flights above 10,000 feet.

These flights moved the standard of American soaring substantially ahead and showed that the thermals over the West and Southwest offered great possibilities for altitude and distance flights.

Emil A. Lehecka and his German-built Sperber sailplane in which he won the 1938 National. The Sperber was named the Gunther Groenhoff, after the famous German soaring pilot.
(NSM Loomis Collection)

Controversy over the Nationals

For some time a controversy within the SSA had been developing with regard to the purpose of the national contest. Du Pont, Barringer, and Lange led a group that felt that the Nationals should be mainly for experienced pilots with high-performance sailplanes, and that separate regional contests should be conducted to give pilots experience in their lower-performance ships before coming to the Nationals.

Others, such as Ralph Barnaby, Earl Southee, and Larry Lawrence, argued that at this stage in the growth of the soaring movement, the Nationals should welcome all soaring pilots, regardless of the type of glider they were flying. They felt that the Nationals were really like a convention, one purpose of which was to promote soaring. It also provided an opportunity for pilots to gain experience and to exchange information that would be beneficial to their home clubs. They noted that utility and intermediate sailplanes had good soaring potential, if flown by experienced pilots. Few could afford the cost of high-perfor-

mance sailplanes and they felt that stiffer entry requirements would seriously limit the number of pilots who would compete.

Fifty-four ships had entered the 1937 Nationals, more than twice the previous number. However, at the 1938 annual meeting in January the directors voted to also have an American Open Soaring Contest at Frankfort, Michigan. Two successful contests had been held there in 1936 and 1937, along the sand dunes of that area. In order to encourage those with limited soaring experience and low-performance sailplanes to attend the American Open rather than the Nationals, the minimum requirements for points at the Nationals were increased to Silver "C" requirements, and a point-award fund of $1,500 was made an added attraction.

Ninth National, 1938

Because of these changes, there were only 20 entries in the Ninth National Contest: 7 sailplanes, 5 intermediates, 4 utilities, 3 two-place sailplanes, and 1 two-place utility. This was 34 less

than had competed in 1937, and there was concern that this new policy was hurting the soaring movement.

It was a competitive meet, however, and the total mileage flown was 2½ times that of the previous year. Peter Riedel finished first again, but Emil Lehecka, flying a German Rhoensperber sailplane, was named the champion, with du Pont and Decker, flying Minimoas, close behind. O'Meara was fourth in a Baby Bowlus, and Stan Corcoran finished 10th in his new Cinema, demonstrating again that intermediates could do well at the Nationals.

The design and construction of the Baby Albatross was based on the concept of a low-priced kit sailplane with better performance than a utility. It had a "boom-tail" design with a laminated plywood pod fuselage and wooden wings, similar to the Grunau Baby. The Baby, when flown by experienced pilots, could do very well, but it was not the ship for those who had little flying experience. The "flying" tail surface (without a stabilizer) proved too sensitive for the inexperienced pilot. The rather light construction of the pod made it susceptible to damage in hard landings, and the aluminum casting used for the critical wing and the strut fitting in the earlier models did not hold up in service. One pilot who learned to fly the Baby well was Woody Brown, who set a new national distance record of 280 miles in the 1939 Southwest Soaring Contest. The Baby caught the imagination of many pilots and it was the most popular Bowlus, with over 100 kits sold.

Two-Place Sailplanes

Peter Riedel and Alfred Bayer from Germany flew Kranich two-place sail-

planes in the 1938 Nationals and finished in first and seventh place. Their performance greatly boosted interest in two-place sailplanes. Most of the glider training during the 1930s was done with single-place sailplanes using auto or winch tow. Many instructors were tired of this slow and tedious method and were looking for two-place trainers. Two instructors who did something about this were Dave

Top: Jay Buxton and Jack O'Meara with the prototype Baby Albatross at the 1938 National. O'Meara finished in fourth place.

Don Stevens and Stan Corcoran in front of the "Cinima" sailplane, which Corcoran designed and built and which finished 10th in the 1938 National.

The Gross two-place "Sky Ghost" is shock-cord launched from "old no. 6" to catch the ridge winds. It showed that two people could soar as easily as one.

(NSM Loomis Collection)

Robertson and Henry Severin of San Diego, California, who built a two-place primary and taught Johnny Robinson and many others to fly. The San Diego club later bought a Grunau 8 two-place sailplane and used it for club training.

The first two-place sailplane to appear at a National was the Gross *Sky Ghost*, which was entered in 1932. It demonstrated that two could soar as easily as one. It was painted a dull nonreflecting black and it was named *Sky Ghost* because of its eerie appearance in flight.

The Funk brothers' two-place and Dick du Pont's new Bowlus-du Pont two-place entered the 1933 Nationals. The Funk had provisions for attaching wheels and racks to hold the wings so

it could be towed behind an auto; no trailer was required. The Buxton Transporter first appeared in 1936, and its great span and tapered wing gave it improved performance. Jack Laister and a group of other students at Lawrence School of Technology built a two-place that appeared the 1937 National. The Purdue University Glider Club was using a Moore two-place for club instruction and later bought the Gross four-place, which had appeared at Harris Hill for the first time in 1935. Stan Smith, when director of the Utica Aviation Ground School, designed a side-by-side trainer called the *City of Utica*. It was built by the school and flown at the 1937 Nationals. It was painted bright gold, and Earl Southee jokingly referred to it as the "golden monstrosity" because of its large size and brilliant color. Many referred to it as the "golden goose."

Although some of these two-places were used for student training, the technique for two-place instruction had not yet been fully developed and the CAA requirements still called for a large number of flights. However, the benefits of two-place training were beginning to be recognized.

In the fall of 1937 the Airhoppers Club of Long Island, New York, came to the Schweizer Metal Aircraft Company to see about a new two-place design. Schweizer had previously recognized the need and had a proposed design. The Airhoppers placed an order for one, which was designated the SGS 2-8. It was completed in June and flown the last few days of the 1938 contest by Jack Brookhart.

Big Meadows

In July of 1938, R. Barnaby received a letter from Arno B. Cammerer, director of the National Park Service, asking what the SSA's intentions were concerning the Big Meadows soaring site that they had cleared for glider use in 1934. Soaring contests had been held there in 1934 and 1935, but thereafter the site was unused.

Barnaby replied that he was assigned to the Canal Zone and was not up to date on SSA activities and so passed the letter on to President du Pont. He added that he had "always believed . . . Big Meadows to be one of the finest soaring sites in the country and would hate to see anything happen to it that would make it no longer available for that purpose."

Barnaby then forwarded Cammerer's letter to du Pont along with the following comment: "There is no

doubt that the Big Meadow site is a good one, unfortunately most of the attempts to use the site have occurred at poor seasons of the year. . . . I think a mid-summer expedition next year would serve to keep up the interest, and its proximity to Washington DC is an asset not to be lightly overlooked." In his reply, du Pont stated:

> It is my belief that the days of slope soaring in this country are rapidly passing away, and we will in the very near future see soaring development take place very near the center of population. . . .
>
> Lehecka's numerous soaring flights from winch launchings at Hicksville, Long Island NY—Barringer's soaring flights from winch launching at airports in Tennessee and Texas—have indicated to me that the day of old type soaring site is nearly gone. At many of our Executive Committee meetings we have seriously discussed moving the National Contest to some large airport. . . .
>
> Immediately after this year's contest Peter Riedel came to Wilmington with his 2-seater Kranich and for two consecutive days made soaring flights from the du Pont Airport, carrying with him such people as—Col. Olds, Igor Sikorsky and Henry du Pont. These people were amazed at the progress that has been made in soaring within the last few years. . . .

The Buxton Transporter two-place sailplane at Harris Hill with Red Slatter in the cockpit and Jay Buxton on the wing tip.

(NSM Collection)

The Schweizer brothers brought a very good all-metal two-place to the contest this year. However, they arrived during the last few days of the meet which was too late to get into the running. . . .

I think Ralph, you can deduce from the foregoing my feelings regarding trying to keep the Big Meadows soaring site open. I fear there are few boys who would be interested in going there on an expedition since most of them realize that they can soar from their local airport so long as they can obtain a plane of good performance.

Barnaby replied to du Pont on August 31. He pointed out that the lower-performance ships were far in the majority and that "everybody who is interested in gliding at all hopes someday to have available for their use a high performance soaring plane, but the chances are against them." Du Pont had mentioned that he knew of at least eight new high-performance sailplanes that would probably be completed by the next contest, and Barnaby replied, "That may bring the total to about 20 or 25 which would be a very small percentage of the membership of SSA. While the results of the 1938 contest have been most gratifying I still feel that the SSA is becoming a club for the few who are privileged to own and to fly high performance soaring craft and not an organization for all those interested in gliding and soaring. I still feel that it would be a good move to keep the National Park Service interested and the Big Meadows soaring site available for use."

Du Pont's comments that "the days of slope soaring in this country are rapidly passing away" was premature. Not only have ridges continued to be used, but in the 1970s Karl Striedieck and many others showed that with new techniques and high-perfor-

mance sailplanes, flights of 800 to 1,000 miles were possible along the ridges. His assessment that "the day of the old type soaring site is nearly gone" has also been disproven, since these sites have also demonstrated the advantages of wave and ridge soaring, in addition to thermal flying, over most flat-country sites.

One factor that du Pont overlooked in pushing high-performance sailplanes was the impact that airplane tow would have. In those days, most launchings were made by auto or winch tow and the chance of catching a thermal was not very good unless you had a higher-performance sailplane and a very high tow. Although airplane towing was beginning to be used more each year at the Nationals, it was restricted to ships that had the Bureau of Aeronautics approval for aero towing. This eliminated most of the utilities and secondaries. At that time aero towing was considered to be more demanding of the glider and of the pilot than auto or winch towing, but, as we now know, the reverse is actually true. With the coming of aero towing, the chances of soaring in utilities and intermediate sailplanes increased tremendously and minimized the performance difference for local soaring.

Directors' Summer Meeting, 1938

The summer directors' meeting was held in New York City on August 4, 1938, and focused mainly on minor changes in the bylaws and the appointment of special committees.

Dr. Lange, who had been chairman of the contest committee, which had run the 1937 and 1938 Nationals, said that he would be unable to continue, and Larry Lawrence was chosen to replace him. The executive committee was changed to include R. du Pont as chairman, Gale as vice-chairman, with Decker, Lange, and Lawrence as members.

The last subject of the meeting was the 10th National Soaring Contest. All agreed that the SSA was not in a position to make this an international contest. Dr. Lange was authorized to inform the ISTUS that the U.S. group was withdrawing its reservation for an international contest in 1939.

Elmira was chosen as the site of the 10th National on the condition that a satisfactory agreement could be arranged with the SSA. The meeting concluded with a discussion of the type of contest that should be held in 1939. The fact that a small number of sailplanes had entered the 1938 Nationals added weight to the argument that the contest should be open to all types of sailplanes. The consensus was that a compromise should be reached that would meet the needs of an inexperienced new pilot as well as the veteran with high-performance equipment.

Another directors' meeting was held on September 30 at Gale's office, but it was not well attended. Du Pont himself was not present to chair the meeting because of the pressure of his All American Aviation business.

In 1938 du Pont had been approached by Dr. L. S. Adams, designer of an airmail pickup device, who convinced du Pont that his system could be used to fulfill the Post Office Department contract. This device had been used daily for an entire summer at the Chicago World Fair and for ship-to-shore service, with mail being delivered and picked up from the decks of the *Leviathan*. The idea appealed to du Pont and he formed All American Aviation, Inc., to carry out the development of this system.

This all took considerable time so that little was left for SSA matters.

As du Pont became less and less involved in SSA in late 1937 and 1938, there was a gradual change in attitude of some of the directors regarding how du Pont and Barringer were running the SSA. One criticism was that du Pont tended to operate with executive meetings rather than directors' meetings. He also had stopped having directors' meetings at the time of the Nationals, in spite of the fact that this was the best time for getting the greatest number of directors together.

Lawrence discussed ways of making the 10th National Soaring Contest serve the interest of the soaring movement more effectively. His believed that a large contest, open to all classes of pilots and gliders, could be conducted and that the prize money should be spread out among more pilots under a carefully worked out point award system that would reward "C" pilots with utilities on a different basis than Silver "C" pilots with sailplanes. He hoped that this would attract more contestants and provide continuous flying at the contest. The directors agreed that the 10th Annual National Soaring Contest should be open to all gliders and pilots as outlined in Lawrence's plan. The advisability of tying the national contest to Elmira for the next three years was discussed since this would facilitate the raising of adequate finances and might make possible the erection of a new hangar. The directors voted unanimously that the national contest was to be held at Elmira for the next three years under the condition that the EAC raise adequate funds for the conduct of these contests.

Lawrence proposed that a policy be established that the American Open Soaring Contest be bid for annually by communities with established soaring facilities. A minimum guarantee of $3,000 would be asked—half for operation and half for prize money. The motion was carried unanimously.

Lewin Barringer outlined the financial situation of the SSA, stating that prospects were not too encouraging for continued financial support through the next year. However, he said that he would be able to make substantial savings through a new contract for the publication of *Soaring* and by reducing office expenses so that a budget of $8,000 would be sufficient for the next year. This would be exclusive of prize money, which it was felt should be raised separately in the future.

Lawrence's article "What Will We Do in 39" in the November *Soaring* asked:

> How about the soaring movement itself and can we do anything to advance it other than by piling up a fine record of performance? Where do we now stand after ten years of organized soaring for seven of which the SSA has been responsible? The writer still holds to his belief first expressed in 1930 that before any extensive soaring movement develops in this country, more good yet inexpensive gliders must be manufactured, and more opportunities must be provided for people to become associated with the sport through efficiently operated school facilities. What kind of a contest do we want? Let's try to get back to fundamentals in deciding. The chief excuse for soaring is that it's a sport. Our inferiority complex over not having performances that compare favorably with the international ones has made us "record conscious" which is alright in its place, but wouldn't we get further in the future if we had contests that gave each pilot, no matter what degree his skill is and what type of glider he flies, a chance to do his best in competition with the best.

General Activity

A record number of meets were held in 1938. In addition to the Nationals and the American Open there were meets in Bakersfield California, Wichita Falls, Texas; Wenatchee, Washington, and Ellenville, New York. There were also sailplane events at the national races. Hanna Reitsch put on an aerobatic show each day in her Habich stunt sailplane and a three-sailplane aerobatic show was put on by Emil Lehecka in his Rhoensperber and Decker and Bellak in Minimoas.

Barringer used Hanna's remarks to a distinguished aircraft manufacturer "that soaring is more than a sport" as the theme of his editorial "Much More than a Sport" in the October *Soaring*. He said,

> We use it now to show how very much more there really is to this field than at first appears to the public eye.
>
> First of all, remarkable willingness for considerable physical labor on the part of many to get a few into the air, which is of undoubted value in character building.
>
> Good pilots—and we know that soaring pilots make the best airplane pilots—will always be in demand in peacetime flying.
>
> New sailplane designs are having a far reaching effect in helping to develop new airplanes.
>
> Meteorology, which became second nature to the skilled soaring pilot who, of necessity, has a more fundamental knowledge of air movements than the majority of pilots, is of considerable advantage.
>
> We know of so much to be learned—that none of us should ever have any difficulty in convincing the skeptical laymen of the undoubted value of soaring, which makes it so much more than a sport.

The SSA board had long recognized the need for a gliding and soaring manual for operations and one for glider construction and maintenance. It took considerable time to get the drafts to the CAA, which finally approved the operations manual in the spring of 1938. Since there was no assurance as to when it would be printed, the Stone Aircraft Company of Detroit, which was putting the Detroit Gull primary back into production, offered to print 2,000 copies of the manual. This was approved by the board and the manual was published in the fall of 1938. The construction manual was never published as such, but was included in the glider handbook, which was later put out by the CAA.

While Barnaby was stationed in Panama, Gale kept him informed on developments in the SSA. He wrote Barnaby on December 17 and mentioned Barringer's dolorous report at the September 30 directors' meeting that du Pont was fast losing interest:

> I think most of the people got the idea that therefore, soaring was about to die. I know Lew gave that impression. However, I reminded him that while it might be necessary to drop the magazine and toss him out in the cold, the good old SSA was far, far from dead.
>
> I had a chat with Dick [du Pont] in Washington DC a few weeks ago and found that his interest is as keen as ever, but he feels he must pull in his horns financially. He says he will continue to contribute, but not at the rate to which we have been accustomed.
>
> I was surprised Dick replied so arbitrarily to Cammerer. . . . We should keep up such contacts as Cammerer fresh, so that we will not lose any facilities.

Summary of 1938

Barringer's editorial in the December issue, "A Review of 1938," sums up

the year. He mentions that although the membership had not grown between 1937 and 1938, because business continued to be depressed and membership and subscription rates had increased, there were other advances. For example, in 1937 there were 88 clubs in 27 states, whereas in 1938 there were 148 clubs in 35 states. Interest had been stimulated by another article in the July 1938 issue of *National Geographic* entitled "Men-Birds Soar on Boiling Air."

Henry Wightman Becomes Manager, 1939

Lewin Barringer resigned his position at the end of 1938. Although du Pont and Barringer had hoped that the two of them could get the SSA going, it proved to be too big a task, and two years was too short a time in which to expect the SSA to become self-sustaining.

Barringer was the "complete" aviation enthusiast, and flying had been his main activity up to that time. The position of general manager of the SSA and editor of *Soaring* magazine suited his talents, but the SSA was too small to be able to afford him. Toward the end of 1939 he had received an offer of an executive position with a paper manufacturing company of which he said, "The financial considerations are such that I cannot afford to turn it down." He reluctantly resigned, effective the end of 1938.

Directors' Winter Meeting, 1939

Beside finding a replacement for Barringer, the directors meeting on February 10–11, 1939, saw the need to develop a national program for soaring and to plan celebrations for the SSA's

A SGS 2-8 takeoff from Harris Hill. The 2-8 became the military TG-2, which played an important part in getting the Army Glider Training Program under way.

(Hans Groenhoff)

10th anniversary. A meeting of the executive committee was held on January 14 to prepare for the coming annual meetings. This would include the directors' meeting, the annual membership meeting, and the Second National Gliding and Soaring Conference, to be held at the same time in February.

The committee assigned five chairmen to lead discussions on a national program: Henry Wightman, instruction; Jay Buxton, construction; Wolfgang Klemperer, gliding research; Karl Lange, meteorology; and Charles Gale, airports.

At the directors' meeting in New York on February 10–12, du Pont said that it was imperative for the SSA to increase its membership by a considerable number. Although the 400 percent increase since January 1937 was a significant one, it was not good enough. Du Pont said that the cost per member in 1936, before he took over, was only

$2 per member, whereas in 1938 it was $9.11. He hoped that through an increase in membership and some planned reduction in the cost of running the SSA office, it would be possible to cut in half the cost of servicing a member. Additional advertising revenue was expected to reduce costs further.

The board had received a request from Henry Wightman that he be considered a candidate for general manager. It decided to act on this matter before the conclusion of the annual meeting and conference. Enyart outlined a plan in which the SSA might share the officers of the NAA in Washington, D.C.

Those who attended the conference remembered that while the meetings were going on Capt. Ben Kelsey, an Air Force pilot, received some unwanted publicity when he clipped a tree in landing the secret prototype Lockhead P-38 at Mitchell Field on

Long Island, about a mile from where the conference was being held. He had set a speed record for nonstop flight from the West Coast with this new Air Force fighter. Kelsey, a soaring enthusiast, had been a frequent visitor at the National Soaring Contest and had landed military airplanes at Harris Hill. He became an Air Force general and continued to be active in soaring with the Middle Atlantic Soaring Association.

A National Soaring Program

At the conference, each of the chairman led a discussion period on his phase of the proposed program and, at the end, a program was approved. Its main objectives were to establish a motorless flight institute at Harris Hill, operate an approved soaring school for instructors, encourage the location of a sailplane manufacturer there, carry out research in sailplane design with the NACA and soaring meteorology with the Weather Bureau, and establish schools for gliding and soaring throughout the country.

The program's overall goal was to create a reserve of experienced soaring pilots that would constitute an important national aviation asset and thus would justify continued support of motorless flight by the various government agencies.

Henry Wightman was confirmed as executive secretary and the SSA office was moved to the NAA office in Washington, D.C. The directors also decided to order a Schweizer 2-8 two-place sailplane. SSA had purchased the Ross *Ibis* in 1938 and it was used principally by Barringer. It was felt that the SSA's general manager should have a two-place sailplane, particularly in view of the possibility that the government might become interested in a

training program. All agreed to sell the *Ibis* and to order the two-place.

CAA's CPTP Glider Program

The first evidence that the CAA was listening to SSA occurred on June 16, when the Elmira Area Soaring Corporation and the Frankfort Sailplane Group each received a telegram requesting a bid for the sailplane training of 12 airplane pilots who had graduated from the Civil Pilots Training Program (CPTP).

The EASC and the SSA submitted a combined proposal to train 12 students at the Big Flats airport and at Harris Hill. Wightman was to be in charge of instruction and the primary

---

The Schweizers were told to go ahead on the SSA two-place at the time of the directors' meeting. It was important to get this sailplane delivered by the 10th National Contest. It was finished in time to be delivered to Hank Wightman during the contest. At that time, the bill of sale had to be notarized, and Bob McDowell, a local attorney who had helped launch O'Meara, did so. He asked the Schweizers why they did not build their gliders in Elmira. They told him that they would like to, for their barn was getting crowded, but they didn't have the money to swing it. However, McDowell convinced the Elmira Industries, the business development organization, to provide space on the second floor of the Elmira Knitting Mill building in Elmira Heights for two years in return for stock in the company.

Thus a new corporation, the Schweizer Aircraft Corporation, was formed, and stock was sold to a number of soaring people and Elmira businessmen. Ernie and Paul moved to Elmira in early December of 1939 with two employees, Atlee Hauck and Paul Nissen. Bill Schweizer was still attending Syracuse University. The 2-8 was certified in May 1940 and put into production. Orders were received from a group of Bell Aircraft employees that included Stan Smith, Bob Distin, and Howie Burr. In addition, one came from Ed Knight of Toledo, several orders came from Joe Steinhauser for his Chicago school; and one order from Dick Johnson and his brother Dave. Also, an order for three 2-8 kits was received from a Michigan youth group with which Ted Belak was associated.

---

training was to be carried out in two Franklins using auto and winch towing. Airplane tow was to be demonstrated in the Schweizer 2-8 sailplane. The school at Frankfort was under the direction of Stan Corcoran and Ted Bellak, who used a Franklin glider and a Wolf sailplane for their training. Both these experimental programs were carried out successfully even though the staff had had little time to prepare for them.

10th National, 1939

The 10th National Soaring Contest was held at Harris Hill, June 24 to July 9, 1939, with 36 ships (13 in Group I and 23 in Group II) and 88 pilots entered. There were a number of outstanding performances: a national altitude record of 17,264 feet by Bob Stanley in his *Nomad* sailplane, a national goal flight record of 233 miles by Chester Decker in his *Minimoa,* and a national two-place altitude and distance record of 6,560 feet and 101 miles by Lewin Barringer in the Airhoppers 2-8 sailplane.

Chet Decker won the national championship and set a record of 1,149 miles, the greatest total mileage flown by an individual during a national meet. The first three Gold "C" awards in the United States were completed during the contest by Robert Stanley, John Robinson, and Chester Decker. The requirements for the new award were a five-hour flight, a distance flight of 187 miles, and a 3,000-meter (9,843-foot) climb.

For the first time since 1933, du Pont did not fly in the National, nor did Peter Riedel. Instead, Riedel attempted to soar across the United States in his *Kranich* sailplane, using auto-tow launchings. He became the first person to soar across the continental divide. It was generally agreed that as a result of Riedel's participation in the two previous Nationals, U.S. pilots started improving their soaring techniques, particularly by spiraling tighter in thermals.

Wolf Hirth was at the Nationals to help celebrate the 10th anniversary, as well as his "Blue Sky" thermaling flight. He was no longer competing, but he did get a chance to fly Joe Steinhauser's *Wolf* and proceeded to do a "loop" off winch tow. He had done a similar maneuver in Germany a few years earlier, but it had ended in a crash and left him seriously injured.

Other Soaring Contests

In 1939 there was a marked increase in the number of soaring contests held

Bob Stanley, Bell Aircraft Co. test pilot and later chief engineer, by the cockpit of his homebuilt *Nomad*. It was the first aircraft in the United States to use a "V" tail.
(NSM Loomis Collection)

throughout the United States. The Associated Glider Club of Southern California's three-day New Year contest included the dedication of the Torrey Pines soaring field.

The Third Annual Western Spring Soaring Contest was held near Arvin, California, in April. In June the second South Western Soaring Contest was held in Wichita Falls, Texas. The Second American Open Contest was held near Frankfort, Michigan, and the Eastern State Meet at Schley Field,

Liberty Corners, New Jersey, over Labor Day. This was the field that Gus Scheurer and the Aero Club Albatross had developed. That Labor Day weekend Germany invaded Poland, and this event cast a cloud over the contest. In the fall the Hudson Valley group conducted a soaring contest at Wurtsboro, New York, the Chicagoland Glider Council ran a meet at Benton Harbor, and over the Thanksgiving Day weekend Harris Hill held its first Snowbird Contest.

Johnny Robinson flies the Zanonia at Torrey Pines, California, one of the oldest soaring sites in the United States. When the tide was out, the beach was used for emergency landings.

(NSM Collection)

Parker Leonard and Wolf
Hirth at the 1939 National.
The 10th anniversary of the
first National and Hirth's
"blue-sky" thermal flight.
(NSM Loomis Collection)

SSA's Financial Problems

In the fall of 1939 Wightman started to run into financial difficulties since he came to the end of the $8,000 that du Pont had earmarked for 1939 and he had to let his secretary go. Wightman pointed out in his editorial in the December issue of *Soaring:*

> The SSA cannot sit back and expect a complete magazine to be dropped, prepaid into its lap, or to have a National organization to represent its need and to conduct contests unless it goes out and works hard. . . . You, individually, are the SSA—On your interest and your activity depends the whole future of the organiztion. . . . Our problem is partly one of organization. . . . to unite the increased Regional activity into a single National program—It is still, however, mainly a problem of starting activity where there has previously been nothing but interest, and of enlisting the support of the hundreds who have been actively flying and receiving benefits from the SSA without contributing anything to its support. We have made a fine start in many sections of the country but if our efforts are to be successful there is still much to be done.

Chapter 5

The World War II Period, 1940–1946

Soaring Adjusts to the Prewar Buildup, 1940

The war in Europe had little effect on soaring in the United States until 1940, when the U.S. aircraft industry was told to expand and to supply aircraft to our allies in Europe. This increase in aviation activity stimulated participation in gliding and soaring.

At that time, the SSA was experiencing serious financial problems since du Pont was no longer providing funds to supplement SSA income. Wightman realized that the SSA could not support a paid manager and in his last editorial in the January *Soaring* he asked about the future of the SSA:

> We have a magazine the cost of which is just about equal to the SSA's average income, leaving nothing for paid employees. We have nine Regional Associations and many well established clubs. We have more skilled pilots, more interest, more potential soaring enthusiasts than ever before in our history. The picture is hardly as black as some would have you imagine. Why—may we ask—if there is so much interest and spirit, has there been so much complaining about the inactivity of the members in general? There have been two reasons: First— When the General Manager was hired everybody thought he was being paid for it—let him take care of it! However, it was impossible for one man to do everything single-handed—. Second—There has been, since 1937, the

Floyd J. Sweet, director of the Elmira Aviation Ground School, and Maurice Waters, general manager of the EASC, in front of the Elmira Glider Club's Rhonebuzzard sailplane at the 1940 National.

(NSM Loomis Collection)

attitude that SSA has not been an organization of soaring enthusiasts but a "rich man's toy."

Wightman was frustrated for he had worked hard to help the SSA grow. He had taken over while du Pont's interest was on the decline and did not have as much support as Barringer had had.

Annual Meeting, 1940

The 1940 annual meeting was held in New York City at the Hotel Breslin on

The Briegleb BG-6 flying over a California dry lake. The sailplane was ATC'd a short time later.
(Richard Miller Collection)

January 27–28. The major items of business were the election of officers, how to keep *Soaring* going, and SSA operations under the new financial conditions. Earl R. Southee was elected president. When first nominated, he had stated that in spite of his work with the CAA he was in a position to devote the time to the job as president. Southee, with his friendly but brusque style, was not a du Pont "man."

This was brought out in Southee's letter to Barnaby of August 1938: "The good old SSA seems to have boiled itself down to a very select group. . . . As far as I am concerned, Dick is paying the bills and I have taken the stand that as long as he does that it is not up to me to criticize him. . . . Ted Bellak told me in confidence that Dick is just about through. . . . I understand both from Dick himself and from others, that his family is constantly after him because he devoted so much of his time to the SSA activities."

Floyd Sweet was elected secretary and took over the major job of running the SSA office and editing *Soaring* from his home, as Eaton, Southee, and Barnaby had done before. His wife, Frances, acted as his assistant. Robert Stanley and Shelly Charles were elected vice-presidents, and Chester Decker treasurer.

Southee, in his presidential message, noted that "it now becomes incumbent upon our organization to adopt a 'Pay as we go policy'. . . . This society is yours—you will have to provide the nourishment necessary for its growth and success—We have no place in the commercial phase of motorless flight. . . . Consequently, we offer for sale to the highest bidder a 2-place Schweizer sailplane and a Franklin Utility glider."

It was decided to go to a bimonthly magazine to ease the transfer from a paid editor to a voluntary part-time editor. The first issue published by Sweet was for February–March 1940.

New Glider Schools and Manufacturers

Although Southee was concerned about the future, the soaring movement was growing. As Wightman had indicated, there were nine active regional associations: Associated Glider Clubs of Southern California, the Chicagoland Glider Council, Detroit Glider Council, Eastern States Soaring Association, Elmira Area Soaring Corporation (EASC), Hudson Valley Soaring Association, Pacific Northern Soaring Association, Soaring Society of Northern California, and the Southern California Soaring Association.

As soaring gained more adherents, the number of sailplane companies increased. Among them was Frankfort Sailplane Corp. of Jolliet, Illinois, which had been formed to take over the glider manufacturing that Stan Corcoran had started at Frankfort, Michigan. Another, a new company, called the Bowlus Sailplane, Inc., was formed by Bowlus, who asked some of the leaders of the California aviation industries to be honorary board members. At the same time, The Briegleb Aircraft Company was carrying out ATC work on its BG-6, and the BG-7 and BG-8 were well under way. In addition, SAC was operating in the loft of the Knitting Mills building in Elmira Heights above the Elmira Aviation Ground School, which was directed by Floyd J. Sweet. The school provided a convenient source of aviation mechanics for SAC.

Southee Resigns

On May 13, 1940, Southee resigned as SSA president. His position with the CAA required him to advise over 100 CPTP flight operations, which were spread over 13 states, and Southee had been instructed to retire from all outside activities.

Directors' Spring Meeting, 1940

Vice-President Stanley called for a directors' meeting on May 25 at Gales's office in New York City, but only seven directors attended. Southee's resignation was accepted and Stanley was elected president pro-tem. Executive powers for SSA were delegated to Sweet, the secretary, until the next meeting. Barringer was delegated to draw up a plan for affiliating with the NAA.

At the start, SAC employees were a group of bachelors who rented space at purchasing agent Bill Brown's house at 1030 Hoffman Street, Elmira, New York. This became the gathering place for visiting soaring enthusiasts and was known as the "1030 Club." The original group consisted of Atlee Hauck and Paul Nissen, SAC's first employees; Bill Skinner, an engineer who soon gave up bachelorhood by marrying the girl next door; Bob Yellott, a Mercury Club member; Brown; and the Schweizers.

11th National, 1940

The 11th National Soaring Contest was officially opened when Lewin Barringer, master of ceremonies, introduced Grant Mason, member of the Civil Aeronautics Board (CAB), who gave the principal address. Barringer then took Mason on a flight in a 2-8, which had been equipped with a two-way radio so Mason could describe the flight over the public address system.

The two outstanding flights of the meet were covered in *Soaring*:

> Saturday, July 13, was one of those days that always makes a successful meet. The wind was from the northwest, cumuli were forming at about 4,000 ft. and the wind was fairly strong. This meant but one thing, that if national records were to be broken, this was the day! John Robinson was first off by airplane tow at 11:45 AM. He was immediately followed by Chester Decker. . . . Following in rapid succession were Robert Stanley with Ernest Schweizer as passenger in a 2-8, Udo Fischer in his "Wolf," William Putnam in a "Midwest" and Richard Johnson in a "Baby Albatross."
>
> As the day wore on and all but two pilots (Robinson & Stanley) had reported in, great tension was felt at headquarters. Officials, pilots and crew members were busily computing speeds and distances against time and as the hours rolled by, it became more and more apparent that the two pilots were lost or were establishing new records. As dusk was settling on Har-

Top: John Robinson won the first of his three national soaring championships in 1940 flying the RS-1 called the *Zanonia*.

(Ross-Pix, NSM Collection)

Dick Johnson the youngest pilot in the 1940 Nationals with his brother Dave and a friend in front of the Baby Bowlus that they had built from a kit. Dick arrived with little experience and without a license, but ended up in third place in the Nationals.

(NSM Loomis Collection)

ris Hill, two phone calls came in rapid succession. The first to report was Robert Stanley who had landed near Washington DC, a distance of 216 miles, establishing a new American distance record for 2-plane sailplane with passenger. . . . The second call, a few minutes later, was from John Robinson who had landed his "*Zanonia*" at Mineral, VA, a distance of 290 air miles which established a new American single place distance record.

John Robinson was the winner of the contest, followed by Chet Decker,

Richard Johnson, Randall Chapman, William Putnam, Stan Smith, and Floyd Sweet. Twenty-six ships were entered.

Directors' Summer Meeting, 1940

Ralph S. Barnaby was elected president on July 7, 1940. He had been assigned to the Naval aircraft factory in Philadelphia and thus had the time to devote to the presidency. All the other officers were reelected. The major action at the meeting was the approval of the SSA-NAA agreement for a period of three years with a $300 franchise fee. There was no joint membership requirement, and the SSA membership rates were set at $4.00 a year, with associate membership at $2.50.

Barringer

Barringer continued to be active in soaring. Since his new position was in New Jersey, he was only a few hours' drive from Wurtsboro, New York, and he attended the various regional meets held there. At the 1940 Eastern State Meet over the Memorial Day weekend he used the Airhoppers 2-8 to give Winthrop Rockefeller, president of the Air Youth of America (AYA), a flight. Barringer was trying to interest Rockefeller in adding motorless flight to the AYA's main activity, which was model airplane building.

Later that summer Barringer organized a soaring expedition to Sun Valley, Idaho. Averell Harriman of the Union Pacific Railroad was promoting the new ski resort, Sun Valley, and thought soaring might be another suitable activity for the area. He provided railroad transportation for the 2-8 sailplane and the Wing's Club winch. John Robinson stopped off on his way back from the Nationals, and Buxton came to operate the winch. The soaring conditions were excellent and a number of records were set. One of these, to 21,000 feet, exceeded the world two-plane record, but for some reason this never became official.

At this time Barringer was editing a book, *Flight without Power.* Chapters were written by Barringer and six other specialists: Charles Colvin, Karl O. Lange, N. H. Randers-Pehrson, Ernest and Paul A. Schweizer, and Milton Stoughton. (The Schweizers wrote the chapters on aerodynamics, and on design, construction, and maintenance; glider manufacturing at that time was tough going financially and the possibility of royalties from the book made it of special interest.) Published in the summer of 1940, it sold quite well since there were no other American books on soaring available. Later it was used in the military glider training program and was reprinted three times.

Toward the end of the year Barringer was approached by James A. Leftwich and Frank Blunk, who had developed a national defense plan that involved a youth glider program. Leftwich worked for a public relations agency and Blunk had been involved with J. C. Penney, Jr., in the Cape Cod Soaring School.

A few weeks later Chas. T. Malone, a former World War I pilot, proposed a similar program. In late December, Barringer had a meeting with the Air Youth of America, and as the year closed, it looked as though there might soon be a major national gliding and soaring program.

Start of Military Use of Gliders, 1941

A change in the public's perception of gliding and soaring was now taking place. Up to that time it had been considered mainly a sport, but numerous articles in newspapers and magazines told about the German Air Force and how it was being built up through a glider program.

In the spring of 1941 the Germans made a lightning thrust into Belgium and Holland using paratroops supported by gliders carrying troops and field equipment. Using the new "shaped" charges, demolition teams brought in by gliders made it possible to take over the impregnable Fort Eben Emael, and the German Army poured into Belgium.

Many were impressed with the effectiveness of the German Luftwaffe in the European war and wondered why the United States did not have a glider program under way to build up its pilot reserve and to allow part of its airborne Army to use gliders.

The CAA had its CPTP program for teaching power flying to college students and civilians in high gear, but the program was still relatively small. The need for building up the U.S. pilot reserve was much in the public mind and so the time was right for proposals on national youth glider programs.

Proposed Glider Training Programs

The feature story in the 1941 January-February issue of *Soaring* was written by Ralph Barnaby and titled "Another Glider Boom?" He noted:

> Interest is being shown in our Congress which now has before it three Bills pertaining to gliding. The first is S-290 introduced in the Senate on Jan 10th 1941 by Sen. McCarran. This bill would establish a Civilian Glider Training Division of the U.S. Office of Education and be involved in a National Gliding and Soaring Program.
>
> The second, H.R. 3300, was intro-

One afternoon in early April of 1941 when the Schweizers were leaving their plant, they noticed a small military plane flying overhead and saw it head to the northwest, toward the airport. When they got home they received a call from a Maj. Fred Dent who said that he was at the airport and it was urgent for him to see them.

At the airport they found Dent in civilian clothes standing by his military airplane. He said that he wanted to talk to them about important defense matters. Dent explained that owing to the Germans' successful use of gliders in warfare, the U.S. Army Air Forces wanted to get into gliding immediately and would need training gliders, large gliders for carrying troops and equipment, and they wanted to train some glider pilots right away. The Schweizers said that their 2-8 would be ideal for the Army Air Corps to use as a trainer and that John Robinson was operating the EASC school on Harris Hill and could train their pilots. A short time later the military glider program was under way. On August 10, 1941, the Air Corps issued the following statement: "What is probably a record in procurement was established in the case of the contract with the Schweizer Aircraft Corporation of Elmira, New York. This contract, covering three two-place gliders to CAA Class 2 requirements, with certain modifications, was signed in Washington DC on June 27, 1941. The first glider under the contract had its initial flight test July 2, at the Big Flats Airport, Elmira, New York, and is now at Wright Field."

duced in the House of Representatives on Feb. 12th by Rep. Hamilton Fish. This is a companion bill to that submitted by Sen. McCarran, the only difference being that Mr. Fish added another zero to the proposed authorization making it $5,000,000. Frankly, these bills as introduced don't stand a chance of the proverbial snowball of getting serious consideration, much less of being passed. They attempt to cram down the CAA's throat something about which the CAA has not been consulted and in a form in which it's not in sympathy.

These two bills are primarily the work of Mr. Charles F. Malone. Malone falls in the class of those interested persons whose efforts have been somewhat misguided. For instance, he is the founder and President of a

newly formed American Glider Association. While Malone stated that he feels his organization will not be duplicating the work of SSA, since he plans it to be a trade organization to represent the glider and sailplane manufacturers, we note that at the time of incorporation, the AFA had not circularized these manufacturers to find out whether they wanted this representation.

The third Bill, H.R. 2601, was introduced in the House of Representatives on Jan. 24th 1941 by Rep. Costello of California. This bill was to provide for the training of civil glider pilots and for other purposes, seems a much more reasonable proposition than the first bills cited and one which the CAA might take more kindly to, inasmuch as it leaves the general organization and finances, etc. within their control.

Proposals to the SSA

The SSA investigated the Leftwich-Blunk proposal and found that it was just a money-making proposition for Leftwich. The Air Youth of America had much better possibilities and looked like the answer to SSA's financial problems.

At a meeting in New York City on February 1 the directors officially turned down the Leftwich-Blunk agreement and authorized Barnaby to negotiate an agreement with the AYA. Although the 9 directors at the meeting gave Barnaby authority to go ahead, he sent a night letter to the 11 directors who were not present to inform them of the decision. Barnaby then proceeded to negotiate with the AYA, but, when he learned that the AYA expected the SSA to finance the program, he said that the SSA was not able to do so. A possible factor in this change in AYA's position was that

Winthrop Rockefeller had enlisted in the Army and his brother Lawrence had become chairman.

Although it was not possible to work out an SSA-AYA agreement, Winthrop Rockefeller did not lose his interest in soaring. In the fall of 1966 he arranged to have Schweizer Aircraft send some of its school personnel and equipment to his Petti-Jean Ranch in Arkansas to try out the conditions there. Although the location was excellent for soaring and Rockefeller was enthusiastic, he was unexpectedly elected governor of the state of Arkansas shortly thereafter and unfortunately became too busy to do anything about a soaring program.

The U.S. Army Air Forces Get into Gliding

The reports of the successful use of gliders by the Germans in taking Belgium and Holland impressed Gen. H. H. Arnold and he felt that the U.S. military should investigate the use of gliders in its own military program. A study of the German glider program was made and a set of specifications for troop and cargo gliders was developed. In early April the USAAF contacted the active glider manufacturers about trainers. They also approached a number of aircraft manufacturers who might build troop-carrying gliders. It was not long before contracts were issued to the Frankfort Sailplane Corp. and Schweizer Aircraft Corp. for the first training gliders. The Frankfort got the TG-1 designation, although Schweizer Aircraft delivered the first glider, the TG-2, to the military many months before a Frankfort glider was delivered. The government had restricted the use of strategic materials on trainers and so another contract was arranged with Schweizer Aircraft

to develop the TG-3 glider, which used wood in place of the aluminum alloy in the TG-2. A new company was formed by Jack Laister in St. Louis, Missouri, called the Laister-Kauffman Company, and it received a contract for the TG-4A glider.

Glider Demonstration

A special glider demonstration sponsored by the SSA, the EASC, and SAC was conducted at the Big Flats Airport on April 26. High-ranking officials of the Army, Navy, the House Naval Affairs Committee, and Civil Aeronautics Authority were present. The main feature was a triple tow of three 2-8 two-place sailplanes by a J-5 Standard airplane to demonstrate how gliders could be used in warfare. The pilots on the triple tow were John Robinson, Stanley Smith, and Joe Steinhauser. The three sailplanes, with a total of six people aboard, were towed to 1,600 feet, where they released and then made a spot landing in a restricted area on the airport.

The reaction of the three congressmen from the House Naval Affairs Committee were very favorable. Congressman Maas said, "I did think the potential value of glider training had

The triple-tow of three SGS 2-8 sailplanes, which was part of the demonstrations conducted for the congressional committee that helped get the U.S. military glider program under way.

(NSM Loomis Collection)

The prototype Pratt-Read side-by-side two-place training glider designated the LNE-1. This was principally the brainchild of Parker Leonard and Jay Buxton and is shown taking off on a test flight with pilot Emil Lehecka.

(Pratt-Read Co.)

been exaggerated, but I don't now." Congressman Jacobsen said he was as enthusiastic about gliders now as he was when he first saw the Navy's mosquito fleet of torpedo boats.

Charles Malone wrote Barnaby:

The testimony of Commander Durgin, who said that in view of the failure of the Pensacola glider pilot training experiments, the Navy Department did not consider that the proposed legislation (S.290) has sufficient merit to warrant its support. Congressmen Maas, Cole and Sutphin tore this guy apart and made him say that as a matter of fact, he did not know whether or not the Pensacola experiments were a success or a failure. I want to tell you that you did gliding a lot of good with your testimony. Congressman Sutphin told me today that his committee had written their report and that they definitely recommended glider pilot training, and the building of troop carrying gliders by the Navy.

The congressional hearing was attended by a number of soaring people, including R. S. Barnaby, Y. Sekella, R. E. Franklin, E. S. Evans, and P. A. Schweizer. The House Naval Affairs Committee was a friendly one since three members had been at the demonstration at Elmira earlier that spring.

How the Navy would use gliders was apparently not given much thought, but the wartime requirements of the Navy and the Marines would add to the demand for training and troop-carrying gliders.

The Navy glider program was started shortly thereafter with the purchase of a number of Schweizer 2-8 sailplanes designated the LNS-1 and a side-by-side trainer designated the LNE-1 from the Pratt-Read Company. They set up requirements for a 12-place amphibious assault glider for the Marines and contracted with Allied Corp. for the LRA-1 and Bristol Aeronautical Company for the LTQ-1.

Germany's successful invasion of the island of Crete in May with the aid of 70 gliders spurred the Air Corps to put its glider program into high gear. It was anxious to train glider pilots and in May of 1941 awarded contracts to the EASC and the Lewis School in Lockport, Illinois, for each to train 12 pilots beginning in June. Major Fred Dent took the course in Elmira, and while there he took delivery of the first TG-2.

12th National, 1941

A report in *Soaring* on the 12th National from June 28 to July 13, 1941, noted: "The contest had a more serious spirit than in previous years". A good number of soaring people were already in the services and Major Dent, flying the TG-2 with its military markings, added to this mood.

John Robinson, in the Zanonia, won the National for the second time, defeating Bill Putnam in the Orlik and Chet Decker in his Minimoa. Dick Johnson, flying his new 2-8, was fourth. Stan Smith set a two-place goal flight record of 73 miles in a 2-8.

On the last day of the contest

General Arnold flew up from Washington, D.C., to be the principal speaker at the banquet that evening. He and his adjutant were picked up at the airport by two 2-8 sailplanes and flown to Harris Hill.

Edward S. Evans awarded the Evans Trophy to John Robinson. He also presented another Evans Trophy to General Arnold and asked that it be given each year to the military's outstanding glider pilot.

Directors' Meeting, 1941

What was to be the last directors' meeting until after World War II was held July 1941. Floyd J. Sweet, who was in the Ordnance Corps, could no longer carry out the work of secretary of SSA and editor of *Soaring*. The hope was that with the buildup of military gliding, financial support might be available from the expanding glider industry. An executive committee composed of Stanley, Sweet, and Corcoran was to investigate ways of obtaining sufficient support to hire a manager. Parker Leonard was elected president, secretary, and editor of *Soaring*. Don Hamilton and Jay Buxton were elected vice-presidents and Art Schultz treasurer.

The U.S. Military Glider Program Accelerates

As the U.S. Army Air Forces expanded its glider program, more training schools were needed and the EASC was asked to expand its school. Another school was set up at 29 Palms, California. Capt. Floyd J. Sweet transferred to the Air Corps and was appointed its director of flying. In the beginning they used sailplanes purchased from civilian owners. Dick and Dave Johnson sold them their 2-8 sailplane and became instructors there. The Air Corps recommended that the EASC set up a larger school in the south so they could train year round. EASC representatives E. A. Mooers, Youston Sekella, and James Beecher chose Mobile, Alabama, as the site for the school. Other intermediate schools were also set up in Lamesa, Texas; Wickenburg, Arkansas; and Ft. Sumner, New Mexico.

Even with the accelerated production of training gliders, however, there would not be enough to handle the students scheduled for training. Thus the Air Corps investigated converting lightplanes into gliders and while doing this contracted with 18 CPTP civilian schools to train pilots in lightplanes with the emphasis on dead-

Left: Bill Schweizer, right, readies the first TG-2 for test while Major Fred Dent and Milt Girton of the CAA inspect the instrumentation.
(NSM Loomis Collection)

Right: Left to right: Comdr. Ralph S. Barnaby, Maj. Gen. H. H. Arnold, and Edward S. Evans, immediately after General Arnold had been flown from the airport to Harris Hill in a two-place sailplane at the end of the 1941 National.
(NSM Loomis Collection)

stick landings. After completing this preliminary training phase, the students attended an intermediate school where they were trained in TG-1s, 2s, 3s, or 4s. The lightplane gliders had three seats since the engine in the nose of the lightplanes was replaced with a seat and controls for the student. These gliders were designated the TG-5, TG-6, and TG-8 and were modifications of the Aeronca, Taylorcraft, and Piper lightplanes, respectively. They often beat the tow plane to the ground, but their performance was closer to that of the CG-4 glider, which made them ideal for training pilots for the CG-4As. A total of 750 lightplane gliders were built, whereas only 350 of the sailplane type were delivered.

The Air Corps set specifications for two types of troop transport gliders—a 9-place and a 15-place glider, which were intended to glide in for a landing at night. The landing speed was not to exceed 38 miles per hour without the use of flaps in order to keep the glider cheap and simple, and even if it did strike trees or buildings, the low speed and relatively low energy were expected to enable the troops to survive. This meant that the gliders would be very large and lightly loaded, which would make them difficult to manage on the ground, particularly in windy conditions.

SAC made a design study of these two types, which were designated the SGC 9-10 and the SGC 15-11. Although SAC submitted these designs to the USAAF, it considered them impractical owing to the unrealistic requirements. SAC was tied up getting the TG-2 into full production and developing the new TG-3A, so did not think it should become involved in the troop-carrying glider program at that time.

The Waco nine-place CG-3 was the first troop-carrying glider delivered, and it was designed to the original specifications. After some modifications, flaps were added and a higher speed landing speed was acceptable, so its size could be reduced. The CG-3 was followed by the 15-place CG-4, designed to the revised requirements. The CG-3 had been intended as a training glider for the transition to the larger type. However, it turned out that the CG-4 was satisfactory for training, with the result that only 100 CG-3s were produced.

The Air Corps decided to standardize on the Waco CG-4A and then set up a crash program to get these ships into volume production. Many large corporations besides Waco became involved in producing CG-4As or major components for them, notably, the Ford Motor Co., Commonwealth Aircraft, Laister-Kauffman, Cessna, G & A Aircraft, General, Gibson, North Western, Pratt-Read, Robertson, and Timm. A total of almost 10,000 CG-4As were built.

Development of the Pickup

The first pickup launch of a sailplane took place in September 1941. At du Pont's request, Arthur B. Schultz came to Wright Field with a Midwest sailplane. A standard AAA Stinson pickup plane picked Lewin Barringer up in the Midwest. Du Pont hired Shultz as chief engineer of AAA and gave him the task of designing and building a pickup unit for the Waco CG-4A. Walter Setz also joined the AAA as a special project engineer.

Barringer Heads Military Program

In October 1941 General Arnold appointed Lewin Barringer to coordinate

Top right: A modified surplus TG-1A sailplane in a winch tow from the Torrey Pines site.

(G. Uveges)

Top left: The SGS 2-12 takes off from Harris Hill. This was the only commercial version of the TG-3A that was built after the completion of the TG-3A contract.

(Hans Groenhoff)

Center,: A TG-4A with the original military markings. These Laister-Kauffman designed training gliders were popular surplus gliders because of their small size and the opportunities of improving them for better soaring performance.

(NSM Collection)

Bottom, : The TG-5A, a modification of the Taylorcraft light plane that was one of the three types of light plane gliders that were the mainstay of the final phase of the military glider training program.

(Don Downie)

Those soaring enthusiasts who were at Wurtsboro Airport for the "Keep 'Em Flying" meet will always associate that day with the attack on Pearl Harbor. It was a cold day and Ginny Mayer was sitting in a car near the flight line keeping the flight log. She had the radio on and heard the Pearl Harbor announcement. She spread the word among those at the meet. That included the Schweizers, who had dropped by on their way back to Elmira from New York City, where they had been buying spruce for the TG-3A. The shocking news made everyone realize that now they would have to "keep 'em flying" for war rather than for fun.

and administer the entire glider program. Barringer chose Eliot B. Noyes to assist him. Noyes had been the artist and cartographer on the Persian expedition on which Barringer had been the pilot. They became good friends, and a year after they had returned to the United States Barringer soloed Noyes in a sailplane at Wing Field. Noyes obtained his 5-hour duration leg for his Silver "C" at the 1937 Sleeping Bear Meet in Michigan, and thereafter became a life-long soaring enthusiast.

Noyes was assigned to the USAAF Glider Headquarters in Washington during the entire war. At the end of the war, Noyes was asked for a story on the wartime glider program, which was to be used in a revision of the book *Flight without Power*. Although the book was never repub-

The WACO CG-3A training glider, the first U.S. cargo glider.

(U.S. Army)

lished, Noyes wrote a brief but excellent summary of the military glider program, which is quoted in appropriate places in this history.

"Keep 'em Flying" Meet

By the fall of 1941 soaring activity around the United States had waned. Efforts to keep private flying and soaring going were highlighted by a series of "Keep 'em Flying" meets that were held around the country on the weekend of December 6–7, 1941. Ironically, the Japanese attack on Pearl Harbor that Sunday brought all private flying along the coasts to a halt.

The Military Glider Program, 1942–1945

In the spring of 1942 the USAAF decided to buy up existing private gliders for its training program. It purchased all the flyable sailplanes it could find, offering prices in excess of their current value. Needless to say, the owners offered little resistance to selling them. The only sailplanes left were those being constructed or repaired.

Unfortunately, the schools could not use them effectively since there were so many different types.

Soaring and the SSA

With most of the soaring people in the United States involved in the war effort, the soaring movement was now held together by the continued publication of *Soaring*. Attempts to obtain financial support for the SSA from the expanding military glider industry had not been successful, and so the SSA was unable to hire a general manager.

Parker Leonard and a group of soaring enthusiasts at the Pratt-Read plant ran the SSA as an after-work project. Jay Buxton, who was one of the most active members of the group, became assistant editor of *Soaring*. However, work at the plant made it increasingly difficult to get the magazine out on time. Early in 1942, Leonard turned over the editorship of *Soaring* to Alexis Dawydoff and the secretaryship to Ben Shupack. The May-June 1942 issue was Dawydoff's first.

Alexis Dawydoff was a White Russian prince who had escaped to England during the Russian Revolution. He had an aviation background as well as experience in writing and he immediately joined the RAF in England as a flight observer and interpreter. After World War I he came to the United States, where he worked with Sikorsky Aircraft. In 1930 he became a test pilot for the Peel Gliderboat Company, but later joined Street and Smith Publications, where he worked on *Air Trails* and *Air Progress* magazines. Shupack was a high school science teacher and a member of the Airhoppers Club.

Buxton died a few months after the changeover. During his involve-

Early in 1942, SAC was concentrating on building up the production of the TG-2 and getting started on the TG-3. It received a visit from General Knudson of the War Production Board, who was inspecting the plants in the area that had military contracts. When he saw the antiquated facilities on the second floor of the Knitting Mill building, he told the Schweizers to "get out of here" and informed them who might be able to help them find a new location. It was not long before the Defense Plants Corporation started building a plant for SAC at the Chemung County Airport, which was also under construction at that time.

ment with the soaring movement he had made many important contributions to soaring. His *Transporter* two-place sailplane was a bold step ahead for that time and it played a part in the development of two-place sailplanes in the United States.

As the military training program expanded, many soaring enthusiasts became instructors in the military glider schools. Production of training gliders was increasing and deliveries started on the modified lightplane gliders. Col. Mike Murphy was in charge of instructor training at Lockbourne, Ohio, which was to start as soon as CG-4As were available.

The first CG-4A glider was delivered in September 1941. As more CG-4As were delivered, advanced schools were set up in Stutgart, Arkansas; Lubbock, Texas; Delhart, Texas; Victorville, California; and Ft. Sumner, New Mexico. In the fall of 1942, CG-4As were used in airborne maneuvers in San Antonio, Texas, where some top military observers had mixed feelings as to how effective gliders would be in actual warfare.

1943

In January 1943 the U.S. Army Air Corps, and the U.S. soaring movement in particular, suffered a severe loss. Barringer, who had been commissioned a major a few months before,

The WACO CG-4A being towed by a C-47.
(NSM Collection)

was lost when the C-47 in which he was flying from Europe disappeared between Puerto Rico and Trinidad. Du Pont wrote an obituary in the March-April 1943 *Soaring*: "Lewin's many outstanding contributions to the advancement of gliding and soaring . . . are a matter of public record. . . . We know of the great contribution that Lewin, working in his quiet and characteristically modest way, has made to this progress. . . . Learning to fly in 1929, Lewin entered into a wide and varied aviation career. . . . He always remained true to his first love—gliding and soaring. . . . Lewin Barringer is gone but his contribution to aviation will live on, not only in aviation history, but in the hearts of those of us who have been privileged to know him."

By February of 1943, the CG-4As were not yet available in large enough quantities to be able to give advance training to all the pilots that the schools graduated. The task of cutting the pilot training program from 10,000

students to 5,000 fell to Col. Don Hamilton of the Glider Office in Washington, D.C. Subsequently, some schools were shut down. The training glider manufacturers' orders were not cut, although no new orders were forthcoming.

After Lewin Barringer's death, no one replaced him until April, when General Arnold appointed Richard C. du Pont. One of du Pont's first actions was to set up an advanced training course at the Laurinburg Maxton Air Force Base in North Carolina. Col. Mike Murphy was in charge and developed a very effective program for training glider pilots by landing CG-4As under simulated war conditions.

Philadelphia Conference, 1943

Soaring enthusiasts not in uniform were interested in finding a public service that they could perform. The possibility of a youth glider training program had been discussed, and a glider conference, sponsored by the SSA and the Philadelphia Glider Council, was held at the Franklin Institute on March 27, 1943, to consider this idea.

Thirty representatives were present. The main problem in starting such a program was the lack of gliders, launching equipment, gliderports outside the defense zone, and personnel to conduct the courses. Committees were set up to study these factors and report to the SSA directors.

Soaring *Magazine*

Shupack, who took over as editor of *Soaring* early in 1943, depended on stories about the military use of gliders and scientific and technical articles to fill up *Soaring*. Soaring news was always popular, whether it was about

---

After Barringer left his SSA position of general manager, the Schweizers got to know him better as they saw him quite often at Wurtsboro, New York, and at other soaring events. They worked closely with him on the book Flight without Power *and found him congenial. After he was lost over the Atlantic, all the authors agreed to turn over future royalties from the book to Lewin's wife, Helen. Soaring lost one of its most effective supporters, and many in soaring had lost a good friend.*

Frank Kelsey test flying his Super Albatross, Gus Briegleb receiving the ATC on the BG-8, or Ralph Barnaby being promoted to captain.

A few soaring pilots were able to soar outside of the air defense zones. Shelly Charles, an Eastern Airline pilot, flying a Minimoa, set a new U.S. altitude record in a thunderstorm over Atlanta, Georgia, with a gain of height over release of 19,434 feet. Out west a group of California pilots held the Sixth Annual Western States Meet at Bishop, California, on September 4–5, 1943. However, flying was limited by the 150-mile coastal defense area. John Robinson, using thermals, flew his Zanonia to 19,200 feet. Paul Tuntland, flying a Baby Bowlus, got his Silver "C" distance in a flight to Nevada.

With the training glider production going at high speed, the manufacturers soon started running out of orders. The only exception was the Laister-Kaufmann Corp., which was building CG-4As and developing the new CG-10A cargo glider. Pratt-Read continued to work on the CG-4A. Frankfort Sailplane Corp. went into other defense work, and the Schweizer Aircraft Corp. switched to aircraft subcontract work.

First Military Use of Gliders

On the night of July 9, 1943 the allies used gliders for the first time when they invaded Sicily—127 CG-4As and 10 Horsa (British) gliders were used to carry 2,000 troops. Unexpected winds and "friendly fire" caused many gliders to land in the sea, but enough troops got there to help the paratroopers carry out a successful attack.

In September, du Pont and Col. P. E. Gabel flew to California to look over the XCG-16, the 42-place Bowlus-designed glider. Du Pont went along

Schweizer Aircraft moved into its new plant on March 1, 1943, and soon after that was producing one TG-3A a day. The official plant opening was celebrated on May 22, with representatives from the government, the military, and the community present. The soaring movement was represented by Parker Leonard, SSA president, and a contingent from the Airhoppers Club of New York, which included Emil Lehecka (who did the test flying for SAC), Alexis Dawydoff, Steve and Ginny Bennis, and Ted Pfeiffer. The USAAF sent a Vultee L-1 equipped for glider pickup and All American Aviation sent Taylor Boyer and Fred Tietzel to assist with the pickups. Two production TG-3As were used for the pickup launching and the Schweizers, Bennis, Lehecka, and Leonard all experienced their first pickup flight.

At the Philadelphia conference it was agreed that if a civilian program such as this was to be permitted to continue during the war, it could not interfere with the war effort. This eliminated the use of aero tow. It was recommended that instead a single-place utility glider be used with auto or winch towing. It was suggested that SAC look into the possibility of building such a glider with a minimum of strategic materials. The 1-19 was the result, but because of the wartime limitations, developing it was a slow process and the prototype was not completed and flown until the summer of 1944. By this time there was no longer enough interest in a wartime youth program. SAC therefore decided to get it type certificated and to put it into production after the war as a completed utility glider and as a simplified kit.

on a test flight as an observer with Col. Gabel, as pilot, Howard Morrison copilot, Harry Perl flight engineer, Curley Chandler crew chief, and Paul Wells observer. Gabel, who had had limited experience with gliders, let the glider get caught in the prop wash of the Lockheed C-60 tow plane. It began to oscillate and then became detached from the towline. The ballast shifted aft, and the tail-heavy glider went into a flat spin. Perl and Wells parachuted successfully, but du Pont's parachute was just opening when he struck the ground and he was killed. The others failed to get out of the glider—Gable and Chandler were killed instantly, and Morrison died a short while later.

The loss of du Pont was another

and a force of Wingate's Raiders were double-towed over the Chin Hills and landed on the night of March 5th in a rutted jungle clearing 100 miles behind Japanese lines. This field was dubbed "Broadway." For twenty-four hours after the landing, the engineers worked frantically to prepare an air strip, which enabled U.S. and British transport planes to land. Another glider team went in nearby at "Chowringhee" and by the sixth day after the initial landing, 9,000 troops, 175 ponies, 1,183 mules and 509,083 lbs. of supplies had been brought in, undetected by the Japs.

This was a new kind of airborne operation. In this case, an airhead was established behind enemy lines and the entire assault force moved in by air. As distinguished from the Sicily landing, which was diversionary in intent, this was a new type of attack, particularly suited to sparsely held territory and almost impossible to prevent except by alertness and overwhelming air superiority on the part of the defenders. In this operation, gliders were the only key to success. In no other way could the bulldozers and engineering equipment have been successfully landed on rugged terrain.

Top: Frank Kelsey and his Bowlus Super Albatross after a flying demonstration on Armed Force Day in 1945 at Fresno, California. This second "Super" was built by Kelsey in his spare time while working at the Bowlus plant. He added flaps and a number of other changes to this sailplane, which is now part of the National Soaring Museum collection.

(Frank Lelsey)

severe blow to the Army's glider program as well as the U.S. soaring world. Du Pont's enthusiasm, leadership, and financial support had enabled the SSA to become self-sufficient. The SSA would sorely miss his "faith, courage, enthusiasm, and sincerity," which his wife Allaire referred to in the obituary that she wrote for the September-October 1943 issue of *Soaring*.

Felix du Pont, Dick's brother, was appointed to take over for him. Good progress was being made in the production of the CG-4A and the training was ahead of schedule. To quote from Elliot Noyes's story:

> Through the fall of 1943, the emphasis was on the tactical training of glider pilots, the standardization of techniques, and the making of as many improvements as possible in the equipment. No one knew what the deadline would be for this intensive activity but the invasion of "Festung Europa" had been promised and no one doubted the importance of the role gliders would play.

1944

It was the China-Burma-India theater that produced the next glider activity. In one of the most dramatic actions of the war, 54 CG-4As loaded with U.S. Airborne Aviation engineers

Bottom, right: Shelley Charles with his Minimoa sailplane at the 1946 National. He set the U.S. national altitude record in the Minimoa in 1943.

(NSM Loomis Collection)

While this exciting activity was going on in Burma, intensive preparations were under way in England for the invasion of the continent. Lieut. Col. Murphy had been summoned to England by General Eisenhower to help organize the glider phase of the assault. The airborne attack on Normandy was originally planned to be a daylight landing. As the day approached, a German panzer outfit was reported to be moving up into the area where the gliders were to land. Despite anticipation of heavy losses, it was considered important enough to revise the plan and make the landing at night. The best available fields were not very large and almost all were bordered with high trees. The assault was launched on the night of June 6, 1944. Lieut. Col. Murphy piloted the first of the 512 gliders into Normandy. Of all glider missions to date, this was the most critical, since the communication lines back of the beach had to be cut to assist the landing of troops from the sea. Although the hazards were tremendous, the glider landings succeeded brilliantly, with unusually light losses. Three fully equipped divisions were deposited squarely across the German communication lines. . . . Two months later, another airborne landing was made on the continent. Taking off from Italy, some 9,000 paratroopers and 408 gliders landed in Southern France on the high ground which controlled the land approaches to the points of seaborne attack.

The final airborne operation in Europe took place during the Rhine crossing. Ground troops had surged across the Rhine before the gliders and paratroopers made their landing which was only a very short distance in advance of the ground units.

Little further use was made of gliders in the Pacific. The final operation in which they were put to use was the mopping-up of northern Luzon in the Philippines in the spring of 1945. It is possible that a more extensive role might have been found for gliders had an invasion of the Japanese home island of Kyushu or Honshu been necessary.

First Motorless Flight Conference, 1944

In an effort to encourage scientific and technical development in motorless flight, Raspet and Shupack made arrangements with Dr. R. P. Harrington, Head of the Department of Aeronautical Engineering, and Dr. Nicholas J. Hoff, associate professor of aeronautical engineering, both of the Polytechnical Institute of Brooklyn, to hold a two-day technical conference on motorless flight on August 5–6, 1944.

The conference drew a good number of SSA members, although wartime travel difficulties kept the attendance down. Dr. Klemperer gave an introductory paper on the contribution of gliding and soaring to aviation. He listed 49 common items on powered planes that were first used on gliders and sailplanes. He also mentioned that gliders were an excellent vehicle for research and for the testing of new ideas that could have application on powered aircraft.

The conference was divided into five sections, and a total of 18 papers were delivered.

An actual combat photo of troop gliders landing in Europe during World War II.
(NSM Collection)

Left to right: August "Gus" Raspet and Ben Shupack with Thermal Sniffer on wingtip of SGS 2-8 sailplane.

(NSM Loomis Collection)

5. **Research Contributions**—C. K. Kolstad, Sperry Gyroscope Co., chairman; "Reaction Propulsion for Gliders," M. Z. Krzywoblacki, Brooklyn Poly; "Sandwich Construction," N. J. Hoff and S. E. Mautner, Skydyne, Inc.; "Research Problems of the SSA," A. Raspet, technical editor, *Soaring*; "Miniature Barograph," A. L. Lawrence, Kenyan Instrument Co.

1945

The January-February 1945 issue of *Soaring* was Ben Shupack's last issue. The new editor was Taylor Boyer of AAA. He had the assistance of Arthur Schultz who was SSA treasurer and AAA's chief engineer, and a number of other soaring enthusiasts who were at AAA at that time, including Wally Setz, Don Doolittle, and Vic Saudek. The masthead of that issue was changed to add the name of the Soaring Association of Canada, which had become an affiliate of the SSA. It had been formed the previous year at a meeting in Ottawa on April 21.

With victory in Europe, gas rationing and the restrictions of flying were eased up. The government started to sell its surplus training aircraft and before long soaring enthusiasts around the country were flying military training gliders and being towed by the primary training airplanes, such as the Stearman PT-17 and the Fairchild PT-19.

A number of soaring pilots in the northeast were drawn to Harris Hill over the 4th of July holiday, the traditional time for the Nationals. They had brought fourteen sailplanes for informal flying. Included were seven TG-4As, one TG-2, one TG-3A, a Kirby Kite, and Dawydoff Cadet, a SGU1-7 and SGU1-19, and Parker Leonard's new two-place. There was no set competition, just local soaring with attempts for "C" and Silver "C" badges.

At an informal "banquet" on the evening of July 4, Bill Nesbitt of the

1. **Operational Techniques**—A. B. Schultz, AAA, chairman; "Glider Tactics," Maj. Eliot F. Noyes, Army Air Force; "Single-Place Glider Training in Europe," Jerzy Illaszewicz, Canadian Wooden Aircraft, Ltd; "Instruments and Flight Technique in Thermal Soaring," R. F. Blaine, SCSA.

2. **Commercial Applications**—P. Leonard, Ludington Griswold, Inc., chairman; "Glider Pickups," A. B. Schultz, All American Aviation, Inc.; "Improved Efficiencies in Glider Structures," I. Bouton, L-K Aircraft Corp; "Value of Glider Background to Airline Flying," L. V. Petry, TWA.

3. **Gliding and Soaring**—L. Hull, Philadelphia Glider Council, chairman; "Calibration of Barographs," V. M. Saudek, All American Aviation, Inc.; "One Design Class," P. A. Schweizer, Schweizer Aircraft Corp.; "Gliding in War-Torn Europe," A. Dawydoff, Cadet Aeronautics; "Practical Thought on Thermals," K. O. Lange, Meteorologist.

4. **Design and Aerodynamics**—Dr. Harrington, Brooklyn Poly, chairman; "Glider, Tug Performance Studies," A. Raspet, technical editor, *Soaring*; "Powered Gliders," S. Corcoran, Frankfort Sailplanes; "Utility Gliders," W. Czerwinski, Canadian Wooden Aircraft, Ltd; "Variable Incidence Wings," G. W. Cornelius, Cornelius Aircraft Corp.

Laister-Kaufmann Corp. presented a TG-4A to the SSA for the purpose of carrying out scientific research. It was officially accepted by Dr. August Raspet. That evening the Herbert Sargent Award was presented to Ben Shupack for his untiring work in keeping the SSA and *Soaring* going during the war.

Most of those present had known Herb Sargent, for whom the trophy was named. He had started flying with the NYU Glider Club in 1932 and became the inspiring leader of the Hudson Valley Soaring Club, which had been formed from the old Mercury Glider Club. The club operated at Wurtsboro, New York, and used the Schweizer SGU1-2 (called the "brick") for training and the prototype SGU-1-7 for soaring. Herb Sargent, with the aid of Frank Hurtt and other club members, had built a winch for the club and its was used for the first time at the Eastern States Soaring Meet over Decoration Day. After a very busy day of operating the winch and flying, Herb took his fiancee for a ride in a Piper Cub and hit a tree at the edge of the airport. Both died as a result of the accident. Because of his great dedication to soaring, this award was given in his name by the members of the club.

By the end of the war there was only one glider in production—the Laister-Kaufmann CG-10A, the "Trojan Horse." The Air Corps at Wright Field was developing a new concept of assault aircraft, and the contract for the CG-10A was soon canceled.

There were no Navy (Marine) gliders in production. Their amphibious assault gliders never got beyond the prototype stage, mainly because Congress had forced the Navy to get into gliding, but the Navy did not have a place for gliders in its plans.

The biggest drawback of gliders in war was the logistical problem of getting them to where they were to be used, and, once used, getting back the undamaged ones. At first, gliders were considered expendable, but their high cost as well as the need for them at the front prompted the military to recover whatever they could. When available, C-47s equipped with the AAA pickup gear were used to snatch CG-4As out of small clearings.

Efforts to improve the mobility of the gliders were carried out at Wright Field. Two 125-horsepower Franklin engines were put on the CG-4A, which was then designated the PG-1. Later, two 175-horsepower Rangers were used and called the PG-2. Flight tests showed that this modification had promises as it greatly improved their mobility. Two 225-horsepower Jacobs engines were tried on the CG-15, which was then designated the PG-3A, and it flew well, but by the time these designs were developed the war had come to an end.

The only glider project that continued after the war was the Chase XCG-14. It was designed by Mike Stroukoff, who had formed Chase Aircraft. Maj. Floyd Sweet, who was project engineer on the new assault aircraft section at Wright Field, worked

The CG-10 glider tied down at the airport during the 1946 National Soaring Contest.
(NSM Collection)

with Stroukoff on this project and later encouraged him to give the Larissa Stroukoff Trophy in honor of his wife for the best out-and-return flight at the Nationals.

The CG-14 led to the new concept of assault aircraft—unpowered and powered—which were developed after the war. Chase Aircraft received contracts for two different types of military unpowered assault aircraft, the CG-18 and the CG-20. These were later powered and became the C-122 and C-123 military assault aircraft.

How Effective Was the Military Glider Program?

Whether the military glider program can be considered successful depends to a large extent on where the gliders were used. In the Burma invasion, where the gliders were vital, they were a brilliant success. On the other hand, the results of the Sicily invasion were disappointing since most of the gliders were released over the sea, and the paratroopers had to save the day. It is difficult to assess how important any particular weapon is in war. The important thing is that the war was won, and gliders played a part in the victory.

In evaluating the military glider program from the point of view of the soaring movement, one can point to both plus and minus factors. The following were some of the plus factors:

1. Prewar soaring pilots who became involved in the military training program in gliding or powerplane flying benefited from this experience and were convinced of the many advantages of two-place training.

2. Many training gliders, the TG-1, 2, 3, and 4 and the Pratt-Read LNE-1, were declared surplus and could be purchased at very low prices. In many cases, they were unused and included a trailer. This made available two-place sail-planes with fairly good performance that could be used for training or that could be cleaned up and flown in soaring competitions.

3. Surplus airplanes such as the Stearman PT-17, N3Ns, L5s, and other types that made good towplanes were available at low costs.

There were also minus factors:

1. One of the most severe blows to gliding was the bad publicity from an accident at the St. Louis airport. A CG-4A on a demonstration flight carrying the mayor of St. Louis, some of his aldermen, and military personnel had a wing strut fail and crashed in front of the large crowd that had gathered to watch the flight. The front page of almost every newspaper and *Life* magazine carried a picture of the CG-4A, minus one wing, diving for the ground. Although this flight had nothing to do with sport soaring, it would take a long time for the public to forget the accident.

2. With many surplus training gliders suddenly available at very low prices, the few glider manufacturers that had started up again at the end of the war were hard hit. In addition, others were discouraged from forming new companies.

3. Many pilots and troops who had lived through glider missions brought back tales of horror, and many were happy to get as far away from gliders as they could.

4. Although the surplus training gliders were well built and were licensed by the CAA, they were much heavier and faster than the prewar type. Many who bought them had little or no gliding experience, and many serious accidents occurred.

Another result of World War II was that soaring never got into the Olympics, although it was scheduled for the 1940 Olympics. Soaring was a logical sport for the Olympics, since it was to be a contest between men using one design of sailplane built to standard specifications and drawings, and would therefore test the skill of the sailplane pilots. However, the 1940 Olympics were never held. Although adding soaring to the Olympics has often been proposed since then, the idea has not yet received adequate support.

Second Motorless Flight Conference, 1945

The success of the first motorless flight conference led the participants to hold another conference at Brooklyn Polytechnic Institute in 1945. It was scheduled for October 12–13, and the number of papers presented was reduced from 18 to 12 so as to allow more time for discussion. Ralph Barnaby gave the introductory talk, "The Promise of Gliding and Soaring."

The conference was divided into four sections, and three papers were given in each section:

1. **Airframes**—Arthur B. Schultz, AAA, chairman; "Production Methods in Glider Manufacture," William Schweizer, SAC; "Shoulder Harness for Gliders," Howard Burr, SAC; "Steel Tube Fuselage Design," N. J. Hoff, Brooklyn Poly.

2. **Cargo Gliders**—Maj. Eliot F. Noyes, AAF, chairman; "Outlook for the Postwar Glider," J. W. Laister, LK Aircraft Corp.; "Cargo Glider versus Cargo Plane and Helicopter," R. H. Rush, AAA; "Commercial Glider Operations," A. E. Blomquist, Eastern Airlines.

3. **Research**—Roger Griswold, Luddington-Griswold Corp., chairman; "The Athodyd, as a Velocity Transformer," Zygmon Fonberg, A & R Corp.; "Research Problems of the SSA," August Raspet, SSA technical editor; "Meteorological Aspects of Soaring," B. L. Wiggin, U.S. Weather Bureau.

4. **Design and Aerodynamics**—R. P. Harrington, Brooklyn Poly, chairman; "Optimum Sailplane Design," Felix Chardin, Waco Aircraft Co.; "Stability of Canard Gliders," Robert Lopez, Luddington-Griswold Corp.; "Glider Airworthiness Regulations," A. A. Vollmecke, CAA.

Three of the conference papers dealt with the commercial use of cargo gliders. In 1941, when the military decided to use cargo gliders, the idea caught the imagination of the public and some envisioned the use of "glider trains" at the end of World War II.

Some "experts" improperly used the railroad train analogy that "you can pull more than you can carry." It was generally accepted that moving a given amount of cargo from one point to another could be done most efficiently by an airplane designed for this

The AAA Stinson about to pick up Bipps Boyer and the modified TG-3A with its load of lobsters.

(AAA, NSM Collection)

The easiest record to beat was the national multiplace duration. It stood at 8 hours and 48 minutes and had been set in 1936 by Slatter and Buxton in the Transporter. Frank Hurtt and Paul A. Schweizer made a try on the Harris Hill ridge in a TG-3 on November 4, 1945. A northwest wind enabled them to stay up for 9 hours and 17 minutes, the first postwar national record set. Although it was done for fun, the flight received good publicity and may have encouraged others to try soaring.

specific purpose, rather than by a tow plane–glider combination. The advantage that the glider train had was its ability to drop gliders off at different fields not suitable for cargo airplanes and then to pick them up later.

A few days after the conference All American Aviation ran some pickup tests. A modified TG-3A with its front cockpit full of lobsters was picked up from the beach at Hull, Massachusetts, and towed to "Teterboro" Airport near New York City. Three test trips carrying 400 pounds of lobster per trip were made for the Hull Lobster Co. The TG-3A wings were shortened and the front cockpit modified into one cargo bin. Taylor Boyer, the pilot, flew from the rear seat.

Although such an operation was feasible, the economic factors made it an impractical way of transporting such cargo. A truck could have taken the lobster from the Hull Lobster Company to a nearby airport for loading on the Stinson. It could have carried twice the amount of lobster without the pickup operator, the glider pilot, the glider, or the special ground handling crew needed at each end.

Soaring Starts Up Again, 1945–1946

Soaring enthusiasts felt that soaring would "take off" because the war had stimulated interest in aviation and had provided a large reservoir of potential

soaring pilots. Although many of the prewar gliding clubs were revived, some did not survive owing to the loss of key members. The availability, at low cost, of surplus gliders and training airplanes suitable for aero tow, made it possible for many to start without having to form a club. Soaring could be done readily from the local airport, where its novelty often made it an attraction. As traffic increased and the novelty wore off, some airports prohibited glider flying, and pilots then had to form clubs in order to get places to fly.

Record Flying

Favorable publicity was needed to give gliding a boost, and one way of doing this was to make some record flights. Thus far the United States had not broken any of the 20 possible world soaring records in the following categories: (1) distance in a straight line, (2) altitude gain, (3) duration with return to starting point, (4) distance with return to starting point, or (5) distance to a predetermined point. These records could be made in single and multiplace sailplanes, and by men and women. The Russians held 12 of the 20 possible records, the Germans 5, and Poland 1. No women records had been set in two-place goal and two-place out-and-return categories.

Since the world records were much superior to the U.S. national records, the first attempts concentrated on improving the national records, in the hope that the world records would soon follow.

Record flying has always been a highly visible part of soaring, and it began when the Germans tried to beat Orville Wright's duration record. Klemperer broke that record in 1921, and one year later Martens made the first flight lasting over an hour. During the next five years this record was broken five times. It stood at 14 hours 7 minutes in May of 1927. The United States won back the record on December 17–18, 1931, when Lt. W. A. Cocke, Jr., U.S. Navy, stayed up for 21 hours and 30 minutes on the east slope of Oahu in the Hawaiian Islands.

As the duration records increased, accidents began to occur and interest in duration flights declined. Many felt that further extension of the duration records proved nothing and that it was very much like "flag pole sitting," which was much in the news at that time.

SSA Looks Ahead

The SSA was looking ahead to a rapid growth of motorless flight. The SSA had been run during the war by the officers who had been elected in 1941, but no directors' meetings or elections were held so that by 1944 all directors' terms had expired and the SSA was technically without a board. Ben Shupack, the SSA secretary, who had kept SSA operating, announced in the January-February 1946 *Soaring* that an election would be held for 20 directors; the first 6 were to be elected for a three-year term, the next 6 for a two-year term, and the last 6, plus 2 "at large" directors, for a one-year term.

The election was based on proportional representation, a "pet" idea of Ben Shupack. He said that this method of election would "automatically reflect the distribution of glider enthusiasts geographically and according to active interest. This method of voting ensured that any area sufficiently interested will automatically secure representation on the board of directors." However, the low vote from the West and the heavy voting in New York State meant that the majority of members on the board were from the East.

All the new directors except for two, Charles and Hammond, had been active in the SSA before the war:

R. Barnaby, Philadelphia
W. Klemperer, Los Angeles
P. Leonard, Essex, Connecticut
A. Raspet, Locust Valley, New York
A. Schultz, Wilmington, Delaware
B. Shupack, Brooklyn

Elected through 1947:
S. Corcoran, Chicago
A. Dawydoff, New York
W. Hammond, Retsoff, New York
P. Schweizer, Elmira
E. Schweizer, Elmira
Sweet, Dayton, Ohio

Elected through 1946:
W. Briegleb, Van Nuys, California
J. S.Charles, Atlanta
C. Gale, Darien, Connecticut
E. Lehecka, New York
J. Robinson, Altadena, California
S. Smith, Tonawanda, New York

Directors-at-large
T. M. Boyer, Wilmington, Delaware
J. W. Laister, St. Louis, Missouri

Directors' First Postwar Meeting, 1946

The first postwar directors' meeting was held in New York City on April 13, 1946. For the third time, the directors called upon Captain Barnaby to be president. Ben Shupack was elected East Coast vice-president and Dr. Klemperer West Coast vice-president. Charles Gale was elected secretary and Emil Lehecka treasurer. Taylor Boyer continued as editor of *Soaring* and Dr. Raspet was made chairman of the Records Committee.

This directors' meeting was held at Charlie Gale's office at the Haire Publication Co. It had been only 14 years earlier that the founders of the SSA had gathered in the office of Gale's bosses at *Aviation* magazine to form the SSA. There was an air of excitement at this meeting, as there must have been at that first meeting. It was the first step in getting the SSA going again and all were hoping to see soaring gain a new following around the country.

The major action taken by the board was to determine the location of the 1946 Nationals. Eight cities had submitted proposals: Seattle, Oklahoma City, Casper, Dallas, Denver, Louisville, Elmira, and Muskogee. Elmira and Muskogee were the only ones that were willing to meet the SSA requirement of contributing $10,000 toward the expenses and prizes and that could provide an adequate airport and sufficient housing for pilots and crew. Elmira was chosen when Muskogee was unable to obtain the use of an airport.

A review of the SSA dues structure was made, and because of the growing number of husbands and wives active in soaring, it was decided to institute a family membership at $6. The regular membership was set at $4 and a subscription of *Soaring* was available at $2.50 per year. Schools, libraries, and commercial institutions could get a subscription for $2.

Commercialization

Many of the wartime glider manufacturers, such as Frankfort, Laister, and Pratt-Read, did not continue to manufacture sailplanes. Although Gus Briegleb planned to get his BG-7 glider into production, he was busy operating the Briegleb Soaring School. Thus, the only manufacturer that moved aggressively into a postwar glider program was SAC. It had the 1-19 glider ready for production and a new two-place trainer, the 2-22, under design.

The Two-Place Trainers

The surplus sailplanes were used mainly for fun flying, competition, and passenger rides, since they had certain limitations when used for training. Their higher wing loading and faster flying speeds, although satisfactory for training pilots for the military gliders, were not the most desirable characteristics for training beginners and made them impractical to use with car or winch tow, unless a very large field or airport was available. Furthermore, the instructors did not like the poor rear seat visibility in most of the surplus training gliders, and the wooden wings made them impractical for storing outside.

The 2-22 was built to fill the specific need that the surplus two-place trainers failed to do. Its design was based on the belief that more people would get into soaring if they could start in a trainer that was easy to fly and easy to soar, and one that gave them the confidence to continue.

Commercial Schools

Commercial soaring operations started soon after. The Briegleb Soaring School, which had been in operation before the war, started up again in 1946 at Rosamond Dry Lake, California. Owner and chief instructor Gus Briegleb, used a BG-8 and TG-1 two-place sailplanes. The launchings were made from the dry lake by auto tow using a 215-horsepower Duesenburg auto that had once been owned by Howard Hughes.

SAC started its school in the spring of 1946. It used the single-place 1-19 to begin with, but added a 2-22 as soon as it was available. Using both auto and aero tow, SAC operated at the Chemung County Airport adjacent to its plant.

The Gliding and Soaring Service, Inc., located at Ellenville, 90 miles northwest of New York City, was founded by Steve and Ginny Bennis, Alexis Dawydoff, Don Lawrence, and Guy Storer (all members of the Air-hoppers Club). Their equipment included a Franklin Utility, a Dawydoff Cadet, a Kirby Kite, two L-Ks, one Pratt-Read, and an Olympia. Launchings were made by winch or Stearman airplane from the top of Mt. Menagha at Ellenville—1,875 feet above the valley floor. At this time, other commercial operations were also being established around the country.

In the spring of 1946, interest in aviation was at an all-time high. SAC had signed up 15 dealers, most of whom were power operators who saw the possibility of a glider and soaring operation. The dealers had to start with the single-place 1-19. Some dealers were optimistic—one dealer in Georgia ordered a carload of 1-19s.

13th National, 1946

The 1946 National was held in Elmira from August 3 to August 18. Of the 48 ships that competed, 38 were surplus military trainers. The top three finishers were John Robinson in the Zanonia, Fritz Compton in a LK-10A, and Maurice Waters in a LK-10A. Only four high-performance sailplanes were entered, and they all finished in the top six places. A new pilot named Paul

SAC expected its sailplane manufacturing to become an important part of its business and had started to prepare for this toward the end of the war. Franklin Hurtt was hired to help with subcontract administration, do graphic artwork, his specialty, and to assist with advertising and promotion. Hurtt was a member of the Hudson Valley Soaring Club. He had been a glider instructor for the EASC military glider school in Mobile and later a power instructor for a primary training school. When SAC's glider program started, he became the company test pilot and the first chief instructor at the Schweizer Soaring School.

The 2-22 was test flown successfully in early March of 1946. In order to give the new sailplane publicity, Hurtt and Dick Powell, an SAC engineering department employee, set a new duration record of 10 hours and 9 minutes on April 10 in the prototype 2-22. As in the first National, an attempt was made to lower sandwiches and hot coffee to them from another glider, but the rough air made it too difficult.

MacCready ended up in eleventh place flying a Pratt-Read.

Contest rules allowed extra points for goal flights, goal-and-return flights, and records. This tended to distort the results and became a controversial issue.

The 1946 performances were not up to those of the 1941 contest and *Soaring* said that "this year was just the ice breaker and that future contests would bring a steady improvement." However, two new national records were set. The first was an out-and-return record of 100 miles, set by John Robinson and Clarence See. The second was a woman's distance record of 37 miles set by Virginia Bennis on the first woman Silver "C" distance flight in United States.

In order to promote attendance, an air show was staged every day after the contest sailplanes had left the field. The Army Air Force and Navy both had exhibition teams there, and daily pickups of a CG-15 by a C-47 were made from Harris Hill. A mock assault by five C-46s, each towing two CG-4As, was carried out each afternoon. A Laister-Kaufmann CG-10A

The U.S. Air Force "invades" Harris Hill as five C-46 transports, each towing two CG-4As, pass over the field. This demonstration was part of an air show that was put on every afternoon during the 1946 National when competing pilots were away from the field.

(NSM Loomis Collection)

Trojan Horse and a captured German Gotha 242 troop-carrying glider were also part of the military show. On one flight, the CG-10A, with its 105-foot span, came close to soaring the Harris Hill ridge and was a striking contrast to the contest sailplanes flying there.

The total cost of running the 1946 National was $16,400. At that time entry fees were only $10 and contest tows were free, and considerable prize money was offered to get pilots to come from distant parts of the country. In order to finance contests at Elmira it was necessary to develop income from a number of sources: gate receipts ($5,229), contest programs ($1,844), concession fees ($529), cabin fees ($478), and entry fees ($480), with the balance donated by the community.

Thunderstorm Project

In the summer of 1946 the SSA carried out its Thunderstorm Project at the Pine Castle Army Air Field at Orlando, Florida. Ben Shupack was in charge of the glider activities and Paul Tuntland was project pilot. On one flight he established what he thought was a new national two-place altitude record of 18,700 feet. However, his application was not allowed since he carried ballast instead of a passenger. Although this project attracted considerable attention, it lasted only a short time, and little specific information was released to the soaring world.

SSA Activity

There was no formal directors' meeting at the time of the Nationals, but a meeting was held on September 13 in Philadelphia. President Barnaby, who would be retiring from the Navy on January 1, pointed out that the SSA would have to renew its agreement with the NAA, which had expired during the war. It was announced that the Federal Aeronautique International (FAI) was to take over the gliding and soaring functions of ISTUS.

A bid to hold the 1947 National Soaring Contest had been received from Wichita Falls, Texas, and Muskogee, Oklahoma, and Louisville, Kentucky, were also interested.

Barnaby reported that the Army Air Corps proposed to turn over to the SSA a number of captured German sailplanes. The sailplanes were a Weihe, Windspiel, and Olympia, and two MU-13s. These ships were in very poor condition and it was recommended that they be sent to soaring centers in different parts of the country to acquaint designers and builders with the latest German prewar designs.

The matter of CAA glider regulations was also discussed, and Stanley was appointed chairman of an SSA Glider Regulation Committee that included Klemperer, Sweet, an additional member from the SCSA, and E. Schweizer.

SAC submitted a set of proposed standards for "GI" Glider Schools that Robert Taylor of SAC had developed, and they were accepted by the Veterans Administration.

The future of SSA was discussed, and Bob Stanley felt that SSA should employ a full-time general manager. He suggested that necessary funds could be raised by engaging the services of a professional promoter. The Executive Committee was instructed to investigate this possibility.

1-21 Sailplane

If the United States was to become important in the international soaring world, it would have to acquire some high-performance sailplanes. From what SAC had learned of metal construction, it was convinced that it could make a high-performance sailplane that would be a step ahead of other sailplanes of that time. The company designed the 1-21, and announced in the September–October *Soaring* its plan to produce this model, if sufficient orders were received. The price was set at $2,750, and two orders were received—one from Richard Comey, who had been a World War II bomber pilot and a member of the Harvard Glider Club, and the other from David Stacey, who had organized the Harvard Glider Club. The 1-21 was an all-metal design with a high aspect

ratio wing that incorporated water ballast, which was being used for the first time in the United States. In spite of having only two orders, SAC decided to go ahead with the project—hoping that more orders would be forthcoming.

Single- vs. Two-Place Training

After the war there was considerable controversy about whether training should be done in two-place or single-place sailplanes. Most people were sold on the two-place training method, but a few still believed in the single-place training technique, which had been used before the war.

The CAA requirements were based on the single-place training with auto or winch launchings, which required 100 flights for a private rating and 250 flights, or 150 flights with 5 hours soaring, for a commercial rating. This meant an unnecessarily large number of flights for those training with two-place trainers using aero tow. Most members of Stanley's committee preferred two-place training. Their recommendation would have eliminated single-place training, but Ben Shupack objected, and the matter was then scheduled to be taken up at the next directors' meeting.

While this controversy was going on, those active in training had to live with the existing CAA regulations. Some worked around this problem by using a combination of single-place training sailplanes and surplus World War II two-place training sailplanes, with surplus tow planes. This method was used by Gliding and Soaring Service of Sanford, Florida, the first school to have a GI-approved glider school program. It required dedicated instructors, a lot of ground work, and

Single-place training at the University of Illinois Glider Club in a SGU 1-19A training glider. Tom Page, the instructor in the tow car, signals information to the student.

(Steve Moreland, NSM Collection)

a large airport to minimize the interference between glider and airplane traffic. Adjustment of the CAA regulations and the introduction of the 2-22 in 1946 eased the problem.

New National Record

In the fall of 1946 Dick Johnson of Pan American Airways, his brother Dave, and Bob Sparling attempted to set some two-place distance records in the Southwest. They used Prescott, Arizona, as their starting point. On September 8, Dick, with Bob Sparling as copilot, took off in their TG-2 behind Dave's Waco tow plane. They had set Durango, Colorado, as their goal. After a difficult start, conditions improved and they landed in the northeast corner of New Mexico to set a new multiplace national distance record of 314 miles.

Directors' Winter Meeting, 1946

The main purpose of the meeting on December 13, 1946, was to determine the site of the 1947 contest. Representatives from Wichita Falls and Elmira were present to make their proposals. Wichita Falls was chosen by a vote of

13 to 4, and for the first time the National was to be held away from Elmira. The SSA-NAA relationships were discussed and it appeared that the NAA was willing to continue the previous agreement without the $300 per year sanction fee, since the SSA would sanction the contests and issue the badges.

A discussion was held about the advisability of hiring a paid manager, and the Executive Committee was instructed to find ways and means to finance a paid manager, and to look further into the CAA regulations.

Chapter 6

The Postwar Period, 1947–1951

The Center of Activity Moves West, 1947

The year 1947 saw the center of soaring activity move toward the West. Before that time the main areas of activity had been on the East Coast, in the midwestern states of Ohio, Indiana, Illinois, and Michigan, and on the West Coast. Barringer had shown in 1938 that soaring could be done over the plains and in the Southwest. Contests that followed at Wichita Falls, Texas, in 1939 and 1940 confirmed this. However, it took the 1947 Nationals to convince many soaring people of the excellent soaring conditions in the West.

A National Gliding and Soaring Program Proposed

The main concern during 1946 had been to get soaring going again and to have a national contest. Now that this had been accomplished, Barnaby felt it was important to restate the purposes and goals of the SSA. He listed them in the January-February 1947 *Soaring*:

1. Encourage people to bring world soaring records to the United States.

2. Urge the Congress to pass legislation in support of a national gliding and soaring movement.

3. Help the CAB develop new regulations in order to encourage gliding and soaring flight.

4. Encourage the formation of approved gliding schools so as to make gliding training available to as many GIs as possible.

The legislation that he referred to was the McCarran bill, which was pulled out of the files by Charles Malone and reintroduced in the Senate in January 1947 by Sen. McCarran.

The SSA did little about the McCarran bill until 10 months later when Barnaby stressed the value of a national glider program in his letter of November 6, 1947, to Thomas Finletter, chairman of the President's Air Policy Commission.

SSA Developments

Early in March Taylor Boyer wrote Barnaby that he could no longer edit *Soaring* because of the great amount of time that he and his wife were spending on it. On March 16, 1947, Richard Comey wrote to Captain Barnaby expressing his interest in the position of general manager and said that he would be willing to assist the editor of *Soaring*. In view of these developments, Barnaby set an SSA directors' meeting for Elmira on April 12–13.

The directors voted to give Comey a four-year contract as general manager and editor. A formula was developed for his salary that was based on the number of members in SSA. The dues were to be increased from $4 to $5 a year, and Comey was to receive

Dick Comey, competing in his first national contest, won the 1947 national championship, which was held at Wichita Falls, Texas. He flew the new Schweizer SGS-1-21 all-metal sailplane.

(NSM Collection)

$1 for each of the first thousand members and $2 for each member above one thousand. He was to start work in August of 1947, and his first issue of *Soaring* would be the September-October 1947 issue.

The SSA Committee on CAA regulations proposed revisions that would have required instruction in two-place sailplanes. The single-place adherents objected to this change, maintaining that past experience did not indicate that dual training was safer, and that the glider regulations at that time permitted both two-place and single-place training. Shupack put forth a motion that the SSA withdraw their recommendations to the CAA. The motion was defeated, but another motion was passed that authorized the committee to continue to work with the CAA to develop satisfactory rules.

The bylaws were amended to set the membership rates at $5 for active, $3 associate, $25 sustaining, $100 sponsoring member, and $100 for life memberships. The bylaws were further changed to provide for the election of directors prior to the directors' meeting held at the national contest.

The question of the amateur status of glider pilots was discussed in connection with the possibility of soaring being authorized again in the Olympics. The Record Committee was asked to secure a definite statement on this matter from the Olympic Committee.

14th National, 1947

The 14th National at Wichita Falls on July 4–20 was the largest contest to date. Eighty pilots and 65 sailplanes were entered, of which over 40 were surplus military trainers. Two EON Olympias came from England and two AIR-100s and an all-metal SO-P1 from France. The other U.S. sailplanes that appeared at the National for the first time were the 1-21, the Prue-160, Vernie Ross's Ranger, a BG-6, the Super-Albatross, a Lawrence XS-2, and the Nelson Dragonfly power glider.

The contest was scheduled for 17 days, the longest ever, and it was "blessed" with exceptionally good soaring weather. Of the 17 days, 14 were contest days, with every day being an "open" day, meaning that the contestants could chose their own tasks. Most pilots chose distance flights each day in order to get the most points, but the long flights and even longer retrieves caused the pilots to become very tired, so that only the most competitive kept going.

Bonus points were given for goal, and goal-and-return flights. There were many cash goal prizes. One pilot made the contest secondary and each day went after a lucrative goal prize.

Bob Blaine was the contest director, assisted by Johnny Nowak, Joe Steinhauser, Gus Scheurer, Stan Corcoran, Bill Putnam, Art Hoffman, and Gene Ardelt, with Hawley Bowlus as chief timer.

The contest was won by Dick Comey, flying the 1–21. MacCready finished second in the Screamin Weiner, Ray Parker third in the Rigid Midget, and John Robinson was fourth in the Zanonia. These were all-American designed sailplanes and showed the way sailplane design would go.

The western soaring conditions were ideal, and it was clear that new sailplane designs would have to achieve greater speeds and distances. Although some surplus sailplanes flown by good pilots did quite well, it was evident that the war surplus sailplanes were no longer competitive.

Comey was the first one to win the Richard C. du Pont Trophy. This was given in du Pont's memory by his wife Allaire and his father A. Felix du Pont, as the perpetual trophy for the national soaring champion.

Comey won mainly because of his persistence and that of his crew, Bill Frutchy and Don Quigley. They got little sleep during this grueling contest. Quigley, an SAC employee, had helped build the 1–21 and spent his vacation to help the 1–21 win the championship. The 1–21, and the Screaming Weiner, Rigid Midget, and Zanonia had all shown that they were good for western conditions, and it was clear that thinner airfoils, higher wing loading, and cleaner design were necessary to achieve greater speeds and distances.

A total of 40,192 cross-country miles was flown. Paul MacCready set a world out-and-return record of 230 miles, and Virginia Bennis set a women's world altitude record with a gain of 7,200 feet in her British-designed Kirby Kite. Herman Kursawe of Long Island, New York, had built this classic wooden sailplane from plans. Bennis became the first woman in the United States to earn an FAI Silver "C." A national distance record of 300.25 miles was set by Comey, but before the contest was over E. Nessler raised it to 319 miles, and then Robinson to 332 miles.

Virginia "Ginny" Bennis and her Kirby Kite in which she earned the first U.S. Women's Silver "C" badge and exceeded the women's world altitude record, at the 1947 National.

(Ken Eden)

When the Wichita Falls Chamber of Commerce had bid on the Nationals, it anticipated a good income from admission charges. However, not many local people came to the contest because they had seen many gliders during the war, since Sheppard Field had been one of the advanced glider training bases. As a result, the contest quickly ran into financial difficulties, community support declined, and the final banquet was canceled. A banquet was held, however, after E. J. Reeves, Jon Carsey, and Jim Simmons of the Dallas Soaring Society agreed to underwrite it.

The National was a great success in many respects: It substantiated the excellent soaring conditions in the Southwest, justified that part of Barnaby's program that urged U.S. pilots to set international soaring records, and proved the claim that a central location would encourage pilots to attend from all parts of the country. Of the 74 U.S. pilots who entered, 39 came from the eastern half of the country and 35 from the western half.

There were some shortcomings, however. The unlimited distance flying was just "too much of a good thing." The safety of the pilots was endan-

Paul A. Schweizer attended the first directors' meeting and accepted the position of secretary. He and Howie Burr of SAC had come to the contest with the Schweizer 1–20 (a 1–19 with extended wings) to fly the first week of the contest. They hoped to get some experience at contest flying and to try out the soaring conditions in the Southwest.

On the way down, as they were approaching the Wichita Falls Airport, they saw a pilot standing along the road with an open parachute bunched under his arms. They stopped and found that it was Scott Royce who had just "bailed out" of his Baby Albatross, which had come apart in the air when he hit some strong lift.

In a very short time both extended their individual distance records, the best one being a 136-mile flight, which the contest management referred to as a new utility record, since it had beaten Hank Wightman's 1936 utility record.

gered when pilots, tired from the long flights and retrieves, were forced to fly in order to have a chance of winning.

A Paris Newspaper correspondent, who attended the contest to report on the three French pilots who had entered, complained about the rules in a letter to the editor in the September-October, 1947 *Soaring*. He felt that some rules were changed as the contest progressed, which was a disadvantage to some of the competitors. He also claimed that some pilots were towed an unnecessarily long time in the direction of their proposed flight and that other pilots made use of aero tows for retrieves. It was evident that changes were required. The one most talked about was the need to do away with duration. The rules gave points for duration, which meant that, if two pilots flew to the same point, the one who took the longest time would get the most points.

Directors' Summer Meeting, 1947

At the meeting on July 9–10, 1947, in Wichita Falls, Texas, officers were elected and the drift to the West continued when E. J. Reeves of Dallas was elected president. The other officers elected were Robert Stanley, East Coast vice-president; Bob Blaine, West Coast vice-president; Shelly Charles, treasurer; and Paul A. Schweizer, secretary.

The main actions of the board were to work out the details for Dick Comey's start as general manager and to approve some bylaw changes. These included the new membership rates that had been set at the April meeting and the addition of a junior membership at $1 per year.

A second meeting was held on Sunday July 20 and included the decision to sell the L-K and two of the three Pratt-Reads that the SSA owned. Dr. Klemperer and Captain Barnaby were named to the Technical Committee, which was to prepare a platform for approval of the directors. This was done as a result of the directors' concern that Raspet, the chairman, and Shupack, who worked very closely with him, were venturing off into too many different areas and that the board should have some control over these activities.

Contest Rules Change

The 1947 contest rules were based on the previous Nationals at Elmira and were designed to encourage new distance records. It became apparent, as the 14th National progressed, that the rules needed to be changed extensively if they were to ensure a fair, safe, and competitive meet.

Fritz Compton, the chairman of the Contest Committee, proposed the following changes: (1) Only each pilot's five best flights would be counted, and (2) the pilots entering the meet should be divided into two groups—contestants and participants—in order to speed up the takeoff lines of the serious contestants. He asked for comments on the proposed rules changes.

Although the SSA was concerned about the rules and the importance of running a good competition, it did not seem worried about the problems of the sponsors of the Nationals. Even though the Wichita Falls Junior Association of Commerce had serious financial problems, the SSA increased the requirements for bidders for the next Nationals so that the sponsor would have had to put $5,000 in escrow for the point-award fund, guaranteed an operating fund of at least $12,000, and pay a $500 sanction fee. These were much in excess of what Wichita Falls had been required to do.

SSA Activities

E. J. Reeves began his presidency by calling for a directors' meeting at the Northeastern Soaring Contest set for Harris Hill in the last week of August. The meeting opened with a discussion on SSA-NAA relations. A committee was set up to carry on the negotiations with the NAA. Choosing the site of the 1948 National was discussed next. In order to give the sponsor adequate time, it was decided to make the decision in October.

Reeves Bulletins

President Reeves started the practice of issuing numbered bulletins to the directors. The first was issued in October, and it covered the possibility of a bid for the National coming from the Dallas area. He mentioned that the $17,500 required contribution caused the would-be sponsors to look at the potential gate very carefully. He pointed out that a procedure for hom-

ologating records was needed since only one of the two world record flights made at Wichita Falls had been accepted.

In late October, Fritz Compton sent a letter with an attached ballot to all directors. The choice was either to vote for Elmira as the site of the 15th National or to wait and see if any other bids might be forthcoming. All but one director voted for Elmira. Reeves's Bulletin No. 3 advised the directors that since the site of the contest had been set the next meeting would be held at the time of the southeast contest at Sanford, Florida, in January.

Reeves pointed out that the "chief purpose of our National Contest is for the selection of an American Soaring Champion. Record breaking, though highly desirable, is merely an adjunct to the main purpose of the National Contest." Reeves also mentioned that a paper on gliding and soaring in America was to be presented at the President's Air Policy Commission and Congressional Aviation Committee. This report was compiled by Captain Barnaby, the SSA general manager, and the society's secretary and was to appear in an early issue of *Soaring*.

Activity around the Country

Soaring got some good national exposure when four sailplanes opened the show each day at the 1947 National Races in Cleveland over the Labor Day weekend. The 1–21, flown by Emil Lehecka and three L-Ks flown by George Tabery, Fritz Sebeck, and Fred Brittain were towed aloft in a quadruple-tow by a BT-13. After release, Lehecka put on a solo aerobatic show while the three L-Ks did team aerobatics.

That year Joe Steinhauser re-

Bob Symons of Bishop, California, with his Pratt-Read.
(NSM Collection)

opened his Motorless Flight Institute at the Chicagoland Airport, and the Schweizer school and the Cromelins Air Activity in Augusta, Georgia, received "GI" approval. In addition, Aerojet Engineering Corp. launched a P-R glider to 1,500 feet with a 500-pound-thrust 30-second rocket. As the rocket weighed 150 pounds and cost $145.00, there was little enthusiasm for this method of launching.

Wave Flying Starts

The first wave flying was done in March of 1933 over an area near Hirschberg, Germany, where a farmer named Moaz had reported seeing wave clouds. Wolf Hirth's Grunau Soaring School was located nearby and the students there made many wave flights in the next few years, the highest being J. Kuettner's flight to 22,310 feet (without oxygen) in a Grunau Baby.

Bob Symons, a native of Bishop, California, had felt unusual air currents while flying in the Bishop area

and suspected that they might be waves. In early 1947, Harland Ross, who had learned to fly at the early Bowlus School, moved to Bishop. While instructing in a Cessna 140, he confirmed the spectacular soaring conditions there—both thermal and waves.

The town of Bishop, at an elevation of 4,000 feet, lies in the Owens Valley, between the 12,500-foot-high Sierra Nevada mountains to the west and the White Mountains to the east. The Owens Valley is very dry since the air masses coming from the Pacific deposit their moisture in the form of rain or snow as they move up the western Sierra slopes. Little moisture is left for the Owens Valley and Nevada to the east. This situation gives rise to good thermals with high cloud bases.

When the winds come from the west and are over 25 miles per hour, they set up wave motions as they drop down the east slopes of the Sierras. They are often marked by lenticular (lens-shaped) clouds, which are called "Lennies," or "Moazagotl Clouds" after farmer Moaz. These clouds appear stationary to the eye, but form at the windward edge and dissipate at the leeward edge, much like the stationary wave that forms downstream from a submerged stone in a shallow but fast-moving stream.

On one occasion Ross soared to 18,000 feet in the 140 with the engine stopped. Symons, who made snow observation flights in a P-38 fighter for the Los Angeles Water Department, was once able to hold his own at 30,000 feet with the propellers feathered.

Paul MacCready came to Bishop later that December with his Orlik sailplane. It was equipped with oxygen, and MacCready had cold weather flying equipment. On December 29 he

Paul MacCready, in the Polish Orlik sailplane, explores the waves near Bishop, California, in December 1947. The Orlik was on exhibit at the 1939 World Fair in New York City at the time that Poland was invaded at the start of World War II. It was given to a Polish-American group headed by Dr. Zbikowski, and Bill Ptunam flew it to second place in the 1941 National.

(Bob Symons, NSM Collection)

was climbing in a wave when his canopy cracked at 21,000 feet. He cut short his flight rather than risk the danger of exposure at that altitude. This ended the wave flying for 1947, but thereafter many were convinced that altitude records would be set when properly equipped pilots made more attempts to fly the Bishop wave.

The Expected Boom That Did Not Develop, 1948

Many aviation and soaring boosters had expected private flying and soaring to undergo tremendous growth after the war. By 1948 it was evident that the market for airplanes and sailplanes had been overstated. Lightplane manufacturers were making more airplanes than they could sell, and the airplanes produced up to that time were being used mainly to fill the distributors', dealers', and operator "pipeline." Very few airplanes were actually being sold to ultimate customers.

The surplus sailplanes continued

to provide price competition for SAC and discouraged other manufacturers from going into the business. Once SAC had filled its dealer requirements, its sales also diminished.

One factor that hurt this first Schweizer dealer program was that the 2–22 did not go into production until late in 1946, and most dealers and operators did not get to use them until the spring of 1947. If the dealers could have started their program with the two-place 2–22 rather than the single-place 1–19, they probably would have been more successful. Most of the Schweizer dealers did not continue. However, subcontracts kept SAC going.

Elsewhere in the aircraft industry adjustments were severe, and some of the newly established aircraft companies with a limited product line could not stay in business.

A news item in *Soaring* announced that in February of 1948 Schweizer Aircraft Corporation had purchased from the War Assets Administration the plant it had occupied since 1943. It included 10 acres of land adjacent to the

Chemung County Airport. This purchase assured a permanent home for SAC at Elmira, New York.

Gus Briegleb's Soaring School was also assured a home when Briegleb bought the surplus Victoryville Air Base that was on the War Assets Administration surplus list. This 640-acre plot became El Mirage and the home of the Brieglebs, and one of the most active soaring sites on the West Coast. Soaring continued there until 1984, when it was sold and used for other purposes.

National Program

The plan that Barnaby had announced in early 1947 was expanded during the year and the full program was announced in an editorial entitled "A Fundamental For Air Policy" in the January-February 1948 issue of *Soaring*. It included the following comments:

> The SSA feels that it is its duty to do all it can to see that gliding and soaring achieves its rightful place in the National Air Policy now being determined.
>
> Motorless flight's position in such a program is justified by the definite contributions that it can make to (1) national security, (2) safety in the air, (3) scientific progress, and, (4) society in general.
>
> Unlike the situation in most other countries, where motorless flight is subsidized by the government, in the United States, the SSA has had to struggle along by itself. In spite of this, it has progressed steadily and has made many contributions to aviation. It provided the know-how and nucleus of personnel about which the Army glider program in the last war was developed.
>
> Perhaps the largest and most important benefit that motorless flight can give is to provide a medium

through which the United States can build up a thoroughly trained civilian air reserve with the greatest possible safety and the lowest overall cost.

The editorial encouraged members to contact their senator and congressmen to get them to vote for the McCarran Bill and suggested sending them a copy of the January-February *Soaring* issue in which a series of articles expanded upon the editorial.

One article by William C. Lazarus, aviation supervisor of Florida, urged the CAA to provide for the issuance of air agency certificates to glider schools. The CAA did not act on this, however, since there were only about 12 gliding schools, and of these only 3 were approved under the GI Bill.

First Southeastern Championships

The first Southeastern Championships were held at Sanford, Florida, on January 15–18. "Pop" Krohne, president of the Florida Soaring Association—assisted by Steve Bennis of the Gliding and Soaring Service, Inc. school based there—conducted a very successful contest. Seventeen sailplanes and 24 pilots were entered. Among the competitors was Suzanne Melk, one of France's most famous women soaring pilots, who flew an AIR-100. Fred Brittain was the winner, with Suzanne Melk second and Bill Coverdale third.

SSA-NAA Agreement

There was no directors' meeting in the winter of 1948, since not enough directors had been present at the Southeastern Championship. However, a special SSA-NAA meeting was held in Washington, D.C., on January 20 to negotiate a new SSA-NAA agreement.

Attending that meeting were President Reeves and Comey, Captain Barnaby, Sweet, Stanley, and Compton. The final agreement authorized the SSA to "exercise exclusive jurisdiction over gliding and soaring in the United States," on the condition that national records would be finally approved by the NAA and world records by the NAA and FAI. The agreement was to run for a period of one year and the fee would be $200 plus one-third of the total record and contest sanction fees collected by SSA in excess of $600. A vote by mail later approved the agreement.

Paul MacCready, alongside the Orlik sailplane in which he won the national championship in 1948 and 1949. The Polish Orlik placed second to the German "Meise" sailplane in the design competition in 1939, which was held to choose the "Olympic" sailplane.

(NSM Loomis Collection)

15th National, 1948

The 1948 National at Harris Hill, June 20 to July 11, was shortened from 17 to 12 days. Seventy-one pilots and 51 sailplanes were entered. The contest incorporated many changes in rules and procedure. Paul A. Schweizer, contest director, wrote the following report of the meet in the July-August *Soaring*:

> The Championship was won by *Paul MacCready,* flying his *Orlik* sailplane. Hard on his heels was *John Robinson* in his familiar *Zanonia.* Third place was won by *Don Pollard* in the AIR-100. Defending champion, *Dick Comey* put service above self and worked on SSA matters at the contest.
>
> The high points of the 15th National were: (1) the keen competition and good fellowship that prevailed, (2) the largest prize fund on record (about $12,500) and (3) good soaring weather for the full period of the meet.
>
> July 8th was the greatest single day in Elmira soaring history. The best flight was a 222 mile trip by MacCready to Middlefield OH. . . . On the same day eight other flights were made in excess of 100 miles and a total of 2,600 miles were flown.

> Important rules changed were: (1) only distance counted for points, (2) the pilots were divided into two groups, Contestants and Participants (those entered for fun and experience), (3) only five best flights of each pilot counted for point score, (4) in order to receive point award money contestants had to have at least 25 percent of the average of the top three pilots' scores, (5) travel points were granted to those who came over 300 miles with their glider.
>
> Another new idea was the use of a "guinea pig" pilot. Clarence See, flying his TG-2 "Little Butch," was first up each morning to check the soaring conditions. Decision on when to start take-off line was made by consultation of Contest Officials and the "guinea pig." Later on this service was improved by the use of radio.
>
> Another way of reducing the costs would be to reduce the prize fund requirements. Most European Soaring Contests have little prize money.

The actual costs of the meet totaled $20,101. This meant a loss of $7,000, which had to be absorbed by the community. As a result, Elmira was not ready to accept such financial requirements for future contests.

At the 15th National, a joint SSA-

Clarence See and his TG-2, the first "Guinea Pig." The practice of having an experienced pilot, not in the contest, test the conditions to determine when the contest takeoffs should start, was first used at the 1948 National.

(NSM Collection)

Institute of Aeronautical Science meeting was held on July 1. The subject was the design of the ultimate sailplane.

One pilot who was thinking about a new sailplane design was Dick Johnson, for his Tiny Mite was not doing well. It was too "fast" for the Elmira conditions. After seven days of very poor results, during which his best flight was only 28 miles, Dick Johnson asked the Schweizers if he could fly the 1–20 for the remainder of the contest. The 1–20 was a "floater," and on Johnson's first flight with it he made 78 miles; he averaged 61 miles on his last three flights.

He no doubt wished that he had something better. It was not long after the contest that he got together with Harland Ross to talk about a new sailplane.

Directors' Summer Meeting, 1948

The directors' summer meeting was held on July 3. It was probably the shortest SSA meeting ever—it lasted a little over an hour. It covered only the election of two directors-at-large and the election of officers. All were re-elected, except the two vice-presidents: the new West Coast vice-president was Dr. Klemperer and the East Coast vice-president was Fritz Compton.

Swiss International, 1948

The first postwar International Invitational Meet was held in Samedan, Switzerland, in July. Twenty-eight pilots from nine countries competed with France, Great Britain, and Switzerland, each of which entered a full team of six pilots. Egypt, Finland, Italy, Spain, Poland, and Sweden entered one or more pilots. Although the SSA was invited to the event, it did not send a team.

There were six types of tasks, including the new 100-kilometer speed triangle. Axel Persson won the meet, and two Swiss pilots, M. Schackenmann and A. Kuhn finished second and third. There was much enthusiasm for international soaring competition, and all looked ahead to the World Championship that was scheduled for Sweden in 1950.

Sailplane Manufacturing

The U.S. sailplane inventory at the start of 1948 totaled about 400, the majority being five- or six-year-old surplus trainers. There were only about a dozen high-performance sailplanes, half of which were at least 10 years old and of European design. The 1–21 had been well received, but it did not sell, because of its $3,000 price tag. The only foreign ships available were the Swedish-built Weihes and Olympias, the British-built Olympias and the French AIR-100s, and they were not selling either. The cost of the Weihe was $4,000 ($2,000 in kit form), and the Olympia cost $2,000 in Sweden and $1,980 in England.

SAC, with no orders for 1–21s and with a slowdown in the sale of its 1–19s and 2–22s, was anxious to develop sailplane volume. It felt that there was

The construction of the prototype 1–23 was started in May of 1948 and was completed on July 5, nine weeks later. Bill Frutchy of Elmira had ordered the first one and was able to fly it in the last half of the 1948 National. The first production 1–23 was ordered by E. J. Reeves, which stimulated sales. These sailplanes were sold on a direct sale basis, which permitted lower prices than the original dealer arrangements allowed.

a market for a high-performance sailplane if the cost could be substantially lower than the 1–21. Benefiting from the experience with the 1–21, it designed the 1–23, which was of smaller size and simpler construction. The price was to be in the $2,000–2,400 range. SAC soon received a sufficient number of orders to justify going ahead with production.

Activity around the Country

Dick Johnson won the Second Annual Pacific Coast Championship in his TG-2 with a 45-mile flight to Tecate, Mexico. That was the first soaring flight to a point outside the United States.

El Mirage, California, ran a series of soaring regattas with a number of "heats" during the year. At one of the regattas, Robinson encountered waves over the area and got to 14,000 feet.

Herman Stiglmeier and his brother set a new duration record of 12 hours and 52 minutes, flying over the Palos Verdes Hills in California in their Pratt-Read. This flight broke Hurtt and Powell's duration record set two years earlier.

SSA Business

E. J. Reeves in Bulletin no. 7 mentioned that "Comey hopes to get the Sept-Oct issue out in early December, and the Nov-Dec. issue out by the end of the year." Some SSA members were critical of Comey, since he was so late

E. J. Reeves takes his turn in a PT-17 tow plane for the Texas Soaring Association at the Grand Prairie Airport in Texas. A power pilot first, he transitioned to glider after World War II.

(NSM Collection)

U.S. Position in Records Improves, 1949

The year 1949 started out auspiciously when on January 1 John Robinson flew the Bishop wave in his Zanonia to a world's absolute altitude of 33,500 feet, a new record category that had been added by FAI. His altitude gain beyond release was 1,800 feet short of the Swedish Axel Persson's existing record of 26,411 feet.

The FAI created a new record category of speed around a 100-kilometer triangle. The first official world record in this category was set in a BG-8 by Gus Briegleb and Jack LaMare at El Mirage, California, on August 12, 1949. They achieved a speed of 27.83 miles per hour.

These records started a move toward improving the U.S. position in world records held, which then totaled three.

with *Soaring*. At that time, *Soaring* was about the only communication that the members had with SSA and the soaring movement.

Directors' Meeting, 1949

The SSA directors had drifted away from the practice followed before World War II of having a winter meeting in January or February and a summer meeting at the time of the Nationals. It was a year and a half since the directors had had a full-scale meeting and so there was much to be covered at the meeting at the Astor Hotel in New York City on January 28–29, 1949.

The main problem facing the directors at this meeting was the slow growth of the SSA. President Reeves said he would conduct a drive in an attempt to increase the membership.

The membership categories of "chapter" and "affiliate" were created, but there were no financial benefits assigned to these memberships. Because Comey was late in issuing *Soaring*, the directors voted that he should put out a newsletter for a trial period to keep the members informed.

There was considerable discussion on an SSA youth program, and Reeves was to investigate the possibilities of tying in with the Civil Air Patrol program.

The directors decided to appoint an SSA governor for each state to help stimulate interest in soaring and to coordinate activities in their area with the general manager, officers, and directors.

Elmira, Grand Prairie, and Muskogee had expressed interest in the 16th National Soaring Contest, but had not submitted firm bids. Grand Prairie, Texas, and Elmira said they would be interested if the financial requirements were reduced. The directors felt that the contest should alternate between the East and the West and that it was important to decide on the 17th National at that time. President Reeves was to get firm bids from Grand Prairie and Elmira and submit them to the directors for a vote by mail. The chairman of the Contest Committee was authorized to set new financial requirements subject to the approval of the president. The directors also urged the Contest Committee to initiate limited task flying in the 16th National. The meeting closed with the directors setting up a category of state records and instructed the president to renew SSA's agreement with the NAA.

At a Crossroad

"Today we are at a crossroad," wrote Comey in his editorial in the March-April 1949 issue of *Soaring*. He continued:

> Up to the present time, the Society has been operating on such a limited budget that its work has been severely hampered. However, to carry out our activities on a current basis we have recently invested every penny available in setting up a central office with a secretary, an Associate Editor and a full-time General Manager.
>
> Whether we are able to keep this staff together in 1950 to coordinate activities, publish *Soaring* and handle the day-to-day functions of the Society will depend directly on how many new members you are able and willing to sign up this year.
>
> The CAA has over 3,000 licensed glider pilots entered in its files. Interest in our great sport is growing. We need every glider pilot, every would-be glider pilot, and every potentially interested individual as "a member." Our minimum goal for 1949 is 500 new Active Members.

16th National, 1949

By the third week of March, no decision on the location of the Nationals

Three pilots in the 1949 National wait for their crews to retrieve them from the Ithaca Airport. Left to right: Dick Comey (1-21), Kim Scribner (1-23), and Fred Tietzel (L-K).

(Kurt Forester, NSM Collection)

had yet been made. This left only three months to organize the meet. Immediate action was required, so Reeves sent out Bulletin no. 8 in the form of a telegram requesting an immediate vote on the issue. The majority of directors voted in favor of Elmira, and preparations began immediately.

The contest story in *Soaring* noted:

> The Sixteenth Annual National Soaring Contest was held at Harris Hill, Elmira NY from July 2 thru July 10th 1949. Twenty-nine (29) sailplanes were entered, all having flown in previous Nationals. Paul MacCready, Jr. won the National Championship for the second year in a row in his Polish built *Orlik*. Paul made the longest flight on each of the free distance days. [Dick Comey was second in his 1–21 and Bill Coverdale third in his Minimoa.]
>
> The 16th National will stand out as the one in which "set task" flying was tried for the first time. It proved to be very competitive, reduced the expense of the contestants and was generally liked by all. . . . Set task flying seems here to stay.
>
> The banquet featured Secretary of Air Stuart Symington as principal speaker. He spoke of the contributions made by the glider fraternity during the last war and expressed the Air Force's continued interest in soaring. Also on the program was Bill Odum, who presented the Beechcraft Award.

Directors' Summer Meeting, 1949

One of the most important matters discussed at the Harris Hill meeting of July 9–10, 1949, was the SSA's financial problem due to the very slow increase in membership. Comey commented on the vital importance of building up membership in order to meet the current expenses of the society. Alternate ways of raising funds were discussed, but again no definite action was taken.

Capt. R. S. Barnaby was voted to replace Compton as East Coast vice-president. Otherwise, all the officers were reelected.

A committee was appointed to start planning for the possible entry of a soaring team in the 1950 international meet scheduled for Sweden. The committee included Captain Barnaby, Dr. Klemperer, and Wally Setz.

The need to set up a national program was discussed at length. However, no definite action was taken at the meeting.

Floyd Sweet reported on the progress of his committee's plan to submit a suggested youth glider program to CAP.

With the FAI general conference scheduled for Cleveland, Ohio, over Labor Day, a committee was appointed to develop plans and to make recommendations for the meeting of the Gliding Committee of the FAI.

Since members of the Technical Committee were acting on technical matters with which they had only limited experience, two separate committees were set up. The Scientific Committee was to replace what was then called the Technical Committee, and the new Technical Committee would cover "technical" matters related to sailplanes and flight operations. Gus Raspet was appointed chairman of the Scientific Committee and Paul Bikle chairman of the Technical Committee.

George Haddaway, a member of the Aviation Development Advisory Committee to D. W. Rentzel, administrator of the CAA, wanted to get SSA's recommendations on any change in CAA regulations that his committee could carry to the CAA. It was pointed out that many of the people getting into soaring were power pilots but that no credits were being given for their power flying experience at that time.

Recommendations made to George Haddaway were that (a) the experience requirements for glider pilot ratings for a person having a valid power pilot certificate be reduced to one hour and include five landings, and (b) a third category (similar to the previous "R" category) be created to permit limited production of special type sailplanes and power gliders.

The FAI General Conference, 1949

The FAI Gliding Committee, with Pirat Gehriger as chairman, met at the same time as the FAI general conference, which was held in Cleveland on September 2–4, 1949, during the National Air Race. Delegates attending the Gliding Committee meeting came from Belgium, Canada, France, Holland, Hungary, Poland, Switzerland, and the United States. The U.S. delegate was E. J. Reeves, and he was accompanied by a group of SSA observers that included Barnaby, Carsey, Klemperer, Sweet, and P. A. Schweizer. The gliding Committee held a very productive meeting: It proposed that the powered glider category of records be reinstated; created the diamond "C" award; changed the contest rules to permit flying starts for speed records; decided to name the international contest the World Championship Soaring Contest; worked out the details for the First World Championship Soaring Contest, the Gliding Committee meeting, and the meeting of the International Scientific and Technical Organization (OSTIV) to be held in Sweden at the same time.

E. J. Reeves extended an invitation to the FAI Gliding Committee to hold the World Championship Soaring Contest in the United States in 1952.

Comey's Last Editorial

It was becoming evident that Comey's position as general manager and editor was not working out as originally proposed. In his editorial in the November-December issue of *Soaring,* he announced that Fred Obarr was to be the new editor of *Soaring,* beginning with the January-February 1950 issue. The growing dissatisfaction over the late and irregular publication of *Soaring* led the directors to accept unanimously Obarr's offer to take over the editorship.

In an Editorial entitled "49–50-and You," Comey pointed out that the SSA was growing too slowly and needed many more members if it was to accomplish its goals. Active membership had only risen from 580 in 1946 to 700 in 1949. He therefore appealed to all members to encourage others to join and existing members to renew on time. He said, "Let's not rest on our oars. With your Help *We Can Go Forward from '50.*"

It was evident that he was uncertain as to how long he would continue in his general manager position since he wrote: "The Office of General Manager will be continued to expedite correspondence and other basic functions, at least until the SSA Directors' Meet-ing in Aug., at which time the financial resources of the Society will be reviewed."

U.S. Assault on Altitude Records, 1950

A wave expedition was held at Bishop, California, during the Christmas–New Year week. This period had become popular as a combination holiday and wave camp since there seemed to be a good chance that waves would develop sometime during that period.

John Robinson reached 33,800 feet absolute altitude; this was 300 feet above his world record, but not high enough to establish a new one. Bill Ivans reached 30,500 feet, and the inside of his canopy iced up with 1/16 inch of ice.

Strong wave conditions on January 27 enabled Harland Ross and George Deibert to set two new world two-place altitude records by reaching an absolute altitude of 36,000 feet after achieving a gain of 24,300 feet. They used a TG-3A that they had modified for wave flying and had installed some Maxey-Prue "clear vision" panels on their canopy. They worked effectively, and Ross reported that at their maximum height the outside air temperature was −69 degrees Farenheit.

Irv Prue remembered from his boyhood days in northern Vermont that the double-glaze windows in their farmhouse did not frost up in the coldest weather. He talked to Lyle Maxey about this, and they developed a way of maintaining visibility when frost or ice formed inside the canopy from the pilot's breath. They taped a 4- to 5-inch-square plastic panel to the inside of the canopy with a slight air space between canopy and panel. This eliminated the frost and ice and soon became standard equipment on sailplanes flying the wave.

On April 7, Betsy Woodward and Vera Gere set two world altitude records for women, flying from El Mirage Gliderport. They reached an absolute altitude record of 17,598 feet, which represented a gain of 10,797 feet also in a TG-3A.

New Editor

Obarr took over as editor on January 1, 1950, beginning with the January-February issue. He was a student at Mississippi State when Gus Raspet was the sailplane project leader there. Although Obarr was unproven as an editor, it was felt that he would have the support of Raspet and the other soaring enthusiasts at Mississippi State.

With his academic load plus his other soaring activities, however, Obarr quickly found that he had bitten off too much. He was able to get out the March-April issue, but that was his last.

First World Soaring Championship, 1950

The First World Soaring Championship was held in Orebro, Sweden, July 3–16, 1950. It was sponsored by the Swedish Aero Club and the operations were conducted by the Swedish Air Force. Eleven countries were entered and 29 pilots competed. This marked the first time since Eddie Allen had flown in the International in Frane in 1922 that a U.S. pilot was flying in an international contest. The SSA had not been able to enter a team but encouraged qualified contest pilots to do so if they could finance themselves.

The only American pilot to enter was Paul MacCready, with his father as a crew chief. They financed themselves and did most of the liaison work with the Swedish Aero Club to arrange for a sailplane. Captain Barnaby was the team captain.

The MacCreadys arrived early so that they could prepare their new Swedish-built Weihe, which they had rented from the Swedish Aero Club for the competitions. They spent a great deal of time "cleaning up" the Weihe by taping, sealing, smoothing, and polishing to improve the L/D (glide-ratio) and the high-speed performance. Dr. Raspet worked with MacCready on this cleanup program, which Raspet claimed had improved the performance about 7 percent. On two of the contest days, which involved a speed-to-goal task, MacCready beat the field by large margins. Some of this success, no doubt, was due to the cleanup, but it was also due to MacCready's aggressive flying and the use of his best-speed-to-fly technique. At the start of the last day, MacCready was in the lead with Nilsson of Sweden also flying a Weihe close behind. The final task was a choice of goal, and the strong south wind put the pilots over rugged country to the north. Nilsson made a 427.6-kilometer flight to win the championship. MacCready was fifth for the day with a 350-kilometer flight and finished in second place in the contest.

Portions of Barnaby's report of the championship to the chief of the Bureau of Aeronautics were printed in *Soaring*: "It was a great disappointment to the European contestants that no U.S. designed and built sailplanes were present. They all had hoped to see at least one of our Schweizer all metal sailplanes. I believe a 1–21 or 1–23 could have made a very creditable showing in this contest. On the other hand, it was a great tribute to Paul MacCready's skill as a pilot that he was able to make such a splendid showing with a sailplane of the same type as that used by 12 of his competitors."

The part of Barnaby's report that was not printed in *Soaring* dealt with Dr. MacCready's letter of complaint to the Swedish Aero Club. It was very critical of the club's conduct of the meet, but this criticism was not shared by Barnaby and Setz of the committee. The directors realized that in the future they would have to send an organized team with a captain who could act as the liaison between the team and the contest officials.

John Robinson Earns First Diamond "C"

John Robinson became the first three-Diamond "C" pilot in the world by making a 221-mile goal flight in his Zanonia on July 1, 1950, from El Mirage Field, California, to Overton, Nevada. He had used his 1947 American record flight of 325 miles for his distance Diamond and his 1949 altitude-gained record of 24,200 feet for his altitude Diamond. That gave Robinson and U.S. soaring another first!

International Meetings

The FAI Gliding Committee, (CVSM), held a meeting and approved the complete FAI sporting code for soaring developed by Gehriger. They also drafted and adopted a proposed set of bylaws with which OSTIV would operate under CVSM. Captain Barnaby was elected vice-president of CVSM.

At the CVSM meeting there was strong opposition to having the 1952 World Soaring Championships in Finland in connection with the Olympic

Games. Many wanted it to be held in the United States, but they realized that this would not be possible unless the United States was able to finance the cost of getting the teams there.

Nine countries were represented at the OSTIV Meeting that followed. Dr. Klemperer, Dr. Raspet, and Captain Barnaby were present and during the proceedings Dr. Klemperer was elected a trustee-at-large and Dr. Raspet was made the chairman of the Scientific Committee. At a technical session held later five papers were read, including two by Raspet.

17th National, 1950

The 17th National Soaring Contest was held from August 2 to 12 at Grand Prairie, Texas. The Texas Soaring Association (TSA) ran the contest, which attracted 59 pilots and 42 sailplanes. The weather was poor at the outset but improved considerably later in the contest. On the last day, Dick Johnson made the longest flight of the contest, a goal flight to Odessa, setting a national goal record of 317 miles, and won the National Championship for the first time. Finishing behind Johnson, all flying 1–23s, were Coverdale, Ivans, and Reeves, in that order. Wally Wiberg was fifth in the Bunny Nose L-K.

Johnson was flying the new RJ-5 that he and Harland Ross had designed and built. Between flights, Johnson and his crew continued to sand, fill, and smooth the wings. The sailplane did not look very attractive with its different shades of primer and sanded areas—but it did perform well. The other new high-performance sailplane in the contest was the Prue 215, flown by Lyle Maxey, who tied for sixth place.

Eugart Yerian had been a soaring enthusiast for some time. When the military gliders were put on surplus, he bought a large number of TG-3A's and became a glider broker, reselling them in the United States and foreign countries. Shortly after the war he visited Elmira on a spring Sunday, eager to fly. He was given some flights in an early production 2–22 just off the line. Since no aero tows were available, auto tows were made from Harris Hill. The conditions were poor and a landing had to be made in a farmer's field in the valley. In landing, they touched down on some "cow flop," and since the 2–22s at that time did not have wheel cover or cockpit liners, Yerian, sitting in the back seat, "got it all." Yerian and the 2–22 required a thorough washing to get rid of the barnyard aroma. Since he was traveling, he had to borrow some clothes. Yerian did a lot of flying with his TG-3As and has been a long-time member of the Memphis Soaring Club.

Single-Place vs. Two-Place Training

Wednesday, August 9, had been scheduled as a noncontest day in order to hold a joint technical session of the SSA and the Institute of Aeronautical Sciences (IAS), which was organized and conducted by Dr. Gus Raspet and Ben Shupack. One topic of considerable interest was the controversy over single-place versus two-place training, which had continued for a number of years since it had taken time for the U.S. soaring movement to make the transition to two-place training. Shupack, Raspet, and a small following were pushing the single-place method and called on Dr. Lippisch to explain the German technique for single-place training.

In his defense of single-place training, Dr. Lippisch explained that the student was told how to move the controls and then once launched, if he should make the wrong movement and crash, "the student knows not to move the stick so much." He was surprised that this comment was received with loud laughter. It is doubtful that the single-place adherents gained any converts that afternoon.

Directors' Summer Meeting, 1950

The first meeting was held on August 9 at the TSA clubroom at the Grand Prairie Airport. Jon Carsey was elected president, Barnaby, East Coast vice-president, and Shupack, treasurer. Klemperer, the West Coast vice-president, and Paul A. Schweizer, secretary, were reelected.

The board appointed Eugart Yerian as the new editor. Yerian, who was the speech and drama instructor at Memphis State Teachers College had become active in soaring after World War II.

After reviewing the general manager's performance and the state of the SSA, the directors decided to abolish the position of general manager and to divide Comey's work between the secretary and the director.

Some directors felt that the Technical Committee should be given specific projects. The board decided that its first project should be to simplify the requirements and procedure for getting CAA approval for tow planes. John Paul Jones of the CAA was at the meeting and asked for a list of the SSA recommendations and requests that he could pass on to the CAA administrator. High on the list was the recommendation that a central person or office in Washington, D.C., act as the coordinator of gliding and that the CAA add gliding to its Oklahoma school so that all field inspectors would become familiar with gliding.

Powered Sailplane

One Significant development at the 1950 National Soaring Contest was the performance of the Hummingbird, Ted Nelson's new two-place powered sailplane. Nelson, with Harry Perl and

Les Arnold as alternate team members, finished in eighth place and won the team championship. For the first time a powered sailplane had effectively competed in a national contest. What had led up to the development of the Hummingbird?

Interest in powered gliders had existed almost from the start of gliding in the United States. Designers had many reasons for creating them. Some were looking for a method of self-launching their gliders so that they could enjoy the sport of soaring without having to use a launching crew. Others saw the convenience of operating like an airplane from a busy airport. Still others were not yet ready to accept the challenge of motorless flight and needed a "crutch" to overcome the glider's natural tendency to descend. Finally, there were those who were looking for a low-price airplane.

The numerous designs that came out during the 1930s and 1940s did not meet with much success because performance was generally low and there was a lack of suitable engines.

In 1931, Ted Nelson, who had built a glider in the late 1920s, built a glider similar to a Waco primary and put a Salmson Aircraft engine on it and successfully flew it. His interest in gliding and power gliders continued, and shortly before the end of the war he and Hawley Bowlus formed the Nelson Aircraft Corp. in San Fernando, California. Their purpose was to develop a two-place power glider version of the Baby Bowlus. This was called the Bumblebee and had side-by-side seating, retractable tri-cycle landing gear and a Ryder 36-horsepower, 4-cylinder 2-cycle engine mounted in the aft end of the pod. However, the engine was only able to develop about 16 horsepower. Nelson decided to develop his own 4-cylinder engine,

which he installed in a refined version of the Bumblebee, which he renamed the Dragonfly.

In 1948 the Dragonfly received the CAA type certificate, the first for a power glider. Seven of these were built before production was stopped owing to economic factors. Gus Briegleb leased one to evaluate it in his school, and a number of powered glider records were set with the Dragonfly at that time.

Ted Nelson and Harry Perl in the prototype Hummingbird at the 1952 National, in which they set a new two-place goal-and-return record of 158 miles.

(*Dallas Morning News*, NSM Collection)

As SSA secretary, Schweizer worked closely with Comey and found him to be a dedicated soaring enthusiast who became deeply involved in his new responsibilities. He had a good grasp of the whole soaring picture. He accepted the position of general manager and editor with enthusiasm and put a great deal of effort into it.

With the slow growth of the SSA membership, it became obvious to Comey that he could not afford to stay in this position. Reluctantly, he accepted the SSA's board decision to terminate his general managership. He had given his "all" for almost three years; still, many members of SSA did not appreciate how much he had contributed to the organization.

After the directors' meeting, Schweizer went to Cambridge to carry out the transfer of the SSA office to Elmira. Dick was sorry to see the files go for they included so much of his hard work over the last three years. To try to cheer him up Paul went with him to see the Boston Red Sox play!

Paul Tuntland in the Screamin Weiner in which Paul MacCready set the out-and-return world record in 1947.
(Florida News and Photo Service Photo, NSM Collection)

In 1949, with the help of Harry Perl and Don Mitchell, Nelson completed the first Hummingbird. This had a larger span, an all-metal wing, a more powerful retractable Nelson engine, side-by-side seating, and a retractable gear. Nelson and Perl took it to the 1949 Nationals at Elmira, where they made a large number of exhibition flights. The Hummingbird was definitely an improvement over the Dragonfly, but Nelson wanted to further improve the performance. He changed the fuselage to a tandem design with a single-wheel landing gear,

and this was then flown successfully at the 1950 National.

New SSA Operations

When the secretary was authorized to carry out the transfer of the SSA office from Cambridge to Elmira, the Elmira Association of Commerce (EAC) agreed to assign Katherine Jones to handle the clerical functions. "Katy" had taken care of the clerical phase of the EASC and the National Soaring Contests at Harris Hill since the late 1930s. Under this arrangement, the SSA paid the Elmira Association of Commerce $50.00 a month. This was a real bargain for SSA and a fine contribution to soaring by Katy and the EAC.

The SSA secretary took over all the other functions of the general manager, except for publishing *Soaring*. It was possible to operate SSA this way since there were less than 1,000 members.

Paul Tuntland's Accident

After the Prue 215 had returned from the 17th National, it was being tested at El Mirage by Paul Tuntland. At the end of one 2¾-hour flight, one wing broke off and Tuntland's parachute did not open in time and he was killed. The exact cause was never determined, but it was clear that the tests should have been run at much higher altitude for safety reasons. Tuntland was a very popular figure and his loss was covered in a special section of the September-October 1950 *Soaring*.

New Altitude Records

On December 30, Bill Ivans, in his new 1–23, set two world records at Bishop, California, by reaching an ab-

SAC had a fling at powered gliding. In 1946, when an Andover Auxiliary power unit became available the SAC tried it in a 1–19. The company made a simple power unit that bolted on to the fuselage-wing fitting. With the low performance of the 1–19, an engine that only had 12 horsepower and turned at 4,000 rpm, a homemade prop, plus a quick-and-dirty installation, performance was disappointing. It could fly nicely at an altitude of 10 feet in the "ground effect," but just could not get higher. One day, however, when strong thermals were present and with a new Sensenich prop, Frank Hurtt managed to catch a thermal at 10 feet and climbed the powered 1–19 to over 2,000 feet. This was the only time that it got out of the "ground effect," except when it was auto-towed once with the engine going full speed. Making these trial flights was a lot of "fun," but the airport manager was becoming annoyed at seeing the 1–19 flying all over the airport at an altitude of 10 feet. The power unit was unbolted and the 1–19 became a glider again!

solute altitude of 42,100 feet and a gain of 30,100 feet. On the way down, he celebrated the records with a series of loops and rolls. For these records Ivans was awarded the Lilienthal Medal, the FAI's top soaring award, and he was the first American to be chosen.

The number of world records held by the United States now totaled eight, which made it second to the Russians, who held nine; France was third with five and Switzerland, Poland, and Germany each had one. In the 2½ years since Paul MacCready's out-and-return record, the United States had made a remarkable gain from no world records to eight!

CAA Regulations Reviewed, 1951

On reviewing the glider pilot regulations, the CAA proposed that an instructor's rating be required for instructing pilots instead of the commercial glider pilot rating in effect at that time. The CAA had few personnel experienced in gliding, and some of the present regulations were inconsistent. For example, power pilots could obtain an additional category rating in gliders without any minimum experience, whereas the same pilots would be required to have 10 hours, including 50 flights for a private glider certificate. Also, a power pilot could get a commercial glider rating without any experience and would then be allowed to instruct. There was much controversy over the regulations, and this subject was to be one of the main concerns at the forthcoming directors' meeting.

Directors' Winter Meeting, 1951

Memphis was chosen for the meeting of February 16–17, 1951, as it was cen-

Bill Ivans in his 1-23 in which he set two world altitude records.

(NSM Collection)

trally located and was the home of the editor, Eugart Yerian. This was the first SSA directors' meeting to be conducted by Carsey as SSA president.

The CAA regulations were discussed first. Many wanted the minimum requirements, whereas others, such as the SCSA Regulation Committee, were all for tightening up the regulations even more than the CAA had proposed. Stan Hall, president of the Southern California Soaring Association (SCSA), in a letter to the SSA, explained that the SCSA committee felt

---

During World War II, Tuntland visited Elmira to see if he could do some soaring. He was a very pleasant person and eager to fly, and he and Paul Schweizer made a number of auto tows from Harris Hill in a TG-3A. On one flight they caught a good thermal and when they got sufficiently high Tuntland did some aerobatics. On one maneuver he pulled up so sharply that there was a loud cracking noise. The glue joints on both wooden seats had cracked from the "g" loads. There was no other damage, but Schweizer was not impressed with the way Tuntland handled the TG-3. He seemed to let his speed build up unnecessarily and this trait may have had some bearing on the Prue 215 accident, in which the combination of high speed plus a gust or high maneuvering load may have caused the wing to fail.

---

that all glider pilots should have a minimum physical examination, that instructors' ratings should be required and instruction by commercial glider pilots outlawed, and that flight tests be made much stricter. Nothing was settled at the meeting, but the matter was referred to the Technical Committee.

Carsey was effectively using the SSA governors in his program to expand soaring and his request for permission to appoint lieutenant governors in the larger and more active states was approved.

Eugart Yerian explained that the editorship of *Soaring* was turning into a full-time job and he needed secretarial assistance. The board voted to approve $100 a month for this purpose and at the same time approved $50 a month for operating the secretary's office.

The secretary reported that active members now stood at 961. He mentioned that there had been a large increase in the number of inquiries received and that there was a need for an information booklet that could be used to answer these inquiries. It was decided to make the May-June issue of *Soaring* a special one that could be used for that purpose.

Contest matters were discussed next, and it was decided to assign permanent contest numbers. It was also proposed that shoulder straps be made mandatory for pilots and passengers, but some of the directors objected to this on the grounds that they did not want to get the SSA into a policing position.

18th National, 1951

The 18th National was held at Harris Hill, Elmira, New York, on July 4–12,

1951. Thirty-five sailplanes were entered, of which approximately half were still World War II gliders. The other entries were Johnson's RJ-5, nine 1–23s, Stan Smith's XS-2, and Trager's T-3.

Johnson won the championship for the second year in a row. He made the outstanding flight of the meet—a 360-mile hop to Roanoke, Virginia, a new national distance record. Stan Smith was second in his SX-2, Bill Coverdale third in a 1–23, Wally Wiberg fourth in his modified L-K, and Paul A. Schweizer fifth in a 1–23. The competition was a mixture of set tasks and open days and the demand takeoff system was used, whereby the pilot selected his takeoff time. This contest was operated on a much reduced budget, which set the pattern for coming contests.

A scientific session was held on the last day with Dr. Raspet chairing the meteorological session, and Ernest Schweizer chairing the aerodynamic session. Papers were presented by Kuettner, Carmichael, Raspet, Johnson, and Seredinsky.

Directors' Summer Meeting, 1951

At the July 3–5 meeting in Elmira, the president, treasurer, and secretary were reelected. Ralph Barnaby was elected East Coast vice-president and Ted Nelson West Coast vice-president; Dr. Klemperer was voted honorary vice-president and life member.

For the first time in SSA history, a budget was presented to the directors, by E. J. Reeves, chairman of the Finance Committee. He recommended that membership rates be increased.

President Jon Carsey presented a three-point program for the year: (1) to increase interest in soaring through local club and associated activities; (2) to realize more from SSA by contributing more to it; and (3) to develop a greater and more dependable means of financial support for the American soaring activity.

A copy of Paul Bikle's Technical Committee report was presented to the directors and included the following comments:

> A wide difference of opinion as to the purpose, necessity, and desired contents of the regulations was expressed. The difference of opinion breaks down into two primary groups; one in favor of regulations; the other in favor of no regulations other than the minimum possible to satisfy the CAA.
>
> The first group is composed primarily of long standing, experienced pilots of the SSA and appears to be stronger on the west coast. The second group, by far the majority as far as numbers are concerned, is also supported by long standing and experienced pilots of the Society. If this question were to be decided by vote, the regulations would be held to a minimum. It appears that the reason for this is that most feel the movement is too small for more rigid regulation; that the CAA inspectors, with a few exceptions, are not sufficiently familiar with gliders and soaring to properly administer the more rigid regulations; and also that no real benefit would be derived other than a decrease in participation in soaring. I, for one, would vote for minimum regulations for these reasons.

The directors accepted the Technical Committee's report and decided that the matter would be aired in *Soaring*.

International Competition

Interest in the World Soaring Championships (WSC) for 1952 had increased a

The meeting was held at Bonnie Brook, the home of the secretary, where he lived with his father, a retired Swiss chef and restaurateur. It was a large farmhouse with ample space for the meeting and it was conveniently located halfway between Harris Hill and the airport. Its chief attraction, as a meeting site, in addition to being away from the activities of the contest, was the promise of one of "Papa" Schweizer's excellent dinner that he liked to serve every now and then to keep his hand in cooking. The second meeting, to cover some unfinished business, was held at Harris Hill on July 5.

great deal as a result of the Swedish World Soaring Championship.

At the CIVV meeting in Belgium in July of 1951 Col. Lawrence Ely, representing the SSA, proposed that the Internationals be held in Elmira in 1952. Spain also made a proposal, which included supplying twelve Weihes and fifty Kranichs with trailers. The contest would be held at their national site called Montflorite near Huesca, although another site near Madrid might be used. Their bid contained the provision that each pilot would be provided with two carrier pigeons and, in the event that other communications were not available at the landing site, the pigeons would be

SSA President John Carsey with members of the SSA Board of Directors who were present at the 1951 winter meeting in Memphis, Tennessee. Left to right: Eugart Yerian (*Soaring* editor), Bill Coverdale, Fritz Compton, and E. J. Reeves. Bottom Row: Paul A. Schweizer, John Carsey, Floyd Sweet, and August Raspet.

(Lou Lowry, NSM Collection)

Dick Johnson and the RJ5 in which he set the world distance record in 1951 and won the 1950–52 and 1954 Nationals.

(Ed Walty, NSM Collection)

used to bring back information on the pilots' landing location.

The Spanish bid was an excellent one and since Elmira had made few firm commitments, the decision was made to hold the next WSC in Spain in 1952.

New Distance Records

Between May 1937 and July 6, 1939, the Russians had raised the distance record four times, the last being Olga Klepikova's flight of 465 miles.

With the RJ-5 continuously being improved and after his record distance flight of 360 miles at Elmira, Johnson was ready for a try at the world distance record. A record camp was organized at Odessa, Texas, in August and a number of other pilots joined Johnson for some serious distance flying. On August 5, 1951, Johnson beat Klepikova's world record by flying 545 miles in a straight line, which gave Dick Johnson and the U.S. soaring movement worldwide attention.

The Mountain Wave Project I

The Southern California Soaring Association was eager to learn more about standing waves and so held meetings with the Los Angeles branch of the American Meteorological Society (AMS) on this subject. The SCSA proposed to initiate a lee-wave research project. Unknown to the association, the Office of Naval Research (ONR) had been doing some upper-air research, flying modified B-29 airplanes on constant altitude flights at 30,000 feet west to east across the Sierras and White Mountains. The ONR test pilots noticed that with some strong west winds it was necessary to vary the

power as they passed over the Owens Valley.

The ONR heard that gliders had been used in Germany for researching lee waves, so proposed using gliders. Two of the captured German sailplanes had been received and the SCSA was asked to evaluate them. However, the sailplanes were so badly damaged that they were unusable. Klemperer and Saudek, who had been called by the Navy to look over the gliders, told them about SCSA's interest in a wave project and that they had pilots and better sailplanes for such a project.

On a return trip from Europe, Dr. Klemperer met with Captain Hutchinson of the ONR at the U.S. Weather Bureau in Washington, D.C. They proposed meeting the next day at Harris Hill, where the 1949 National was in progress. At Elmira, Klemperer met the ONR and Weather Bureau people as well as Dr. J. Kuettner of the USAF Cambridge Research Center, who was to give a paper at the conference on lee-wave research.

As a result of these meetings, the wave project got under way the following year. The University of California at Los Angeles was given the prime contract. The SCSA was to be the subcontractor conducting all flight operations and was to provide many personnel and all flight equipment. The USAF Cambridge Research Center was a sponsor of the project, and the Naval Ordinance Test Station was to do the tracking and to give other support. Phase I of the project started on October 31, 1950, and ran for one year. Phase II would start on October 31, 1951, and run for one year.

The project had an experienced team, many of whom were soaring enthusiasts. Dr. Klemperer was the "spiritual" leader, Dr. J. Kuettner of the USAF was project scientist, and Vic Saudek project supervisor. The operation crew consisted of Ray Parker, chief of field operations; John Robinson, chief pilot; Larry Edgar, pilot and project technician; and Betsy Woodward and Richard Eldredge, pilots and ground workers. The project used two Pratt-Read sailplanes that were specially modified and equipped for wave flying. A local flying service provided towing.

The first phase of the project was to develop the procedures to be used on the project flights, including practice in tracking the sailplanes. When conditions were very good, attempts were made to establish new records.

On March 5, 1951, Bob Symon invited Dr. Kuettner to go along on a wave flight. Conditions were better than expected and they were able to reach 38,000 feet—a new two-place world record.

Phase II operations in the Owens Valley began on November 1. At that time Karl-Erik Ovgard of Sweden, a visitor, was eager to be involved in wave flying and to set some Swedish altitude records. It was regrettable that Ovgard, who was not a part of the wave project, lost his life in a record attempt and thus the perfect Bishop wave safety record was broken.

Ovgard first stopped at Elmira, New York, on his way from Sweden to Bishop, California. He was a pleasant young man and had a consuming desire to set sailplane records. He had no idea of the economics of the U.S. sailplane movement nor did he understand the sacrifices that most U.S. soaring pilots had to make in order to be active in soaring.

On December 18, 1951, he rented Bob Symons' Pratt-Read. After being instructed in the ship's oxygen system, he took off on a day with very strong waves. He disappeared, and it took several days of intense searching to find him, dead, in the wrecked fuselage that had crashed in a nearby valley. He had taken a photograph of the instrument panel at 33,000 feet, which showed the oxygen pressure gauge at zero. The regulator was set at normal, instead of 100 percent, as he had been instructed to do at 30,000 feet. With an empty tank, the normal setting gives the user no indication that he is not getting any oxygen, whereas the 100 percent setting would have warned him of an empty tank. The barograph trace showed a maximum height of 37,000 feet, at which point he must have fallen against the controls and put the Pratt-Read into its fatal dive. A few years later, a wing tip was found 20 miles from where the fuselage had crashed.

His experience is a classic case of a pilot letting his enthusiasm overtake the cool thinking and strict discipline needed in high-altitude flying. The extreme turbulence and low temperature and the need for proper use of the oxygen life-support system are conditions not normally found in soaring.

Other Activities during 1951

What was to be the last U.S. duration record was flown on April 29,1951. Les Arnold and Harry Perl stayed up for 12 hours and 3 minutes on the Warm Springs, California, ridge in Les's TG-3A called *Redwing*. Before anyone could break this record, the FAI abolished duration records.

The Allied High Commission permitted motorless flight to resume in West Germany on April 26, 1951. Being able to glide again caused great excitement among the German glider enthusiasts, and this set in motion the postwar German glider movement, which was to have a great impact on world soaring in the years to come.

Chapter 7

The SSA Goes International 1952–1956

First Team in the World Soaring Championships

The editorial in the January–February 1952 *Soaring* was entitled "Spain in 1952," a reprint of an article that E. J. Reeves had written for *Spirals,* the Texas Soaring Association (TSA) newsletter.

It set the tone for SSA's first effort to send a full team to a WSC. There had been some feeling that the SSA had "missed the boat" in not sending a team to Sweden in 1950, even though the MacCreadys had done a good job of showing what Americans could do on their own.

Carsey had already started to solicit support and to organize a team. The Board of Directors had decided not to use regular SSA funds for international team purposes. To quote from the editorial: "The fund so raised will be spent only for pilot participation by proven performers and in American designed and built sailplanes." At that time it was the practice for each country to use their own sailplanes if they had a sailplane industry.

A Committee on International Participation was set up with Walter Setz as chairman and Dr. Klemperer and Captain Barnaby as members. Questionnaires were mailed to potential team pilots, and fourteen pilots signified interest in competing.

A jury of peers (top pilots, not

candidates for the team) was composed of Fritz Compton, Bill Coverdale, Bill Ivans, E. J. Reeves and Floyd Sweet. Carsey instructed the committee: "You are requested to very carefully give consideration to each of the following attributes—First and foremost—all other considerations are to be considered secondary: Piloting Ability—Contest Experience—Diplomacy—and Sportsmanship." The seeding order was (1) R. Johnson, (2) S. Smith, (3) P. MacCready, (4) P. Schweizer, (5) W. Wiberg and S. Charles, (6) R. Ball, (7) L. Maxey, (8) J. Robinson, (9) R. Parker, and (10) W. Beuby.

Directors' Winter Meeting, 1952

One of the continuing problems of the SSA board was how to make sure that a two-thirds majority (14 directors) would be present to act on changes in the bylaws. The meeting on February 29 to March 1, 1952, in Memphis, Tennessee, had only 13 directors present and so they could not act on the changes proposed at that time, which included (1) bringing the bylaws in line with established operating procedures, (2) increasing the number of directors at large from two to four, and (3) changing the quorum from five to eight with an instructed proxy to count on previously announced agenda items. The board decided to vote on these changes by mail.

The principals of the Mountain Wave Project at Bishop, California. Top, Left to right: Dr. J. P. Kuettner, Dr. Wolfgang B. Klemperer, Lawrence Edgar, and John Robinson. Bottom: Victor M. Saudek, Richard C. Eldridge, and Raymond Parker.

(NSM Collection)

The Technical Committee was instructed to study the operational problems with a view to issuing standard interpretations of CAA regulations, particularly with respect to the approval of tow planes and tow pilots. Reeves presented the financial report and the proposed budget and again stressed the need for an increase in membership rates. Next, Eugart Yerian advised that he might not be able to continue as editor if his plan for a new position developed. Finally, Carsey presented a plan to expand *Soaring*. The directors instructed Carsey to proceed with the plan.

Mountain Wave Project

There were many accomplishments in Phase II of the project in early 1952. The project workers were now an experienced team, and considerable flight data were recorded, in part because there were some outstanding waves in March.

On March 19, Larry Edgar, and Harold Klieforth as observer, reached a maximum altitude of 44,255 feet with a gain of 34,426 feet in a Pratt-Read sail-plane. These became world records. On the same day, the first significant distance flight from a high-altitude wave start was made by Dr. Kuettner, who flew to Williams, Arizona, in a TG-3A (a distance of 375 miles) in 4 hours, 10 minutes. It showed the great potential of distance flights using waves, particularly if much higher performance sailplanes were used.

The Mountain Wave Project closed flight operations on April 15. The balance of the contract was spent reducing the data into reports. Betsy Woodward and Dick Eldredge spent another year (1951) at UCLA completing additional reports. During that time they also put together the Phase II Mountain Wave Film with the help of Kuettner and Saudek.

A $250,000 Phase III project proposed the construction of a pressurized stratospheric sailplane designed to soar to 70,000 feet. Apparently this was too big a step for that time since the Korean War had limited the funds available for new projects and the cost of the Mountain Wave Project had taken up a major share of the funds available to the Cambridge Research Center. Another factor was that the U-2 spy plane had become available and could be used for upper air research. As a result, the Mountain Wave Project came to an end. It was a significant achievement in soaring and in meteorological research, carried out by a dedicated team. A great deal of credit for the success of the program must go to all those soaring enthusiasts who were involved, particularly to Vic Saudek who spent just about all his available spare time on the project.

Preparations for Spain

Preparations for the internationals were soon under way. Johnson continued making improvements on the RJ-5; Stan Smith had the 1-21 flat-topped and some span added to the wings; SAC built the 1-23B for Mac-Cready, which had the wings extended to about 50 feet; and a "C" model was made for Schweizer with thicker wing skins and a stiffer spar with the expectation that a smoother wing would improve the performance. Larry Gehrlein volunteered to build two special trailers for the "B" and the "C" models.

The team consisted of Capt. R. S. Barnaby, CVSM representative; Walter Setz, team captain; Richard Johnson, Pilot, and Earl Bailey, crew chief; Paul B. MacCready, Jr., pilot, and Dr. Paul MacCready, Sr., crew chief; Stanley W. Smith, pilot, and Tom Eaton, crew chief; Paul A. Schweizer, pilot, and Hugh Whitney, crew chief; William Beuby and Shelly Charles, pilots, and Kirk Harris, crew chief. Additional crew and specialists were Ernest Schweizer (repairs), Richard Ball (radio), Walter Hausler (photography), and crew members Doug Craig, Erwin Authofer, and Hans Stolberger.

1952 Internationals

The contest was held at the Cuatros Vientos Airport at Carabanchel, a few miles southwest of Madrid. The first team project was to unload the sailplanes and trailers when they arrived at the Barcelona docks. The contest organization provided a Spanish driver and a Unimog tow car for each sailplane. The Unimog was a European "jeep" powered by a low-horsepower diesel engine with four-wheel drive. On the trip from Barcelona to Madrid it became clear that the heavy trailers and hilly country would be a problem for the Unimogs. They could just seat a driver and a passenger on each side

of the hot engine. Any extra crew would have to find room in the 5-foot-square wooden box in the rear, which the driver lined with straw to increase the "comfort." It was a tight fit for two crew members and the barrel of reserve diesel fuel that was standard equipment.

As it turned out, the sailplanes arrived at Barcelona behind schedule and it took an extra day to get them to Madrid, so that the pilots had only one day to check out the sailplanes, radios, and crew. Most of the other teams had taken advantage of the unannounced two-week practice period to become acquainted with the conditions. However, it had not been possible to work out an earlier sailing for the U.S. team that would still allow enough time to get the sailplanes ready.

There were eight scheduled contest days, but only five were used since many pilots needed a second day for retrieving because of the poor communications, the "country" roads, and the slow Unimogs. Phillip Wills won the single-place championship, Pierre of France was second, Jock Forbes of Great Britain was third, Quadrado of Argentina was fourth, and Gehriger of Switzerland was fifth.

The British team had its own meteorologist, and its effective Pye radio enabled the crews to stay within range of their pilots so that they were able to return the same day. It had also come early with its own tow plane and had considerable practice before the competition started.

The U.S. team did not do well. MacCready finished 6th, Schweizer 19th, and Smith (who missed the first day because of trailer damage from the Barcelona-Madrid trip), 24th. Dick Johnson damaged his fuselage in a difficult landing on the first day and

Little America at the WSC, Madrid, Spain, the tiedown area for the U.S. sailplanes. The Unimog tow cars are in the foreground; the center tent contained the base radio station. The Aero Club is across the field and the Guadarrama Mountain area, where much of Hemingway's *For Whom the Bell Tolls* takes place, is not too far away.

(Paul A. Schweizer)

missed two days, and ended in 31st position. Twenty sailplanes were damaged during the contest as a result of poor landing conditions and unpredictable local weather.

Seventeen two-place sailplanes competed, with Juez of Spain the winner. Frowein and Hanna Reitsch of Germany were second and third. Beuby and Charles finished in sixth place.

However, the U.S. single-place pilots did well on the last day's task, a 75-mile race to a goal at Torresavinan. Johnson was first and outclassed the field with a speed of 66.9 miles per hour. MacCready was second at 55.5 miles per hour, Smith seventh at 49.1 miles per hour, and Schweizer eighth at 49 miles per hour. These good performances showed that the American pilots and sailplanes were ahead of their field in speed flying. Moreover, Johnson's performance confirmed that he and the RJ-5 were of record caliber.

However, many problems plagued the team. Not having an interpreter,

they had to obtain the weather briefing thirdhand—via two other languages. On the second day, a free distance day, MacCready and Schweizer independently chose to go west from the information they received. They were forced to land early when increasingly strong west winds developed. Almost everybody else went to the northeast and made good flights.

In addition, the U.S. radios and ground stations did not work well and so were of limited value. The contest administration had not provided carrier pigeons as originally planned; instead they gave each pilot a formal-looking document that was equivalent to a disaster clearance and that got results when shown to the civil guards.

Still another problem was that Spain had only been open to visitors for a short while after enduring 15 years of warfare and reconstruction. On the other hand, the costs in Spain were very low, so that the U.S. team was able to obtain rooms in the deluxe

Palace Hotel at a fraction of the cost of rooms in a comparable hotel back home. Liability insurance for the team was also very low since there was a low legal limit on the value of human life.

The Spanish people were generally friendly and helpful, even to the point of advising the team on how to dress—a Spanish taxi driver in Barcelona would not take Smith and Schweizer to the Ritz Hotel until they put on their ties. In one of Schweizer's landings near a small farm town, a family he met would not let him pay for his dinner or night's lodging, but treated him like a guest. After another landing, the entire population of the town gathered, and after the crew arrived they followed the trailer to the police station in a "Pied Piper" procession, with the youngest at the front and the oldest trailing far behind.

A foreign sailplane and pilot landing near a village was the biggest event in the town since the Civil War.

Fred Hoinville, an Australian pilot, told of the farmer who sent his son to the next village on a bicycle to get something to celebrate his landing—it turned out to be a can of Del Monte peaches.

A New Editor Chosen

Convinced that something had to be done to stimulate SSA growth, John Carsey talked Julian Stag of Dallas, a writer and public relations consultant, into studying the SSA and *Soaring* operation. Stag concluded that what *Soaring* needed was "a professional editing and publishing arrangement. . . . I propose that I be retained to render professional service in editing and publishing *Soaring,* including editorial, advertising and circulation direction,

on a retainer fee of $300 per month, effective June 15th."

Jon Carsey sent Stag's proposal to all the directors. His memo stated: "Under the authority given me at the Board Meeting in Memphis, I am accepting Mr. Stag's proposal and am instructing him to proceed. . . . My agreement with him regarding his remunerations and cost of publication is that these things will depend upon revenue from the magazine including advertising and subscriptions, and that his compensations will increase or decrease on an agreed basis as revenue is increased or decreased."

19th National, 1952

The National of 1952 was to be the latest ever scheduled—August 19–29. However, the weather at Grand Prairie, Texas, was excellent, and a total of 26,000 miles were flown in the 10 contest days. This compared favorably with the record 1947 Wichita Falls contest, at which over 40,000 miles had been flown, since there were 4 less contest days and 37 fewer sailplanes at the Grand Prairie contest.

Only 28 sailplanes were entered (this was the smallest number in a National since 1941), and the only new sailplanes at this contest were the rebuilt prewar Horton IV that Rudy Opitz flew and the 1-23C, just returned from Spain, flown by Larry Gehrlein.

The contest consisted of four task days, six open days, and one rest day. The winner would be the one who had the most points on his three best task days and the four best open days. This allowed pilots to eliminate three poor days or days on which the pilot chose not to fly. On Sunday, the rest day, Gus Raspet and Bruce Carmichael ran the SSA technical session.

Nelson needed a copilot and asked Paul A. Schweizer to fly the Hummingbird while he made a radio broadcast for the Sunday show. During the climb there was an explosion. Nelson tried to restart the engine but was unable to do so. While Schweizer soared the Hummingbird, Nelson made his broadcast. They landed at the end of the field, away from the crowd, and when they got out they saw that one cylinder head had blown off.

A few years later, George Downsbrough was flying his Hummingbird at the Chemung County Airport. He invited Schweizer to take a flight to Harris Hill. When Downsbrough applied power on takeoff there was another explosion, and this time both occupants saw the cylinder head flying across the airport.

Nelson wrote Schweizer, kidding him about being a jinx. He said that the next time he was out West he should drop in at Hummingbird Haven so he could get a "proper" demonstration of the Hummingbird.

On a visit to Les Arnold's Sky Sailing in Fremont, California, a while later, he was flown to Hummingbird Haven, Nelson's home and gliderport, about 20 miles away. After touring Hummingbird Haven and hearing about the changes on the engine, they flew back to Sky Sailing in the Hummingbird. The engine was at full throttle the whole way. Upon landing, Schweizer said he was convinced, and after a friendly handshake, Nelson returned to Hummingbird Haven with the engine going full throttle!

Dick Johnson, who had just returned from Spain, won the contest in his RJ-5. He had to fight off Ivans and Coverdale, who finished a close second and third in their 1-23s. Paul Bikle was fourth in a 1-23 and Ray Parker fifth in the Tiny Mite. Two world records were set at the contest—Bill Coverdale set a world out-and-return record of 268 miles in his Standard 1-23, and Dick Johnson set a triangle speed record of 54.7 miles per hour.

Ted Nelson and Harry Perl set a new two-place goal-and-return record of 158 miles in the Hummingbird, but in a demonstration for the public on the Sunday rest day, an engine problem developed and the Hummingbird had to withdraw.

Directors' Summer Meeting, 1952

All officers were reelected at the August 23–24, 1952, meeting in Dallas, Texas, except that J. W. Simmons replaced Shupack as treasurer. Julian Stag was introduced to the directors and gave a report on his plans for *Soaring*.

E. J. Reeves gave a report on the financial condition of the SSA and made a motion to increase the dues from $5 to $7.50. The motion was tabled, since it was felt that Stag's program, if successful, might allow the society to hold membership fees at the same level.

The SSA would have to increase its income in order to be able to carry out its program, but this was to be done by increasing membership and by obtaining support from the aircraft industry through grants and advertising. This was what Evans had tried to do to build up the NGA 23 years earlier.

CAA Regulations

The controversy over glider regulations continued into 1952 and was highlighted in the January–February issue of *Soaring* in letters to the editor from Gus Briegleb, who supported the stricter SCSA position, and Ben Shupack, who objected to what he called the unnecessary tightening of glider regulations. The Technical Committee report appeared in the March–April *Soaring*, and comments from the members were expected by the time of the summer directors' meeting, but there was no report.

Sailplane Production

At the start of the Korean War in 1950, the use of strategic materials became restricted, and this affected the production of the 1-23 and 2-22. Few other sailplanes were being built at the time and almost none were imported. As soon as the war began to wind down, SAC went back into production.

Ted Nelson proposed building a limited number of Hummingbirds at a price of $7,000 each. Wolf Hirth announced the availability of three types of sailplanes from Nabern Tech, West Germany: the Doppel-Raab, the Goevier, and the MU-13E, the first German sailplanes available in the U.S. since the late 1930s.

Youth and Soaring, 1953

In 1934 the SSA had proposed that there should be a National Youth Gliding and Soaring Program, and Warren Eaton submitted an overall plan to the presidential committee. The idea was again suggested just before World War II, when the Air Youth of America proposed to add gliding to its program and the McCarren bill was being considered. Immediately after the war, so much effort was put into reviving the soaring movement that little was done about a youth program until Barnaby tried again in 1947 and submitted a proposal to the presidential commission.

When Jon Carsey became president of SSA in 1950, one of his goals was to get more young people into soaring. He developed a program in 1952 and pushed ahead with it in 1953. The editorial in the January–February 1953 issue of *Soaring* promoted the idea of a youth aviation program based on gliding and soaring.

Gus Raspet's talk to the National Association of State Aviation officials in 1952 entitled "The Sailplane in Research, Training and Sport" was reprinted in the January–February 1953 *Soaring*. He indicated that gliding and soaring for young people had an important role to play, as illustrated in other countries: "In Russia 50% of the high school students take up gliding as a diversion, but behind this apparently pure sport is a wide use of gliding for screening of pilot material. . . .

Before World War II the Germans depended on their glider program to provide their pilots. From the glider schools came the 'Abbeyville boys' and the pilots of ME163s."

First SSA Directory

In 1946 a roster of the SSA membership had been issued for the first time. The expense of this project had put the SSA in debt for a year, and so there were no further rosters until 1952. At that time the roster was developed by the secretary's office. By using volunteer help and mimeographing it, the SSA was able to keep the roster within the secretary's budget. It was well received and useful and there were requests to include additional information in future issues. The secretary expanded the roster and in 1953 made it into a directory, which was available to SSA members at $3 per copy.

SSA-IAS Meeting

A joint SSA-IAS meeting was held in New York City on January 29 at the Astor Hotel just before the SSA directors' meeting. Ben Shupack chaired the meeting, which included papers by August Raspet, Glen Bryant, Bruce Carmichael, and Charles B. Cliett, all members of the Aero Physics Department of Mississippi State College. All of the papers were related to various aspects of boundary layer control. Despite the success of the session, some soaring people felt that it was too specialized and should have included other aspects of sailplane aerodynamics.

Directors' Winter Meeting, 1953

Only eight directors were able to attend the meeting in New York on January 3, 1953, because of bad weather. However, with four SSA governors present, the instructed proxies, and five regional reports, the meeting was national in scope.

The secretary reported a 20 percent increase in membership during 1952. A large volume of inquiries was causing more work for the EAC offices and it needed more funds to handle the services being provided. The directors therefore authorized an increased payment of up to $75 per month.

The treasurer's report showed that, with the increase in membership, the SSA was close to breaking even.

Julian Stag presented a proposal for a full-time editor with a budget of $15,000 ($7,500 for the editor, and $6,000 for publishing *Soaring,* and the remaining $1,500 for office operations). Some felt that this was too high a cost for producing only six issues a year, and they proposed that the editor should be the general manager as well.

SSA's tight financial situation made it important to consider increasing the membership rates, which had been the same since 1947. A committee, chaired by Floyd Sweet, was set up to make recommendations to the president.

The editor's report included details on Carsey's Get Youth Into the Air program, and proposed a $50,000 two-year program that assumed dues

would increase to $10 and on a fund drive aimed at the aviation industry and other private sources. This was too ambitious a program for the directors to consider and so no action was taken.

During the general discussion of the youth program, Wally Setz spoke about the Philadelphia Glider Council's plans for conducting a two-week summer training camp. The board commended PGC for this action and encouraged other groups to sponsor similar camps.

Barnaby proposed that the United States should again enter a team in the World Soaring Championships and that steps should be taken to get plans under way at the earliest possible time. Wally Setz was named chairman of the Advance Planning Committee.

The Technical Committee was given three special projects: (1) to develop a set of rules and regulations for a glider design competition with a view to identifying a design that could be built in the schools so as to attract youth into aviation; (2) collect data on tow hooks installations, which could then be made available to members; and (3) ask CAA to put gliding in the Oklahoma Flight Center so that standard and simplified CAA regulations could be established.

A West Coast club proposed a Plutonium "C" as the next step beyond the Diamond "C" since the number in the Diamond class were steadily increasing.

Insignia Contest

The design contest for an SSA insignia that had been announced in 1952 was judged during the directors' meeting. Seventeen members entered 52 designs. The winning design was sub-

National Airlines officials greeting the three "visitors" from Elmira standing by Stan Smith's 1-21 at New York's Idlewild Airport. Left to right: A. Gossette (NAL), Stan Smith, Steve J. Bennis, A. Peterson (NAL), Comdr. Nick Goodhart, and J. O. O'Brien (NAL).

(National Airlines, NSM Collection)

mitted by Millard Wells, and Frank Hurtt was the runner up. The design was to be displayed in *Soaring* to test member reaction, and if it was favorable, the design was to be accepted as the official SSA insignia.

One of the unsuccessful designs entered was expertly carved into a wood panel. Although the rules of the contest did not require designs to be returned, the secretary contacted the person who submitted this design to see if he wanted the panel back. It turned out that he was a "lifer" at the Trenton State Prison. He was an SSA member and a soaring enthusiast who yearned to do some soaring. He said he wanted the secretary to have it, and so it became a part of the secretary's collection of soaring memorabilia.

Midwinter Membership Meeting

The SSA midwinter membership meeting was well attended, and the featured speaker was Charles Horne, CAA administrator, who talked about getting more people into flying. He felt that gliding and soaring was the way to do this and commended the SSA on its planned youth gliding program.

Gill Robb Wilson, the editor of *Flying* magazine, was also a guest speaker. He told of his experience while visiting the prewar youth training in Germany and paid high tribute to the planned program.

Changes in Editor of Soaring

The proposal that Julian Stag act as both editor and general manager was not acceptable to Stag, and so the March–April, 1953 issue was his last. He was replaced by Jack Kemp of Dallas. Kemp edited only the May–June issue before Carsey and Reeves decided to take over the editorship themselves.

The 1954 World Soaring Championships

The CIVV met in The Hague, Holland, and chose England as the site of the WSC for 1954. It would be held at

Having been born in New York and having gone to college there, Paul Schweizer had often dreamed of soaring over the city. He had read the story of Wolf Hirth's 1930 soaring flight over Riverside Drive many times. On the first day of the contest there were strong northwest winds and it was an open day. Bill Schweizer suggested a "business flight" to Grumman Aircraft to see Hank Kurt, the subcontract manager. So Schweizer picked Grumman Airport at Bethpage, Long Island, as his goal, and brother Bill let Kurt know of the coming visit. The flight proceeded well until late afternoon, when Schweizer found himself low over the swamps south of Teterboro Airport in New Jersey. He thought that he would have to land there, but did manage to catch a good thermal, which he worked to 6,000 feet, directly over the George Washington Bridge. When he looked down he could see the area where Wolf Hirth had made his famous flight. It was a great thrill for him to fly over this spot and over New York City. He used Flushing Airport and then Mitchell Field as possible emergency landing points, but the general thermal lift from the hot city kept him going. It was well after six o'clock when he reached Bethpage. Kurt had left for the day but he returned when he learned that Schweizer had kept his appointment. The headlines in the Long Island Newsday *the next day told of the business trip via sailplane!*

Camphill, the Derbyshire and Lancashire Club site near Great Hucklow in the Peak District. Factors that favored England over the United States and Argentina bids were the lower travel cost and the practice at that time of giving preference to the country of the previous champion.

20th National, 1953

The 20th National Soaring Contest received widespread publicity when three pilots landed at Idlewild (Kennedy) Airport. National Airlines had put up three prizes for the first pilots to reach an airport that it served. Stan Smith in his 1-21, Steve Bennis in a new 1-23D, and Comdr. "Nick" Goodhart of England flying an old L-K all landed at the airport, which was 191 miles from Harris Hill. Their landing caused quite a stir and the New York Port Authority, which operates the New York airports, later that day added the following sentence to its regulations: "No motorless aircraft may land or take off at an air terminal without permission."

The following day a *New York Herald Tribune* editorial entitled "Visitors from Elmira" commented on the incident: "Idlewild Airport authorities doubtless had good reason to be displeased at the landing there Tuesday of three gliders from upstate. This airport has no time for visiting firemen from Elmira who drop in on powerless wings expecting a fraternal greeting. World-girdling superliner pilots and faster-than-sound jet men, yes; but not eccentrics who come to town in glider, kites, or balloons."

The *Binghamton Sun* said: "Unannounced arrival of glider enthusiasts from Elmira proved upsetting to those in charge of the Idlewild Airport. . . . Yesterday's Herald Tribune was a bit sarcastic about it. . . . The same can be said for the Airport officials who scolded them for not picking out a safer place among the skyscrapers, or out on the broad Atlantic."

MacCready made the best flight of the day with a goal flight of 212 miles to Simmsbury Airport, Connecticut. Schweizer was second with a 201-mile "business trip" to Grumman Aircraft, Bethpage, Long Island, and S. Smith, S. Bennis, and N. Goodhart tied for third.

Paul MacCready won the championship in a 1-23D, Stan Smith was second, P. A. Schweizer third in a 1-23D, Steve Bennis fourth, and Nick Goodhart fifth.

Two new types of sailplanes were entered in the National. Howie Burr flew his new 1-24, a 55-foot development from the 1-23 series, which he named *Brigadoon*. Emil Lehecka flew the *Watzit*, a wooden gull winged sailplane that Volmer Jensen had built for

Jim Martin. Another first was the use of an FAA-operated portable tower at a National, using a light gun to control traffic.

Directors' Summer Meeting, 1953

The officers were reelected at the next directors' meeting, with the exception of the treasurer, who was replaced by E. J. Reeves. The secretary reported that the membership was at an all-time high and that "the activity at the two Elmira SSA offices has been steadily increasing with a great increase in the number of inquiries received. . . . It would seem that if *Soaring* can continue to appear on a regular basis . . . and the push on new members continues, that we should have no trouble in steadily increasing our memberships. . . . The matter of changing the rate structure of SSA should be given real careful consideration in view of the great improvement in the number of members."

Carsey's report advised that for the immediate present he and E. J. Reeves would carry on as editors until someone else could be found.

August Raspet advised that because of his heavy research responsibilities he wished to be relieved of his duties as chairman of the Scientific Committee. He recommended Ben

Shupack to replace him. The report was accepted but no action taken.

Membership Rates

After studying the membership rates, Sweet's committee recommended that they be increased as follows: "Life Membership $100.00, Industrial Membership $50.00, Patron or Sustaining Membership $25.00, Active Membership $10.00, Associate Membership $5.00 & Subscription to *Soaring* $3.00."

The committee also proposed that the funds raised from the SSA life memberships be invested so that the earnings would be sufficient to cover the cost of servicing those memberships.

It was decided to list the proposed rates in *Soaring* so that the directors could get an idea of how members might respond to the new rates.

Soaring Photographic Library

Jon Carsey had formed a Photographic Committee at the directors' meeting in January 1952, with Walter Hausler as chairman. In his report to the directors, Hausler gave a short history of the committee's activities since the start. Although the original purpose of the committee was to cover both pho-

Emil A. Lehecka in the 1953 National flying the "Watsit," the 9th of Volmer Jensen's 24 designs. Jensen has been building hand gliders, sailplanes, light aircraft, and ultra-lights for almost 60 years, and built the *Enterprise* starship of the Star Trek Series. He flew gliders with Cloyd Artman in Washington State and is one of the "senior statesman of home-building" in the United States.

(Albert Rosse)

tography and films, Hausler's main interest was in the film phase. In February 1953 the SSA films were sent to Hausler to start the SSA Film Library.

International Contest

E. J. Reeves proposed that SSA make every effort to enter a team in the 1954 WSC. Carsey was to write the Weather Bureau to request that Barney Wiggin be named meteorologist for the U.S. team.

50th Anniversary of the Wrights

To commemorate the 50th anniversary of the Wright Brothers' first airplane flight, Floyd Sweet and Nick Goodhart piloted a sailplane over Kitty Hawk, and later Sweet laid a wreath at the base of the flagpole from which the SSA flag was flying. The wind was so strong that the powered aircraft portion of the air show was canceled and so in 1953, as in 1903, the only machines in the air at Kitty Hawk were flown by glider pilots.

Carsey's Youth Efforts

In spite of Carsey's many efforts to get a youth program under way, only small pockets of youth activity in gliding developed in the country: (1) Guy Storer's Youth Program at Mississippi State, (2) the Air Scout Program in Washington State, (3) the Texas Soaring Association Youth Program, and (4) The PGC successful summer camp.

A Need for Low-Cost Sailplanes, 1954

In 1954 the 1-23 was the only sailplane being produced in the United States.

Few sailplanes were being sold and none were being imported, mainly because of the high cost. At the same time, the inventory of U.S. sailplanes was declining as a result of the fast attrition of the surplus gliders. Powerplane production was also experiencing a slowdown at this time.

Nonetheless, the SSA membership had almost doubled and the number of inquiries about SSA membership was steadily increasing. It was clear that a demand for lower-priced sailplanes was developing.

American Designers Respond

This need was recognized by a number of American sailplane designers. Stan Hall was working on the Cherokee, an all-wood and fabric intermediate sailplane that could be built from drawings using readily available materials. Gus Briegleb was in the early design stage of his BG-12, a higher performance all-wood sailplane for homebuilders. Al Backstrom was designing his flying Plank, and Art Schultz was working on his Nucleon sailplane.

SAC revived the idea of a one-design class sailplane that it had proposed at the 1945 Motorless Flight Conference.

Once the war ended, SAC concentrated on building trainers since they were most needed. As interest in high-performance sailplanes grew, SAC developed the 1-21 and followed this with the 1-23 series in an effort to bring the cost down. After selling about 25 1-23s, SAC found sales dropping off because of the relatively high price. SAC knew that it would be necessary to produce something significantly lower in cost in order to get a higher sales volume. The only way it

could do this would be to produce a kit.

In an advertisement in the November–December 1953 *Soaring*, SAC announced a proposed 1-26 kit sailplane. The ad suggested that the 1-26 low-cost kit might initiate a one-design class that could lead to class competition. It mentioned that the prototype was being built and would include the following features: (1) be available in a kit; (2) be small in size and light in weight for ease of construction, handling, and storage, with rugged design for safety and pilot protection; (3) have good auto and winch tow characteristics as well as the ability to be towed by light aircraft; and (4) have performance suitable for Golden "C" flights but with minimum flying speed and low sink to permit soaring under light conditions.

The prototype made its first flight on January 16, 1954. Many soaring pilots flew the prototype, and the concept of a 1-26 kit was enthusiastically received. From past experience, SAC knew that the average person would take from three to five years to build a sailplane from scratch and that many never were completed. Therefore SAC believed that a kit should have the following features:

1. It should be designed so that no critical parts or important lineup work would need to be done by the builder. This would ensure reliability of the final product, minimize the jigs required, and simplify construction.

2. The kit would have to be set up so that it could be completed in a period of six months by a person working in his spare time.

3. All material and parts were to be included, so that the builder would not have to locate the material himself.

A full report on the 1-26 appear-

ing in the March–April 1954 *Soaring* said the kit price would probably be in the range of $1,250 to $1,500 and that if sufficient orders were received the 1-26 would be put into production.

Directors' Winter Meeting, 1954

Several important points were raised at the February 19–20, 1954, meeting in Dallas. First, the committee's recommended membership rates were approved, except that life membership was increased from $100 to $200. It was also agreed that $400 from the SSA general fund should be invested each year until the full amount of all life memberships was reached.

Second, the method of electing directors was changed. There had been considerable discussion for a number of years on the method of electing directors. A proportional representation system had been used by Ben Shupack since World War II, but some directors were opposed to the system, and so it was decided that directors should be elected by a majority vote of the membership.

Third, the directors agreed that the SSA should encourage one-design class competition and recommended that, in national or regional meets in which there were at least five of the same class of gliders, special one-design awards should be considered.

In addition, flight training for young people was discussed at length.

The first flight of the 1-26 prototype made on January 16, 1954.

(Schweizer Aircraft Corporation)

Top: The Nimbus sailplane designed and built by Don Mitchel, who had worked for H. Bowlus in the 1930's. He later designed and built a number of other sailplanes and assisted with building the prototype Nelson Hummingbird.

(Pete M. Bowers, NSM Collection)

Wally Wiberg in his *Lil Dogie* sailplane with his wife June at Elsinore, California, National.

(NSM Collection)

It was pointed out that the Office of Naval Research, CAA, and the National Organization of State Aviation officials were considering flight training programs for young people.

The directors also decided that the United States should enter a team in the 1954 WSC. A committee composed of Reeves, Sweet, and P. A. Schweizer was to set policy for the international team and carry out liaison with the Department of State and the BGA.

The Seeding Committee composed of Compton, Coverdale, Ivans, John-

son, and Sweet rated the 14 top pilots. The final team consisted of MacCready and Schweizer, single-place pilots; and Stan Smith and Bob Kidder, two-place pilots. SAC made available a 1-23E for MacCready, a 1-23D for Schweizer, and a 2-25 that Smith and Kidder would fly as a team. Barney Wiggin was to be team manager and meteorologist.

The 21st National, 1954

Thirty-six sailplanes entered the 21st National on July 27 to August 6, 1954, at Elsinore Gliderport, California. This was the first national competition to be held on the West Coast. The new sailplanes entered were the all-metal Maxey-Prue Jenny Mae, the Perl Penetrator, the Mitchel Nimbus, and the 1-26 prototype.

The Dick Johnson RJ-5 combination was at its best. Having five of the nine contest days open was to Johnson's advantage. He had so many points that he did not have to fly on the last day. He left the RJ-5 at Blythe, where he had landed, and would pick it up on his way home to Texas. However, Ed Butts asked Johnson to try out his new 1-23D. Johnson agreed and won the last day too!

Ray Parker, flying his Tiny Mite,

which he had improved at Mississippi State, won second place, and Lyle Maxey showed the potential of the new Jenny Mae by finishing third. The Jenny Mae was the combined effort of Irv Prue, Lyle Maxey, and Frank Kerns. Kerns had built a new Prue 215 fuselage and Maxey designed a new wing, which Prue built. Three 1-23s flown by Bikle, Ivans, and Hoverman finished next; Wally Wiberg was seventh in his Lil Dogie, and Clarence See finished eighth in the 1-26 prototype.

Directors' Summer Meeting, 1954

The first West Coast SSA directors' meeting was held on July 26, 1954, in Elsinore, California, the day before the start of the Nationals. Floyd Sweet was elected president to succeed Carsey, who had held the position for four years. All the other officers were reelected. Sweet accepted the presidency on the condition that Carsey and Reeves would see that *Soaring* continued to be published for the next year.

When Carsey and Reeves had edited *Soaring*, it was a soaring community effort. One of those who helped was Jock Forbes, a former British soaring pilot who had immigrated to the United States and lived in the Dallas area. He became the unofficial editor with the March–April 1954 issue. After Sweet was elected president, Forbes agreed to continue as editor with a salary of $200 for each issue.

Proposals were made to return to proportional voting and to limit directors' terms to a maximum of three years. Both were turned down. A Standing Award Committee was established to review and recommend to the board the name of worthy candidates for the awards.

Carsey

In summing up his term as president, Carsey said that during his four-year term, memberships had increased "in all types of memberships and subscribers from approximately 700 in 1950 to 1800 in 1954." He started the film library and gave strong support to the international team. His great disappointment was that he could not get a national youth program going.

Carsey had been a very active and dedicated president, and many wondered whether he was neglecting his architectural business, since he spent so much time on soaring, as did his wife, Mary, who was of great assistance to him. He didn't have the benefit of a general manager, as Reeves had had, although in fairness to Reeves, Comey created many problems for Reeves since *Soaring* was always so late.

Carsey built up the membership by creating contact with SSA members and interested prospects and getting *Soaring* out on time with the aid of E. J. Reeves and others, and through his growing SSA governors' organization.

The Hall of Fame

During 1954 the Helmes Athletic Foundation of Los Angeles, at Dave Matlin's suggestion, invited the SSA to nominate famous soaring people to the Helms Hall of Fame. Some directors were reluctant to have soaring tied in with an athletic Hall of Fame that was sponsored by a baking company, but the board accepted the offer, and SSA's first six nominees—Eaton, du Pont, Klemperer, Bowlus, Robinson, and MacCready—were inducted at a ceremony after the completion of

Members of the 1954 WSC team assist with the loading of sailplanes at the Montreal, Canada, docks for trip to Liverpool, England. Left to right: Ernie Schweizer, Hugh Whitney, Robert Kidder, Stanley W. Smith, and Bernard L. Wiggin.

(Canadian Pacific Railway, NSM Collection)

the 21st Nationals. The SSA directors could nominate two persons each year after a catch-up period.

Sweet

Sweet's first act as president occurred early in the 1954 contest when he ruled that the contest committee, which had made some rules of its own, should return to the published rules. Making last-minute changes had been the practice at earlier contests until the Compton committee developed a set of standard rules. These were reviewed and revised each year before the start of the contest.

Sweet's method of operation would be different from Carsey's easygoing, "folksy" style. Sweet's background as an Air Force officer would show through at times during his presidency. In this first editorial in *Soaring* he listed his plans for SSA:

There is much work to be done in the

awakening of the leaders of the aviation industry, educators, and sportsmen to the value of soaring.

The interest of youth must be captured in its early teens and fostered to maturity. This can be done by interesting youth in soaring. Our efforts in this direction must be continued.

Improve our relations with CAA, promote a better safety record and provide the guidance necessary for the instruction of glider pilots.

Every effort will be made to improve the financial condition of the Society toward the end that we may once more establish a paid staff.

World Soaring Championship, 1954

The 1954 WSC was held at Camphill at Great Hucklow, England, from July 20 to August 4. Each country was permitted two single-place and one two-place sailplane. Nineteen countries were represented with a total of 33 single-place and 9 two-place sailplanes. The United States sent a full team, but all except three pilots and the manager-meteorologist and the assistant manager had to pay their own way as not even half of the budget was raised in the fund drive.

The competition was plagued with the worst English weather in 50 years. Although the contest lasted 14 days, each category had only four contest days, the minimum for an official contest.

Before the contest started, Ray Young, a Pan American pilot based in England, offered to fly the U.S. pilots around the courses in his Fairchild 24 stationed at Derby. Young, who knew England well, with MacCready, Smith, and Schweizer as navigators, flew the courses during the practice period. The ceiling was low with hazy conditions and on the flight to the first turn-point there was much conversation as check points were confirmed along the way. However, after leaving the second point everything became very quiet. Finally, after a few minutes of silence, someone said—"Where in the hell are we?" The problem was not navigation—but the weather.

· The contest started well with two flying days, but was followed by a solid week of rain. There was growing concern as to whether there would be enough contest days to make it an official contest. The two-place ships were given preference since they had one less contest day completed, so the single-place ships were not allowed to take off until all two-place ships had gone. On one afternoon with an overcast ceiling of less than one thousand feet, the single-place sailplanes were winch-launched to soar on the mile-long ridge. Thirty-three sailplanes flying in that small amount of air space were truly a crowd. The only sailplane that had enough room was South African Helli Lasch's AIR-100. It had a dark tinted canopy and his face could not be seen. The other pilots gave him a wide berth as they did not know if he could see them! Fortunately, there were no midair collisions.

Gerard-Pierre of France was the winner of the single-place class in the new Bruguet 901, P. A. Wills was 2d in a Sky, and Wiethucher of Germany was 3d in a Weihe-50; MacCready finished 4th and Schweizer 15th. Z. Rain and B. Komac of Yugoslavia were the winners in the two-place competition. Mantelli and Broghini of Italy were 2d and Smith and Kidder finished 3d.

On MacCready's last flight he surprised everyone by landing at the tip of Flamborough Head Peninsula close to the water's edge, the farthest he could get from Camphill in that direction. He won the day and added 1,000 points to his score.

Paul MacCready, Sr. (left) and Paul MacCready, Jr., by the 1-23E at Camphill, England, the site of the 1954 WSC.

(J.D. Grave, NSM Collection)

Smith and Kidder were in second place when they made the best flight on the third contest day. Unfortunately, this flight did not count since there were not enough finishers. They hit a fence in landing and damaged the 2-25. This prevented them from flying the last day.

Most English fields are quite small in comparison with fields in the United States. The one that Stan Smith picked was surrounded by a heavy timber fence. With the limited power of the original brakes, Smith could not stop the 2-25 and it slid into the fence. A heavy timber ended on top of the canopy but did not break it. Smith and Kidder tried to get out, but could not raise the canopy. They were trapped! After a while, an elderly gentleman approached cautiously and from a distance asked if they were all right. They said that they were, and with that he said "Tallyho," turned, and started to walk away. Smith and Kidder shouted, asking him to help get them out.

Since there was no single-place competition that day, the Schweizers arrived to help retrieve them. Smith was most disturbed by the mishap, which put them out of the contest. Gloom prevailed as they trailered back to Camphill. En route they stopped for gas. There was more gloom when, on leaving the station, they smashed the fin and rudder on the low canopy over the gas pumps. Kidder's comment was, "That Smith. What a vocabulary!"

Chance was a major factor in determining the outcome of this competition. The ever-changing weather and the 2 to 3 hours it took to get all the sailplanes winch-launched created problems. The result was that only seven of the 43 competing pilots scored points on each of the four days, and only 12 scored on three days.

The contest rules were written to minimize the "chance element" by allowing each pilot to throw away at least two days. However, this did not apply, since each class flew only the minimum of four days.

Unlike the Spanish WSC, Camphill provided an opportunity for the team members to get to know each other: Everyone lived on the site in tents or caravans, ate together in a large wedding tent, and drank beer at one of the three bars on the field. With seven days of rain, things got so friendly that at one evening meal they all sang "Happy Birthday" when one of the U.S. pilots was given a birthday cake.

Other Activities during 1954

Stan Smith, chief engineer of Bell, made a two-way business flight in his 1-21. He flew from Batavia, N.Y. to Elmira, New York and back on the following day. His purpose was a visit to SAC, which was a subcontractor for Bell, but most of the discussion was about a two-place sailplane for the coming WSC.

The SSA took part in a joint IAS-SSA session in New York City on January 28, 1954, which included papers by MacCready, Raspet, and Kidder. Earlier that day a joint session was held with the American Meteorological Society at which Klieforth, MacCready, and Wiggin had presented papers.

A number of youth activities took place in the United States during 1954. A glider club was formed at Mississippi State to give students actual flight experience. TSA and the PGC both ran youth programs. An article by L. deLange in the November–December '54 *Soaring* told of the value of gliding and soaring training for selecting airline and military trainees in Holland. In the same issue an article entitled "Youth Must Fly" reported on a number of cases of young people involved in motorless flight including the two Klemperer children.

MacCready wrote about the optimum airspeed selector in soaring giving all the details of this device, which later was called the best-speed-to-fly indicator.

The Jet Stream Project, 1955

The second Sierra wave project was called the Jet Stream Project. Six comprehensive articles appeared in successive issues of *Soaring* about this project, which was organized principally by Kuettner of the Air Force Cambridge Research Center, using the same team from UCLA's Department of Meteorology and SCSA. The main purpose of the project was to study the influence of the jet stream on waves and the possibility of such conditions causing tornadoes and other severe weather downstream a day or two later. The team also wanted to investigate the possibility of "pressure

SSA President Floyd Sweet with members of the board and John Agnew of the Soaring Association of Canada at the 1955 winter directors' meeting in New York City. Front row left to right: E. J. Reeves, F. J. Sweet, P. A. Schweizer, J. D. Carsey; *back row*: R. Symons, B. Shupack, P. B. MacCready, Jr., Dr. P. B. MacCready, Sr., J. Agnew, W. Coverdale, T. Nelson, and H. Burr.

(NSM Collection)

jump" waves, which had been suspected for some time.

Retarded Growth of Soaring

Sweet's first editorial in 1955 asked why there was such limited participation in soaring in this country. He said the first reason was the *shortage of gliders:*

> The 1954 inventory of gliders in the U.S. was reported as 428, of which 242 were listed as being active. Of this number, less than 200 carried CAA certificates of airworthiness, so we must assume that less than 200 gliders were actively being flown in the U.S., at least legally.
>
> The next reason is the limited places where soaring can be done and the third is the *cost*. The answers to the first and last problems are interrelated. There will be no production of gliders unless there is a demand for gliders, and there will be no demand until the price can be *brought within the means* of the many who would like to participate in soaring. The *answer then is* to *create* a demand for gliders

through a nationwide program using the glider as a means of stimulating and retaining youth interest in aviation.

> The answer to the second problem is: "If there are enough people with gliders who want to fly, they will band together and purchase or lease land convenient to their communities for the purpose of establishing gliderports."

IAS-SSA Session

The joint IAS-SSA session on soaring flight was held in New York City just before the directors' meeting. Harry N. Perl gave a paper and showed a 25-minute color film on the story of the Hummingbird.

The second session was a panel discussion, "Contributions of Soaring to Aviation Progress—Past, Present, and Future." Sweet, pinch-hitting for Klemperer, gave a history of the past contributions. E. Schweizer spoke on current contributions since the end of

Top: Dr. Joachim Kuettner, R. Rados, and Betsy Woodward of the Jetstream Project by their Pratt-Read in April 1955.

(NSM Collection)

Larry Edgar in the Pratt-Read that disintegrated after hitting severe turbulance in the Sierra wave.

(NSM Collection)

World War II. E. Stout, staff engineer of Consolidated-Vultee, talked about possible future contributions, including the further development of boundary layer countrol. MacCready discussed future contributions of soaring to meteorology, including the use of pressurized sailplanes and possibly pilotless sailplanes for high-altitude investigations. Lt. Fred Obarr discussed

the future role of gliders in the field of aviation and training.

Directors' Winter Meeting, 1955

At the directors' meeting in New York on January 28–29, 1955, the treasurer reported that SSA was holding its own financially, and the secretary announced that the membership was substantially the same as a year ago.

Sweet reported that government officials were beginning to show interest in the American Youth Glider Training Program. SSA bylaws were changed to increase the subscription price for *Soaring* to $4.

The directors reaffirmed the objectives of SSA as stated by Warren E. Eaton. They also established its goal for 1955: "To provide every American boy with the opportunity to get into aviation through gliding and soaring—a National Air Youth Program."

Review of SSA Structure

At the Elsinore meeting in 1954 the directors had recognized that the structure of SSA would have to be changed if it was to grow faster and be able to carry out its programs. At that time many people who were active in motorless flight were not members of SSA. Since one could borrow a copy of *Soaring* to read, many did not bother to join SSA until they earned their first award. An ad hoc committee was authorized to study the problem.

Klemperer Heads Ad Hoc Committee

Sweet appointed Dr. Klemperer to chair the ad hoc committee and to develop a plan that would correct this problem. His proposed plan included three types of groups: *affiliates, chapters,* and *clubs.* A variety of responses came in from both SSA members and directors, and so Klemperer felt that it was not possible to recommend a specific plan at that time. Unfortunately, he was not able to attend the meeting of the directors, who thought that much more had to be done on this proposal and thus tabled it for further study.

Sailplane Developments

In the January–February *Soaring* Art Shultz reported on his Nucleon sailplane, an intermediate-performance sailplane that was designed for home construction. It was the first to use styrofoam planking to get a smooth wing and possible laminar flow. Art Shultz died during 1955 and nothing further was done with this project.

Six Nelson Hummingbirds were ordered and Nelson decided to go ahead and produce a limited quantity. A two-part story in *Soaring* by Harry Perl entitled "The Powered Sailplane" gave the details on its design and production.

The Jet Stream Project

The Jet Stream Project used a B47 and B29 meteorological research aircraft. The SCSA provided a Pratt-Read, which had been used in the Mountain Wave Project. Schweizer Aircraft loaned the 2-25, which Frank Kerns equipped for high-altitude flying. Kuettner hoped to be able to use it to exceed his 375-mile wave flight of 1951 by a significant amount. Kuettner, Lyle Maxey, Larry Edgar, and Betsy Woodward did the flying and Vic Saudek

supervised the SCSA part of the project.

In addition to the Air Force, the SCSA, the UCLA Meteorological Department, represented by Professor Holmboe, Dr. Wurtele, Dr. Edinger, and Harold Klieforth were also part of the project. Some preliminary flying had been done in March and April of 1954 to test the equipment and technique to be used. The period between March 29 and April 25, 1955, proved to be a fantastic wave period. Waves were flown to over 40,000 feet on four different days, and close to 40,000 feet on four other days. These flights gave ample opportunity to carry out the planned program.

On April 14, Betsy Woodward set two world records with a flight to 39,994 feet and an altitude gain of 27,994 feet in the Pratt-Read.

On April 25, however, Kuettner flying in a 2-25 and Edgar in the Pratt-Read encountered very strong conditions. Kuettner ran into "fantastic turbulence" at 14,000 feet and called Edgar to tell him of this, whereupon Edgar headed to the forward edge of the lenticular cloud at 14,000 feet. As he approached the roll cloud, the Pratt-Read was suddenly engulfed in the cloud and the turbulence tore the Pratt-Read apart. It was later estimated that the Pratt-Read was subjected to about 16 g's acceleration, and medical specialists estimated that Edgar had taken minus 20 g's for at least 0.4 seconds. Although the exact sequence was never known, when the turbulence hit, the left wing and tail boom were broken off and the nose sheared off from the center section directly behind the pilot seats. Edgar was thrown out, still attached to the nose section by his flying boots. The negative g had temporarily blinded him, but he found the D ring of his parachute and gave it a pull. As the chute opened, the nose section fell free and his feet came out of his boots. He was concerned about being lifted up in the wave and found that his bailout bottle hose had been ripped off, so he tried to spill his chute, but had difficulty since his left arm was almost useless. When he finally broke out of the cloud, he saw parts of the Pratt-Read flying past him. He saw that he was drifting east very fast. However, his easterly drift decreased and soon reversed as he got into the westerly flow at the bottom of the rotor. He landed going backward at about 25 miles an hour and was dragged over the ground until two nearby workers helped spill his chute. Although he had been subject to extremely high positive and negative g's and was quite battered, he fully recovered from this harrowing experience.

Edgar's flight was in a wave of the pressure jump variety and it was the last flight of the project. A great mass of information had been accumulated and Kuettner's reports in *Soaring* gave some idea of the extent of the information gained.

Vic Saudek evaluated the success and benefits of the wave project in his report "The Sierra Wave Project from Concept to Fruition," presented at the National Soaring Museum (NSM) Symposium in May of 1975: "Was it worth the zealous effort, risks and dollars? There is no proof, but, from the viewpoint of a quarter of a century later, if there had been only one airliner which was saved from these destructive forces by weather reports about waves, or by knowledge of how to avoid them, or to recognize them—and stay out of the danger zones—then it has been worthwhile. The Air Force's Cambridge Research Center

distributed a total of 42,000 copies of their document: AFCREA Technical Report 53-56, No. 35 'Flight Aspects of the Mountain Wave' by Kuettner and Jenkins. In 1953 every American owned airline and ATR and Military pilot in this country was given a copy."

Directors' Summer Meeting, 1955

At the meeting held from July 3 to 14 at Elmira, a proposed revision of the bylaws, to provide that "a director may serve no longer than two consecutive three year terms but may be eligible for reelection after a lapse of one year," was defeated. An amendment proposed and passed was that "the Board of Directors shall meet during the first quarter of the calendar year and elect from their number the officers who will then start serving their term at the summer directors meeting". An amendment to "legalize the SSA State Governors" was passed. In addition, "The Secretary recommended that the Board should seriously consider the addition of a paid manager since he could justify his cost by expanding the membership. The President and Secretary were authorized to investigate this possibility."

The report of the ad hoc committee on national structure was again tabled as the directors were still unable to agree on this plan.

22d National, 1955

A comprehensive article by E. J. Reeves in the July–August issue of *Soaring* commemorated the 25th anniversary of the First National Contest and set the stage for the 22nd National, to be held on July 2–14, 1955 at Elmira. Twenty-seven sailplanes com-

peted. The new sailplanes included the V-tail Alibi, which Kemp Trager built around a set of L-K spars, a home-built Prue 215, and a new British Skylark II, flown by Bill Coverdale and the first sailplane imported to the United States in a number of years.

With good weather, each day was a "contest day." The R. C. du Pont Goal Flight Award was given for the fastest flight to du Pont Airport, Wilmington, Delaware. Cmdr. Nick Goodhart was the winner.

On the last day a special task was set with the Stroukoff Trophy as the prize. Mike Stroukoff had given this trophy in memory of his wife, Larissa, for the best out-and-return flight. Steve Bennis was the first winner of the award.

Nick Goodhart, a British Naval officer stationed in Washington, D.C.,

flying a 1-23 that Bill Ivans had loaned him, earned the most points. Kempes Trager, who had finished second to Goodhart, became the national soaring champion. Ivans was third in his 1-23E, and Bob Smith, flying a flat-top L-K, was second.

The rules continued to include two drop days—one task day and one open day. Since there were two days on which almost everyone had poor performances, the rule did not have much effect on the standings.

Records

Since flights of more than two days were no longer a rarity, the CIVV abolished duration records in 1955, arguing that the hazards involved did not justify continuing this record category. Instead, it added two new record categories for speed around a 200- and 300-kilometer triangle. That summer, Dick Johnson claimed a 200-kilometer triangle record of 44.8 miles per hour at the annual southwest meet in Grand Prairie. However, this record was never homologated. On September 4, *Lyle Maxey* set a world record in the Jenney Mae with a flight of 310 miles from El Mirage to Independance, California, and back. Although the United States had gained another world record, it was losing ground in the number of world records held because soaring activity in Europe was increasing.

World's First One-Design Regatta

Also in 1955, SAC ran the first 1-26 Regatta over the Labor Day weekend at Harris Hill. Seven 1-26s entered, and Dave McNay, an Air Force pilot and former Purdue University Glider

Kempes Trager and his Alibi sailplane, which he designed and built and in which he won the 1955 national soaring championship.

(All American Engineering)

The 1-26 Regatta Trophy, a painting of a regatta scene by Frank Hurtt. Each year's winner is listed on a brass plate attached to the frame.
(Schweizer Aircraft Corporation)

lar sailplanes and all those involved in the first regatta were eager for another one to be held the next Labor Day. With over 39 kits and five complete 1-26s already delivered, a much larger regatta was forecast for 1956.

1955 Snowbird Meet

The last contest of the year was the Snowbird Meet held on Thanksgiving weekend at Harris Hill. It was the largest one yet with 25 sailplanes entered. Tom Smith was the winner in his flat-top L-K. Howie Burr flew to second place in his 1-24, and Dave McNay was third in the double-bubble flat-top.

SSA President Sweet presented the trophies at the awards banquet. The contest had an international flavor with 5 ships and 15 pilots from Canada and visiting pilots from Australia and South Africa.

First U.S. World Soaring Champion, 1956

SSA began planning for the 1956 WSC in France early in the year. A new system was used for choosing the pilots for the team, as some SSA members had been dissatisfied with the previous system. The first 10 finishers in the 1954 and 1955 Nationals plus the pilots of the previous international team were put on a list and each pilot on the list graded the names after eliminating his own name. The only factor to be considered in this seeding was each pilot's ability in competition flying. The voting produced the following seeding: (1) Paul F. Bikle, (2) Paul B. MacCready, (3) William S. Ivans, (4) Richard H. Johnson, (5) Kemp Trager, and (6) Raymond H. Parker. However, the final team was

Club member, won the regatta. Don Pollard was second and Otto Zauner third. A newcomer to soaring, Harner Selvidge, took delivery of a 1-26 No. 43 the day before the regatta and finished fourth in his first contest. Other contestants at this historical event were Joe Perrucci, Art Millay, and Tennis Mahoney.

The regatta principle of fleet racing among sportsmen in the same type of craft was enthusiastically received by those at the organization meeting of the 1-26 Association held during the regatta. Otto Zauner was elected the first president and Don Ryan was elected secretary.

One of the purposes of the 1-26 project was to encourage one-design competition. The concept had been so successful in sailing that it seemed natural to apply it to sailplanes. Although it was less than a year since production had started, of the seven 1-26s entered, five had been built from kits, one of which was completed in less than six months. The tasks chosen for the first regatta were not very ambitious since most of the pilots had little experience flying their 1-26s. However, the regatta demonstrated the fun and satisfaction of competing in simi-

not selected until the place and date of the contest were made known, along with the number of entries allowed, the availability of gliders, pilots' availability, and the funds available for the team.

The MacCready combination of Paul, Jr., pilot, and Paul, Sr., crew chief, after finishing second, sixth, and fourth in the previous three WSCs were determined to win this one. Seeded No. 2, Paul, Jr., was sure to be on the team, and Paul, Sr., was ready to finance the trip, if necessary, so they started to get organized early. Paul, Jr. was impressed with the Breguet 901 that Pierre had used to win at Camphill and was able to rent one. Bill Ivans arranged to borrow a new British "laminar flow" Olympia IV that was reported to be better than the Skylark IIIs that the British team would fly.

Up to that time, it had been the practice for the competing countries with sailplanes of their own design and manufacture to use them in the WSC. At Camp Hill, for example, nine countries (Belgium, England, France, Finland, Germany, Italy, Yugoslavia, Switzerland, and the United States) had used their own sailplanes.

There were exceptions, when it was not possible for financial or other reasons for a team to bring their own sailplanes. The popular feeling, however, was that winning the WSC was not the pilot's victory alone, but a total victory of the pilot, the sailplane, and the supporting team, as in the America's Cup sailboat race.

A change was under way, however, for the growing competitiveness of the WSC and the rapid improvement in sailplane performance put those with the higher-performance sailplanes at an advantage. Before this, superior piloting, good team work, and the "breaks" could offset higher performance. Unfortunately, the high cost of staying in the "performance race" prevented many sailplane companies from continuing to build high-performance sailplanes for use in the WSC.

Developing the 1-21 and the different versions of the 1-23, which were competitive for a number of years had cost SAC a considerable amount of money. It was not possible, however, to continue producing top competitive sailplanes since it cost a great deal to manufacture relatively limited quantities. Some foreign sailplane manufacturers, with either government help or large market potential, were able to continue to develop competition sailplanes. SAC put its effort in the 1-26 project, which it hoped would help to broaden the sport in the United States and had a much better possibility of paying its way. Even the costs of a "one-off" type, such as the 2-25, were getting more expensive to make!

Directors' Winter Meeting, 1956

At the January 26–28 meeting in New York, the secretary reported that there had been a 10 percent reduction in the total number of members, but an increase in the number of inquiries received. He felt that if SSA had a full-time person to work on these prospects and to follow up on those who did not renew, this person's salary could soon be justified. The possibility of a paid manager was discussed but was tabled until the next meeting to give more time to locate prospects for this position.

The treasurer's report showed that the SSA had a cash balance and that the increased membership rates had offset the loss of members. A $12,500 budget was approved.

The directors decided to accept Klemperer's ad hoc report on national structure but not to accept the recommendations. The two vice-presidents, Bikle and S. Smith, were delegated to study the report and to submit their recommendations at the summer directors' meeting.

The directors approved the seeding list for the 1956 WSC. If Johnson (and later Bikle) had not decided to pass up this WSC, Trager, the current U.S. champion, would not have been on the team. In the absence of a policy on the standing of the current national champion, it was voted that in the future he should be a member of the WSC team, if he wanted to compete! E. J. Reeves agreed to conduct the $15,000 national team fund drive.

Sailplane Developments

SISU-1.   Leonard Niemi, a Bell Helicopter engineer, gave a report on the all-metal SISU sailplane in the March–April 1956 issue of *Soaring*. The SISU was to exceed the RJ-5 in overall performance and was under construction.

XBG-12.   Jack Wolfe wrote about the test flight of the XBG-12 in the May–June issue of *Soaring*. Gus Briegleb and Paul Bikle test-flew the XBG-12 and reported good performance.

CHEROKEE.   Stan Hall reported on his first flight in the Cherokee II in the November–December *Soaring*. The prototype had been built at Frank Kern's shop, and Hall's first flight was a three-hour soaring flight from an auto tow start from El Mirage Dry Lake. Hall called the Cherokee II a "Sunday afternoon soarer." He also stated "that anybody who has a 20 ft. garage, has access to a table saw, a drill press and a band saw and has ever built a model airplane, can build her." Stan hoped that the Cherokee would "bring soaring to high school youngsters the country over."

1-26.   SAC announced that the first fifty 1-26 kits had been sold and a second run of 50 was in production.

As a result of the growing interest in one-design competition, some overenthusiastic supporters proposed that a 1-26 contest could replace the National Soaring Contest. SAC and some soaring people did not approve of the idea. One of these was Dick Johnson, who pointed out in the January–February 1956 *Soaring* the continued need for an open contest to improve the breed of sailplanes. No doubt the misunderstanding developed from an SAC proposal for a 1-26 National.

World Soaring Championships, 1956

The French Aero Club had originally allowed each country three single-place and one two-place entries for the 1956 WSC, held June 29 to July 13 at St. Yan, France. However, it also stipulated that should more than 60 entries be received, each team would be allowed only two single-place and one two-place entrant.

The U.S. team was composed of MacCready, flying a Brequet 901, with his father as crew chief and Charles Willard as crew; Bill Ivans in an Olympia IV with Bill Kramp as crew chief and Sterling Starr as crew; Trager, with Gene Miller, a soaring companion, as copilot, in the Schweizer 2-25, with John Bierens as crew chief and Howard Hayes as crew; Barney Wiggin as captain and meteorologist; Floyd Sweet manager; and Ray Parker reserve pilot and assistant captain.

The task of July 3 was a distance flight along a straight line through Cuers Airport, approximately 250 miles south southeast of St. Yan, close to the Mediterranean Sea. The excitement of this flight was recorded by Barney Wiggin in the September–October 1956 *Soaring*:

Saradic, Wills and Ivans reported in from the Toulon-Cuers Airport. . . . No report on MacCready. Finally MacCready was the only pilot not reported! The sun had set. It grew dark. Some of little faith shivered in the evening chill as they thought of the mountain crags and ravines along the course, one of them possibly holding MacCready. Suddenly excitement boiled in the telephone room. . . . M. Boissinado ordinarily a poker-faced gentleman and normally not speaking one word of English was radiant as he shouted—"MacCready at Mediterranean!" For one glorious moment MacCready was on everybody's team.

MacCready himself agreed that "this was probably the most interesting flight during any contest. It lasted almost 9 hours, and featured thermal soaring, then low slope soaring, and finally wave soaring. At the end of the flight I landed at 9:15 PM after dark at a Navy air station on the Mediterranean while jet training flights were under way."

MacCready had correctly assumed that most of the pilots would consider the task ended at Coers, since it was only 9 miles from the Mediterranean shore. MacCready continued along the line past Coers until he landed at the air station, to earn 1,000 points for the day. The flight was reminiscent of his landing at Flamborough Head on the shore of the North Sea at the WSC two years before.

At the end of this task MacCready was in first place, Ivans in second, and Trager in first place in the two-place class. MacCready stayed in first place for the rest of the contest. It is no wonder the French began calling him "La Machine."

The last day's task was a 187-mile race to St. Auban. A strong "mistral" wind meant rough conditions in the mountains. The first portion of the

The U.S. team pilots and captain at the awards ceremony at the end of the 1956 WSC at St. Yan. Left to right: ceremony at the end of the 1956 WSC at St. Yan. Left to right: Gene Miller (second pilot two-place), Kempes Trager (first pilot two-place), Sterling Starr (standing in for the injured Bill Ivans), Paul MacCready, Jr. (world champion), and Bernard Wiggin (team captain and meteorologist.)

(Teddy Heimgartner, NSM Collection)

task took the contestants over flat lands, where thermal conditions were good. However, an unexpected overcast developed over the edge of the mountains, and the tops of the ridges were in the clouds. It was necessary to fly the ridges and find passes through which the sailplane could fly downwind to the next ridge.

Ivans and Persson, the Swedish pilot, were flying in the same area near Crest. Ivans went through a very small pass followed by Persson. They were unable to find any lift and in attempting to land in the turbulent air, Ivans was stalled out by a gust and crashed into the rocky ground. Persson landed a few miles from Ivans and, since he could speak French, was able to get help for Ivans, who had fractured a vertebrae. Ivans was taken to the hospital at Crest and after a number of days there, Sweet arrange for an Air Force ambulance plane (which was made by Convair, Ivans's employer!) to fly him to the U.S. military hospital at Weisbaden. He received good care there and made a successful recovery.

MacCready, who did not have to fly that day since he led the contest by more than 1,000 points, decided to fly anyway and said that it was the most fatiguing flight he had ever experienced. In the remaining top five places were L. V. Juez of Spain, second; Gorzelak of Poland, third; Saradic of Yugoslavia fourth, and Ivans, fifth. The top four in the two-place category were N. Goodhart and F. Foster of Great Britain, first; Z. Rain and Stepanovic of Yugoslavia, second; Saudoux and Baset of Argentina third; and Kempes Trager and Eugene Miller of the United States, fourth. This was a superb performance by the American team. MacCready was later awarded the Lilienthal Medal for his victory.

The contest had presented the entrants with every possible type of weather and a great variety of soaring conditions, including thermal, cloud flying, thunderstorms, and ridge and wave soaring. It was a complete test for soaring pilots—and thus much different from the contests of today. The task of July 9, however, raised questions about the safety of cloud flying at internationals. Philip Wills reported that on one occasion about 25 sailplanes were in the same cloud. Fortunately, no midair collisions occurred!

FAI Gliding Committee and OSTIV Meet at St. Yan

The FAI Gliding Committee accepted the U.S. recommendation that the two-place category be eliminated from future WSCs in view of the limited interest in this class. The possibility of having a restricted class of single-seat sailplanes instead was discussed. OSTIV was asked to study the problem and recommend rules.

Attention at the OSTIV meeting

was centered on the papers by Lorne Welch and Boris Cijan concerning the proposed restricted class of competition sailplanes. OSTIV was asked to set up the requirements for such a restricted class and did so soon after the meeting. The requirements were for a 15-meter, low cost, easy-to-fly, club-type of sailplane. This new class was expected to make its appearance at the 1960 WSC.

23d National, 1956

The weather was excellent for the TSA-sponsored National of July 31 to August 10 in Grand Prairie, Texas. The 46 sailplanes entered flew a total of 42,200 miles cross-country, with 15 flights covering over 300 miles and 45 flights over 200 miles. This broke the record set at the 1947 Nationals at Wichita Falls.

Lyle Maxey came first in the Jenny Mae, Graham Thomson was second in the RJ-5, and Dick Schreder from Toledo, Ohio, flying his first national, was third in a 1-23D. Next in order were Bikle in a 1-23B, Schweizer in a 1-23F, and Stan Smith in the 1-21. Ross Briegleb, 17-year-old son of Gus, flying his first national in the prototype BG-12, came in eighth. Marshall Claybourn, flying a kit built 1-26, finished in thirteenth place. Seven sailplanes competed for the two-place championship, which was won by Harold Hutchinson in a modified LK.

Lloyd Licher was signed up to fly the Cherokee prototype in the contest, but the FAA forced him to withdraw this since the sailplane did not have the necessary flying hours in its local test area. Other sailplanes appearing for the first time included the Nucleon, flown by Harold Jensen; the R-6, flown single-place by Harland Ross; the Mitchell Nimbus II and III, flown by Dr. Sawyer and Vic Swierkowski. A newcomer at the contest was Joe Lincoln of Scottsdale, Arizona, who flew a Baby Albatross.

Directors' Summer Meeting, 1956

The directors' meeting was held on the rest day, August 5, which happened to be the middle Sunday of the Nationals. However, it was not possible to get a quorum of directors until 3 p.m., since some were still returning from

Scene at the 1956 National with Dick Schreder's 1-23D alongside the operations building at the Grand Prairie Airport.

(E. J. Reeves, NSM Collection)

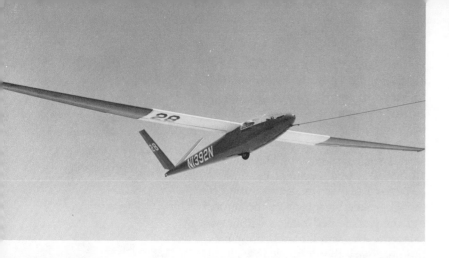

Top: Lyle Maxey taking off in the Jenney Mae at the 1956 National, where he won the championship.

(Henry Dittmer, SSA Files)

Two Briegleb BG-12A sailplanes just after landing at El Mirage Field, California. William G. "Gus" Briegleb, designer, is in the nearest BG-12A and his eldest son Ross is in the other BG-12A.

(Paul W. Heasley, NSM Collection)

the previous day's flights. It was proposed that the bylaws eliminate the requirement that a directors' meeting be held at the time and place of the Nationals.

No agenda had been sent for the meeting, although Sweet had indicated a few weeks earlier that he wanted vice-presidents Bikle and Smith to present their report on the proposed national structure. Because the time was short, no discussion was held on this matter. Barnaby was elected honorary vice-president.

The directors approved a program to publish a gliding and soaring manual developed by the University of Illinois Glider Club. The board voted to issue certificates of merit to Paul B. MacCready and his father for their outstanding performance. They also authorized the president to take positive steps to hold the WSC in the United States.

Chapter 8

Start of the Golden Decade, 1957–1961

The Transition, 1957

During 1957 the SSA moved from 25 years of very slow growth into a period of rapid increase averaging almost 500 new members a year for the next 10 years, which have been called the golden decade. This abrupt change was spawned by a number of events in 1957.

SSA started the year with only about 650 active members. Because of its small size, its limited finances, and the fact that it was a volunteer organization without any government support, SSA was limited in what it could do. It could not sustain a drive for new members, it was too small to get much attention in Washington, D.C., and it could not get a youth program going or support a sailplane industry. It obviously had to grow if it was to carry out its mission.

Nonetheless, by the end of its first 25 years, U.S. soaring was on top internationally. For one thing, Mac-Cready's victory and the good team showing at St. Yan had shown that American soaring pilots were up with the best. The United States now shared the lead with Poland in the number of world records held—it had eight; France had five; and Russia four. Another notable accomplishment was that a U.S. pilot was the first to win the three-diamond award, and by the end of 1956 the United States was in third place in the number held.

Only two other countries, Poland and France, both with government-supported programs, had more. Furthermore, U.S. soaring was well regarded for its scientific and technical advances, having taken the lead in the development of laminar flow sailplanes, all-metal sailplanes, and home-built sailplanes produced from drawings and kits.

In fact, the size of the SSA was not a good indication of the soaring activity around the country, since many who were actively soaring were not members. Most clubs at that time did not require 100 percent SSA membership. If the number of inquiries received at the two SSA Elmira offices was any indication, soaring was on the rise. SAC was also receiving more soaring inquiries, as it had started doing some national advertising in *Flying* and *AOPA Pilot* magazines.

The problem was how to convince all those active in soaring to join SSA and to sign up new prospects. What the SSA needed was a full-time employee to do this, as well as some restructuring. As the directors prepared for the coming board meeting, they sensed that action had to be taken on these two important items.

Directors' Winter Meeting, 1957

The first directors' meeting of 1957 took place on March 8–9 in Holly-

Rose Marie and Lloyd Licher, who were the key players in transitioning the SSA from a volunteer group to a growing organization. Both were soaring pilots, but a health condition limited Lloyd's participation. Rose Marie became very active and she set a woman's distance record in 1963.

(George Uveges)

wood, California, two weeks short of the 25th anniversary of the SSA's founding meeting in 1932. Dr. Klemperer, one of the founding directors, was present along with all the other directors, Bikle, Briegleb, Fuchs, Ivans, MacCready, Nelson, Robertson, P. A. Schweizer, Selvidge, Stan Smith, and Sweet.

The first session of the meeting was routine, but in the following one the directors devoted a full day to SSA's major problems. After considerable deliberation—for there was no assurance that funds would be available—the board voted to employ a full time executive secretary. It felt, however, that with the executive secretary conducting an aggressive membership drive, things would work out. To fill this post, the board hired Lloyd Licher at a yearly salary of $7,200, with an annual travel allowance not to exceed $2,000 and an allowance of up to $3,000 a year for clerical and secretarial help.

Licher had started his soaring ac-

tivity with the MIT Glider Club in 1949, and after graduation he moved to the Los Angeles area. He and his wife Rose Marie, who had also been a member of the MIT Club, both worked as engineers in the aircraft industry. He owned a 1-7 sailplane and became very active in soaring. He became SSA governor for southern California in 1954 and was appointed chairman of the SSA Record and Homologation Committee in 1955. In 1956 he started his column "West Words" in *Soaring*. He had already proved his enthusiasm and devotion to soaring, and he seemed to be the right person for the SSA.

The following officers were elected at the March meeting: Paul A. Schweizer, president; W. S. Ivans, vice-president; S. W. Smith, vice-president; H. Selvidge, Treasurer; and W. Fuchs, secretary. It might have seemed to some that the former secretary was "jumping out of the frying pan and into the fire" when he accepted the nomination for president. Actually, now that SSA had an executive secretary, the president's SSA work load would be lighter, and he thought that he was in the best position to help Licher with the transition.

Up to that time the position of SSA secretary had carried many responsibilities and involved day-to-day operations. For the past three years, he had seen the work load building up, and in his secretary's reports he had repeatedly recommended that the directors consider hiring a full-time person. He was convinced that there were enough potential members to increase membership in a reasonable time and to the point where the SSA could support this new position. He was willing to help prove this point.

The Board of Directors then proceeded to restructure the SSA on a regional basis with regionally elected directors. Up to that time, the 18 directors were elected by all the voting members. Some referred to the system as a "popularity contest" and also pointed out there was no assurance that all areas of the country were represented on the board. Therefore the directors decided to establish geographical areas based on the SSA member population and to base the number of directors on the number of members. That is to say, the total number of directors would remain constant, but as the SSA grew, redistribution of the directors might be necessary from time to time to take care of membership changes. A committee was appointed, with Paul Bikle as chairman, to prepare the bylaw revisions needed to accomplish this change.

The agenda of the next OSTIV meeting was reviewed and it was moved that the SSA should take a negative view on the proposal to include a standard class at the 1960 WSC. This decision was due mainly to the fact that little time was available to discuss the proposal for a standard class. As a result, the Standard Class in the United States got off on the wrong foot.

Barnaby's award handbook, which described all SSA awards, was approved for publication. Stan Smith was appointed chairman of a committee to develop plans to celebrate the 25th anniversary of SSA.

Fiberglass-Reinforced Plastic

Jim H. Gray, member of the EASC, wrote an article in the March-April *Soaring* on the possible use of fiberglass-reinforced plastic (FRP) for sailplane construction. Gray was with the Corning Glass Works and had access to the latest developments in fiberglass. At that time, FRP was used on boats, fishing poles, skis, bows for archery, and other sporting equipment. Fiberglass cloth impregnated with plastic provided a smooth finish and had been used as a covering for a Taylorcraft experimental airplane.

New FAI Requirements

A change in rules permitted the use of cameras for record flights and FAI awards, to prove that a turn-point had been made. This change made it much more convenient to carry out record or badge flights, since a qualified observer was not required at the turn-point.

SAC Dealer Program

SAC announced its new dealer program in the May-June *Soaring*. The four original Schweizer dealers listed were Les Arnold Enterprises, which operated at Hummingbird Haven east of San Francisco; Frank Kern's company Glider Aero in southern California; the Hudson Valley Aircraft formed by Steve and Ginny Bennis and Bill Terry, operated at Middletown, New York; and the Thermal Gliderport formed by Larry Gehrlein near Erie, Pennsylvania.

SAC had been selling directly to the sailplane customer, since the sales volume did not warrant having dealers and the elimination of dealer commissions helped to reduce the cost to the customer. After operating that way for about 10 years, SAC came to the realization that if soaring was to expand to the point where it could support U.S. sailplane manufacturers, there had to be a way to encourage many more

Major William Fuchs assists Air Force Academy cadets in removing their 1-26 from its special enclosure, which was necessary to keep the antelopes from gnawing the fabric.

(U.S. Air Force, NSM Collection)

new people to participate in soaring and to teach them to fly sailplanes. The few soaring clubs that were active in the United States were hard-pressed to handle their own members, and some were even closed to new members. SAC believed that the answer was to form commercial soaring schools around the country so that introductory sailplane rides would be available to the public as well as sailplane flying courses for those who wanted to get into the sport. This meant that people would not have to join a club if the were not sure whether they wanted to become more deeply involved. The commercial operators would therefore need sailplanes to use themselves as well as to sell to students, clubs, and other prospects. Under the new agreements, dealers who had a soaring operation were given discounts to encourage them to go out and sell.

The Airmate HP-7

Richard Schreder of Toledo, Ohio, described his high-performance design, the HP-7, in the May-June *Soaring* of 1957. Schreder had started soaring in 1955, finished third in the 1956 Nationals, and was building the HP-7 for the 1957 Nationals. The design incorporated all-metal construction with a high aspect ratio wing having flaps for approach control.

Air Force Academy Gets Sailplanes

The SSA had not yet been successful in its efforts to start a national youth glider program, although there was some youth activity around the country in clubs that sponsored such programs. One bright spot developed in June of 1957 when Maj. William Fuch accepted delivery of the first sailplanes for use in an Air Force Academy program. A 2-22 trainer and a 1-26B sailplane were to be used to introduce motorless flying to the cadets. The previous year Fuchs and a group of officers had formed the Falcon Glider Club and purchased a used 2-22. With the arrival of the new sailplanes, gliding would become both a scheduled part of the curriculum for the second-year cadets and an extracurricular activity.

Gift of 1-21

The first of two generous gifts to the SSA occurred just before the summer directors' meeting. David Stacey, one of the soaring pioneers in New England in the 1930s, in an open letter to the SSA membership, announced that he was giving his 1-21 to the SSA so it could be sold and the proceeds used to help finance the cost of the new executive secretary. The directors decided to sell it to the highest bidder, Bob Moore of Richland, Washington.

Transfer of SSA Office

At a meeting in Elmira early in May, Licher, Sweet, and Schweizer arranged to transfer SSA functions and files from the Elmira offices to Licher's home in Santa Monica, California. For seven years, Katy Jones had handled the SSA membership and other routine SSA functions at the EAC and had made an outstanding contribution to the soaring movement.

Licher had driven to Elmira to pick up the files and on his way back, Schweizer met him in Dallas to work out the move of *Soaring* magazine. Lloyd had to spend some time in Dallas to get out the July-August issue since Jack Forbes had developed an ulcer and had gone to Canada for a rest. The transition was carried out smoothly and Lloyd Licher's first issue of *Soaring* from Los Angeles met the September-October deadlines.

24th National, 1957

Licher's report on the 24th National, held on July 2–11 in Elmira, appeared in *Soaring*. It began, "Each National Contest seems to be different in a fairly distinctive way. This one was marked by the seeming singularity of purpose, that of selecting the National Soaring Champion. Although provisions had been made in the rules for selecting champions in two-place, feminine, junior and club categories, there were no entries for any of them. The whole emphasis was on the main event."

Howie Burr was contest director and the 31 sailplanes entered included Dick Schreder's new HP-7 and 2 foreign LO-150s. The miles flown on July 6, the open day, totaled 4,956, a record for one day's flying at Harris Hill. Compton made the best flight of the meet with a 320-mile flight to Plymouth, Massachusetts, in his modified LK. Schreder came second with a 305.5-mile flight to Logan International

While the contest was going on, "Papa" Schweizer passed away. His many friends at the contest were saddened by this news. He liked his three boys' soaring friends, and some had had the opportunity to partake of one of his meals, or to take a tour through his garden. P. A. Schweizer, who had been flying Howie Burr's long-wing modification of the 1-23, the 1-24, withdrew from the contest.

Airport in Boston, and Stan Smith was third with a 244-mile flight to Hiller Airport at Barre.

Stan Smith won the championship in his 1-21. It was 21 years since he had won the 1933 Nationals in a Franklin glider. He flew very consistently but only won one day. Bikle was second in his 1-23E, Compton third.

Directors' Summer Meeting, 1957

The principal business of the July 11 meeting in Elmira was the revision of

Catherine "Katy" Jones is honored for her efforts beyond the call of duty for the EASC and the SSA. Edward A. "Eddie" Mooers, one of the EASC's founders, presents her an award at the 1951 National Soaring Contest at Harris Hill. Earl Southee, standing nearby, was the toastmaster.

(NSM Collection)

Top: Lyle A. Maxey, left, 1956 national champion, presenting the duPont Trophy to the 1957 champion, Stanley W. Smith.

(*Elmira Star-Gazette*, NSM Collection)

The premier of Poland greeting Johnny Nowak, U.S. team interpreter, and the U.S. team at Leszno, Poland, at the 1958 WSC.

(SSA files)

New President

Paul A. Schweizer took over as president at the directors' meeting. His first editorial in *Soaring* commented:

> The employment of full-time Executive Secretary is a big step forward in putting the SSA on a more business-like basis and giving more service to our members. The recent change in the bylaws, putting the election of Directors on a Regional basis, should do a lot to emphasize the fact that the SSA is basically the organization of soaring enthusiasts all over the country.
>
> Our main task for the year is to increase our income in order for us to continue to pay for these improved services and those to come. It seems that the best way to do this is to start an "EVERY MEMBER GET A MEMBER" Campaign, with the goal of doubling our membership by the end of next year. It is estimated that less than 1/3rd of the people actively interested in soaring are SSA Members, and so the goal stated above is far from an impossible one.
>
> Even though we do have a full-time General Manager, there are just too many items for one man to do, and he needs your continuing cooperation.

World Soaring Championships in Poland, 1958

the bylaws to provide for 18 regional directors. Advertising rates were set and a master insurance plan for the membership was investigated.

Because the bylaws cut all terms of office back by six months, the board elected the existing slate of officers for the calendar year 1958.

David A. Matlin, a Los Angeles attorney, active in the SCSA and former SSA director, was named general counsel for the SSA.

Only two bids had been received by the CIVV, one from the Aero Club of Poland and one from the United States. The Poles had offered to lend 15 high-performance sailplanes to the competing nations, and so it was decided to hold the 1958 WSC in Poland.

The method for seeding the U.S. team was the same as the one used for the 1956 team, except that the two lowest scores were eliminated from each pilot's list to minimize any possible unfair ratings. Stan Smith, the current national champion, and Paul MacCready, the world champion, would automatically be on the team. The seeding by the pilots for the top 10 places was as follows: (1) P. S. MacCready, (2) P. Bikle, (3) L. Maxey, (4) W. S. Ivans, (5) S. W. Smith, (6) F. B. Compton, (7) R. E. Schreder, (8) P. A. Schweizer, (9) K. Trager, and (10) R. B. Smith.

Chichester du Pont Foundation Gift

The second generous gift was received from the Chichester du Pont Foundation. In June, Floyd Sweet had lunch with Felix du Pont, Dick's brother, in order to bring him up to date on the SSA and to ask for financial support. He followed this up on June 16 with these comments in a letter:

> Three items on which the Society would like financial support from the Chichester du Pont Foundation . . . the endowment of the Richard C. du Pont Memorial Trophy . . . the continuation of the annual Sponsoring Membership of the Foundation . . . and the possibility of an increase in support, at least for the next several years, in order to give our new Executive Secretary an opportunity to establish himself.
>
> While our future plans are far from complete, they include the following: To re-establish SOARING on a monthly basis; to increase the service and films available from the film library; to prepare information sheets and pamphlets on soaring to adequately answer the many inquiries received; to encourage the formation of many gliding clubs; to encourage the design and manufacture of new sailplanes; and to seek new outlets for soaring. . . .

On November 25, 1957, the SSA was informed that the foundation was making a gift of $15,000 for 1957,

$5,000 to endow the du Pont trophy and $10,000 to help finance the office of the executive secretary. For operating purposes, they also would contribute $8,000 in 1958, $4,000 in 1959, and $2,000 in 1960. These grants, together with a reasonable growth in members, more or less ensured that SSA could be "on its own" within three years.

Harner Selvidge, the SSA treasurer, thanked the foundation in an editorial in the November-December *Soaring* entitled "No Excuses Anymore":

> The du Pont Foundation aid is arriving in the nick of time, and has been very thoughtfully planned by them to give us the maximum assistance this year, with decreasing amounts in the future when we will be more able to support ourselves.
>
> There must be no relaxing in our "Every Member Get A Member" contest. The du Pont Foundation has made it possible for us to get around the problem of which comes first, the chicken or the egg. We have the egg now. It's up to us to decide whether it hatches into a Dodo, or a Soaring Eagle. We've no excuse anymore.

Sweet Presidency

In Sweet's last editorial as president he looked back at some significant accomplishments that had helped to further his goal of "improving the financial condition of the Society toward the end that we may establish a paid staff." His continuing efforts to obtain an executive secretary and his successful approach to the du Pont Foundation were important achievements and made possible the transition from a period of low growth to one of accelerated growth that would continue for many years.

The Standard Class, 1958

The CIVV adopted the OSTIV proposal for a new class, and called it the Standard Class. It was to be included in the 1958 WSC, which was two years ahead of schedule as a result of the enthusiasm that it had generated in European soaring circles. The idea of an inexpensive, easy-to-fly, club-type sailplane appealed particularly to the smaller countries. It would give them an opportunity to compete on a more equal basis with the larger countries, and provided a practical sailplane that could be used in each country's soaring program.

U.S. soaring had not given much serious thought to the Standard Class since it had originally been scheduled to start in 1960. As a result, there were no American Standard Class sailplanes available for the 1958 WSC. It was decided, however, to include a 15-meter class in the 1958 U.S. Nationals in order to compare the 15-meter sailplanes with the open sailplanes.

Directors' Winter Meeting, 1958

The meeting of January 31 to February 1 was held in the boardroom of the Bendix Aviation Corp. in the RCA Building, New York, and was the first to be held under the new regional director plan. The executive secretary reported that the active membership totaled 840 at the end of 1957, which represented a 30 percent gain in one year. The EMGAM program was working, but not as well as was expected.

In order to encourage memberships, the board decided that subscriptions to *Soaring* would no longer be sold to individuals in the United States, but only to libraries, the Soaring Association of Canada, and for foreign distribution.

Licher's performance during 1957 was reviewed, and he was rehired for an indefinite period and his yearly salary increased by $500. The board said that his first responsibility was to get *Soaring* out on time. In addition, board members decided to go ahead with the publication of the *American Gliding and Soaring Handbook*.

It was noted that more discipline in sailplane flying was needed in view of the CAA's tightening of airspace regulations. The board decided to notify the CAA that it wished to be consulted in any future rule making that would affect motorless flight. In order to show its cooperation, the board voted to prohibit instrument flying at future sanctioned contests.

To fill the gap between issues of *Soaring* until a monthly *Soaring* became feasible, it was decided to publish a bimonthly newsletter, which was to be edited by Selvidge. The first issue came out on February 9, 1958.

An insurance program for SSA members for liability and hull coverage was inaugurated with Lloyd's of London through the Cosgrove General Agency in Los Angeles.

Preparations for Poland

Some directors were concerned about sending a team to Poland because of the unsettled conditions there, but the board decided to do so after Sweet had reported that the State Department, although not able to assist financially, encouraged SSA to participate.

The pilots of the U.S. team were S. Smith, P. Bikle, and L. Maxey, in the Open Class; and F. Compton in the Standard Class. The respective crew chiefs were R. Parker, J. Robinett, I. Prue, and J. Nowak. John Graves was captain-business manager and

John Aldrich was team meteorologist. Other crew members were Dick Johnson, Fred Matteson, and George Lambros. Gus Briegleb was a reserve crewman and an OSTIV delegate.

By working through Jacqueline Cochran and the NAA, it was possible, for the first time to arrange for military air transportation for the team personnel. However, the pilots had to rent sailplanes in Europe. Smith and Bikle rented Breguet 901s, Maxey a Zugvobel, and Compton arranged to borrow a Mucha from the Polish Aero Club.

A fund drive was under way to raise $10,000 for the team, and an appeal was made to the 2,000 readers of *Soaring* for each one to give $4 to support the team.

Every Member Get a Member

The EMGAM membership drive started on August 5, 1957. When it was conceived, there was no assurance that any other financial help would be available, so increasing the membership was the only immediate way that SSA's income could be increased. To stimulate interest in the drive, $600 worth of prizes were put up by SSA. By the time the contest ended (March 31), the active membership totaled almost 1,000, which was a gain of over 300 members in $7\frac{1}{2}$ months, a significant increase but not enough to achieve the EMGAM goal. It is quite possible that the Stacey and du Pont gifts caused the members to ease up in their efforts to get new members, but the contest helped to start an accelerated growth of SSA that would continue for many years. Winners of the contest were John Williams of San Diego and Howie Burr of Elmira, who each received a life membership in SSA.

MacCready's Optimum Airspeed

Paul MacCready, Jr., explained his optimum airspeed indicator in the January-February *Soaring*. At that time it was the general practice to fly thermals at minimum sinking speed and to fly between thermals at the best gliding angle. His indicator permitted greater speeds in tasks and greater distance on open days.

SAC Report

In the March-April 1958 issue of *Soaring* SAC reported that 80 of its 1-26s had already been delivered in kit and complete form. The other sailplanes in production were the 2-22C and 1-23G. Development of a laminar experimental sailplane known as the 1-29 was under way. The SAC dealer program now totaled 14 dealers.

Bobby Symons's Fatal Accident

Bob Symons was killed in a sailplane at El Mirage Dry Lake on April 19, 1958. The accident was investigated by a special committee composed of Bruce Carmichael, Bob Schnelker, and Irv Culver. There was no clear cause of the accident, except that some type of structural failure of the wings had occurred.

Bill Ivans said in his Memorial to Symons in the May-June 1958 *Soaring*:

> The soaring world lost one of its most distinguished and best loved citizens with the death of Bob Symons at El Mirage.
>
> We shall sorely miss the warmth and candor of his counsel, his infectious enthusiasm, his willingness to share with all of us the mysteries of wind and cloud which were opened to him in his career as mountain pilot.

*The OSTIV delegates stayed at an old palace on the Lake of Os-
ieczno, seven miles from Leszno. The two U.S. delegates, Briegleb and
Schweizer, had a large palace room and took part each morning in a cat-
and-mouse action with the other OSTIV members, to see who could get
to the only bathroom in the palace. Briegleb and Schweizer were friendly
competitors in U.S. sailplane manufacturing and got to know each other
better during that two-week stay. Wolf Hirth was present for the CIVV
and OSTIV meetings, which were the last such meetings that he would
attend.*

Bob Symons made deep and lasting contributions to his community
and to the growth of soaring. We
mourn him as a fallen hero, and as a
dear friend.

World Soaring Championships, 1958

The first World Soaring Championship
to be held behind the Iron Curtain
took place at Leszno, Poland, on June
15–29. It was the largest WSC to date,
and most of the Iron Curtain countries
were entered, including—for the first
time—Russia.

Members of the U.S. team were
flown to Paris or Frankfurt by MATS,
so they could pick up their sailplanes
and tow cars. They proceeded to
Leszno via Czechoslovakia, since the
USAF discouraged them from going
through East Germany. Two military
officers were assigned to the team—
Col. Mitchel Giblo, who was the official interpreter, and Capt. John Dono-
hue, who assisted in many ways.

Twenty-two countries entered 37
Open and 24 Standard Class sailplanes. The weather for the meet was
not the best: Out of 13 possible competition days, only 6 days counted.

The winner of the Open Class was
Ernst Haase of West Germany, flying
the HKS. Nick Goodhart of Great Britain, flying a Skylark IV, was 2d and
Rudolf Mestan of Czechoslovakia was
3d in a Demant. Of the U.S. team,
Lyle Maxey finished 9th, Bikle 25th,
and Smith 34th.

Standard Class Sailplanes at the WSC

Twenty-four Standard Class sailplanes,
of 10 different designs, were entered.
Both classes flew the same task, and
the performances turned in by the
Standard Class sailplanes were surprisingly good. In some cases, they
equaled the performance of the Open
Class, even though their takeoffs
started 20 minutes after the Open
Class each day.

The winner was Witek of Poland
in a Mucha Standard I. Persson of
Sweden was 2d in a Zugvogel IV, and
Huth of Germany was 3d in a Ka-6B.
Compton finished 16th just below the
Russian pilot, Victor Goncharenko, a
baritone in the Kiev opera.

The Polish Aero Club conducted a
well-run contest, but the U.S. team
found it difficult to adjust to living in
tents, particularly in wet weather. It
also had to contend with flying borrowed sailplanes. There just wasn't
time to get the sailplane, instrumentation, and pilot "tuned" for the best
possible performance.

Evaluation of the Standard Class Sailplanes

To encourage the new Standard Class,
the OSTIV had announced in 1957 that
a cup donated by the Royal Aero Club
of Great Britain would be awarded for
the best Standard Class design of the
1958 WSC. The following Standard
Class sailplanes were evaluated: Breguet 905, France: Olympia 415, Great
Britain: PIK-3c, Finland: Skylark 2,
Great Britain: Ka-6BR, Germany: Standard Futar, Hungary: Zugvogel IV,
Germany; Mucha Standard I, Poland:
EON-Olympia, Great Britain: and Ilin-
denka IT, Yugoslavia.

The OSTIV jury was composed of
George Abrial of France, Julian Bohan-

owski of Poland, Boris Cijan of Yugoslavia, P. A. Schweizer of the United States, and Lorne Welch of Great Britain. The evaluation procedure started with a review of the assembly of the sailplane, which gave the jury an opportunity to inspect as much of the internal structure and controls as possible. The assembled ship was then weighed and carefully inspected and the cockpit checked for visibility, control movement, and comfort. The ship was then derigged by four men against a stopwatch.

The following three sailplanes were picked for the flight tests: the Ka-6BR, Mucha Standard I, and the PIK-3c. Each of these ships was flight-tested by the jury. When the jurors rated the three ships in order of preference, the Ka-6BR was the winner.

It was generally agreed that the Standard Class was a definite benefit to soaring and that it should be encouraged. The jury could see, however, that much stricter requirements were needed to enable it to meet its original purposes.

In picking the Ka-6BR as the winner, the jury didn't realize that the elevator controls were designed so that forward stick movement lifted up the ailerons slightly, which would help the high-speed flight, and rearward stick movement would droop the ailerons somewhat, which would help slow-speed flight. This was not an attempt to bypass the OSTIV rules, for Rudy Kaiser had designed the Ka-6 before the Standard Class requirements had been set.

The OSTIV Meeting

Briegleb gave a paper on the BG-12 and Schweizer represented Dr. Klemperer at the OSTIV board meeting and Captain Barnaby at the meeting of the FAI Gliding Committee. Betsy Woodward, who was living in England, was appointed to take care of the publication of technical and meteorological papers in the *Swiss Aero Review*. Efforts were to be made to build up the industrial membership in OSTIV around the world.

25th National, 1958

This was the second national contest to be held on the West Coast. It took place on July 29 to August 7, 1958, at Bishop Airport, California, and 46 sailplanes were entered. All were U.S.-built sailplanes except for an L0150 and three Ka-6Bs.

On one day both Schreder and Jensen flew a 360-mile out-and-return flight to El Mirage, which beat the world record by over 60 miles. Unfortunately, the pilots were released too far from the takeoff site and so could not qualify.

Schreder was flying his new HP-8 and was the winner of the contest by edging out Harold Hutchinson and his Prue 215 on the last day.

"Cowboy" Jensen, flying a L0150, was 3d, Graham Thomson in the RJ-5 was 4th, and Bob Moore in the 1-21 was 5th. Sterling Starr finished 6th in his 1-26, and Les Arnold 10th in the Nelson Hummingbird power glider.

In the separately scored 15-Meter Class (there was not much difference between the 15-Meter and Open Class results), Harold Hutchinson easily won, with Dewey Mancuso second in a 1-23 and Sterling Starr third.

Directors' Summer Meeting, 1958

At the August 7 meeting in Bishop, Licher reported that he was having difficulty keeping *Soaring* up to date

Schweizer was present for the last few days of the contest and was busy with SSA matters. A special meeting was held with Lloyd Licher and Mary Cosgrove of the Cosgrove Insurance Agency. She reported that the insurance claims to date were three times the premiums. An SSA member had been refused payment on his damaged sailplane since it was rumored that he had wrecked it in order to collect the insurance. The owner threatened to sue the SSA, and since there was no proof that he had done this, payment was authorized.

George Deibert, contest manager, asked Schweizer to address the Bishop Rotary Club luncheon. During the talk he noticed that Diebert had hurriedly left the room. It turned out that there had been a wing brushing between Dr. Sawyer in a Nimbus II and Harner Selvidge in a 1-26. In an abrupt recovery maneuver, the Nimbus experienced a structural failure and Sawyer was killed when he went down with the ship in the White Mountains. The day after the accident the FAA wanted the wreckage burned so pilots would not continue to report a crash. Since the helicopter that had taken the FAA up to the crash site had left the area, SSA Safety Committee chairman Joe Robertson asked Pete Bowers and Schweizer to climb up the mountain with him to burn the wreckage.

Although the SSA avoided one lawsuit, it was named in another when the Sawyer estate sued the SSA, Selvidge, SAC, and Schweizer as president of SSA.

because of the great amount of other SSA work he had to do. The directors set a deadline for *Soaring* so it would come out regularly. The membership growth of SSA was reported to be large enough for SSA to operate close to break-even without the help of the contributions. As a result, the president was directed to appoint a committee to investigate the possibility of a separate editor for *Soaring*.

The directors, impressed with the success of the Standard Class in the Polish WSC, decided that a separately scored OSTIV Standard Class should be included in the U.S. National Soaring Contest as soon as possible.

Heasley Entz submitted a report that proposed a regional contest system for selecting contestants for the national contest, and this was to be published in *Soaring* for membership reaction.

The following officers were elected for 1959: H. Selvidge, president; Joe Lincoln, Paul A. Schweizer, vice-presidents; Ted Sharp, treasurer; and Joe Robertson, secretary.

Three World Records in Three Successive Days

"Sandbaging the Ross Racer" was the title of the article in the September-October *Soaring* about the three two-place world records that Harland Ross had set in his R-6 sailplane on August 12, 13, and 14 at Odessa, Texas.

With Mikey Jensen and Paul A. Wilson of the Wichita Soaring Association alternating as passengers (ballast), Ross's first record was a 200-kilometer triangle flight at 50.6 miles per hour, the second a 300-kilometer triangle at 51.1 miles per hour, and the third a 100-kilometer triangle at 53.9 miles per hour.

These records put the United States far ahead in the number of men's world records held, with 9 out of 16. Yugoslavia was second with 2. For both men's and women's records, the United States was still in the lead with 11 out of 31. Poland was second with 10 world records, 9 of which were women's.

FAA Requirements for Glider Assembly

In some regions the FAA agents did not permit pilots to assemble their sailplanes without having each operation signed off in the ship's log by an aircraft mechanic.

The SSA worked with the FAA on this matter and an amendment to Manual 18 added a preventive maintenance option that permitted "The Removal and Installation of Glider Wings and Tail Surfaces which are Specifically

Designed for Quick Removal and Installation, may be accomplished by the pilot." Licher reminded the readers that SSA, in this case, provided a valuable service to its members.

Soaring Magazine Goes Monthly, 1959

In his first *Soaring* Editorial as president, Selvidge stated:

> With the continued help of those who have contributed so much in the past and with additional assistance from our newer members, I am sure we can collectively continue to advance the soaring movement in the United States. . . .
>
> While our financial position is good at the present, thanks to the duPont Foundation contributions, we would need more than 750 fully paid new members to permanently finance a monthly magazine. . . .
>
> Every SSA member should realize that the more people we have in the

Society the smaller will be the cost of soaring to everyone concerned. . . . It is equally important to point out that the greater our numbers, the more influential will be our voice in regulatory circles.

The first full year of operations with an executive secretary ended with a total membership of 2,046. This exceptional growth of about 80 percent was due to a number of reasons: the EMGAM contest, the elimination of subscriptions, the increase in new members introduced to soaring by the commercial operators, and an executive secretary who made increased membership one of his important goals.

Directors' Winter Meeting, 1959

At the next directors' meeting in Denver from January 31 to February 1, the directors were convinced that *Soaring* should be published monthly. The changeover was to start with the July 1959 issue, and Licher was authorized to hire an assistant editor and to discontinue the newsletter with the April issue (No. 9).

A number of bylaw amendments were approved, the most significant

Top, left: Dr. Harner Selvidge, president, and Theodore E. Sharp, treasurer of SSA, in front of their 2-22E.

(SSA files)

Harland Ross in the R-6 that he used to set the three world two-place records. The passenger sits beneath the wing with a plastic bubble on top of the wing for visibility.

(NSM Collection)

being the change in chapter status, which would allow a $2 per member rebate for chapters with 100 percent SSA membership. Although the chapter category had been established a number of years earlier, the lack of any financial benefit caused it to be unused.

The directors voted to encourage regional contests by guaranteeing entry into the National for the top three pilots of each regional contest.

A resolution was passed recommending that SSA strongly urge the FAA to require an hour of instruction in the recovery from stalls and spins prior to solo. An ad hoc committee was formed to submit to the FAA recommendations for cloud flying.

The American Soaring Handbook

The need for a gliding and soaring manual to standardize sailplane operations and to increase safety had been talked about for some time. In January of 1956 Jim Redway had written to Dr. L. A. Bryan, proposing a manual. Bryan asked Tom Page for suggestions and in April 1956 a detailed outline developed by Page and the University of Illinois Glider Club was sent to the directors. The project was endorsed at the directors' summer meeting and the

go-ahead was given at the 1958 directors' winter meeting. The appointment of Alice Fuchs as editor was announced in the March-April 1959 *Soaring*, along with the receipt of the $1,500 grant from Link Foundation and a gift of $1,000 from R. C. du Pont, Jr. The name was changed from the *American Gliding and Soaring Manual* to the *American Soaring Handbook*, or *ASH* as it is often called. Editor Fuchs planned to have each subject written by one or more authorities in the field.

Sailplane Developments

Sailplane developments were on the increase both here and abroad. Len Neimi completed and test-flew his Sisu. Irv Prue surprised the soaring world by flight-testing the Prue Two, a 64-foot-span, high-performance, all-metal two-place sailplane. At SAC the 1-29 experimental laminar sailplane was also undergoing flight tests, and the 100th 1-26 was scheduled for delivery in the summer. Stan Hall said that almost a dozen Cherokees were flying and almost 100 sets of prints had been sold. In addition, Briegleb reported that a good number of BG-12s were in production.

American designers were watching what was going on in Europe, where some designers were moving further into sandwich construction that the HKS had pioneered in the early 1950s. The Phoenix used balsa core with a fiberglass-reinforced polyester resin plastic covering, which provided light structural weight. This was the start of a trend toward all-fiberglass sailplanes.

26th National, 1959

The 15-meter class that was added in 1959 at Harris Hill during the competi-

Tom Page, the faculty advisor of the University of Illinois Soaring Club, in his "flat-topped, double bubble" LK. Becoming interested in soaring in the early 1930s, he became an instructor in a World War II military glider school. He later played an important part in putting together the *American Soaring Handbook* and was an SSA director for many years. He was vice-president in 1962 and secretary from 1966 to the end of 1968.
(Alan Karr, *Champaign-Urbana News Gazette*, NSM Collection)

tion from July 1 to 10 did little to encourage the development of sailplanes in the International Standard Class. The SSA board had previously decided to include the Standard Class in the 1959 Nationals, but at the winter meeting it realized that owing to some unresolved problems in the limiting speed dive-brakes requirements, this was not advisable. It authorized the contest board to determine a reasonable intrim speed-brake requirement. This was written up in the March-April 1959 *Soaring* by Paul Bikle. Unfortunately, only one U.S. sailplane, the 1-23H, met the requirement, and of the 35 entries there were only five Standard Class sailplanes entered, a 1-23H and four Ka-6s.

As proposed by the EASC, the SSA provided the competition director (John Graves), as well as the personnel for the scoring and technical phases of the contest. This put the competition functions into the SSA's hands, where it should have been. The EASC provided the contest director, Hugh Whitney, and the other personnel necessary to carry out the Nationals.

The generally light soaring conditions favored the lighter sailplanes, and Dick Johnson won the championship in a pre–World War II Weihe. Dick Schreder was second in his HP-8, and A. J. Smith third in a Lo-150. Kit Drew won the Standard Class in a Ka-6. There was not much difference in performance between the two classes, which prompted some board members to feel there was not much reason to push the Standard Class.

Directors' Summer Meeting, 1959

At the meeting in Elmira on June 30, the SSA general council, David Matlin, raised the point that SSA's practice of permitting directors to vote by proxy

In August of 1958 Hirth came to the United States to buy a Cessna airplane for a friend in Germany. On his flight back from Texas he had many problems. He had poor eyesight but was not allowed to use a radio, since he was an alien. He was forced to use uncontrolled airports and in Tennessee he mistook a road in a housing development for a runway and landed there. He got lost over West Virginia and had to land in a hayfield and stay overnight with a farmer. The next morning he called to make arrangements for landing at Elmira. When he got there, he was worn out and seemed aged beyond his 59 years. He rested for three days at P. A. Schweizer's home. He agreed to an informal meeting with the local soaring enthusiasts, where he told many stories, including the one about the secret "variometer" he had on board when he made his famous "Blue Sky" thermal flight in 1930. It was an unforgetable evening for those fortunate enough to be there.

On his last hop to New Jersey to see Gus Scheurer, Schweizer taxied Hirth's Cessna to the end of the runway for takeoff, since it was a physical problem for Hirth, with only one "good" leg, to taxi the Cessna. They said goodbye—for the last time—and he took off and successfully met up with Scheurer.

A few years later, during a trip to the United States, his daughter Barbara was taken to Elmira by Wally Setz. She said that her father considered Elmira his second home and she wanted to have a soaring flight over the area that her father loved so much. P. A. Schweizer had the pleasure of taking her on a soaring flight, and after they landed it was clear that she had just completed a personal mission.

was of questionable legality and he advised discontinuing it. The bylaws were amended to change the quorum for a board meeting from two-fifths (10) to one-third (9) and to eliminate the practice of allowing directors to be present by proxy. The irony was that this motion was passed with 17 affirmative votes that included 6 proxies. This change did not solve the real problem, which was that two-thirds of the directors (17) had to be present to pass changes in the bylaws.

All officers were reelected, except Ted Sharp, who was replaced by Bertha Ryan as treasurer. Sharp was called way to sea duty with the Navy Pacific Fleet.

In order to give more attention to safety problems it was decided to publish accident reports in *Soaring*.

per hour; and the 300-kilometer triangle, 57.9 miles per hour. Later that year these records were accepted by the FAI, and Schreder was awarded the Lilienthal medal for 1959 for these performances.

Another outstanding flight was made by Harland Ross in his R-6 sailplane. By aero towing 122 miles southwest to Kent, Texas, Ross was able to contact the Marfa dewpoint front. He rode this front for 365.5 miles to earn his Diamond "C" (no. 14).

Wolf Hirth's Last Flight

On July 25, 1959, Wolf Hirth had a fatal accident while flying a sailplane in Germany. He had been one of the great pioneers of soaring. In the United States he is remembered most for being the first one to use the spiraling technique for thermal soaring at the time of the 1930 National and for designing the Minimoa.

Odessa Soaring Camp

A soaring camp was held from August 1 to 15 at Al Parker's operation at Odessa Airport, with E. J. Reeves as the director. It was informal and distinctly different from a National. The weather was good in a 175-mile radius around Odessa, but beyond that it was disappointing.

As a result, there were no record distances or out-and-return records made. Dick Schreder, flying the HP-8, duplicated Harland Ross's feat of a year ago by setting three world records in less than a week's time. His records for single-place sailplanes were 100-kilometer triangle, 66.6 miles per hour; 200 kilometer triangle, 66.9 miles

1959 Technical Symposium

The joint SSA-IAS sessions that were held in the early 1950s had been discontinued owing to the limited interest and the lack of quality "papers." A renewed interest in the scientific and technical phases of soaring prompted the SSA to sponsor a Technical Symposium on September 12 at the IAS building in Los Angeles. Eight papers were presented, and it was hoped that this symposium would inspire others in SSA to do similar technical work and to prepare papers for future meetings.

Preparations for the 1960 World Soaring Championships

At the CVSM annual meeting held in Paris in March, Germany was chosen as the host country for the 1960 WSC. A few months later, the German Aero Club announced that the WSC would be held from May 19 to 29 at the Butzweilerhoff Airport in Cologne. There was no indication whether pilots could fly over the German frontier or whether blind flying would be allowed.

In October, Ivans reported on the pilot seeding for the 1960 WSC. The

Briegleb School lineup at El Mirage, California. Left to right: BG-8 two-place with Ken and Ross Briegleb; A TG-1A two-place; a BG-12; two modified PT-19 tow planes and a Piper tow plane.

(NSM Collection)

first five pilots seeded were R. H. Johnson, R. Schreder, P. F. Bikle, L. Maxey, and A. J. Smith. Since all were interested in competing, the team pilots were Johnson and Schreder, who chose to fly in the Open Class; and P. F. Bikle, who would fly Standard Class. Johnson was well along on his Adadtra sailplane and Schreder was rushing to complete the HP-9. Paul Bikle chose to fly a Schweizer 1-23H-15. The promise of MATS transportation made it possible to take American sailplanes along to the meet.

In a special meeting with Jacqueline Cochran, who was the NAA president-elect and also FAI president, help was requested in order to get MATS transportation from the U.S. team and its three sailplanes. She promised her assistance. Knowing of her ability to get things done in Washington, they were confident that she would be successful. Colonel Giblo was to be available to her to work out the details between the U.S. team and the Air Force.

NAA Support

Selvidge and Schweizer attended the NAA convention in Washington, D.C., in December. Discussions were held concerning cooperation between NAA's affiliated groups and the need for financial assistance for sending teams to international competitions. NAA believed that by presenting a united front it might be able to get more support. The NAA also explained its plan of having a Washington aviation center for the NAA and its affiliates.

Club Activity

The "West Words" column that Licher had started in 1956 was turned over to Bertha Ryan when Licher took over as executive secretary. Ryan was a former member of the MIT Glider Club and had migrated to California at the same time as Licher. In the September-October 1958 *Soaring*, the column name was changed to "Club News" to cover the entire country. This column reported on the growing activity of clubs, which then totaled 100.

Growth of Commercial Operators

Commercial operations were growing. The Briegleb Soaring School was expanding, and Gus Briegleb's two sons Ross and Ken were helping in the operation. In the August-September 1954 *Soaring*, it was reported that Les Arnold Enterprises had ordered a freight carload of seven sailplanes from SAC: "It is interesting to note that of the last 87 FAI badges issued in the U.S., 40 were earned in 1-26's and another 34 were earned in other Schweizer models. . . . Many of these badges are the result of commercial operations such as those conducted by Les Arnold and other Schweizer dealers. They are creating a new pool of soaring enthusiasts, ones that are buying sailplanes, as this shipment indicates."

W. E. "Tony" Doherty, a former World War II pilot, sailing enthusiast, and winemaker from Hammondsport, joined SAC in 1959 as sales manager and was responsible for SAC's sailplane sales and the dealer organization.

Regional and Other Contests

The year 1959 saw a twofold increase in the number of sanctioned contests held in comparison with 1958. In addition to the 12 sanctioned regional contests there also were a total of 16 other contests, including local and area contests as well as camps and get-togethers.

Promotion

The membership committee under Chairman Bob Moore, working with the SSA office, carried out a number of promotional programs during 1959 that helped the membership grow.

The booklet *Soaring in America* had been revised and reprinted and was effectively used to answer inquiries. An experimental classified ad program

in a selected number of aviation magazines was tried out with good results. One ad offered a sample copy of *Soaring* for 25¢.

Bob Buck, a Trans World Airlines captain, wrote an article in *Air Facts* magazine about transitioning to soaring. This was reprinted in the *Reader's Digest*. A similar article entitled "Transition to Soaring Flight" by *Chuck McKinnon*, corporate pilot for IBM, appeared in *Flying* magazine. Beside helping to draw in new members, these articles also gave soaring favorable national publicity.

The Start of the Soaring Sixties, 1960

In his January editorial entitled "The Soaring Sixties," Harner Selvidge commented:

> What of soaring in the sixties? . . . If this new era of greater prosperity and more leisure time . . . is actually realized, it cannot help but benefit the soaring movement. . . . From this point of view the prospects look rosy.
>
> The really clouded part . . . is the murky depth labeled "Government Regulations.". . . As the skies get more crowded with aircraft, we get closer to the time when "100% Positive Control" will be the battle-cry.
>
> It is imperative that we be prepared to speak in Washington with one strong united voice. . . . Here is one of the best arguments for a strong national Soaring Society to which everyone in soaring belongs.

Directors' Winter Meeting, 1960

A record 18 directors were present at the meeting on January 30–31 in Kansas City, Missouri. They were concerned about the problem of getting *Soaring* out on time. The hiring of an editor was considered, but it was agreed that the president should look into hiring a full-time assistant secretary so that between Licher and his assistant, the magazine should come out on time.

A proposal was made that the "A" and "B" badges be revived and awarded as a mark of progress in training. An ad hoc committee of J. Robertson, L. Arnold, and L. Licher were appointed to study this matter.

In his comments on the agenda Selvidge noted: "It has been suggested that the Standard Class concept, while laudable in purpose, has failed to achieve the goal for which it was intended. It has been suggested that we discontinue all Std Cl activities in the U.S. and concentrate on Open and One-class competition."

In his report for the meeting, Paul Bikle, chairman of the Rules subcommittee of the Contest Committee said: "The stated objective of a cheap, simple and easy-to-fly sailplane are not being accomplished by the present Std C. The imposition of large terminal velocity speed brakes, the prohibition of flaps for this purpose, the rule against radio, and the possibility of spending any amount of money and effort for structural and aerodynamic refinement do not make sense to many of the soaring people in this country. Instead, many feel a cheap, simple, easy-to-fly sailplane should be encouraged without trying to regulate the way in which this should be done. Others feel that Std Cl objectives should include a provision for a standard of performance which would permit pilots to compete on a more equal basis."

These two positions were a complete reversal from the position that the board had taken at the Bishop meeting 18 months earlier. A number of directors did not feel that there was enough difference in performance between the Open and Standard Class to warrant a separate competition, particularly since the U.S. Nationals were never filled to capacity. As a result, the majority felt there was no need to add another championship.

It was agreed that no gyro instruments would be allowed in sailplanes in the 1960 Nationals and that any sailplane entered should be flown by one pilot only, eliminating "teams" from competing. This action did not preclude carrying a passenger in a two-place ship. It was also agreed that the title of the national competition should be changed to "Annual U.S. National Soaring Championship."

Because of operating limitations at the Ector County Airport it was recommended that entries in the 1960 Nationals be limited to those holding a Silver badge with Gold "C" distance leg and that the previous year's ruling, which permitted qualification by placing first, second, or third in regional, be deleted.

Proposals on WSCS were submitted that (1) defined the team captain's responsibilities, (2) stipulated that American sailplanes should be used "if it is possible and reasonable to do so," and (3) approved a team oath similar to the Olympic oath. These proposals were passed unanimously.

Jacqueline Cochran was elected an honorary SSA member in view of her many services to the society.

Members' Reaction to Standard Class Changes

The directors' new position on the Standard Class generated many letters to the editor and considerable objections from the membership. Some felt that the SSA's position was short-

Dr. August "Gus" Raspet with some of his testing paraphernalia alongside the Kirby Kite sailplane that he used for carrying out his flight tests and experiments.
(Ross-Pix, SSA files)

sighted and that the small performance differences between Open and Standard Class sailplanes at that time were not a valid reason for not supporting it. It did not take into account the improved performance possible in the Open Class sailplanes, once designers concentrated on that challenge! Others objected to the new position because of the Standard Class success in the last WSC. In addition, Irv Prue felt that the change was unfair to those who had a Standard Class sailplane, were building one, or had ordered one!

SAC's position on this issue was explained in the May 1960 *Soaring:* "That the present Std Cl specifications are too broad for successful development of a class, and it would seem that these specifications must be tighter to avoid having the Std Cl gradually become very refined and expensive 15 meter super sailplanes. . . . It is difficult to try to control simplification and low cost in a design formula.

However, it is felt that the SSA, as a member of OSTIV, should take a more active interest in development of this Class and take the lead in working on changes to make the class more acceptable."

SAC decided to modify the 1-23H to meet the Standard Class requirement. It took a lot of engineering and flight testing to meet the dive-brake requirements. However, it succeeded, and Paul Bikle chose to fly the 1-23H-15 at the 1960 WSC.

Bernie Carris, SAC test pilot, carried out the dive tests on the dive brakes, as explained in the SAC Report in the May 1960 *Soaring:* "A very extensive flight test program has been carried out to determine the terminal velocity speed with the dive brakes open; as well as to incorporate changes to the dive brakes to reduce this terminal velocity speed to the desired limits and to meet the opening and closing standards as required by the FAI. We have found that it takes considerable practice and careful technique to be able to obtain terminal velocity and it requires 2,000 to 3,000 feet to stabilize out for the 1,000 meter vertical dive as required by the FAI."

The terminal speed with brakes out was around 15,000 feet per minute straight down—which was close to the speed at which a free body would fall. In the dives the pilot aimed at a point on the ground directly below and everything else rushed out radically as he approached the ground, and his field of vision decreased, giving the eerie sensation of a free fall.

Gus Raspet

On April 20, 1960, Gus Raspet had been making a test flight of a specially equipped airplane, and for some reason he stalled and was killed in the resulting crash. He had been the inspirational leader in improving the performance of aircraft and was one of the pioneers in getting laminar flow on sailplane wings.

The laboratories of the Mississippi State College, where Rapset was head of the Aerophysics Department, were later named in his honor.

In the August 1960 *Soaring*, Fred Matteson wrote a tribute to Raspet: "By honest dedicated work and unselfishly encouraging and helping his fellow man, he has earned for himself, for soaring and his country, a position of respect and honor in the world." In the same issue Ben Shupack stated: "The lift that Gus would give was fruitful in stimulating many a person to persist in his research. We lost so much when we lost Gus."

The Schweizers first met Gus when he came to Elmira with Ben Shupack before World War II. He and Ben Shupack were good friends and they seemed to energize each other with ideas and encouragement. One of Gus's first soaring projects was to develop a set of thermal sniffers that were installed on the wing tips of the Air-Hoppers 2-8. The meter in the cockpit indicated which way to turn to get to the thermal by sensing which wing tip was flying in the warmest air. At that time thermistors were not available and he had to use much less sensitive thermocouples. But that did not seem to be the problem. The tests showed that the air on a soaring day was so heterogeneous that the instrument often acted wildly and often called for turning in both directions at one time.

Gus always seemed to have an unlimited number of new ideas that he was eager to try. On one trip to Harris Hill Gus and Ben were studying the formation of thermals by blowing glycerine bubbles at the brow of Harris Hill, to the puzzlement of the onlookers.

Sometimes designers and engineers were annoyed with Gus's "redesigning" their sailplanes and his impatience with the more prosaic factors that engineers are faced with, such as costs, strength requirements, safety factors, FAA requirements, and the like, and they sometimes questioned his conclusions when they seemed to be arrived at with a minimum of testing. But no one questioned his brilliance and enthusiasm, his ability to stimulate others into action, and the impact that he had on the soaring movement.

1960 World Soaring Championships

Jacqueline Cochran made possible MATS transportation for 3 sailplanes and a team of 16 to the 1960 WSC, held from June 4 to 19 in Cologne, West Germany. The fund drive led by John Graves raised $8,500 and ensured that the team's basic costs would be covered. The U.S. team members were pilots Johnson, Schreder, and Bikle and respective crew chiefs Boone, A. J. Smith, and W. Coverdale. P. A. Schweizer was captain, J. Graves team manager, B. L. Wiggin meteorologist, and A. Dawydoff public relations. Other crew members were A. Johnson, J. D. Ryan, H. Stiglmeier, D. McNay, A. Schreder, I. O. Prue. Lt. Col. Floyd Sweet handled liaison with the U.S. Air Force and the German Aero Club.

Dick Johnson took his new ship, the Adastra, to Germany but Dick Schreder was not able to finish the

HP-9 in time and so took the HP-8. The team was met by Floyd and Frances Sweet at the Frankfurt Rhine-Main Airport, with three tow cars and an extra team car. The sailplanes were unloaded and trailed the next day to Butzweilerhof Airport in Cologne.

The U.S. and Finnish teams were about the first to arrive at Butzweilerhoff and over a friendly glass of beer, discussed soaring in the United States and Finland. Only a short time before, Gary Powers had been shot down in his U-2 over Russia. When one of the U.S. team asked whether they soared over the Russian border, the Finnish captain said: "No, we don't have a U-2." This type of good-natured ribbing was typical of the friendly relations between the teams.

Fifty-five sailplanes were entered—20 Open and 35 Standard

Class. The two new Polish Zefirs and the Phoenix seemed to be the ships to beat in the Open Class. In the Standard Class the new types were the Polish Foka and the Standard Austrias. The outstanding features of the meet were the large entry in the Standard Class, greater use of team flying, and "gnats," which played havoc with the performance of some of the laminar flow sailplanes. There was a full spectrum of weather, with fast-changing conditions from strong to light, local thunderstorms, and lots of haze. On days with light conditions, it was difficult for Schreder and Johnson to be competitive.

The WSC and the U.S. team made world news when on a goal flight to Fehmarn, an island off the northeast corner of Germany, Schreder got lost and landed in East Germany. To quote from the WSC report in the September 1960 *Soaring:*

> By 6 PM, everyone had reported in except Schreder. Johnson, along with 18 others, made the Island of Fehmarn. As time went on and still no report from Schreder, telephone conversation with Dick Johnson and Harold Jensen disclosed that Johnson had last seen Schreder approximately 30 miles from the Isle heading to the SE, toward some rows of clouds. Shortly thereafter Johnson received a call from Schreder, advising that he was over water and did not know whether he could make it back to land. Johnson tried to help Schreder orient himself and after a period of silence, Schreder called that he thought he could make it; and then complete silence. When those on the Island did not receive a further call and learned that Schreder had not reported in, they thought he might have ditched in the sea, and Gunter-Haase requested the German Navy to start searching the coast, and the general alarm went out to look for a ditched sailplane.

> As the evening wore on, everyone became more convinced that Schreder was lost in the water. About midnight a call came through that Kiel Radio which had a report from an East Germany Radio Station that a sailplane had landed in East Germany, but no mention made as to whether the pilot or his ship was all right. Request was made to Kiel Radio for clarification and immediate steps were started to get Schreder out. The American Embassy at Bonn, the Air Force at Wiesbaden and the organizers of the meet, were contacted and asked to investigate all possible ways of getting the pilot and sailplane from East Germany. The Embassy was most distressed about the problem because a few weeks earlier a C-47 had come down in almost the same spot. They suggested that since they have no direct diplomatic contact and that their efforts might take a week or ten days, a direct approach be made by having the crew appear on the border and ask to retrieve their pilot and sailplane. Next morning A. J. Smith and John Ryan appeared at the border of Lubeck and approximately 24 hours after landing, Schreder was back in West Germany. Dick had gotten confused as to his position because of the similarity of several bays and when he got out over water looking for Fehmarn he headed for the nearest land which turned out to be East Germany. He was under control of Russians almost the complete time and spent the night in jail. He was treated well and even given a shave. John Ryan's Mercedes attracted more interest than the HP-8.

This set a record for getting a U.S. airman out of East Germany, but the U.S. team unfortunately did not set any other records.

Rudolfo Hossinger of Argentina, flying a Skylark 3, was the winner of the Open Class; Edward Makula and Jerzy Popiel of Poland finished second and third in the Zefirs, and Johnson was 15th and Schreder was 16th. Everyone had expected the Hasse-Phoenix combination to finish at the top, but Hasse ended up in 9th place.

In the Standard Class, Heinz Huth of Germany was 1st in a Ka-6BR, George Munch of Brazil was 2d in a Ka-6B, and Adam Witek of Poland was third in the Foka. Bikle finished 12th. The report noted: "The Std Cl sailplane turned in the best performance on three days and equaled the Open Class on another. In fact, each of the top three Std Cl sailplanes earned more points than Hossinger. They flew the same courses and in many cases got less points because of the greater number of ships in this Class."

The Standard Class design contest was highlighted by the entry of the Polish Foka sailplane, which was not considered to be in the "spirit" of the Standard Class. Its reclining pilot position, low fuselage profile, rudimentary wheel, and generally sophisticated design were far from the basic Standard Class concept. The new Schleicher K-8 sailplane was entered and it was probably the closest to the original concept of this class. However, the jury overlooked this and chose the sleek Austria-Sl, although they privately admitted that the Foka was the outstanding sailplane. It was evident that the Standard Class was fast becoming a high-performance competition sailplane class that provided an appealing challenge for sailplane designers.

27th National, 1960

For the National held on August 2–11 at Odessa, Texas, Oatmar Schwarzenberger was competition director, Beaumont Cooley contest director, and Al Parker modestly called himself the assistant contest director.

The only new sailplanes of the 37 entered were Len Niemi's Sisu, George Tweed's GT-1, and P. A. Wills's Skylark 3F, which added an international flavor to the contest.

The weather was excellent, and 39,741 miles were flown on 7 contest days. Schreder was the winner in his HP-8 with six 1,000-point days and one 945-point day. On the third contest day he set a 338.5-mile out-and-return world record, which was equaled by A. J. Smith an hour later. B. Carris in the RJ-5 was second, A. J. Smith was third in his LO-150, Philip Wills

Richard H. Schreder and his wife "Angie"with the HP-8 on the ramp of the Butzweilerhoff Airport in Cologne, Germany, in 1960. Schreder and the HP-8 had just returned from East Germany, where he had been jailed overnight for an unauthorized landing.

(Schweizer Aircraft Corporation)

With a number of "no contest" days there was ample time for pilots and crew of the various teams to meet. On one occasion Ernst Haase, Schreder, and P. A. Schweizer had a conversation about the relative performance of the sailplanes in the competition. Haase said that he was obliged to fly the Phoenix but he felt he would have done much better with a Ka-6. No doubt, the Phoenix too was the victim of overoptimism that is often present when a new sailplane first appears. Sometimes the "bugs" are worked out and the sailplane will reach its promised performance, but in many cases, as in that of the Phoenix, it is just another step forward in the evolution of sailplane design and construction.

fourth in his Skylark 3F, and Kit Drew fifth in a Ka-6B. Kit Drew had the highest points of the Standard Class sailplanes entered, with Rudy Allemann second. Schreder, in doing a high speed run at the air show developed tail surface flutter. Fortunately, he was able to slow the HP-8 down and land.

Many pilots and crews came to his aid that night, so he was again ready to fly the next day. After this scare, many felt that it was an imposition to expect the contestants to be part of an air show.

Directors' Summer Meeting, 1960

The treasurer's report at the August 12 meeting in Odessa showed that the SSA was still not breaking even. Ways to increase income and to reduce costs were discussed, including the possibility of increasing membership cost, eliminating the directory, and getting more grants to support the ASH Project. A special committee chaired by Ivans with Starr, Briegleb, and Bikle as members was formed to investigate ways to increase income and to streamline the SSA office.

As a result of many objections from the membership it was decided to delay making recommendations to the FAA that would have required licensed instructors to sign off students for solo. FAA had disclosed that it was not planning any changes at that time. The directors felt, however, that the commercial glider rating requirements were not in keeping with the privileges and responsibilities of the rating and that the requirement of 10 glider flights for an additional category rating was inadequate. The SSA Airmen Rule Subcommittee was directed to study the commercial gliding rating, and Lin

Bachtell was appointed chairman of an ad hoc committee to study an SSA instructor rating.

The Schweizer Soaring School also felt that the FAA minimum requirements were too low and had set higher requirements and more flights for its courses. SAC also encouraged its dealers to use these higher requirements. Most commercial operators were not opposed to having instructor ratings. It was the clubs that objected most, since their "instructors" were volunteers, many of whom did not want to have to get a new rating in order to continue to "instruct."

The nomination committee reported that it had no candidate for president. Paul Bikle was nominated, but wanted time to think it over before accepting. He later accepted the nomination and was elected president. Bachtell and Ivans were elected east and west vice-presidents, Robertson and Bertha Ryan were reelected secretary and treasurer. Jacqueline Cochran had been trying to have all the world's flying championships in the United States for 1962, including the WSCs but the board decided that the SSA was not financially ready for this.

The board recommended to the FAI that in future WSCs the Standard Class fly the same tasks and be scored together with the Open Class, and that only one champion be named, whichever class of sailplane that he flew, but that the highest Standard Class finisher be recognized. Also, it was suggested that radios be permitted.

The board agreed that air shows at Nationals should be discouraged, that Gold "C" distance leg requirement for entry should continue, and that competitors in Nationals should be required to attempt the task of the day.

The directors agreed to officially notify the FAA that they objected to the draft release proposing that the base of the continental control area be lowered from 24,000 to 14,500 feet.

First SAC Dealer Meeting

The first SAC dealer meeting was held at the SAC plant in December 1960. Many of the dealers combined pickup trips for new sailplanes to help defray the cost of attending. Of the 17 dealers, 10 had operating schools and the balance planned to start their operations in 1961. All dealers reported that the majority of their students were power pilots transitioning to gliders, and the challenge was to keep them active in the sport.

Philosophy of Soaring

Most soaring pilots have thought about why they soar and what it means to them, but few ever put it into words. Jack Lambie was one of the exceptions. His article, "The Natural Philosophy of Soaring," which appeared in the May 1960 *Soaring*, gives some basic reasons that most soaring pilots would agree with: "Now we engage in quite complex activities, i.e., soaring in which the purpose and meaning are very elusive. These meanings come to be understood when we see that they are of the highest of man's aspirations. They have no practical end, but enable man to experience his world around him more deeply. Attaining this type of awareness is probably the most ultimate drive of man. For the soaring enthusiasts, the measure of these satisfactions is very high indeed in flying motorless aircraft and all that this involves."

44 Exciting Months

Selvidge ended his two-year term as president with an editorial that summed up the 44 months since the SSA board had hired Lloyd Licher. The SSA had continued to grow at a good rate, and by the end of 1960 there were 37 chapters. The 2,000th "C" award had been earned and the soaring activity had increased in many ways.

Selvidge had been a very active president and he played an important part in the growth of SSA. The demands of his new position as vice-president and general manager of Meteorology Research, Inc., the company that Paul MacCready had formed, prevented him from continuing to be as active as he had been in the past.

More Publicity for Soaring, 1961

P. Bikle's "A Message from the President" in the January 1961 *Soaring* explains why he accepted the presidency.

> The Soaring Society has been most fortunate in having been able to find able leaders who have also been in a position to contribute generously of their own time and office or secretarial support in carrying on the business of the Society. Until very recently the conduct of our business was completely dependent on such volunteer effort and contributions. It was recognized that this situation severely restricted the number of capable soaring enthusiasts who might be considered for the Presidency of the Society. . . . I have neither the office resources nor the desire to continue this pattern. Instead, I intend to depend entirely on the efforts of Lloyd Licher and his small staff, the Directors and the Committee Chairmen, doing only those

things myself which the President must do.

It appears that renewed efforts to increase our membership along with a limited curtailment of services and a greater dependence on the SSA working committees should permit us to continue *Soaring* on a monthly basis and reach a balanced operating budget within the next two years.

1961 National Contest Dates

Wichita Municipal Airport, Kansas, was chosen as the site of the 1961 National Soaring Contest. This was the first break in the tradition, which had begun, in 1947, of alternating the nationals between Elmira and other sites in the United States and was due to the growing number of groups that were interested in conducting national contests.

The Elmira Area Soaring Corp. could understand the appeal of the stronger conditions in the West, but it believed that the varied soaring conditions in the East provided more competitive meets and a better way of choosing pilots for the international team when the WSCs were to be held in Europe. The EASC accepted the challenge and would work to improve the Harris Hill field and facilities so that they would continue to attract Nationals. The community was proud of its 27 years of supporting soaring and would continue to do so.

Directors' Winter Meeting, 1961

At the January 28–29 meeting in Dallas the treasurer reported that deficit operations were continuing, but that a balanced budget could be expected for 1962. An NAA divisional agreement with SSA was approved that provided for the NAA to have a director on the SSA board.

Ivans was appointed the U.S. representative at the CVSM to replace Captain Barnaby, who had resigned. Ivans reported on the CVSM meeting held in Paris in November and stated that the SSA proposal on Standard Class would have a better chance of passing if provisions were included for a world Standard Class champion. The board approved this change. There was continued pressure from Jacqueline Cochran to hold the WSC in the United States in 1962, but the directors did not think they could submit a bid unless they had the guarantee of financial support.

The directors accepted the contest board's proposal for permanent contest numbers for sailplanes. It was also decided that gyros would be prohibited in sailplanes competing in the national contest.

The board reviewed Lloyd Licher's performance and was well satisfied with the job he was doing and authorized a 10 percent increase in salary.

Changes in FAA Regulations

The FAA announced that the floor of the continental control area was to be lowered from 24,000 to 14,500 feet effective April 6, 1961. The FAA also announced that a glider pilot holding a limited flight instructor certificate need not wait a year before becoming eligible to receive a flight instructor certificate. He must still, however, have trained at least five successful candidates for pilots' certificates.

Two New World Records

On February 25, 1961, Paul Bikle set two world records. Taking off from Fox Airport near his home, he reached an absolute altitude of 46,267 feet and made an altitude gain of 42,300 feet. The flight was made in the lee of the Sierra-Nevada mountain range between Mohave and Inyokern, California. He used his 1-23E, which was equipped with a low-pressure oxygen system and a pressure demand mask. This flight was at the upper limit of altitude possible without a pressure suit or cabin pressure and so the record would stand for a long time.

As of May 1, 1961, the standings in the world record showed the United States in the lead with 10 records, Russia and Poland tied for second with 6 each, Great Britain next with 5, France 2, and Yugoslavia 1. Bikle won the Lilienthal medal in 1962 for this flight.

Flight Level 460! Paul Bikle's world altitude record flight made on February 25, 1961. This is the first of a series of commemorative paintings by Mike Machet of great soaring events that are available as limited edition lithograph prints.

(Mike Machet)

1961 Membership Contest

A membership contest was held from February 1 to March 31, 1961. Various items of soaring merchandise valued at about $750 were given as prizes. EMGAM was again used as the code word for the contest, which brought in 185 new members at an actual cost of only $200, since most of the prizes were donated.

New Sailplanes

Leonard Niemi had formed Arlington Aircraft Co. to produce the Sisu-1A. The prototype had been flying for two years. Flight tests were conducted by Dick Johnson and were reported in the March 1961 *Soaring*, one of the first Johnson sailplane performance reports.

Dick Schreder announced his fourth sailplane design, the HP-10, in the same issue of *Soaring*. This design made available an all-metal, low-priced, high-performance kit sailplane that Schreder felt could be assembled

in 300 hours. A bonded honeycomb sandwich panel was used as the main stress-carrying unit of the wing, and a rectangular plan form was used to reduce the number of different parts required. It did not meet Standard Class requirements, however, because of its use of flaps, but Schreder had asked CVSM to approve flaps for this class.

Meanwhile, SAC was proceeding with the prototype 2-32, a two-place high-performance sailplane. Although this started out as a more moderate-performance sailplane, the decision was made to go for higher performance. The prototype was to be flown sometime that year.

SAC Report

SAC again presented an annual report of its soaring program in the May 1961 *Soaring*:

> For a country of our size, soaring still is woefully small, and there is a great deal of misinformation to correct. The average person still associates

President Paul Bikle with SSA board members at the directors' meeting at Wichita, Kansas, at the end of the 1961 National. Bottom, left to right: H. Selvidge, W. S. Ivans, H. Ross, F. B. Compton, and J. D. Ryan. Top, left to right: P. A. Schweizer, E. J. Reeves, W. G. Briegleb, L. Bachtell, W. Coverdale, O. Zauner, P. F. Bikle, T. Page, J. Nowak, B. Cohen, and R. L. Moore.

(SSA files)

soaring with windy days and frail contraptions flown by crackpots or daredevils. Typical of this is the paragraph in the book, "Government by the People" by Burns and Peltas, where they discuss the United States as a nation of "joiners" and give a typical list of "oddball" organizations that include such names as American Sunbathers' Association, Blizzard Men of 1888, American Hackney Horse Association and—you guessed it—the Soaring Society of America.

It seems to us that there is an overwhelming number of reasons for building up the soaring movement in this country. Bob Moore, in his editorial in the Feb 1961 issue of *Soaring*, gives many reasons for this. Certainly, a national soaring movement that is too small even to make it economically practical to publish a soaring book has need of growth.

Pilots should work to better the maximum performance possible with the ships they now have, instead of dreaming of the super-ship and not even trying with their present sailplanes. The limiting factor is usually the pilot rather than the performance of the ship. It is a matter of getting experience, and the only way that this can be done is to do a lot of flying. In order to encourage this, Schweizer Aircraft Corp. is offering $1,000 in barographs and other soaring merchandise prizes for best flights made during the year in 2-22's and 1-26's at other than meets or contests.

28th National, 1961

The Kansas Soaring Association conducted the 28th National at the active Wichita Municipal Airport from August 1 to 10, 1961. The airplane and sailplane operations were carried out simultaneously, each using a different runway. This was possible through the cooperation of the FAA, the tower officials, tow pilots, and competition pilots. The timing of the contest was set for the period when Cessna Aircraft was shut down for its summer vacation, since Cessna had made available its company planes for use as tow planes.

Thirty-six pilots entered, including three previous champions. Sailplanes at a National for the first time were the Prue Standard, the HP-10, the Adastra, and the Ka-8B.

Helen Navoy, scorer for the championships, wrote the contest report for *Soaring*:

The 28th National . . . came to a dramatic close on Aug 10th when Andrew J. Smith of Tecumseh MI, and flying a *LO-150* sailplane, shot up from 3rd place to win the Championship from 35 other contenders in a last task upset of the scores and standings. William S. Ivans, Jr. of San Diego CA, flying a borrowed *Skylark 3D*, accomplished a similar feat by moving up from 5th place to 2nd place on the final day.

Dick Schreder, who was in 1st place in his *HP-10*, and John Ryan in 2nd place in his *Sisu*, tumbled to 9th and 8th place on the final day. The task of the day was a downwind goal race to Salina KA, 80.9 miles to the North. A weak dry front lay just south of the goal and as the day progressed the front moved south creating a dead area over the last portion of the course. Only 13 pilots were able to make the goal and it was significant that the 13 who had completed the task landed within 36 minutes of one another. They had used the last thermal that got them high enough so they could glide to the goal. . . . It was a very competitive and well run contest, under Marshall Claybourn, the Contest Manager and E. J. Reeves, the Competition Director.

Directors' Summer Meeting, 1961

During the August 11 meeting in Wichita, E. J. Reeves reported that Charles Abel was making good progress on the Diamond "C" and Gold "C" award plaques for the Smithsonian Institution. Good progress was also reported on the ABC and Integrated Training Program that was being developed. Bachtell reported that he had obtained a ruling from FAA that glider flight test examiners would be appointed where needed upon the recommendation of the local SSA director.

Paul Bikle was reelected president and Tom Page and John Ryan were elected east and west vice-presidents. Bertha Ryan and Joe Robertson were elected treasurer and secretary.

1961 SSA Technical Symposium

A Technical Symposium was held in Los Angeles on September 16 and was organized by Fred Matteson. It was well attended and the nine papers read were to be printed in *Soaring* to keep the SSA membership informed.

CVSM Developments

Bill Ivans reported on the April 15 CVSM meeting:

> No satisfactory bids for the 1962 Championships had been received by the Committee, although Argentina, Italy, Switzerland, and the U.S.A. indicated continued interest. . . . A decision was made to postpone the Championships until 1963.
>
> The SSA had proposed combining the STd and Open Cl contestants in World Championships in order to provide direct comparison of performance and an opportunity for a Std Cl pilot to win both Standard and Open Championships. . . . The final outcome was a vote to strongly recommend to future organizers of championships that equal starting opportunities and identical tasks continue to be granted the two classes.

At the November 23 meeting, the CVSM chose Argentina as the site of the February 1963 World Soaring Championship. Argentina and the United States were the only bidders, but Argentina offered zero cost competition from the moment the teams arrived in Buenos Aires, and the Argentina Aero Club agreed to assume 30–50 percent of all transportation costs. In addition, 27 sailplanes were available for loan, the only charge being $100 each for insurance. The U.S. bid, which included a $400 entry fee, was no match for the Argentina bid. It was obvious that the cost to the teams played an important role in the decision.

To eliminate the entry of exotic prototypes in the WSC Standard Class, a CVSM delegate proposed placing limits on cost, selling price or fabrica-

Alex Dawydoff, SSA governor southern New York, presents Robert Fisher of Moses Lake, Washington, an award for becoming the first man to soar across the country in a sailplane.

(NSM Collection)

tion time, or requiring the prior sale and delivery of at least 10 identical sailplanes at fixed published price. It was pointed out that any new changes would not be effective until an appropriate waiting period had expired so as to avoid problems for those who had new designs under way. This latter point made it very unlikely that any major changes would ever occur.

Promotion and Publicity

One of the reasons for the steady growth of soaring was the increasingly favorable publicity that it was receiving. During 1961 soaring articles appeared in *Sports Aviation*, *Scientific American*, *Flying*, *Aviation Week*, *AOPA Pilot*, *Sports Illustrated*, and *Air Facts*.

Bob Fisher's coast-to-coast flight received wide coverage as he worked his way across the country. Starting near Seattle, Washington, he flew as far as he could each day, and then backtracked to the nearest airport for another takeoff the next day.

It took him 29 hops and 59 days to get across the country. He ended

his flight at Zahn's Airport in Long Island, the first person to really soar across the United States!

Both SSA and SAC had modest national advertising programs in some of the aviation magazines. SSA advertised a copy of the *Soaring* information kit for 35¢. SAC offered an information kit for $1, which included an SAC booklet on how to get into soaring and a copy of *Soaring* magazine.

In 1961 Dick Huppertz produced the film *Sky Sailing* for SAC. It showed what soaring was all about. Over 100 copies were purchased by SAC dealers, film libraries, and clubs.

Getting publicity for soaring sometimes had its problems. The Long Island Soaring Association was proud of the progress that it was making in soaring over the island. On a particularly good soaring day, they had a record number of club sailplanes in one thermal over the field. Rolf Bahrenberg thought that this was an ideal time to get a reporter from the local newspaper to come to the field to see what soaring was all about. He called the newspaper and told them about the record number of sailplanes spiraling together in a thermal overhead, with some of them almost touching. The reporter thought a moment, and then said that when two of them touched they should give him a call!

Chapter 9

The SSA Organization Expands, 1962–1966

The Beginning of the ABC Program, 1962

It has always been the aim of the SSA presidents to get SSA members more involved in carrying out the work of the organization. This voluntary work was necessary if SSA was to exist at its low membership rates. Bikle's report for 1961 in the December *Soaring* encouraged this trend:

> The bulk of the work of the Society is performed by our Executive Secretary and his small, paid staff. A great deal of Society work is also performed by the Officers of the Society and by the various working committees.
>
> Everything considered, 1961 has been a good year. Growth in membership (to 2,750 voting members) has been accompanied by increased soaring activity. Nearly 400 "C" pins and over 90 Silver badges have been earned in the past 12 months. Much of this healthy soaring activity results from the greatly increasing business experienced by the commercial operators in the past year. More new sailplanes have been registered than ever before.

Directors' Winter Meeting, 1962

With the tight financial position of SSA it was suggested at the meeting in Scottsdale, Arizona, on January 22–23, 1962, that chapter rebates be eliminated, but Licher felt strongly that rebates were worthwhile and that he would expect a 20 percent reduction in membership if they were eliminated.

F. J. Sweet was authorized to proceed with a marker at Kitty Hawk to commemorate the first glider flight by the Wrights in 1901.

Attempts to interest CAP in using gliders in its cadet program were ineffective, and no further action was to be taken unless CAP showed more interest.

Joe Lincoln had written the directors expressing concern that only one chapter of the ASH had been printed in the three years since the project had been authorized. At that rate, he said, it would take another 40 years to complete the series. Selvidge reported that nine chapters were in the works and that eight were scheduled for publication during 1962.

Adrian (Michigan), Elmira, and El Mirage bid for the 1962 Nationals and a runoff vote was required since none of the three had had a majority on the first vote. El Mirage was the runoff winner. Voting in the future would be by a preferential ballot.

Compton had proposed a national open contest on one coast and a national class contest (handicapped) on the other. There was little enthusiasm for a handicapped contest, but it was agreed that regional contests should be encouraged. Ivans was directed to set up proposed criteria for regional contests for the board to consider at the next meeting.

Ivans recommended that the SSA should make no regulations that modify, change, or infringe on the regulatory area, as prescribed by the FAA. In particular, the prohibition against gyro instruments during the contest should be removed. He felt that by requiring modifications to certain CARs, SSA was doing two things: (1) assuming the responsibility for the deviation and being prepared to enforce them, and (2) leaving itself open for civil action if damage or injury resulted while following the SSA-imposed deviation. A motion to remove the contest rule prohibiting gyro instruments in sailplanes passed with five dissenting votes.

The Safety and Flight Operation Committee recommended the ABC Program. This was adopted and was to begin by June 1, 1962, on the condition that someone was found to administer the program since Robertson had to resign as chairman.

Ivans recommended two changes in the method of selecting the U.S. soaring team for the WSCs, which were accepted. The team would be chosen as in the past, except that every pilot's lowest score would be removed to eliminate any grudge factors, and a screening committee of competitive pilots would examine the results for possible "weighting" and would recommend the acceptance or alteration to the president.

The question of whether or not the then-current national champion should automatically be on the team was raised and it was decided to change the policy so that he would not be automatically on the team. For the first time, the directors voted unanimously to send a team to the WSC.

F. J. Sweet was appointed chair-

man of the Award Committee on November 10, 1961 and submitted a procedure for obtaining nominations and selecting the winners. The board approved Selvidge's proposed format for presenting the awards at the end of the Nationals. It was also decided to award the Hall of Fame Certificate at some other, more appropriate, time.

A major discussion was held on the FAA's proposal to require a Class III physical for glider pilots. The Safety Committee reported there was no basis for this change in the experience of the last few years. In fact, in several accidents in which a health problem was involved, pilots had had a medical certificate. The majority were willing to accept the requirements of a Class III physical for the private, commercial, and instructor's ratings, but not for students.

The directors were under pressure from the membership to object to the FAA's proposal for Class III physicals for glider pilots. The directors knew that the FAA might insist on physicals and so the majority felt that a compromise proposal was in order.

The main concern of many directors, as well as SAC and its dealers, was that physicals would make it more complicated to get into soaring. Also, not being able to solo without a physical would discourage students right at the time when they would be ready to experience the real thrill—their first solo soaring flight.

The directors felt that not requiring a physical until students were ready for license was not much of a concession for FAA to make, since the students would only be flying dual with an instructor or solo. This would give them ample time to be exposed to soaring and become captivated so that the need for a physical would not discourage them from continuing.

It was agreed that the SSA recommend to FAA that commercial pilots be permitted to instruct if they met the full commercial pilot requirements.

The directors also recommended that someone be appointed as a liaison between the FAA and SSA in Washington, D.C. The board also set up the requirements for glider examiner so that the directors would have a standard for recommending instructors for this position to the FAA.

The ABC Program

Robertson's final report on the ABC program in the May 1962 *Soaring* included the following comments:

> It was decided to use the A B & C Badges as incentive along the path to a FAA Private Glider Pilot Certificate or equivalent. The training program itself was to be published as a chapter to the American Soaring Handbook. . . .
>
> The A Badge is gained when the student solos, the B Badge when the FAA private Glider Pilot Certificate has been gained, and the C Badge for the first solo soaring flight. . . . The operation of the entire program will depend on the availability of qualified and enthusiastic instructors.

Robert Forker, the new chairman of the Flight Training Committee, gave a detailed description of the program in the following issue of *Soaring* and solicited applications for SSA instructors from the clubs and schools.

Heli-Soar HP-10

In early 1961, Steve du Pont, a cousin of Dick du Pont, formed the Heli-Soar Corporation in Danbury, Connecticut. He purchased the manufacturing rights of the HP-10 from Schreder and carried out redesign work for produc-

Joe Robertson, left, head of the ABC Program, with Lloyd Licher in front of the Canadian-registered Ka-6BR sailplane.

(George Uveges)

tion and the type certificate. In the April 1962 issue of *Soaring* an ad announced that the HP-10 and HP-10 kits were now available.

New Sailplanes

Other new sailplanes being built included Schreder's new HP-11, which he planned to have ready for the 1962 Nationals.

Ray Parker was working on his new design, called the "T" Bird, which featured a "T" tail. Parker based this design on the experience he gained in improving the Tiny Mite.

Dick Johnson had made major improvements to his Adastra by modifying the rear portion of his wing and

A Schreder HP-11 being taken to the starting line. Cumulus and lenticular clouds indicate that thermal and wave lift are present in the area.

(George Uveges)

replacing the "T" tail with a conventional tail. This saved about 125 pounds in weight and he expected that the improved wing and lighter weight would enable him to achieve his expected performance.

SAC reported that the 2-32 would be flying by summer. One unusual feature that aroused considerable interest was the rear seat, which provided enough room for two 150-pound passengers.

FAA Developments

The FAA *Glider Criteria Handbook* was issued in 1961. This 139-page booklet became the U.S. sailplane designers' bible.

In Paul Bikle's letter to the FAA regarding Class III physical for glider pilots, he explained that the majority of SSA members felt that there was no need for this requirement, since past experience did not justify it. He also explained that the directors, in trying to be objective about the matter, indicated that the Class III physical would be acceptable for the glider private, commercial, and instructor ratings, but not for the student pilot.

A Schweizer Aircraft Report

Another yearly report of SAC activity appeared in the April 1962 issue of *Soaring*. SAC reported a combined sale of over 100 sailplanes and kits during 1961:

> Our "Best Flight Contest" was carried out last year to encourage cross-country flying in our 2-22 and 1-26 sailplanes. It got off to a good start last spring, in fact, too good. Lt. Roemer flew a 1-26 for 373 miles, and Al Parker flew his 2-22 196 miles. Apparently, the publicity of such good flights at the early part of the season discouraged many from trying. . . .
>
> A special prize was given to Jim Hard of Richland, WA for his outstanding flights in his 1-19. He already has earned his Silver C and has vowed he will get his Gold C in this utility glider. This is the type of flying we had hoped the contest would stimulate. . . . There is no substitute for "sweating out" a weak thermal in a moderate performance sailplane as a means of improving soaring technique. Then, when they have served their apprenticeships, they are ready for a step up to a higher performance ship, and they will be better prepared to make the most of it.
>
> We had another CAP-Air Scout encampment at Elmira during the summer. . . . It is regrettable that so little support is given to help young people to get into soaring. We have found that they are willing to work for it, but they do have to be subsidized to some degree. It would seem that each soaring activity should assist at least a few of its area's most deserving youth to get started in soaring.
>
> We expect the soaring growth rate to increase. We feel that the commercial sailplane operators can play an increasing important part in helping soaring to expand around the country.

Long-Range Planning

Bill Coverdale, chairman of the SSA Long-Range Planning Committee, reported in the April 1962 *Soaring* that, if the present $10 membership fee was to be retained, additional income was needed to balance the budget and take care of inflation. He suggested three methods for raising funds: (1) get more members to switch to life memberships, (2) ask for contributions on the membership renewal blank, and (3) encourage members to include the SSA in their estate planning.

CVSM Meeting, 1962

W. S. Ivans and P. A. Schweizer were the U.S. delegates to the CVSM meeting in Paris on June 22–23, 1962. Garay Sanchaz, Argentina's air attaché assured CVSM that recent changes in Argentina's political and financial situation would enable the WSC to be carried out as planned. The Argentina Aero Club would subsidize round-trip fares for sailplanes and personnel. Entries were expected to be limited to three sailplanes, not more than two in either class. Some eyebrows were raised when they reported that all sailplanes were to be retrieved by aero tow, using mirror signals to get the tow pilot's attention.

Ray Parker with the Screamin Weiner points out a sailplane to a spectator.
(SSA files)

Top: J. Ryan and his Sisu in which he won the 1962 National.

(Ken Shake)

The Flying Gehrleins, left to right, Cindy, Rodney, Jay, Larry, Jr., Gracie, and Larry, Sr., in front of their 1-19.

(NSM Collection)

Phillip Wills of the United Kingdom reported that the United Kingdom had worked out its airspace problem so that there were few restrictions for sailplanes. He recommended that other aero clubs use the same approach to their air traffic control authorities.

The balance of the meeting was concerned with revisions to the sporting code.

29th National, 1962

Thirty-three pilots started the contest at El Mirage, which ran from July 24 to August 2. It was sponsored by the Victorville Chamber of Commerce with support from the Douglas Soaring Club, the Antelope Club, and the SCSA. Othmar Schwarzenberger was competition director and Victor Saudek and Jack Wolfe contest managers.

Excellent weather prevailed for four distance tasks and four speed tasks; there were two welcomed rest days. Over 41,000 cross-country miles were flown, for an average of about 170 miles per ship per day.

It was a very competitive meet, and on the next to last day six ships theoretically had a chance of winning. John D. Ryan, flying a Sisu-1 sailplane, was the winner with Dick Johnson second in the Adastra, 17 points behind. Dick Schreder was third in the HP-11, Carlton Mears was fourth in a Prue Standard, and Paul Bikle fifth in a Prue Standard. There was no separate ranking or prizes given for the 10 Standard Class ships entered.

The new sailplane types at the National included the HP-11, the "T" bird, the Adastra, Vern Oldershaw's 0-2, Vernon Hutchinson's H-127, and Rene Comte's Elfe PM-3.

The complaint heard most often was that there was too much flying. Some thought this was because the average pilot age was 46 years!

Directors' Summer Meeting, 1962

Bikle reported no further developments by FAA on physicals, since the FAA medical office was being moved to Oklahoma City.

It decided that the team captain for the WSC should be selected by the board instead of the team pilots. P. A. Schweizer was elected team captain for the 1963 WSC.

Ivans presented a proposal for regional contests that was approved with minor modifications.

The officers elected for 1963 were W. S. Ivans, president; Nelson J. McLeod and John Ryan, East and West Coast vice-presidents, respectively; J. Robertson, secretary; and Lt. Cmdr. T. E. Sharp, treasurer.

Two New World Records

George B. Moffat, a sailing enthusiast from New Jersey who now owned the HP-8, came back to El Mirage to try to set some records. He felt that the conditions there were much superior to those in Marfa, Texas, where he had been trying for records before the National. He was successful in setting two world records, the 100-kilometer triangle at 79.77 miles per hour on August 16, and the 300-kilometer triangle at 67.18 miles per hour on August 19. After these flights the United States led in the number of worlds records held with 11, Poland was second with 7, and Russia third with 5.

The Gehrlein Winch

Larry Gehrlein, a welder from Erie, Pennslyvania, had started soaring in 1950 with his family and they became known as "the Flying Gehrleins." They established the "Thermal G. Ranch Gliderport" where they used 100 percent winch launching.

Gehrlein provided winches for the Air Force Academy and for the Indonesia Air Force. This improved winch, which he described in the August 1962 Soaring, was available in kit form, and Gehrlein's offer was that he would teach one operator, free of charge, with the purchase of each kit.

Larry Gehrlein's interest in soaring started back in 1929 when he attended the glider meet at the National Air Race in Cleveland, Ohio. Having

Irv Prue, designer and builder of the Prue line of sailplanes, stands by the Super Standard sailplane after its first flight.

(George Uveges)

almost no money, he slept that night in the shelter of a roadside sign. He then started a glider, but never finished it. By 1950 he and his family were all involved in soaring. At the Thermal G. Ranch, Larry had a World War II Link trainer rigged up so that he could give instruction in centering thermals. He generously built the special trailers for two of the U.S. sailplanes used in the WSC in Spain. As an SAC dealer he would challenge a customer to a ping pong game to see how much discount the customer could earn on a needed item if he beat Larry. He has been the perennial SSA governor for western Pennsylvania.

Smithsonian Plaques

On October 24, 1962, Smithsonian Institution accepted two plaques from the SSA that were to be displayed in the National Air Museum. These plaques, which would be updated each year, listed the U.S. soaring pilots who had earned the Gold C and Diamond soaring badges.

Phillip S. Hopkins, director of the museum, introduced the distinguished guests, among them, Jacqueline Cochran, Helen Barringer Shober, and Joe Walker of NASA. The soaring notables

present included Ralph S. Barnaby, Dr. Klemperer, Earl Southee, and many of the past and present SSA officers and directors. Dr. Klemperer gave the presentation address.

The plaques were given by an anonymous donor. Selvidge initiated the project and it was carried out by C. F. Abel and E. J. Reeves.

After the presentation and the renewal of many old soaring friendships, guests toured the old National Air Museum. The SSA officers and directors were then invited to the Sweets' home in McLean, Virginia, for dinner with Klemperer and Barnaby, the guests of honor.

On the way there, one group drove past the White House. It was in the early evening and the brightly lighted White House shone through the hazy fall evening and one wondered what might be going on there.

When they arrived at the Sweets, it was not very long before they were watching President Kennedy make his "Cuban Missile" crisis broadcast from the White House.

The 1963 U.S. Soaring Team

At the top of the seeding list for the 1963 WSC were (1) R. Johnson, (2) R. Schreder, (3) J. Ryan, (4) P. Bikle, (5) A. J. Smith, and (6) G. Thomson. The first three pilots were eager to go and Johnson planned to fly his Adastra, Schreder chose to fly his HP-11, both in the Open Class, and Ryan would fly a new Prue Super Standard in the Standard Class.

The team captain and the pilots chose the crew. The crew chiefs were A. J. Johnson, I. Prue, and G. Abels. Additional crew included R. D. Smith, R. Klemmedson, A. Schreder, W. Coverdale, J. D. Robertson, and

C. R. Doty. The team manager was H. Whitney and the team meteorologist H. Klieforth.

Growth of Cross-Country Flying, 1963

With the growth of soaring, more pilots were going out after Silver "C," Gold "C," and Diamond badge legs. These flights and record attempts, plus the increased number of contests, led to a large increase in cross-country activity. That year would see the continued growth of distance flying, including many outstanding flights.

Financial Problems

Ivan started his presidency with a "Message from the President" in the January 1963 *Soaring*.

> A major problem which will confront Directors is the financial stability of the Society. . . . Directors will be faced with the choice of cutting expenses by curtailing specific services, or raising income by charging more for these services. Happily, our steady growth in membership, nearly one additional member per day, net, offers the hope that the large fixed costs of maintaining a basic staff and publishing a monthly magazine will eventually be spread over a much wider membership base than at present.

Directors' Winter Meeting, 1963

The SSA's financial problems were the topic of discussion at the January 12–13 meeting in Chicago. Some directors favored an immediate increase in membership rates, which had not been increased in nine years. Others felt that operating costs had to be cut to bring the budget in line. The majority,

encouraged by the steady growth in membership, voted to keep the present rate for the immediate future.

P. A. Schweizer reported on the preparations for sending the U.S. team to Argentina, noting that the budget had been cut to $7,500 since the NAA had arranged MATS transportation for the team and three sailplanes.

J. Ryan, chairman of the Governmental Rules and Regulations Committee, reported that the FAA had lowered the floor of the area of positive control to 18,000 feet. The board decided to request exceptions in areas that are used for wave soaring. He reported that the FAA was preparing a draft that would require that glider flight instruction be provided by instructors only. SSA decided to ask FAA for a liberal "grandfather" clause to permit active commercial glider pilots to be able to continue to instruct.

As a result of a number of accidents in which the strength of the towline was a factor, the FAA was proposing that weak links be required for towlines.

Ivans reported that Elmira had been chosen for the 1963 Nationals, and foreign pilots were to be invited to fly in this meet.

It was decided to raise the entry fee for the Nationals to $100. In addition, it was proposed that the U.S. team Standard Class pilots be picked from the top Standard Class finishers in the National. This move was defeated, and instead it was decided that the Standard Class should be encouraged in the Nationals and the score should be listed separately in order to give more emphasis to that class. A suitable Standard Class trophy was to be procured.

It was decided to raise the subscription price for *Soaring* magazine to $5 per year for domestic and foreign

The Air Force C-124 transport plane disgorges its cargo of three sailplanes and trailers and the U.S. team of 15 at the Buenos Aires Airport, Argentina.

(P.A. Schweizer)

subscribers and that the cover price be raised to 50¢.

Dale May recommended in his membership committee report that Alex Aldott be the SSA's official photographer at the 1963 Nationals. Aldott had provided SSA with a set of mounted photos for a travel display, which were exhibited at the directors' meeting.

The 1963 World Soaring Championships

The ninth WSC took place on February 10–24 at the Laguna de Gomez Airport in Junin, Argentina. Thirty-three countries entered 38 pilots in the Standard Class and 25 in the Open Class. The U.S. team was flown to Argentina by an Air Force MATS C-124 leaving from Dover, Delaware.

Quite often an interesting part of a foreign country visit is getting there. The U.S. team made the 7,000-mile trip to Argentina via a USAF C-124. After loading the three sailplanes in subfreezing weather at Dover AFB and having the pre-flight briefing disclose that C-124s do not ditch successfully, they took off for Ramey Air Force Base in Puerto Rico. Tropical conditions welcomed them on their arrival. After a mandatory 14-hour layover, they flew their longest hop to Recife, Brazil, dodging nocturnal tropical thunder-

storms in the unpressurized C-124. After arriving at Recife, they visited the city without their U.S. team jackets since there were many "Yankee Go Home" signs about. They left on the last leg to Argentina. There was concern about a long delay at customs, but upon landing at the Buenos Aires Airport they were impressed to see how effective an SSA Zippo lighter and a carton of cigarettes could be. They later learned that Danilo Frey of Aviquipo, SAC's exporter who a few years before had sold 10 2-22AK kits to FAVAV had arranged for the team to enter and leave on a diplomatic basis.

On the way back, at the stop at Ramey Air Force Base, a team member was apprehended for taking a photo of a U-2 that was being used for shuttle photographic flights over Cuba. The team member was released in time to catch the flight back to Dover.

The team captain's report tells of some of the unusual features of this WSC:

There were apparently many reasons why FAVAV chose to use only aerotow retrieving for the contest. The Argentines had used this technique for their own Nationals, due to the inadequate communications system and the poor secondary roads. They also have an abundance of landing fields in all directions. . . . Also, the 20 new Ka6's did not have any trailers and the availability of more than 60 towplanes certainly was a big factor. . . . It worked amazingly well, if the inconvenience to the pilots is overlooked, for quite often they were absent for a day or two at a time and had to sleep under a wing or stay in primitive quarters out on the pampas."

In general, the towpilots were very capable and cooperative but some were relatively inexperienced at navigation. On one retrieve, a Rhodesian pilot found himself way off course and headed away from Junin. The tow plane ran out of gas and had to land. The sailplane cut off and soared back to Junin to report the towplane' plight; truly a reversal of the normal proceedings.

At the Captain's Meeting the question came up as to what would happen if someone became lost (voluntarily or involuntarily) for three or four days. This problem momentarily stumped the officials. By the next day, a regulation was announced that a retrieve would not be guaranteed for anyone who landed more than 50 km off course or beyond a turning point. This covered everything except the open day, and here the authorities had to gamble that no one would get lost.

Twelve new sailplane designs appeared at the WSC for the first time. In the Standard Class there were the French Edelweiss, the Finnish Vasama, which won the OSTIV design prize, the Dutch Sagitta II, the British Olympia 463, and the Australia Arrow; and in the Open Class, the British Skylark 4, the Italian Eolo, the German SB-7, the Czech Blanik 13, and the three American sailplanes, the HP-11, Sisu, and Prue Super Standard.

The outstanding day at this WSC was the free distance day on February 20. Johnson, who made the second best flight of the day, wrote up his story for the June 1963 *Soaring*.

A good start this day was very important, for even though each pilot could have three tows, they were only allowed one landing away from the airport. In addition, the pilots had to fly a distance amounting to at least 20 percent of that covered by the day's winning pilot in order to get any points.

The following excerpts are from Johnson's story:

The time was 4:20 P.M. and I was approximately 255 miles north of Junin. I called Dick, told him where I was and asked his location. He replied he was doing well, but he did not know quite where he was, but that he was not lost! Several pilots heard that answer and got a chuckle out of it, as I did.

At 5:30 P.M. I was approximately 320 miles north of Junin. The cumulus were starting to die out toward both the east and west, but fortunately for me a line of substantial and active cumuli remained along the course I wanted to fly.

Soon thereafter I was jolted out of my rosy daydream by the sight of a sailplane circling slowly about two miles ahead of me and at my altitude. After all, I rationalized, *this was a world championship,* and for all I knew perhaps a dozen ships could be ahead of me. . . . I found the sailplane to be the slim gray *Polish ZeFir.* . . . It was Edward Makula, who was masterfully inching what altitude he could out of his last bit of convection.

Makula and I could only head downwind along course and stretch our glides as far as possible. . . . At 7:40 P.M. I was down to 300 ft. and had just passed a 2,000 ft. long cultivated field that looked suitable for both the landing and a subsequent aerotow retrieve. . . . My landing location was 5 miles southeast of a small village, El Nochero, and 441 miles from Junin. Makula, with his extra 1,000 ft. of altitude was able to stretch

his ZeFir's glide a bit farther and landed on the northwest edge of El Nochero.

Makula and I shared a room in the gracious home of the Mingo family in El Nochero during that and the following night. Two towplanes arrived almost 24 hours after the sailplanes landed. Early on the third day the towplanes took us part way home, and then a two-motored Bristol Airfreighter finished taking us and the sailplanes the last 300 miles back to Junin. The climax of this free distance day occurred on our landing back at Laguna de Gomez. We were greated by a crowd of around 400 people, lifted bodily above the heads of the greeters by some dozen strong arms, and carried to the swimming pool where we were dumped in, clothes, shoes, and all.

Schreder landed 382 miles out and spent two nights with an Indian family before his retrieve plane arrived. Ryan ran into trouble at the start and flew only 232 miles.

The winner of the Open Class was Edward Makula with Jerzy Popiel second, both from Poland flying Zefirs. Dick Schreder was third and Dick Johnson was fourth.

Heinz Huth of Germany again won the Standard Class in a Ka-6. J. Lachney of France was 2d in an Edelweiss, J. Horma of Finland was 3d in a Vasama. Ryan had one zero point day and finished in 26th place.

The team captain's report noted:

The Standard Class competition was probably more competitive because of the greater number of pilots and due to some countries entering their best pilots in this class.

One of the very satisfying things about the International was the great effort that the Argentine people made to make the visitors' stay at Junin enjoyable. . . .

The first evening at Junin, they

had an open Citroen car for each team, and all the teams paraded through Junin. The streets were completely lined with people all the way from the airport to the city . . . . The people of Junin were all cheering, happy people—throwing flowers— starting off fireworks and blowing horns. It was a most impressive demonstration of a town's welcome.

The Pilots' Meetings were held in a small hangar, which had rather bad acoustics. This, plus a rather poor P.A. system and some limitations of the interpreters, caused a great deal of unnecessary discussion at the Pilots' Meetings. As an example, on the free distance day, with the promise of exceptional conditions, I asked the question as to whether flights would be permitted into other countries. The answer I got was that "pilots could fly as far as where they arrive." We got the point.

On the final Saturday, our hosts had an "asado" for the complete team.

Because of the limited automotive equipment, we attempted to rent some bicycles. Since none were available, we tried to put an ad in the paper, but the editor insisted that we borrow his two bicycles at no charge. These proved to be quite a good-will medium, for the Argentines could not get over the sight of "Nord Americanos" riding bicycles.

Membership Contest

The membership committee conducted a membership and suggestion contest that ran for the last seven months of 1962. The contest gained 150 new members.

30th National, 1963

After a four-year hiatus, the Nationals were again held at Harris Hill, July 2–12. Four previous national champions were entered and the contest had an international flavor with pilots from Canada, Denmark, Germany, Poland, and Switzerland. Twenty-five of the 48 sailplanes entered were of foreign manufacture—the first time that this was over 50 percent. Four sailplane types appeared for the first time: the Skylark 4, the Polish Foka, the French Breguet 905, and the HP-9. Marshall Claybourn was competition director and Bob Owens contest manager.

The contest was not settled until the last day, when Johnson, in his Skylark 4, edged out Bernie Carris in the RJK-5 by 8 points. Carris had trouble with his takeoff dolly and lost an hour in getting started. Johnson was named the champion with Carris in second place. Adam Witek was third in his Foka, Dick Schreder fourth in his HP-11, and George Moffat fifth in the HP-8.

Nineteen Standard Class sailplanes were entered and the final standing of the top five were Witek first, Bikle (in a Prue Std) second, Otto Zauner (in a Ka-6) third, Rudy Allemann (in a Ka-6) fourth, and Walt

Cannon (in a 1-23H) fifth. No trophy was yet available to present to the Standard Class leader. A total of 29,878 miles were flown, a record for Harris Hill.

The famous RJ-5 that Carris flew still held the world distance record. It was purchased by Brad Strauss, an instructor in the Schweizer Soaring School. He damaged the wooden fuselage in an off-field landing accident and then commissioned Adrian Kisovec, an SAC engineer, to design an all-metal fuselage. This was built by Bernie Carris and some friends. It then became known as the RJK-5. It still had only a skid with a launching dolly, which cost Carris the 1963 championship. A retractable gear was later put on it by the next owner, Dietrich Ennulat. The RJK-5 was later given to the National Soaring Museum.

Witek, the Polish pilot, was eager to have American pilots fly the reclined cockpit Foka to promote Polish sailplanes in the United States. On the day after the contest, Witek gave demonstration flights at the airport. When the SSA directors' meeting was over, Paul A. Schweizer had a chance to fly the Foka. The reclining position was strange to him, and after a quick cockpit briefing, Witek closed the canopy and the wing was lifted up for takeoff.

Bernie Carris's RJK, which was modified from the RJ5 in which he finished a close second to Johnson in the 1963 National.

(NSM Collection)

Paul Bikle getting into his Prue Standard sailplane at the Pacific Northwest Regional Soaring Championship at Sun Valley, Idaho, in 1963. Lyle Maxey and his Prue Super-Standard are in the background.
(Sun Valley News Bureau, SSA files)

The view through the canopy seemed very fuzzy, but before Schweizer could open the cockpit, the ship was under way. He was going to release when suddenly everything cleared up momentarily as the ship went over a bump. It was now evident that because of the reclined seating position he had been looking through the bottom part of his bifocal glasses. The Foka obviously was for younger pilots, or at least, pilots without bifocals.

Directors' Summer Meeting, 1963

The directors' meeting was held in Elmira on July 12, the last rest day of the contest. Of the 18 directors present, 9 had just competed in the Nationals and Marshall Claybourn had been competition director.

The SSA's financial condition and the possibility of increasing SSA dues were discussed at length. Since the budget was in balance and the future cost to remain a division of the NAA was uncertain, no action was taken on increasing the dues. The directors received the proposed Symons Wave Memorial Award with Lennie pins and instructed the awards committee to

work out the details with Carl E. Burson, Jr., of Tehachapi, California.

A. Felix du Point, Jr., was elected SSA's second honorary member for his generous financial support.

Unofficial World Distance Record

The 1963 Pacific Northwest Regional Soaring Contest was held at Sun Valley, July 22–26, 1963. Fourteen sailplanes were entered in Open Class and four in Class II. The outstanding flight was made by Paul Bikle on July 24, a free distance day. Portions of his report from the September 1963 *Soaring* follows:

> You all know how the hangar flying stories go: "There I was at 17,000 ft., about a mile back under this big squall line, flying through sleet, rain and lightning at 100 mph to keep from being lifted into the base of the storm; turn needle inoperative, oxygen gone, out of maps, and so on. . . . But, this was no dream—I had been some 300 miles out of Sun Valley, ID, when I first climbed to cloud base along the edge of this storm. Thoughts began to creep into the back of my mind that the 550 miles required to exceed the world distance record for sailplanes and perhaps, the 622 miles for the magic 1000-km distance might be in the cards. These brought forth mixed emotions of elation and frustration as I reminded myself that I had no barograph.
>
> Flying on and on for almost another hour in this dream-like situation it was obvious that the (Canadian) border had been crossed— . . . Although it was only 6:00 P.M., the light was fading rapidly and the visibility was quite restricted. . . . Fifty minutes later, a landing was made in a plowed field.

Bikle received help from a passing motorist in tying down the Prue Standard as best they could before the storm hit: "Leaving the sailplane to the mercy of the storm, we soon reached Smith Airport. Quickly checking the wall map, we determined . . . the distance from take-off (was) in the order of 550 miles. A call was then placed to Maj. Ed Butts at contest headquarters." The phone conversation was terminated because of the storm before Bikle got to such details as a possible record and the fact that no barograph had been carried. Bikle stayed at a motel in Swift Current and in the morning he received a call from Ed Butts:

> Ed informed me that he had contacted Bertha Ryan, Chairman of the SSA Records Committee. . . . She had called back to tell him that the calculated great circle distance was 556.9 miles. Even with an altitude penalty of 6.7 miles for landing at 2,800 ft. (release at 7,500 ft.), this would exceed the claimed record of 543.2 miles by the required 10-km margin so Bertha had sent a cablegram to the FAI making claim for a new record. My reply, that he forget about the whole thing as I had not carried a barograph, was met with something less than enthusiasm.
> The story of this flight should be of interest, not so much for what was accomplished but, because of the indications of what could have been accomplished. With adequate instruments, maps, oxygen and a better prepared pilot, it could have been over 700 miles.

Lyle Maxey was winner in the Open Class in the Prue Super Standard with Bikle second and Bob Moore third in the 1-21. The average flight of the 12 pilots in the Open Class on the free distance day was 289 miles. Rose Marie Licher was winner in Class II in a 1-26 and set a new U.S. Women's distance record of 267 miles.

New World Goal Records

On August 7 Ben Greene of Elizabethtown, N.C., made a 456-mile goal flight in his Standard Austria from Marfa, Texas, to Boise City, Oklahoma. This exceeded the Russian world record and was sent to the NAA and FAI for approval. Twenty days later Al Parker flew 487 miles from Odessa, Texas, to Great Bend, Kansas, which was later accepted as the world goal record. He wrote up his flight in the December 1963 *Soaring:* "Ah was very happy when my friend Ben Greene with his German-built ship captured the world goal record from the Russians, but Ah am much happier to have made it an all-American record by starting out from Texas with a Texas-built *Sisu* and a Texan did the job. If the *Sisu* could be described, Ah would say," concluded Al Parker, "that it thermals like a 1-26 and goes like hell!"

Special 1-26 Issue of Soaring

The October 1963 issue of *Soaring* was called "A Salute To the 1-26." The editorial by Harner Selvidge stated: "Much of the glamour of soaring lies in the realm of high performance, high aspect ratio open class sailplanes, but the backbone of the soaring movement in this country, and any other, lies in the local club operations. These are the weekend fliers who have fun around the airport, make some cross-country flights and enter local contests. For this sort of flying, the 1-26 is unexcelled."

That issue contains the story of Wally Scott's 443-mile flight, the longest 1-26 flight up to that time.

Wright Brothers' Memorial

The gliding and soaring flights of the

Wright brothers on the dunes of Kitty Hawk in 1901–1902 and 1911 are now memorialized by the bronze plaque at Kitty Hawk, which was dedicated on December 16, 1963. Floyd Sweet officially presented it to the U.S. National Park Service on behalf of the SSA. The plaque is a bronze bass relief sculpture by Ralph S. Barnaby, who was at the dedication. A number of other SSA members were present and assisted with a soaring demonstration.

The First 1,000-Kilometer Flight, 1964

An editorial by *Peter Bowers* entitled "Some Comments on Modern Soaring—Heresy or Horse Sense?" appeared in *Towline,* the Seattle Glider Council's newsletter. Because Bower raised so many questions about soaring and the SSA in this thought-provoking editorial, it was reprinted in the January 1964 *Soaring.*

Bill Ivans, in his "President's Message" in the same issue says: "This editorial is frankly critical of the SSA and of some trends in soaring outside of SSA purview. Many will disagree with Pete on some of his points, but his views are to be respected. There is no questioning that his is a thoughtful and serious statement of opinion and intent firmly based on experience. The beginning of a new year is a good time for each member to reappraise SSA activities and objectives and to communicate his views to his Regional Director."

Bowers, a long-time soaring enthusiast—former assistant editor of *Soaring,* airplane homebuilder, and EAA proponent—commented on the soaring movement, suggesting that SSA should be a much larger and more effective organization: "There have been no fundamental improvements in sailplane design since the 'Vampyr' of 1921. True, there have been advances in aerodynamics and structures—and ever-increasing performance—[but] there has been no change in fundamental operating concepts calling for a change in the basic design of the aircraft."

He felt that the current sailplane designs did not meet soaring needs and proposed that lower-cost flying could be achieved through homebuilding of sailplanes. He said that SSA should look at the EAA for pointers, as he considered it very similar to SSA in that it provided recreational flying for amateur sportsmen pilots.

He saw the SSA as an elitest group at the top of a pyramid with a very small base: "Soaring has mostly the custom trade now—a 'top' element with no solid foundation under it. The mass market and the solid bottom of the pyramid must be created from within SSA. . . . Soaring needs three things if it is to grow into anything more than the sport that it is now."

The three things were (1) a "Model T," a simple, low-priced two-place sailplane; (2) soaring sites nearby; (3) appeal to the average man, "the little guy—rather than the expert."

One response to this article appeared in the SAC report in the April 1964 *Soaring:*

> We are first to agree that the soaring movement needs growth. When Pete compares the small number of SSA members to the number of EAA members, he forgets that, with almost 100,000 airplanes and several hundred thousand power pilots, airplanes already are commonplace and accepted in the USA. On the other hand, soaring is a relatively unknown activity to most people, and there is no ready-made market. Hence, it is necessary to expose the public to soaring through publicity, advertisements, introductory

sailplane rides. Who is going to build a sailplane if he hasn't even seen one, let alone flown in one?

We feel the EAA is a fine movement—However, to imply that an EAA soaring movement within the SSA is the complete answer to our growth problem is unrealistic.

It appears to us that the EAA primarily is a designing and building organization with the flying secondary, whereas soaring is principally a flying activity with home-design and construction only one of its many associated activities.

Most people who are getting into soaring . . . are interested in flying—rather than obligating themselves to a number of years of working at the drawing board and in the shop.

Pete complains of the lack of any basic change, or revolutionary new ideas, in sailplane design, since the "Vampyr" and then reverses himself by asking for a "Model T."

We all would like to see cheaper sailplanes, for this certainly would help the movement to grow. However, with the present volume, we can not expect any break-through in cost.

Bowers's article caused quite a stir and brought in many letters to the editor of *Soaring*. It encouraged soaring enthusiasts to take a look at their sport and it developed worthwhile discussions on the future of the soaring movement.

The Symons Wave Memorial

Carl Burson revived the Lennie pins that Symons had started a number of years earlier. A One Lennie pin was given for a flight of 25,000–35,000 feet altitude, a Two Lennie pin for a flight of 35,000–40,000 feet, and a Three Lennie pin for a flight over 40,000 feet. In addition, a plaque was given with each pin. Burson issued pins and plaques to those who made qualifying

flights since Symons's death, and then began issuing pins as flights were made. By the start of 1964, 50 One Lennie pins, 18 Two Lennie pins, and 4 Three Lennie pins had been issued.

Sailplane Flying in Positive Control Air Space

John Ryan reported that a procedure had now been set up by the FAA Air Traffic Service for allocating air space for wave flying. The first such "wave window" was established at Colorado Springs by Wave Flights, and the second one at Tehachapi, California, by Fred Harris, operator of Holiday Soaring School. This would enable wave flights to be made in these areas at specific times cleared by the Air Traffic Control Center.

Director's Winter Meeting, 1964

A record number of 19 directors attended the meeting, on February 8–9, 1964, in Dallas. The directors decided to hire a full-time editor for *Soaring* magazine and to increase its size. This was made possible by separating the cost of *Soaring* from the membership, which would remain at $10 per year. Subscriptions to *Soaring* would be optional at $3 to members and $5 for libraries and foreign subscriptions.

It was decided to return to the five-minute soaring flight for the "C" badge, although the ABC Training Program would continue. The main reason for the change was that the commercial operators felt that more beginners would stay with the sport if they got their "C" and SSA membership right after their "C" flight.

Bernald S. Smith, an airline pilot and Naval Reserve pilot who had flown the Berlin airlift, was elected to the SSA board in 1963. He was appointed chairman of the Flight Training Committee in 1964. This included the ABC Program, which played an important part in the growth of soaring. This was the first of a number of major responsibilities that he would take on for the SSA in his long service as director.

The SSA agreed to pay an annual division fee of $1,000 as its share in supporting the NAA.

In order to encourage widespread bidding for sponsorship of the Nationals and at the same time keep alive the interest of the disappointed bidder, it was decided to solicit bids a year in advance on a letter of intent basis and to select a preferred area by preferential ballots at the summer board meeting. Firm bids would then be received at a later date.

The Safety Committee chairman, Miles Coverdale, promised to once again print summaries of accidents, providing that he would be sent adequate data.

Dawydoff Named New Soaring Editor

In the president's message in the May 1964 *Soaring*, Ivans announced that Alexis Dawydoff had been appointed the first full-time editor of *Soaring*. This would enable Lloyd Licher to spend his complete time on SSA's operations. He had edited 71 issues of *Soaring* and the May 1964 was his last.

Dawydoff came to *Soaring* magazine from *Flying* magazine, where he had been an editor. A soaring enthusiast since his first glider flight at Cape Cod with AMAC in 1929, he had continued his flying at Flushing Airport, New York, where he flew primary gliders. It was there that he had an ac-

cident that left him with a permanently stiff leg. He worked with Sikorsky, Air Associates, and the Peel Glider Boat Co. He then went with *Air Trails* and later *Air Progress* magazine. He was a partner in the G & S Service, which Steve and Ginny Bennis had started. He then flew at Wurtsboro, New York, with the Metropolitan Air-Hoppers Soaring Association while he was with *Flying* magazine. The June 1964 issue of *Soaring* was his first.

Alex was not one to talk about himself, but occasionally, after some "armtwisting" he would tell stories about his past. One was about his family's escape from Russia during the revolution. His natural modesty kept him from divulging that his family was of the nobility. In the early 1930s Bob Kidder was having trouble turning his primary to the right. Alex offered to test it for him and took an auto tow at North Beach Airport and started to make a 360-degree turn to the right. It turned very slowly so that he could not get back to the airport and his only choice was to land on the roof of one of the hundreds of apartments that bordered the airport. The woman who lived in the top story of the one he landed on was having a tea party and she called the police. The police did not know what to do with the glider, so they picked it up and threw it into the street. The newspaper next morning carried the story with the headline RUSSIAN PRINCE DROPS IN FOR TEA.

Alex had some difficulties with the airport manager. One day he was flying his primary over the manager's office when he saw him come outside. Alex took his hand off the stick to thumb his nose at the manager. As he let go, the stick flew forward and Alex could not reach it since the safety belt on his primary went around his chest and he went straight in. He said later that someone had oiled the normally tight stick since he had last flown the primary.

Alex was a true "prince" to the many who knew him.

Sailplane Devlopment

HP-11A. Dick Schreder announced that he was making plans available for the HP-11A as well as components that the kit builder might have trouble making himself.

SGS 2-32. Schweiz Aircraft reported that the 2-32 was getting its type certificate from the FAA. Production had started and two 2-32s were expected to fly in the Nationals.

BG-12B. Gus Briegleb reported on his new "B" version of the BG-12. This included a two-piece wing with flaps and was available in a kit for $1,900. It was being produced by the Soaring Corporation of America at El Mirage, California.

After building five Sisus the Arlington Aircraft Co. was renamed the Astro Corporation and moved to Greenville, South Carolina, with Niemi as project engineer. The Astro Corporation was managed by Clifton McClure and backed by P. J. (Jack) Baugh, Jr., of Charlotte.

31st National, 1964

The 31st National, which took place from June 30 to July 9, 1964, was sponsored by the Nebraska Soaring Association and the McCook Chamber of Commerce. Of the 48 sailplanes entered, 30 were of U.S. manufacture and 18 were foreign-built. Radio was beginning to play a more important part in the Nationals—40 of the sailplanes were equipped with radio.

The weather was termed "unpredictable" because of weak thermals, fast-changing conditions, and occasional squall lines and thunderstorms. Thus it was not surprising that Dick Johnson, in his Skylark 4, was the winner. Close behind in second place was Wally Scott in a Ka-6CR, and A. J. Smith was third in a Sisu-1a. Bob Hupe, Graham Thomson, and Rudy Mozer, all flying Ka-6CRs, followed in that order. The ability to stay in the air was most important. As a result, the heavier and faster ships did not do too well. Seventeen Standard Class sailplanes were entered and the top finishers were Wally Scott, first; R. Hupe, second; G. Thompson, third; and R. Mozer, fourth, all flying Ka-6CRs. C. Mears was fifth in a Prue Standard.

Directors' Summer Meeting, 1964

The officers elected at the meetings of July 10, 1964, in McCook, Nebraska, were J. Ryan, president; B. Greene, vice-president east; R. L. Moore, vice-president west; T. Page, secretary; and T. Sharp, treasurer.

Since all letters of intent to bid for the 1965 Nationals came from the east, it was decided to hold the Nationals east of the Mississippi. Firm bids were to be submitted by September 30.

Life Membership Contest

A life membership contest was organized by Dale May and his Membership Committee and it ran for the first six months of 1964. Prizes of donated merchandise valued at $1,000 were distributed to the first 30 names pulled out of a hat. A total of 56 new life members signed up during that contest, bringing the total life memberships up to 128.

SAC's first contact with Parker was his letter of January 1959 concerning his interest in a Schweizer dealership. P. A. Schweizer wrote him that he would be in the Dallas–Ft. Worth area on business with Bell Helicopter right after the SSA directors' meeting in Denver, so a meeting was arranged in a motel near the Bell plant.

Al brought with him Red Wright of Odessa, Texas, and Charles Adkisson of McCamey, Texas, who were both interested in soaring. The possibility of getting a commercial soaring activity in west Texas with a SAC dealer program was discussed. Parker expressed his interest in setting up an attractive resort soaring center on his ranchland northwest of Odessa and talked about putting up buildings, hangars, and a swimming pool all surrounded by palm trees. It was an exciting idea since Parker apparently had the finances to make such a project possible.

At dinner, the talk changed to their activities during World War II, with each one outdoing the other! Parker told of his exploits as a tank commander in Europe, Red Wright about flying the "Hump" in Burma and Adkisson's activity as a liaison pilot in the European theater. It was a most fascinating evening for Schweizer.

Parker later visited SAC and became a dealer. He started his operation at the Ector County Airport with aero tow, but added auto tow for training in an attempt to reduce the cost and get more people interested.

Al Parker of the Sagebrush Soaring Society who flew his SISU sailplane for a world record, the first flight over 1,000 kilometers.
(Sandor Aldott, NSM Collection)

Three World Records

Within a 15-day period from July 23 to August 6 three new world records were set by U.S. pilots, starting from the Ector County Airport in Odessa, Texas. On July 23, Wally Scott made a goal flight of 505 miles to Goodland, Kansas in his Ka-6, which beat Al Parker's record of 487 miles made the previous August.

The "big one" was flown by Al Parker on July 31. The United States had held this most sought-after world record on two previous occasions, first in 1934 when Dick du Pont flew 158 miles, and then in 1951 when Dick Johnson took the record away from the Russians. Twelve years later, three German pilots broke this record with a team flight of 544 miles.

Parker had not done well in the Nationals at McCook, having finished in 38th place. He said he needed to

learn how to soar, but those who knew him well felt that he would be out there to prove himself. Parker gave the details of his flight to E. J. Reeves who wrote it up for the September 1964 *Soaring* and the quotations are Parker's words.

On the morning of July 31, Parker released from tow at 9:52. Wally Scott and Red Wright, who had also taken off, decided that conditions did not warrant a serious cross-country effort that day. Parker continued on and reached Hobbs at 11:20 and proceeded north over the eastern part of New Mexico. At 2 o'clock he reached a low point of 700 feet and said that at times he was looking up at the canyon rim of the Cimarron River. The desperate scratching technique to stay aloft that he had learned at McCook enabled him to get away. His last chance was a roll of dust 1,900 feet above the ground in front of a thunderstorm. This gave him the best lift of the day— a steady 1,000 foot-per-minute climb to cloud base. With this altitude and the good following winds, he could keep the Sisu up and he could stretch the flight a good distance. Then came the most serious decision of the day.

Another thunderstorm developed across my path and would have forced me to make a considerable detour to the South. I decided to abandon my goal and run North-Northwest to cross the 1,000 km arc.

I climbed slowly back to 8,300 ft. (12,300 ft. MSL). Feeling that this was all the altitude I could use before dark, I drew a bead on the rotating beacon of an airport I thought to be Kimball, WY. At 85 mph indicated after a glide of about 15 miles, the Sisu carried me over the 1,000 km magic arc! I glided into the beacon with about half a mile to spare.

I struggled out of the Sisu after those ten and one half hours and

Sándor A. Aldott

The First 1,000-Kilometer Flight, 1964   207

looked around for landing witnesses. . . . I staggered around hangars to a lighted house trailer and called from a distance, "Anybody home?" Two young men came to the door. I asked them to witness my landing. . . . The younger of the two said, "I didn't hear a plane land." I told him it was not an airplane but a sailplane. He then said, "I didn't hear one of them either. . . . As we walked toward the sailplane, I remarked, "This is Kimball, WY, isn't it?" I then learned that I was in Kimball NB. . . . I am sure both boys thought I was either drunk or crazy. . . . The hostess at the cafe overheard part of my (telephone) conversation (and) seemed to be the only person in town who actually believed my story of a 646 mile sailplane flight.

The third record was made August 6 when George Moffat increased his own 300-kilometer triangle record by almost 10 miles per hour. He was flying the HP-8 and he used Hobbs, New Mexico, and Lamesa, Texas, as turn-points. These three new records added to the six earlier ones enabled the United States to continue to keep the lead in the number of international records held. Parker was awarded the Lilienthal Medal for his record flight.

10th Annual 1-26 Regatta

Every Labor Day weekend since 1954 a 1-26 regatta had been held at Harris Hill. The 10th Annual 1-26 Regatta was the largest yet, with 30 1-26s entered. It was National in scope since three west coast pilots participated, using borrowed 1-26s. Frank Sears was the individual champion and Herb Light and John Tobares were the team champions. The Soaring Dutchmen team of Lowell and Jeff Yund, Luther Moyer, and Don Miller set a new record in the "Le Mans" assembly race.

In this race the 1-26s on trailers were lined up on one side of the field and the assembly teams in a parallel line 150 feet away. The teams raced to their trailers, removed their 1-26 and assembled it while being timed by a stopwatch. The Soaring Dutchmen's record time was 3 minutes 20 seconds!

Present at the regatta was Les Arnold, who planned to aero-tow his new 2-32 back to Fremont, California. Richard Miller and Rus Palmer, both of whom had competed in the regatta, would pilot the 2-32 for the first east-to-west transcontinental towed glider flight.

Stan Hall and the Cherokee Project

Stan Hall reported on his Cherokee II project. His aim had been to "design a sailplane for the 'little people.' " After the sale of 250 sets of plans, Hall decided to end the project because the tracings were worn out, it was taking too much of his time to answer the mail, he had accomplished his mission, and he wanted to go ahead with a "dream ship" for himself. "There is still a place in soaring for the 'little guy,' the guy who hopes to become the 'big guy.' I hope there will always be. If not, we are in trouble."

President's Message

Ivans's last president's message in the December 1964 Soaring stated: "Membership growth has been remarkably steady. Financial operation of SSA remains at a breakeven level. Positive gains including establishment of legal high-altitude soaring areas and the elimination of arbitrary cloud flying restrictions on experimental licensed gliders. As a negative 'gain' we added

our voice in no uncertain fashion to the chorus of protest against a proposed lowering of the positive control altitude floor, and the proposal has been withdrawn."

Fiberglass Sailplanes Arrive, 1965

Germany entered three fiberglass-reinforced plastic (FRP) sailplanes in the 1965 WSC. Two were put into production that year, and started a trend in Europe that would soon see most of the sailplanes there being made of fiberglass. U.S. sailplane kit manufacturers did not feel that FRP was adaptable to their semibuilt kits. SAC was concerned with (1) the high cost of pioneering, through the FAA, the use of such a new material for prime structure, (2) FRP's poor crash resistance under high "g" loads, (3) FRP's unproven service life, and (4) the great amount of skilled hand labor required.

Ryan Starts Presidency

Ryan's first president's message in the January '65 *Soaring* noted: "SSA is extremely fortunate to have a great wealth of talent and ability among its membership. . . . SSA needs your help . . . if we can spread the work around a bit, we will all have more time for our favorite sport!"

Preparations for 1965 WSC

At the fall CVSM meeting, the committee agreed to allow a reduction in the maximum points awarded on days in which fewer than 60 percent of the pilots exceeded a specific distance. This was the start of "devalued days." The SSA proposal to combine tasks and scoring of Standard and Open classes in the WSC was not approved. Opponents of the proposal argued that

Twenty-seven 1-26 sailplanes line up at the 10th annual 1-26 regatta at Harris Hill.
(Schweizer Aircraft Corporation)

SSA President W. S. Ivans presents the Eaton Trophy to Dr. Wolfgang Klemperer in 1964. Left to right: Jack Lambie, Bill Ivans, John Graves, Dr. Klemperer, Ted Sharp, and Howie Burr.

(George Uveges)

class distinction would be lost. The BGA said it would have the same task and equal starting opportunities for both classes, although separate scoring and class awards would continue.

Seeding of Pilots for the 1965 WSC

The top four seeded pilots for the 1965 WSC were R. H. Johnson, A. J. Smith, R. E. Schreder, and W. A. Scott. All were interested in competing and Johnson and Smith chose to fly in the Open Class and Schreder and Scott would fly in the Standard Class. A fund drive was under way and military transportation was expected to be available for the team members and sailplanes.

Directors' Winter Meeting, 1965

Attendance reached a new high at the meeting on January 23–24, in La Jolla, California, when 22 directors arrived. It was decided to expand *Soaring* magazine by adding four more pages. The membership growth curve still continued upward at about the same slope. The treasurer reported that the society was in excellent financial condition.

The *Fauvette* sailplane that Dale

May had given the SSA was to be offered for sale to the membership through a sealed bid.

It was decided that the SSA would provide a suitable trophy for the Standard Class if one were not donated.

The board also adopted a new procedure for bidding for future national soaring contests. This plan divided the country up into three zones, and the preferred zone was to rotate each year.

Soaring Loses a Pioneer

One of the few remaining pioneers of the soaring movement, Dr. Wolfgang B. Klemperer, died from viral pneumonia on March 25 1965. While a graduate student at Aachen University in 1920 he was encouraged by Theodore Von Kármàn, his professor, to build the Schwarze-Teufel. His contributions to motorless flight in Germany and later in the United States were many and well known. Some of his other activities that are not generally known in soaring circles were covered in John Graves's memorial of Dr. Klemperer in the June 1965 *Soaring:*

In the mid-thirties, the Klemperers came to California, where Klemp had accepted a position as head of special research with the Douglas Aircraft Company.

During WW II, he accepted the call of the United States Air Force to participate in the task of retrieval of the scientific data and personnel in Europe.

Then in the early 1950's Klemp worked again with the U.S. Air Force in Europe as a consultant on intelligence matters.

In 1963 Dr. Klemperer was scientific director of the Douglas National Geographic Society expedition which photographed a total solar eclipse from a high flying DC-8 jetliner observatory.

His death will be mourned by all who knew him and worked with him. Rarely was there a man who was so much admired and respected as Klemperer.

Growth of U.S. Soaring Enterprises

Up to 1964 the commercial phase of soaring in the United States included only a few sailplane manufacturers and soaring operators. In June of 1964 John Ryan formed RAINCO, which would handle all types of sailplane instruments, radios, and related equipment. Peter Wessel of Beverly Hills, California, was the U.S. agent for the H-301 Libelle. Graham Thomson was handling radio and instruments. Ken Livingston of Washington, D.C., was agent for the French Edelweiss C-30, Rudy Mozer of Warren, Michigan, handled the sale of the Schleicher Ka-6, K-7, and K-8, and Motorless Flight Enterprises of Glastonbury, Connecticut, represented Schemp Hirth. There were ads by Moto Imports of Poland for the Foka, Zefir, and the Bocian two-place, and Slingsby of England was advertising the Dart. The European sailplane manufacturers had the advantage of a large market in Europe,

After the early 1930s Klemperer did not get to the Elmira area very often as he was active primarily in California, but the Schweizers had had enough contact with Klemperer to learn that he was a kind and capable man and had contributed much to motorless flight.

Klemperer liked new ideas and the Schweizers remember one occasion in the middle 1930s when he and his wife Mia drove to the national meet in a revolutionary new auto, the Chrysler air-flow sedan. This featured the first aerodynamically designed body. Klemperer was a friend of Prof. Alexander Klemin, who had served with him on the Board of Directors of the NGA. Klemin had helped to develop the Chrysler design by running tests of car models in the wind tunnel of the Guggenheim School of Aeronautics of New York University, where he was the director. This was where Ernie and Paul A. Schweizer (and later Leslie Schweizer) earned their engineering degrees. Paul's class was "short changed" one term of wind tunnel time because the tunnel was tied up with the automobile tests. It would have taken too much time to dismantle the moving road bed that had been installed to simulate the effect of the ground on the air flow around the body of the model car.

where the glider programs of many countries were subsidized to various extents by their governments. They would become tough competition for American sailplane and equipment manufacturers.

The SAC Report

The SAC Report in the May 1965 *Soaring* commented:

> Our dealer organization (now 35) continues to expand and made 45,000 flights (in 1964)—a 33% gain over 1963. We had delivered ten 2-32's and are working to increase production to a rate of two per month.
>
> In a delivery flight made by the Chicago Glider Club, towing with a Bonanza, they made the 620 mile non-stop flight from Elmira NY to Naperville IL in four and one half hours at a ground speed of 132 mph.
>
> Our major publicity project in 1964 was the display of a 1-26 at the World's Fair. This is being shown again this year and probably is the most looked-at sailplane in the world.

The U.S. team that went to South Cerney, England, from May 29 to June 13 for the 1965 WSC was led by E. H. "Ed" Butts, captain, and J. W. "Wally" Leland, team manager. Dick Johnson flew a Skylark 4, A. J. Smith a Sisu-1A, Dick Schreder a HP-12, and Wally Scott a Ka-6CR.

The team was airlifted to England by the USAF. On the last day of their practice session at Lasham, the U.S. pilots flew to the RAF's South Cerney training base in the western part of England. This base soon became an international village. RAF flying was shut down for the three weeks of the contest and the 31 Chipmunk trainers were available for tow planes.

For the first time a designated "start" was used. Two "guinea pig" sailplanes were used to check the soaring conditions, which the BGA called the early thermal warning system (ETWS). The weather during the practice period was very cold and rainy, and during the 13 days of the meet there were only 6 contest days. When conditions were flyable, they were typical of England—light thermals, low cloud base, and a lot of haze with resulting difficult navigation.

Eighty-six sailplanes from 28 countries were entered, 41 in the Open Class, and 45 in the Standard Class. The winner of the Open Class was J. Wroblewski of Poland flying a Foka 4. R. Spanig of West Germany was 2d in a D-36 and R. Kuntz of West Germany was 3d in a SHK-1. Dick Johnson was 18th and A. J. Smith 19th.

In the Standard Class, F. Henry of France flying an Edelweiss was 1st, M. Ritzi of Switzerland flying a Standard Elfe was 2d, and F. Kepka of Poland flying a Foka 4 was 3d. Wally Scott was 6th and Dick Schreder was 15th.

The Russians attracted considerable attention with their polished all-metal A-15 and KAI-14 sailplanes, but they did poorly in the contest. Of greatest interest were the new FRP "plastic" sailplanes, the D-36, Libelle H-301, and the Phoebus. The most outstanding sailplane was the D-36, which was designed and built by three Darmstadt students, Klaus Holighaus, Gerhard Waibel, and Wolf Lempke, all of whom would become top sailplane designers in their own right. The D-36 was referred to as the "Gummi Flugel" (rubber wing) sailplane, because of its extremely flexible wings, which took the shape of a scimitar when in flight.

The Polish and German teams had UHF radio direction finders at their base station and on their tow cars and they could give their pilots an exact "fix" on their location. Some of the contestants asked jokingly why the U.S. team did not have a U.S. Air Force AWAC's overhead to monitor the U.S. team's location! Ann Welch, the director of the WSC, noted: "Do we want Championship flying which is submerged in the sea of electronics, met and radio outstations and even aircraft to mark thermals, to the extent that these things become more important than the individual pilot himself? . . . I am sure that this is a matter to which we must give both thought and decision before the next Championships."

1965 OSTIV Trophy

Lorne Welch of Great Britain was the chairman of the Standard Class jury that judged the 13 sailplanes entered in the Standard Class design contest. The other members of the jury were Julian Bojanowski of Poland, Ilbert deBoer of the Netherlands, Hans

Zacher of West Germany, and Paul A. Schweizer of the United States.

The evaluation flights began at 6 a.m. each morning during the practice period so that they would not interfere with the WSC flights. The morning usually started clear but soon a wall of low coulds would come up from the Bristol Channel and put an end to the operations. The only time that they could fly during the day was when the weather prevented practice contest flights.

The jury's final choice was the Slingsby Dart. A special commendation was given to the designer of the Foka, since the jury members agreed that it was the best sailplane entered but was not "in the spirit of the Standard Class." The jury felt that tighter regulations were still required for the Standard Class and they sent their recommendations to CVSM board.

32d National, 1965

Sixty-nine sailplanes entered Nationals held in Adrian, Michigan, on June 29 to July 9, 1965. This was the largest number since the 1947 Nationals. A total of 51,567 miles were flown during the seven contest days. This broke the record of 42,000 miles flown at Grand Prairie in 1956. The soaring conditions were average, and the longest flight, only 272.8 miles, was made by Dale May in his Sisu.

The meet was sponsored by the Adrian Soaring Club and supported by the city of Adrian and the state of Michigan. Gov. George Romney opened the contest and ran the wing tip on a ceremonial takeoff. Marshall Claybourn was the competition director and Werner Sommer was contest manager. The entries of Hans-Werner Grosse of Germany and John Firth of Canada added some international fla-

Since a different sailplane was flown on each flight, often in rainy weather, the jury found the flying a challenge. When there was heavy rain the only parts of the Chipmunk that were visible were the DA-GLOW orange wing tips and rudder.

On one afternoon session, the ceiling was at 1500 feet with just a few holes in the overcast. The jury pilots were towed through these holes, did their testing above the overcast, then came back through the holes to the airport. In one instance, when Bojanowski was flying the Delphin and Schweizer was flying the Olympia 465, they drifted more than they had expected, and when they came out at the bottom of the hole Schweizer could not see the airport. Because the landscape was so green, he did not recognize any of the landmarks. He tried to follow Bojanowski, thinking he knew where the airport was. It turned out that Bojanowski was trying to follow him, since he was also lost. After flying around a bit more, they located another military field and landed there. After a lecture about not landing in restricted fields, the tower operator contacted South Cerney and requested two tow planes. To make the flight back worthwhile, they swapped ships and ran some tests on their flight back.

vor to this contest.

Going into the last day, Moffat was first in an Austria SH-1, Dean Svec was second in a Sisu, and Grosse was third in a Ka-6E. The last day's task was a 160-mile triangle with distance along a fixed course, and the top three positions reversed. The final results were Grosse, first; Svec, second; and Moffat, third—all within a 26-point spread. Since Grosse was a German citizen he was not eligible for the championship and so Svec was named champion, Moffat came second, and Bikle, flying a Prue Standard was third since Firth, who finished after Moffat, was a Canadian. Of the 32 entries in the Standard Class, the top five were Grosse, Mozer, Ray, Scott, and Gertsen. On the final day, 65 sailplanes were launched in 48 minutes by 8 tow planes.

Directors' Summer Meeting, 1965

This meeting was held on July 9, 1965, at the end of the Nationals. Disposi-

Dean Svec who won the 1965 National at Adrian, Michigan, with Francois Henry of France, the world Standard Class champion of 1965.

(George Uveges)

tion of the SSA Fauvette was discussed and the board agreed to sell it for $3,000.

Since no acceptable letters of intent to bid on the 1966 Nationals had been received, bidding was open to the entire country.

All officers were reelected except that Sterling Starr replaced R. L. Moore as West Coast vice-president.

Alex Dawydoff

The soaring world was shocked when Alexis Dawydoff died suddenly of a heart ailment on August 1. He had been active at the SSA office until just a few days before. This must have been his favorite position, for he loved soaring.

Gill Robb Wilson, former Editor of *Flying*, with whom Alex worked for many years, noted in his eulogy: "In all the years I never heard anyone say an unkind word about Alex Dawydoff. What an obituary, what an ambition that would be if each of us could start and fulfill a life like that."

First Annual 1-26 Nationals

The 1-26 Association ran the first 1-26 National Contest, the week before the Labor Day regatta at Harris Hill. W. F. "Bud" Briggs was the winner, R. B. Smith was second, and E. R. Dawson was third. Ted Falk, who was fourth, reported in *Soaring:* "The conventional excuses of the losers—ship too hot for conditions—ship too light for conditions—task chosen to favor certain ships—thermal diameter too small— too big—etc. . . . have been eliminated and we have been forced to admit, although grudgingly, that his skill was greater than ours."

Bud Briggs also won the regatta in which 28 1-26s were entered. The Le Mans assembly race was won by the Soaring Dutchmen, who set a new record of 3.05 minutes.

Gliding and the Civil Air Patrol

The guest editorial in the April 1965 *Soaring* by Paul A. Schweizer was entitled "Youth Must Fly." It explained why young people should be encouraged to fly and why they should begin with a glider program. More pilots were needed in the United States for the expanding airlines, increased business flying, and the military, which Airline and military pilots from World War II were retiring at an increasing rate and not enough new pilots were being trained to replace them.

The New York wing program got its start when Richard Nelson of the Rockland County CAP held an Easter week encampment at Elmira. About 50 cadets were introduced to gliding at the SSS. This partly subsidized program worked out well and was repeated. CAP gliding was sporadic over the next few years, with New York, Il-

Top: Col. Joe Mason, USAF national commander of the CAP, and Bernie Carris, chief instructor of the Schweizer Soaring School in a 2-32 sailplane. Mason was instrumental in starting the CAP National Encampment for cadet glider training.

(Schweizer Aircraft Corporation)

President John D. Ryan with SSA Board of Directors at meeting held in Adrian, Michigan, July 9, 1965. Bottom, left to right: T. E. Sharp, D. E. McNay, J. D. Ryan, W. S. Ivans, and M. Claybourn; top: L. Licher, P. A. Schweizer, D. S. May, B. S. Smith, E. J. Reeves, and F. B. Compton.

(George Uveges)

linois, and Hawaii Wings being the most active.

In 1965 Col. "Joe " Mason, USAF National Commander of CAP, took the initiative and set up a one-month national encampment at Harris Hill. A total of 92 cadets from every state in the union attended this encampment. The course provided 16 cadets with a two-week FAA private glider course, 64 cadets with a one-week introductory gliding course, and 12 cadets with a four-week FAA private power course. Col. Samual H. du Pont (a nephew of R. C. du Pont) was the encampment commander. This program was considered a resounding success

by the Air Force and the CAP, and an expanded program was planned for 1966.

Other Activities during 1965

Richard Miller was appointed editor of *Soaring* beginning with the October 1965 issue.

The first Libelle H-301 was delivered in the United States in September. A new contributor to *Soaring* was Douglas Lamont whose stories had first appeared in the July and November 1954 *Soaring*.

Bernald Smith, chairman of the

ABC Training Program, reported that the 1964 activities included the awarding of 66 "A" badges, 48 "B" badges, 114 five-minute "C" badges, and 135 program "C" badges.

The Base of the Pyramid Grows, 1966

The soaring pyramid that Pete Browers had talked about in "Heresy or Horse Sense?" was beginning to grow. As he had pointed out, there was little room at the top, so the growth had to come at the base.

Soaring activity was spreading out around the country through publicity, advertisement, and word of mouth. The public was now able to give soaring a try at the growing number of commercial soaring operations around the country.

It was recognized, however, that if soaring was to become more popular, it would need much more publicity. The SSA itself had done very little in the way of advertising or promotion, except for issuing an occasional publicity release and some classified ads in aviation magazines. The commercial operators were doing local and regional advertising. The first national advertising was done by the SAC dealer cooperative advertising and promotion program. This 1956 program was expanded to include six full-page ads in *Flying* and *AOPA Pilot* magazines. The ads featured a coupon, which, with $5, would entitle the bearer to a sailplane ride at a dealer's operation.

The films *Sky Sailing* and *Zero Zero Romeo* were being circulated around the country and helped to interest people in the sport. A large number of one dollar kits that SAC advertised in the classified ads were sold and helped to widen the interest.

The most promising developments in 1966 were three projects scheduled for release in 1967: *National Geographic* was to do a story on soaring; Fred Harris and Holiday Soaring had a contract to do the flying for the Disney film, *The Boy Who Flew with the Condor;* and Bob Buck was to do another article on soaring for the *Reader's Digest*.

Directors' Winter Meeting, 1966

An attendance record was set at the January 22–23 meeting in Dallas: 24 directors were present. Since the separation of the SSA membership and *Soaring* magazine created extra work for the SSA office, an effort was made to amend the bylaws and raise the annual dues by $3 and include *Soaring* in the membership. This failed to gain enough support among the directors, many of whom thought that a $13 fee would discourage membership.

Feelings toward the Standard Class were still mixed when the board was asked by CVSM: "Is it still desirable to maintain the standard class as the promoter of cheap, easy-to-handle, club gliders?" The majority voted no. They also decided to eliminate from the U.S. Nationals and all other sanctioned contests special recognition of Standard Class achievements. This rather drastic action was in response to the CVSM board's decision to turn down SSA's recommendation that both Open and Standard Class be given the same task and scored together so that the world champion could be drawn from either class.

Another reversal in policy was that the board set a new rule that would prohibit sailplanes in SSA-sanctioned contests from carrying gyro or other instruments permitting flight without visual reference to the ground. This development was the result of the unfair situations in past contests in which some contestants were suspected of flying clouds illegally, and of the directors' desire to avoid any airspace problems.

The number of entrants in the 1966 Nationals was limited to five times the number of tow planes firmly committed by March 30.

Marshall Claybourn was appointed competition director. The proposal to eliminate the mandatory free distance task from the rules did not pass.

Appeal of Soaring Magazine Broadens

The new editor of *Soaring*, Richard Miller, was working hard to broaden its appeal. He included bits of soaring history in the magazine so that newcomers to the sport could learn about soaring's past, and in the January '66 *Soaring* a famous Barnaby story, "The Cape Code Capers," appeared:

Toward the end of the summer, . . . a time arrived when there were not enough left to muster a launching crew. . . . By hitching a horse to each end of the shock cord (vee) the launching crew could be reduced to five—a rider for each horse, one man on the wing-tip and two to hold the tail.

This worked fine until one fateful day when we were giving short hops to a beginner. As the call "let go!" was given and the glider started forward, it immediately became apparent that there was not quite enough room between the horses for the glider to pass through. In addition the launching was not powerful enough to enable the glider to climb over them.

Hearing the excited screams of the onlookers, the riders looked back over their shoulders—saw the glider bearing down on them, and dove off the horses into the sand. The glider,

whizzing by, was just high enough so that each wing tip clipped a horse on the top of the head as it proceeded on its way to a successful, if somewhat shaky landing.

The horses, . . . lit out at full speed in opposite directions—stretching the shock-cord between them. The further they went the slower their progress, until finally they were pawing the sand but making no headway. At this point, the shock-cord, . . . broke."

Did you ever see a horse turn a summersault? This pair executed two beauties, and then lit out for parts unknown.

Progress with the FAA

Efforts by the SSA Airworthiness and Licensing Committee to improve the FAA regulations for motorless flight were starting to yield results.

A glider flight instructor rating was instituted, but in keeping with the SSA's request, a grandfather clause permitted those who had been instructing to continue to do so.

A change in FAR eliminated the registration numbers on the wings of aircraft, and from then on required 12-inch letters on each side of the fin or fuselage.

The FAA also responded to SSA's request to eliminate the requirement for waiver for towing by proposing a set of regulations for the towing aircraft, the tow pilots, and the towing operation.

John Ryan, Dick Schreder, and Ernest Schweizer met in Washington with W. H. Weeks, chief of the FAA Engineering and Manufacturing Division, to discuss the certification of sailplanes. The SSA agreed to study the present regulations and to propose changes. Schreder also met with an-

A view of the Black Forest Gliderport with Pike's Peak in the background. This site was developed by John Brittingham, Dave Johnson, Wally Leland, and Mark Wild and was called Wave Flights because of its excellent wave soaring.

(NSM Collection)

other branch of the FAA to see about the certification of amateur, homebuilt, and experimental gliders.

Increase in Wave Flying

The creation of "wave windows" was followed by a large increase in wave flying around the United States and in the number of altitude legs earned for the Gold and Diamond "C" badges.

The success of the SSA-FAA-USAF Altitude Training Program, whereby SSA members could be checked out for altitude flying by going through a USAF altitude chamber, made it possible to fly waves with greater safety. Since this program had started in 1964,

over 120 soaring pilots had been through the course.

Wave flights were being made at a number of sites: Holiday Soaring at Tehachopi, California; Sugarbush Soaring at Warren, Vermont; Sky Sailing at Freemont, California, Cumberland, Maryland, and Minden, Nevada; and the Mt. Rainier wave from Issaquah, Washington. One of the most popular was Wave Flights at the Black Forest in Colorado Springs. A noteworthy flight was made there by Bill Cleary on November 15, 1965, when he earned his altitude diamond and became the first pilot to earn all three diamonds in a 1-26. Here are some excerpts from his story of the flight:

After five minutes on tow, heading in the general direction of the Air Force Academy, we were suddenly in the smooth air of the secondary wave and the rate-of-climb indicator . . . suddenly steadied on 1,500 fpm up and Dave's [Johnson] voice on the radio said, "This looks like the part you want, Bill." . . . I released, . . . and watched the rate of climb steady on 1,300 up. Climbing through 20,000 ft. I found that lift tended occasionally to get weak. I then began to probe . . . in an attempt to keep the machine going up.

About two miles north I again found good lift and banged up through 29,000 where my canopy began to ice over. The hose that Dave [Johnson] had thoughtfully stuck in the ventilator to direct cold air to the canopy became a most welcome "optional extra." Around 30,000 feet the air began to get turbulent.

I took a long last look at the Sangre de Cristos 200 miles to the south, at the lenticulars all up and down the Continental Divide, the snow storms in the Aspen area about 100 miles to the west . . . then pulled on the spoilers and started the 20 minute descent to the gliderport.

I had finally cornered the three elusive Diamonds in Schweizer's great little 1-26.

The "Explorer"

Kim Scribner, a Pan American captain, became interested in soaring at the end of World War II. In 1965 he was able to interest some members of the Explorers Club of New York City in the idea of backing a research sailplane for investigating clear air turbulence (CAT).

The Explorers Research Corp. was formed with George Wallace of Fitchburg, Massachusetts the principle backer, as president. They purchased a specially equipped 2-32 that had the

Bill Cleary in a 1-26 with Joe Conn (left) and Dave Johnson at the Black Forest Gliderport, where Cleary completed his third Diamond.
(SSA files)

latest in instruments, radio, and navigational equipment. It also had two oxygen systems, one for 12 hours and the standby for 4 hours. They were to run tests with instrumentation provided by the Air Force Cambridge Research Center and NASA. After the CAT Research Program, the Explorer was given to NCAR in Boulder, Colorado, for upper-air research projects.

Before World War II, Kim Scribner was a parachute jumper and performed at the Cleveland Air Races and other air shows while he was learning to fly. When war surplus gliders became available, he and a fellow Pan American pilot bought an L-K and he was soon doing aerobatics shows in it. When SAC started production on the 1-23, he ordered a special "beefed-up" 1-23 with water tanks so he could jettison the water as he did his aerobatic routine. His special maneuvers were an inverted aero tow and outside loops. He won a number of aerobatic contests held during the national soaring contests and was named the national (aerobatic) champion.

At his yearly show at the Miami Air Races in 1951 he started to roll into inverted flight shortly after takeoff. He had a full load of water and the inexperienced tow pilot slowed up and Scribner's wing caught the ground. He was seriously injured and it took a

Jack Laister with a model of his Standard Class LP-49, which his organization designed, built, type-certificated and put into production. The LP-49 had a considerable reduction of gross weight compared to Laister's previous glider, the 42 place CG-10A.

(George Uveges)

number of months before he was back at his job at PAA, and a longer period before he was back on flying status.

He became interested in the use of sailplanes as a research tool, which resulted in the CAT Program. He also supported youth aviation training and became associated with the Embry Riddle School.

The New Laister LP-49

In 1966 Jack Laister announced the development of the LP-49 sailplane. Laister had been directly involved in developing and producing training gliders and cargo gliders for World War II, including the large U.S. military cargo glider, the CG-10. When the military glider work tapered off at the end of the war, Laister went into the aircraft industry and held a number of executive positions with Aero Commander, Pacific Air Motor, and Weber Aircraft. After 20 years in the industry, he decided to get back into motorless flight and formed the Laister Sailplane Products at Downey, California. The

first product was the LP-49—a 49-foot-span Standard Class sailplane. A story in the July 1966 *Soaring* entitled "Jack Laister Revisited," gave a history of Laister and his many soaring accomplishments. The LP-49 was flown a few months later.

33d National, 1966

Sylvia Colton and Doug Lamont covered the 1966 National at Reno, Nevada, for *Soaring.* Colton handled the routine phases of the meet and Lamont added the color by setting the scenes and giving details of the pilots' experiences during their flights.

Sixty-five sailplanes were entered, making it the second largest NSC held. There were 15 Standard Class ships entered but no separate records or recognition was given to them. Only 4 of these finished in the top 25 positions. It was evident that the long-awaited performance spread between the Open and Standard Class was beginning to develop.

Ed McClanahan made the best flight of 456.5 miles, which was the longest flight ever made in a national contest. There were five other flights over 400 miles and 28 flights over 300 miles. The total mileage flown in the contest was 99,712, which almost doubled the record of the previous contest. Dick Schreder was the winner in his HP-14, Moffat was second in a SH-1, Graham Thomson third in a Libelle, John Ryan fourth in a Sisu, and Ed Makula of Poland was fifth in a Foka 4.

One of the *National Geographic* photographers who had been in Elmira for the soaring story came to Reno to photograph contest scenes. He did some flying with Bernie Carris in the 2-32 to get some special "shots."

Directors' Summer Meeting, 1966

At the July 8 meeting in Reno, directors reviewed two letters of intent bidding for the 1967 Nationals—from Marfa, Texas, and McCook, Nebraska—and a decision was made to accept Marfa's offer.

The flattening of the membership growth curve was discussed at length. The executive director reported that the number of new members had actually increased, but some old members had not renewed.

SSA officers elected for 1967 were Sterling Starr, president; Miles Coverdale, East Coast vice-president; J. C. "Red" Wright, West Coast vice-president; Tom Page, secretary; and Ted Sharp, treasurer.

Region Contests on the Increase

Regional meets, soaring camps, fly-ins, roundups, and other get-togethers of soaring enthusiasts were on the increase. Many of these contests had become regular yearly events with the Snowbird Contest being the oldest, the 1965 Snowbird being the 23d. Other traditional contests held were the 20th Annual Pacific Coast Mid-Winter Championship at Torrey Pines, California; the 18th Annual Wright Memorial Glider Meet in Dayton, Ohio; the 12th 1-26 Regatta; and the 11th Northeastern Labor Day Contest at Hiller Airport, Massachusetts.

This increase in the number of contests was another indication that soaring was growing. These get-to-

Dick Schreder in his HP-14, the winner of the Open National 1966 over Reno Nevada.

(R. Schreder)

Allan MacNicol organized a nine-day wave camp at Mt. Washington, New Hampshire, flying from North Conway Airport. Six diamonds and 14 Gold altitude legs were earned and flights over 30,000 feet were achieved. Twenty-eight years before at the same location Barringer had unknowingly made a wave soaring flight in the Ibis.

Grim Statistics

"Grim Statistics" was the title of John Ryan's last editorial as president of SSA in the December 1966 *Soaring*. He wrote about the large number of serious accidents and the nine fatal accidents that had occurred during the latter part of 1966:

> It is readily apparent that many of these accidents were the result of several different errors in judgment, or mistakes, or lack of training.
>
> A sailplane seems relatively simple, particularly to a transitioning power pilot, and perhaps we become too enthralled with the beauty, joy and simplicity of soaring. We forget that the air is an unforgiving medium and that the sport itself required a great deal of self-discipline from the pilot.
>
> Let's review our flying knowledge, abilities, weaknesses, our good habits and our bad ones too. Let's admit the mistakes we've made and try to understand why we made them.
>
> What else can we do? Well, from time to time we've all seen unsafe operations—a winch cable without a weak link, a pilot about to take-off without the proper check-out . . . . An opportunity to make soaring safer and to eliminate a potential hazard should never be overlooked.
>
> We're not pioneers delving into unknown dangers. And let's not forget our obligations toward the newcomer. We must pass along the lessons we've learned over the years.
>
> The SSA Safety Committee,

Top: Howie Burr and his wife Carolyn are dressed for the cold of a typical Snowbird Meet. They played an important part in making the Snowbird a "fun-type" contest that has become a tradition at Harris Hill.
(NSM Collection)

Three CAP cadets are given a cockpit check of the 2-22 by Holli Nelson of the Schweizer Soaring School during the CAP summer encampment.
(Schweizer Aircraft Corporation)

gethers spread the word about soaring and strengthened the clubs or associations that sponsored them.

Eastern Altitude Diamonds

Most of the wave flying was being done in the western part of the country, but wave flying was increasing in the East. In 1965 Malcolm "Mike" Stevenson got his altitude diamond at Sugarbush, Vermont, where he became the first to get all the legs of his Diamond badge east of the Mississippi!

chaired by Miles Coverdale, was aggressively working on this problem through the monthly column, "The Safety Corner."

Ryan, during his two terms as president of SSA, had worked diligently on various SSA-FAA problems. He was assisted by Doc Mosher, a soaring enthusiast and corporate pilot, and they made many trips to the FAA in Washington, D.C.

Other Activities during 1966

Since the formation of an SSA Archives was long overdue, Dale May, chairman of the Public Information Committee, requested members to send in any historical material to him.

Soaring lost a longtime enthusiast when Bill Placek died of natural causes. He was an FAA general inspector and because of his glider experience he was given the special assignment of preparing new written tests for private and commercial glider pilots.

The 1966 CAP national encampment provided a total of 124 cadets with instruction at Chester, South Carolina; Lawton, Oklahoma; and Elmira, New York.

Chapter 10

A Great Leap Forward,
1967–1971

An Explosion of Interest, 1967

On March 8 it would be 10 years since the directors "stuck their necks out" and hired a full-time executive secretary and committed themselves to get the SSA on a self-sustaining basis. During this period, the membership grew sixfold, an efficient organization was developed, *Soaring* became a monthly publication, and the SSA was able to break even.

Ted Sharp, perennial treasurer of SSA, referred to these 10 years as the golden decade in his article in the May 1967 *Soaring*, noting that "the history of this fantastic growth . . . involves great decisions, a dedicated faith in the future of soaring . . . and [the] hard work and devotion of many SSA members and friends." Other factors that helped to make this possible were the reorganization of SSA on regional director basis, the willingness of sailplane designers and manufacturers to gamble on making a business of selling kits and sailplanes, the stimulus of introductory flights made available by the commercial sailplane operators, and the ABC Program.

Starr's First Editorial

Sterling Starr's first editorial as president listed the accomplishments since the SSA had hired Licher. After sum-marizing what had taken place, he commented:

> SSA has grown to a solid functioning organization on a sound financial basis, with both professional and volunteer personnel providing many and varied tangible and intangible services to the membership. Now, where do we go from here?
>
> The 44 SSA Committees were reorganized into seven Boards . . . with each Board chairman reporting to the SSA President. Committees within each Board have related activities and responsibilities.
>
> Improvement in the soaring safety records is very essential to continued development of the sport. Seventy-two accidents including nine fatalities were reported in 1966.
>
> The encouragement of competition by lower performance sailplanes is to be developed through use of handicapping.
>
> A Business Membership (at $25) has been established to derive mutual benefit to SSA and commercial operators.
>
> The Directors . . . decided that the magazine should go to all members, with the price of the magazine subscription being added to the present dues for members ($13), student members ($4) and associates ($6).

Directors' Winter Meeting, 1967

Special guests at the meeting in San Diego, California, on January 28–29,

Many soaring enthusiasts had been greatly impressed by the original National Geographic *article and were hopeful that the Geographic would do a story on soaring after World War II. In Washington, in the early 1950s, President Carsey and P. A. Schweizer visited the* Geographic *office to encourage them to consider running another story. They expressed interest and said they would consider it in their future plans.*

A telephone call from Young in the spring of 1966 told of his interest in doing a story on soaring, and the Schweizers said that they would be happy to cooperate. Young arrived in a motorhome and parked it for one month next to the SSS. While taking his course, he spent time with Bernie Carris, SSS chief flight instructor, and visited the SAC plant to see how sailplanes were designed and built.

All were impressed with the National Geographic *organization's thoroughness and attention to accuracy. They asked LLoyd Licher, the Schweizers, and other key soaring people to read the draft of the story and check the drawings. This was quite a change from the usual soaring story projects. It seemed that some writers had a preconceived idea of what soaring is about and they did not want to let the "facts get in their way."*

1967, included J. F. Nields, NAA president; Dave Matlin, SSA general counsel; and Col. L. H. McCormack and Maj. Robert Smith of the CAP.

The bylaws were changed to make the immediate past president a director-at-large if he was not otherwise a director.

The board decided to have a die made for an SSA award medal that would go to the top finishers in the national and regional meets each year.

Consideration was given to adopting the Bronze "C" award.

A review was made of the membership dropout problem—over 500 members were being lost every six months.

The Big Three

Three publicity windfalls in 1967 had a great impact on the growth of motorless flight in the United States: the *National Geographic* article, a Disney film,

and Bob Buck's article in the *Reader's Digest*.

"SAILORS OF THE SKY". The January 1967 issue of the *National Geographic* magazine featured an article about soaring entitled "Sailors of the Sky". Gordon Young had become fascinated by soaring after watching it at Sebring, Florida, and was able to convince his editor to run a soaring story. He came to SSS to learn more about it and stayed for a month while he learned to become a soaring pilot. When he left he had two legs on his Silver "C" and needed the five-hour duration. He then spent some time at Gus Briegleb's school at El Mirage, California, and at Les Arnold's school at Sky Sailing, where he was able to get his five-hour flight for the completion of his Silver "C."

It was an excellent (and accurate) article with outstanding drawings and photographs. It followed Young's experiences through his training and, like the 1929 article on soaring, had a great impact.

THE BOY WHO FLEW WITH THE CONDORS. The Disney film, *The Boy Who Flew with the Condors*, was shown on prime-time, February 19, 1967, on the Wonderful World of Color TV program. It is the story of a young girl soaring pilot who, —on her Silver "C" distance flight, lands on a farm field where she meets a boy who is watching the condors soar. She interests him in soaring and the film covers his experience in learning to soar and getting his Silver "C." The training scenes were filmed at Fred Harris's Holiday Soaring School, where both young actors were actually soaring students. The condor scenes were made at nearby Los Padres National Forest, where the remaining condors still fly. Some "Hollywood" got into the picture, with a 2-22

landing in a pond, a Silver "C" distance attempt in what appears to be instrument weather and a "hairy" rope tow from a dry lake north of Bishop. Nonetheless, it is a beautiful film and it conveys what soaring is all about.

"THE SKY IS THEIR LIMIT". Bob Buck, an airline pilot and writer who was converted to soaring in 1959, tells about soaring in this article. It is aimed at the "average" reader and very effectively creates the feeling of soaring. The large circulation of the *Reader's Digest* helped this become another good plug for soaring.

Impact of Publicity on Commercial Operators

The publicity from this film and two stories stimulated an immediate and unprecedented increase in rides and soaring courses at the commercial soaring operations and had a pronounced effect on the growth of soaring.

SAC experienced a 350 percent increase in its sale of the dollar kits during the first three months of 1967. Also, over 1,000 letters of inquiry were received during that period. The $5

The 2-22 production was discontinued at ship no. 258 and production of the 2-33 was scheduled at the rate of six per month. After 19 years in production, with a total of 75 of all types produced, the 1-23 series was discontinued. The other sailplanes in production were the 1-26, of which over 350 had been delivered, and the 2-32, which was at no. 50.

ride coupon that was featured in the ads in *Flying* and *AOPA Pilot* was not needed to stimulate the SAC dealers' business.

Sailplane Development

A full-page ad in the January 1967 *Soaring* announced that Slingsby Sailplane Ltd. in England would produce the HP-14 at the price of $8,995 for east coast delivery. Schreder visited the Slingsby plant in March to assist in preparing three HP-14's for the British Nationals. Irv Prue's new UHP-1 was shown on the front cover of the April 1967 Soaring. This was a new design for light soaring conditions. The first UHP-1 was bought by Dr. Wylie Mullen who competed in it at the 1967 Nationals.

An article by Tony Doherty in the

Fred and Goldie Harris, in the foreground, at the opening of the new location of Holiday Soaring in Tehachapi, California, in 1967. The operations building was placed adjacent to the center of the runways for efficient operations. Site is now operated by Larry and Jane Barrett of Skylark North.

(Reisingers, NSM Collection)

The UHP-1 all-metal prototype that Irv Prue developed for Dr. Wylie Mullen of Chicago. It is shown being tested over a cultivated part of the desert near Prue's home in Pearblossom, California.

(NSM Collection)

Sept 1967 *Soaring* announced the new Schweizer 2-33. It was developed from the 2-22 and was designed to perform about the same as the 1-26.

Changes in FAA Regulations

Ryan and Starr attended meetings in Washington, D.C., with the FAA on the status of changes requested by the SSA. One item of good news was that glider towing could now be done without a waiver and the new regulations set up standards for the tow pilot, the towing procedure, and the requirements for tow ropes.

There were no developments in the regulations on glider instruments and cloud flying nor on simplifying the process of type certification for sailplanes. However, the requirements for experimental license had been clarified so that sailplanes could be issued an experimental license for racing.

The proposal to lower the floor of positive control air space from 24,000 feet to 18,000 feet was withdrawn in face of the objections of many aircraft organizations, including the SSA.

34th National, 1967

The contest at Marfa, Texas, from July 4 to 14, 1967, was the largest National held to date—73 sailplanes were en-

tered, including 7 flown by foreign pilots. In addition, a new record of 112,937 miles flown was set.

Marshall Claybourn was competition director and Fritz Kahl contest manager. The weather was acceptable, despite frequent thunderstorms and a tornado. The distance within a prescribed area task proposed by Bikle, chairman of the Rules Committee, was given a try for the first time. Of the 10 possible flying days, there were 5 speed tasks, 2 prescribed area distance tasks, and a free distance day. On the free distance day, Schreder made the best flight, a distance of 460 miles to Kenton, Oklahoma. He had a friendly reception from the farmer in whose field he landed since he was a member of the National Geographic Society.

A. J. Smith, flying his Sisu, got into first place on the second day and stayed there to become the national soaring champion once again. He described this flight:

> With a lead of about 600 points . . . we were tempted to go up the mountains to the northwest, where conditions would be booming. But the risk was there again, it being probable that thunderstorms would blow up over the mountains, shutting off the track to the north.
>
> So the decision was made before take-off to go a bit east of north along the boundary between the high ground to the west and the irrigated lowland to the east. . . . This was, indeed, the conservative approach. It meant flying without the advantage of a good wind.
>
> A line of growing storms along the south edge of the river canyon was bypassed (Canadian River) in a hurried attempt to make the 20 to 30-mile glide across. It didn't work out. There were no apparent landing places in the canyon, and the glide back out barely got to a good field. . . .
>
> Ross Briegleb landed with me

about an hour later. We had gone 357 miles.

Schreder was second in his HP-14, Johnson third in a HP-13, Moffat fourth in a Diamant, and Ben Greene fifth in his Libelle. Ross Briegleb, who finished eighth in a BG-12B had the highest score on the basis of the Lattimore handicapping system.

Directors' Summer Meeting, 1967

At the July 14 meeting in Marfa, it was agreed that Ivans should continue to push to have the 1970 WSC held in the United States. No site was to be committed, but a decision from CVSM was needed by January 1, 1969. Also at this meeting, Bennett M. Rogers was named the new editor of *Soaring*.

Owing to pressure from the membership, it was decided to recognize the Standard Class in the U.S. national and regional contests again, although there was not to be a separate seeding for the Standard Class pilots for the international team. SSA was to provide a trophy.

The title of executive secretary was changed to executive director since this was more descriptive of the position. All the officers were reelected except for the western vice-president, where Marshall Claybourn replaced Red Wright.

Elmira was chosen as the site of the 1968 Nationals, winning out over Adrian by one vote.

Plans for 1968

At a meeting of the CVSM committee in Paris earlier in the year, Poland was chosen to host the 1968 WSC.

The committee made a number of changes in the sporting code: "Radio is to be allowed in the Std Cl as well as in the Open Cl. All forms of ground-based navaids are prohibited. No navigational instruments other than magnetic or gyro compass are to be used. Radio is to be used for communication only, not navigation. There is to be no help given, in any form, by non-competing aircraft. Team captains are no longer permitted a separate ground-based transmitter."

Most of the above changes or additions to the Sporting Codes reflect the committee's desire to emphasize individual self-reliance in competition.

A proposal to liberalize the Standard Class requirements to permit flaps and retractable wheels was defeated since there was a reluctance to complicate the rules. The committee actually went the other way and set a minimum wheel size on any new Standard Class designs.

The SSA Seeding Committee announced that the top four pilots were (1) R. Schreder, (2) R. Johnson, (3) G. Moffat, and (4) A. J. Smith.

Licher's Summary of 1967

In Licher's report to the directors before their 1968 winter meeting, he summarized the events of 1967:

> The results of our year in the sun are in and make impressive reading. Total membership climbed to 8,200 by year end. . . . The net growth of 2,248 members in 1967 (an average of 187 per month) was 4.6 times the nearly linear average of 488 per year for the preceding eight years.
>
> Even more impressive are the figures for new members gained . . . a total of 3,427; an average of 285 per month.
>
> Five new Chapters were added to the previous total of 71 six months ago. Total Chapter membership is

Hannes Linke in a Libelle after setting a German national record for a 100-kilometer triangle. Linke became very active in the Smirnoff Derby and later in the Hilton Cup activities.

(Don Monroe)

2,794, or 34% of all SSA members.

We now have the equivalent of 9 full-time people doing work for SSA on a paid basis.

Other Activities during 1967

Ann Burns of Great Britain, with Janie Oesch of Colorado Springs as copilot, set a women's multiplace absolute altitude world record on January 1 in a 2-32 at Wave Flights. At the same place in the same sailplane, Janie Oesch with Ruth Wild as copilot set two national multiplace altitude records on November 30.

Ed Minghelli and Bob Semans set a world multiplace out-and-return record in the Prue Two with a flight of 366.9 miles.

Two world speed records were set when Elemor Katinszky set the 500-kilometer triangle record of 75.49 miles per hour in a Libelle, and Hannes M. Linke set the West German 100-kilometer triangle record of 84.91 miles per hour, also in a Libelle.

During 1967 four soaring personalities were lost to soaring. Fred Loomis, who photographed the national soaring contests in Elmira in the 1930s and 1940s died on January 10. His complete photograph and negative files became

part of the NSM archives. Hawley Bowlus died on August 27 at the age of 71. Although he was not active in soaring after World War II, his many sailplane designs made him one of the early pioneers of soaring. George Diebert, a key figure in soaring at Bishop, California, died on November 11. He managed the Bishop airport. Earl Southee, a founder of SSA and president in 1940, died on November 16. He was active in soaring until 1953, when he wrote a 20-page history of soaring for the July-August 1953 *Soaring*.

During the year about 200,000 flights in 1,600 different sailplanes were made without a fatality. This was particularly impressive in view of the expansion of flying during the year.

Ridge Soaring Returns, 1968

The last distance record in ridge flying was set in 1933 when Dick du Pont flew 122 miles along the Blue Ridge Mountains. Larry Lawrence, manager of that expedition, predicted in his report that the distance record would be greatly increased by using the ridges, but thermal soaring was on its ascendency and ridge soaring was soon forgotten.

Thirty-five years later, on March 3, 1968, a world record was set over the Allegheny ridges, and ridge soaring became popular again.

The Air Space

At this time soaring people were becoming concerned by the proposed lowering of the area positive control (APC) to 14,500 feet. Sterling Starr, in his editorial in the February 1968 *Soaring*, explained the problem and told what SSA planned to do:

Two recent airline/light-aircraft collisions, coupled with growing terminal congestion, have added impetus to FAA plans for applying positive control to millions of square miles of airspace.

A major portion of cross-country soaring throughout the U.S.A. would be restricted; soaring sites within 30 miles of major terminals would find operations impossible. . . .

If the sport of soaring is to continue to grow, these restrictions must not occur! The Society is taking positive steps now to prevent such a disaster.

New Awards for Soaring Youth

An article in the January 1968 *Soaring* reported on developments in youth soaring activity:

> It probably will come as a surprise to many to learn that the fastest growing phase of SSA is the student membership. In the last two and a half years, this membership has increased 116%; whereas the total membership of SSA has only increased 42%. As of June 30, 1967 the student membership totaled 1,201, or approximately 17% compared to the total membership of 7,172.
>
> No doubt, this growth has been stimulated by the great publicity last year [and] the growing CAP Cadet Program.
>
> One club, the Colorado Soaring Association, has taken a big step by creating a scholarship fund and a series of special awards for young people in soaring [which] will be carried out from the proceeds of contributions to the "Paul Kolstad Memorial Fund."
>
> The purpose of the fund is twofold: (1) to stimulate youth participation in local club activities, and (2) to reward youth soaring accomplishments. . . . It will be an annual award to an accredited college of the recipient's choice.

Directors' Winter Meeting, 1968

Bill Ivans reported to the meeting of directors on January 20–21, 1968, in Washington, D.C., that the CVSM members felt that if the WSC was to be held in the United States it should be held in the strong conditions of the west, but the cost of sending a team would also be a factor. These requirements created a dilemma for the directors since it was more likely that the eastern bidders could come up with better financial inducements, whereas Marfa, Texas, was desirable because of its excellent soaring conditions. After presentations by representatives of each site, a vote was taken and Marfa received 14 votes, Adrian 5, and Elmira, Reno, and Roswell, one each.

Two officers from the USAF CAP headquarters were present to explain the decision to suspend national CAP glider encampment activities. The reasons were (1) the hourly cost of glider time exceeded that for aiplanes and (2) the cadets had little opportunity to continue glider activity after they returned home.

It had been difficult for soaring people to convince the Air Force officers who administered the CAP program that gliding and soaring had numerous possibilities for the CAP Cadet Program, just as it is difficult to get the "average" power pilot to take up soaring. In 1965, Col. Joe Mason, USAF, became the national commander of the CAP, a position normally held by a brigadier general. Mason had started gliding in a primary in the early 1930s and felt strongly that a glider program would be ideal for the CAP cadets. He set up a one-month national encampment at Harris Hill, where 80 cadets took glider courses and 12 cadets an FAA private power course. Mason was very enthusiastic about the results, particularly the way the cadets were motivated, and he expanded the program in 1966 with encampments at Lawton, Oklahoma; Chester, South Carolina; and Elmira. Since these were also very successful there was hope that they would expand into a national program. However, Colonel Mason retired in 1967, and when the new administration reviewed the program they decided to discontinue it on the grounds of the higher costs per hour of a glider course. The CAP civilian leaders, in contrast, were in favor of continuing the program, since two glider pilots could be certified for the cost of one airplane pilot and they felt that the glider pilots were more motivated toward flying and were "better-adjusted" cadets. However, without support from the top, it was unlikely that gliding in the CAP would continue to grow.

The USAF argued that gliding could be done at the wing (state) level. A report on the ABC Training Program brought out the need to provide more instructors, revalidate existing ones, and to standardize training procedures. The Safety Committee, which was continuing the "Safety Corner" in *Soaring*, announced the start of a series of "Safety of Soaring" cartoons by Gene Planchak.

It was decided to incorporate a modification to the handicap system that Hal Lattimore of the TSA had developed. This would be added to the regional rules so that the contests at that level could be scored both ways, but with only the open scores counting.

The consensus was that a higher achievement award for soaring was needed, and the directors agreed to propose to CVSM that a fourth Diamond be authorized for a flight around a 300-kilometer triangle at some minimum speed.

Jonathan Livingston Seagull

Soaring editor Bennett Rogers was alert for good writing. He had seen the story "Jonathan Livingston Seagull" in the December 1967 *Private Pilot* magazine and was one of the first to recognize it as a masterpiece. He wrote Richard Bach, the author, for permission to run it in *Soaring*. In his reply Bach said: "It would be my deepest honor to see Jonathan in *Soaring* and in as many sailplane magazines as possible around the world. For, if there is in the world one single most skilled type of pilot, it is the man who flies a sailplane. Your big sculptures in the sky are useless for transporting businessmen from A to B on time; they are worthless for showing the rest of the world how rich and powerful you all are; but, my God, you people can FLY!"

It was run in the February 1968 *Soaring* and was later published as a book, and Bach and it soon became literary sensations.

A Timeless Sky

Another piece of good writing appeared in the same issue. Allan MacNicol, who did pioneering work in promoting wave flying in the Mt. Washington area, arranged for Mike Stevenson to take Guy Gosselin, the chief observer of the Mt. Washington Observatory, for his first soaring flight. The flight so impressed him that he wrote an article about it entitled "A Timeless Sky." MacNicol wrote the introduction and said that Gosselin had created "a unique piece of soaring journalism, for seldom are aviation writings graced with such a fine descriptive feel of the actual experience of flight." The following excerpt from the article speaks for itself:

> If there is the slightest bit of humiliation connected with soaring, it is in getting off the ground. One would like to see those long wings give a flap or two, and the craft lurch abruptly into the sky. But, alas, even the gooney bird does better, and the sailplane must decorate the end of a tether. . . . The sensation of being towed is unnatural. . . . When the shock and twang of the cable release occur, it is as though the bird has spit out something distasteful, and it is not until then that a ride begins.
>
> When we had first commenced our flight, I was appalled by the manner in which we can take the miraculous for granted. . . . I longed to reach back into the fifteenth century, grasp da Vinci away from his doomed sketches of flying machines, and say, "Come with me, Leo. I've got something I think you'll be interested in." I tried to imagine him in my place. The miracle would not have been lost.
>
> So there you are—suspended, motionless, alone in a timeless sky.

A World Record on the Ridges

Karl Striedieck's report on his record flight, "Confessions of a Pennsylvania Ridge Runner," appeared in the May 1968 *Soaring* and was prefaced with an interesting comment: "There are some things you can count on, right? Like nobody is going to set any world record soaring on the East Coast . . . particularly not in the winter . . . and especially not in a ship with an L/D in the 20's, for heavens sakes! Right? Wrong."

The article told of his out-and-return record made on March 3, 1968 in a Ka-8. Using the Allegheny ridges that run northeast-southwest, he took off from his strip for a start at Eagleville (near Lock Haven, Pennsylvania) and flew to a turn-point 238 miles away at Mountain Grove, Virginia, then returned to Eagleville for a total flight of 476.6 miles.

Striedieck, a pilot with the Air National Guard, tells of an exciting flight made in cold and turbulent conditions:

> Probably the experience that started me thinking about flying ridges was a trip to Hawk Mountain Sanctuary in eastern PA 16 years ago. The sight of hundreds of hawks sailing effortlessly down the invisible cushion of air captured my fancy, and I longed for a way to join them. This pleasure was realized in 1966 when I bought my Ka-8 and some property from which to launch the bird on top of Bald Eagle Ridge. The possibility of a long ridge flight was obvious the first time we studied the arrangement of the Allegheny ridges in detail. . . . The maps looked good for March 3rd. . . . A call to Phillipsburg FSS at 0515 resulted in a "GO" decision, . . . Sue attached the rope and yanked me into the air. At 0705, I headed north-east to my start point, taking the photograph at 0735. The ridge to Altoona is a piece of cake except for one ticklish place at Milesburg. The Bedford gap is the biggest sweat because it's nine miles to the next ridge. . . . Turbulence was very rough all day, but the stretch from Cumberland to the turn-point and back was the worst. . . . I passed the Mountain Grove turn-point at 1230, took a picture, and headed home.
>
> I had earlier decided not to risk the Bedford and Altoona gaps . . . so I decided to take the 'scenic route' up Tussey Ridge. . . .
>
> I wasn't sure how I could get over the point where the two ridges meet at Altoona, but I went up to find out.
>
> Now I could see the ore pits at Port Matilda and maybe even the

white top of the jeep at my strip. As I
drew closer, it was indeed the jeep,
and I rocked and porpoised my bird as
a happy greeting to [Sue] my faithful
partner.

Near Milesburg I spotted a circling
hawk and deviated enough to identify
him and say hello. . . . Soon I was
swinging out beyond my start point.
Gentle turns brought me down to final
approach, and at 1753 I rolled to a
stop. I wasn't sure if I could still walk,
but who cares!

Marfa Gets World Championship

The CVSM at its March 1 meeting
chose Marfa as the site of the WSC for
1970 by a unanimous vote. The substantial reduction in shipping and fuel
costs guaranteed by the Marfa sponsors and the offer of sailplanes and
tow cars by SSA members all helped
in this choice. A discussion was held
on the emerging class of motor gliders.
Germany had 100 of them flying. An
effort was being made to devise standards by which motor gliders could be
differentiated from light powered
aircraft.

The Record Hoax

Good sportsmanship has long been
synonymous with soaring. The one
characteristic that separates the soaring
pilot from power pilots is that his skill
and flying ability can easily be measured. He has no crutch (engine) to
lean on or to cover up his limitations.
How long he stays up, or how far he
flies is usually a good measure of what
kind of a soaring pilot he is. Most pilots privately evaluate their fellow pilots' ability. Some cannot take this
evaluation and quietly drop out of the
sport. Others might try to cover their
shortcomings by exaggerating their accomplishments. But the majority take
their success or failures as they come
and learn from them.

In 1968 an American pilot claimed
a new world distance record. The
flight was announced by an SSA news
release and reported in *Soaring* and in
the British *Sailplane and Gliding* magazine. One SSA director who lived on
the flight track questioned how the
flight could have been made under the
conditions that existed at that time. He
became suspicious and reported this to
the SSA office. Upon further investiga-

tion, the pilot withdrew his claim. It was hard to see how anyone would have wanted to live with a false claim, when the only purpose of such a flight is the personal satisfaction involved.

The 1968 World Soaring Championship

For the second time, a U.S. pilot became a world champion when A. J. Smith won the Standard Class competition at the WSC in Leszno, Poland, from June 9 to 23, 1968. The other U.S. pilots did well, and unofficially the U.S. team had the best team score, dislodging the Poles, who had dominated the last three WSCs.

The top four U.S.-seeded pilots were on the team, with A. J. Smith and George Moffat both flying Swiss-built Elfe S-3s in the Standard Class and Dick Schreder and Dick Johnson flying HP-14T and HP-13M, respectively, in the Open Class. Marshall Claybourn was the team captain.

This WSC had 105 sailplanes from 32 countries entered, the largest number of sailplanes and countries to date. Through the help of the NAA, the U.S. team was able to get Air Force transportation for the team personnel and two sailplanes.

Because different tasks were given to each class, it was not easy to compare the performance of the two classes. There were 57 competitors in the Standard Class. George Moffat placed fourth. Only 23 more points would have put Moffat behind Smith and given the United States a one-two finish. Per Axel Persson of Sweden was second in a Libelle and Rudy Lindner of West Germany third in a Phoebus A.

In the Open Class of 48 competitors, Harro Wodl of Austria, flying a Cirrus was 1st, Goran Ax of Sweden in a Phoebus C was 2d, and Rudy Seilers of Switzerland, flying a Diamant 18 was 3d. Dick Johnson was 8th and Dick Schreder was 21st.

The OSTIV Congress was held during the championship. The OSTIV finally gave in and picked the Foka as the winner of the OSTIV Standard Class design competition.

35th National, 1968

Sixty-one pilots and sailplanes gathered at the newly improved Harris Hill site for the 1968 contest from July 2–12. Othmar "Oats" Schwartzenberger was the competition director. Ben Greene, flying a Libelle was first, John Ryan was second in a Phoebus, and Neal Ridenaur was third in an HP-13. Twelve Standard Class sailplanes were entered, and Louis Rehr, in a Ka-6E, had the most points of this group.

When Elmira "lost its turn" to have the National in 1961, the EASC became concerned and realized that it had to improve the Harris Hill field. The glider field was originally made by taking down two stone walls that separated three hayfields on the top of Hawes Hill. The fields were grass, but of very uneven grades, which limited the use of the field.

Although the EASC was able to get the 1963 Nationals, this contest demonstrated that the Harris Hill field had to be updated. The contests had more sailplanes entered, required more tow planes, the sailplanes were getting heavier, and the SSA expected the takeoff operation at a National to launch at least one per minute. After four years of work with the community leaders and county officials, the EASC finally convinced the county to approve a $245,000 project to level the hill and to put in a glider takeoff strip and a tow plane runway. The field was closed down in 1967 for construction, and the new field was dedicated at the start of the 1968 Nationals.

While the EASC was searching for support for this project, it encountered some negative reactions from the surrounding communities, since Elmira was getting all the credit. Thus it was decided to change EASC's name to Harris Hill Soaring Corporation (HHSC). This appeased the adjacent communities and brought in support from a 25-mile radius of Harris Hill.

The contest report in the September 1968 *Soaring* was written by Doug Lamont, and Wayne Stettler prepared the maps and drawings. Bennett Rogers said that it was "the most monumental and definitive account of a single soaring event published."

Lamont's explanation of "what doesn't happen at a contest can be equally as important as what does," helped to explain this National:

> With the absence of such names as A. J. Smith, Dick Johnson, George Moffat, Rudy Allemann, Carroll Klein, Wally Scott, Graham Thomson, Al Parker, and Bill Ivans . . . and with Dick Schreder without his proper mount until the end of the contest—there was a suspicion that almost anything could happen, especially in a geographic area where the weather might well turn out to be weak and unpredictable.
>
> But, above all, what did not happen at Elmira was the Big Fluke. For, despite a stage seemingly set for new faces and tricked-up endings, form mercifully held true, and in the end class prevailed. . . . In short, the end result was a Championship, not a Hollywood fairy tale.

Directors' Summer Meeting, 1968

The new slate of officers voted in at the July 12 meeting in Elmira were B. S. Smith, president; Miles Coverdale, East Coast vice-president; Marshall Claybourn, West Coast vice-president; Lewis Hull, secretary; and Ted Sharp, treasurer. E. J. Reeves was elected honorary vice-president in recognition of his great service to SSA over the past 22 years.

The total number of members as of June 1968 had reached the all-time high of 8,540. However, the rate of increase during this period was much less than that in 1967.

Marfa, Texas, was chosen as the site of the 1969 Nationals.

In view of the increased soaring activity in some regions, it was agreed to permit two Regionals a year if the activity justified it.

Dale May, chairman of the Public Information Board, had requested that any archival material be sent to him for safe keeping until an archives could be found. It was pointed out that the University of Wyoming, the University of Texas, and Northrup University might be repositories for the SSA files. Schweizer mentioned that the HHSC had plans for a soaring museum, library, and archives at Harris Hill. The subject was to be an agenda item for the next meeting.

The possibility of a soaring museum, library, and archives at Harris Hill had often been discussed. After World War II, Sherman Voorhees, one of the founders of SSA, promoted the idea. He felt that Harris Hill was the logical spot for such a museum since the U.S. soaring movement had started there and until 1947 had been the center of soaring activity in the United States.

In 1958 a group of Elmirans led by Nellie Mooers, wife of Eddie Mooers, a very active supporter of soaring in the area, started developing a commu-

nity museum at Strathmont, a large el-
egant manorhouse in Elmira. The
EASC was invited to set up a soaring
museum in the adjacent carriage
house. Howie Burr, immediate past
president of the EASC, was the chairman of this project and the soaring
museum portion of the Strathmont
was opened on Decoration Day 1959.
Unfortunately, the museum at Strathmont had to be disbanded after a few
years owing to financial problems. The
soaring exhibits were then divided between the Harris Hill administration
building and the Curtiss Museum at
Hammondsport, where they were sent
on loan. Some items were put into
storage.

Other Activities during 1968

Charles V. Lindsay wrote an article entitled "Satellite Observations used as a
new tool in developing Wave Climatol-
goy" for the January 1968 *Soaring*. In
addition, *Soaring* began running "Regional Rambling," a column by Richard Miller that covered activities in the
12 SSA regions. Rogers had expanded
it and it became a popular part of
Soaring.

The Colorado Soaring Association
and the Kolstad family created a Youth
Soaring Award in memory of Paul Kolstad, one of the outstanding youthful
members who had lost his life in a soaring accident. The Kolstad Award was
awarded for the first time in 1968 to
Michael Opitz.

Hugh Whitney, who had been
manager of the 1968 Nationals, died in
November after a short illness. He had
been a member of three international
teams and was the team manager of
the 1963 WSC in Argentina. He was
active with HHSC and the Rochester
Soaring Club.

Hugh Whitney was one of those
exceptional people who occasionally
appear on the scene. His first exposure
to soaring was at the McGrath lawn
parties that were a feature of the national soaring contests before World
War II. W. L. "Bill" McGrath was the
general manager of the local Bendix
plant and one of the chief boosters of
soaring. Each year he gave a lawn
party at his home for the sailplane pilots, crew, and contest personnel. His
chief engineer, Maurice Whitney, also
a soaring booster, lived next door and
his young sons, Roger and Hugh, attended these parties.

After World War II, Hugh took a
soaring course at the SSS. He helped
form a new soaring club in the Elmira
area called STAG, and Hugh went
after his Silver "C" in their 2-22. While
attending Cornell, he was one of the
crew in the Spanish and English
WSCs. Because of the outstanding job
that he had done there, he was appointed team manager for the Argentina WSC, where he was again a great
asset to the team.

After becoming a military pilot
and completing his stint in the Air
Force as a pilot, he took an engineering job with Eastman Kodak. Soon
after he joined the Rochester Soaring
Club and became its president. In 1968
he took vacation time to be the contest
manager for the National at Harris Hill
and despite ill health, he did his usual
good job. Four months later he died of
cancer.

Standard Class Finally Accepted in the United States, 1969

The Standard Class controversy in the
United States was now in its twelfth
year. Some progress was made when
the SSA directors requested bids for a

Les Arnold of Sky Sailing at Fremont, California, had one of the busiest commercial soaring operations and has contributed much to the growth of soaring in the United States.

(Les Arnold)

full-scale 1970 national Standard Class championship. On the other hand, the CVSM, at its last meeting, had taken two steps that moved the Standard Class further away fom the original concept. The Standard Class was now almost an unlimited 15-meter competition class, and the controversy continued.

President's Message

In his first editorial as president in the 1969 *Soaring*, Bernald Smith wrote:

> As our numbers have grown, so have the numbers of others using all the free airspace. . . . I think what we're really trying to impress upon the regulatory bodies is that soaring is the medium by which that "uninterrupted navigable ocean that comes to the threshold of every man's door" can best be used as a source of human gratification and advantage. (Apologies to Sir George Cayley).
>
> What of the commercial operator? . . . Like the chicken and egg routine of which came first, the question of whether the commercial operator is responsible for the growth of soaring or vice-versa does not seem germane now. One could not exist without the other. But, the expanded list of com-

mercial (operators) . . . is an indication of some devotion on the part of individuals who, although they hope to operate in the block, still are willing to take the lumps along the way.

> The rapid growth in commercial soaring sites has resulted in a large number of adherents finding their pleasure in an occasional rented glider flight; . . . Certainly we would hope to stimulate their interest toward fuller enjoyment and involvement in our sport, . . . the contest pilot is a minority group within the membership of SSA. However, the stimulus of competition provides the improvement to all facets of our sport. . . .
>
> We shall endeavor to instill our own exciting enthusiasm for this sport through the everyday management of Society business.

GI Training

With the increase in military activity related to the cold war, Congress approved funds for a new GI Bill that would help veterans train for a job. To qualify for flight training, the veteran had to establish his intentions of becoming a commercial sailplane pilot or instructor, or to show the need for this training in relation to his work. Under this bill, the United States picked up 90 percent of the cost.

The Return of Jonathan Livingston Seagull

Bennett Rogers, in writing about a sequel to "Jonathan Livingston Seagull" in the January 1968 *Soaring*, said:

> Last February we reprinted "Jonathan Livingston Seagull" from another magazine. The story captured the basic, unspoiled motives and emotions associated with flying. And because soaring pilots deal with flying in its purest state and because for many of them

CVSM Meeting

At the CVSM meeting in London on November 27, 1968, the majority favored having separate tasks for the Open and Standard Class at the 1970 WSC. It was agreed that the "designated start," "photographic identification turn-point procedure," and "prescribed area distant tasks" would be used at this WSC.

Discussions continued on the Standard Class with the usual contradictory philosophies being aired again. The CVSM then decided to allow retractable landing gears, and the use of any types of air brakes, except drag chutes, which opened the way for flaps. The majority was against the fourth Diamond proposed by the United States.

Directors' Winter Meeting, 1969

For the first time the SSA membership meeting and the awards banquet for noncontest awards were held in conjunction with the Winter directors' meeting, which took place February 1–2, 1969, in Colorado Springs. Twenty-four directors were present.

One item on the agenda was the SSA flight training manual, which was well under way. However, since the FAA had not provided financial help, the directors decided that the SSA would go ahead and publish it itself.

An ad hoc committee with Joe Robertson as chairman, was set up to investigate all facets of sailplane competition other than Open Class. Consideration was to be given to the possible development of a new class that would more nearly meet the original Standard Class concept.

It was also decided to increase the maximum number of contestants in

Fred Robinson, owner of Great Western Soaring School in Pearblossom, California, played a major role in promoting soaring at commercial operations. Here Robinson cuts Edward Sloane's shirttail after a successful solo flight at his school.

(Lee Moody)

flying in its fundamental form is virtually a way of life, our readers felt a remarkable sense of kinship and identification with the philosophy expressed in Dick's charming parable. In short, the story had terrific impact and easily won our last reader survey poll.

Now, as an act of personal friendship, Dick has labored (nine rewrites) to give us our very own Jonathan story this month.

While it is, of course, easy to compare the members of "the Flock" with power-flying advocates and to equate Jonathan and his gallant band with gliding enthusiasts, this new story cuts much deeper. Bach recognizes that flying is an attempt to express one's true self and that therefore it represents an urge to attain freedom (in its best sense) by overcoming one's own limitations through practice, learning, and—ultimately—the achievement of excellence.

George and Suzanne Moffat, a top competition team of pilot and crew, won their first National in 1969.

(George Uveges)

the 1969 Nationals to 80. This allowed up to 20 foreign pilots to enter and gave the Marfa group some experience at running a large contest.

It was decided to ask for bids for the 1970 National, even though the 1970 WSC was being held in Marfa. It was felt that the Nationals would have little effect on the WSC.

In view of the fact that only a small amount of auto/pulley/winch towing was being done, the COs requested that the FAA delete this from the commercial glider requirements.

Proposals for an SSA archives were put forth on behalf of Northrop Institute of Technology, the University of Texas, and the HHSC. It was resolved that "the SSA indicates its extreme interest and support of the HHSC's museum program and that SSA is seriously considering the Harris Hill area as the official site of the SSA Archives, Library and Museum."

The treasurer reported that the SSA had operated in the black during 1968 and that the membership had continued to grow, and was now at 8,815 members.

Soaring Symposia

Soaring Symposia was formed by Bill Holbrook and Dr. Edward Byars to put on soaring symposiums. Two were held in 1969, one at White Sulphur Springs, Manns Choice, Pennsylvania, for competitive soaring pilots, and the other, on cross-country flying for less experienced pilots, at Seven Springs in Champion, Pennsylvania.

SAC's Position on Fiberglass Sailplanes

In the June 1969 *Soaring* a letter entitled "Economics" stated that SAC had

underestimated the impact of fiberglass sailplanes and as a consequence a performance gap had developed.

William Schweizer, who was the team member responsible for manufacturing at SAC, explained SAC's position on fiberglass sailplanes in *Soaring:*

In our opinion, fiberglass fabrication techniques have not advanced to the stage where it would be economically sound for us, as a U.S. manufacturer, to use this method of fabrication for the basic structure of a sailplane.

We believe that aluminum construction, in spite of high tooling costs, lends itself well to the fabrication of a more efficient structure and that a smooth aerodynamic surface can now be achieved with some new techniques.

A bonus of metal construction is long airframe life and simple repair. Also, structural integrity (and) pilot safety can more easily be built into the structure.

We have investigated European fiberglass sailplane manufacturing methods and procedures. Also we are familiar with what our U.S. commercial airplane builders are doing in this field and we make various fiberglass parts in our plant. . . .

The problem of meeting U.S. FAA design certification and production reliability requirements would be extremely difficult and costly. This is one of the major reasons why fiberglass airplanes are not in production in this country today.

For a U.S. manufacturer to sell a sailplane for $6,500, it must be built for no more than 600 man-hours. The only way to achieve man-hours in this range is with a completely tooled (all metal) ship and large volume production. It will probably take around 75 ships until the man-hour estimate is achieved and about 200 ships to make up for the starting load (the hours above the estimate for the first 75 ships).

The Standard Class and the 1-34

In an extensive article in *Soaring* P. A. Schweizer traced the history of the Standard Class internationally and domestically. The purpose of the article was to acquaint the members with the complete history in view of the growing interest in the Standard Class in the United States. It points out that the present Standard Class at the WSC was providing an interesting competition for designers, builders, and pilots, but that these sailplanes were a far cry from the original concept.

He proposed that another attempt be made to hold the Standard Class sailplane to the original concept. This would mean more stringent limitations and design standards in order to keep the sailplane within the basic concept, but he was not very optimistic that this would be done.

SAC's 1-34 was designed in the "spirit" of the Standard Class. On a trip to Europe in the summer of 1969, P. A. Schweizer had visited the Schleicher and Schempp-Hirth plants in Germany to see the latest Standard Class sailplanes and to compare them with the 1-34. At the Wasserkuppe, Gerhard Waibel checked him out in the ASW-15. At Schempp-Hirth's, Klaus Holighaus showed him the prototype Standard Cirrus. Schweizer noticed that the dive brakes were obviously not large enough to meet the OSTIV Standard Class requirements. When he asked Holighaus about this, the answer was that they were designed to keep the speed down below placard speed on a 45-degree dive instead of a 90-degree dive. Schweizer asked how this could meet the OSTIV Standard Class requirements, and Holighaus said that the German LFS (equivalent to the U.S. FAA) felt that it was adequate. Schweizer was puzzled about this and tried to find out about the change.

In order to spread out the development costs, it took a number of years to get the 1–34 into production, so that the new Standard Class sailplanes were a step ahead of it in performance by the time it came out. Getting the speed-limiting brakes to meet the OSTIV vertical dive requirements had also required considerable extra time and cost. The 1–34 was an ideal sailplane for badge flights and would have become another one-design class if enough had been built.

At that time, SAC saw a growing need for a "next-step" sailplane beyond the 1-26 and it went ahead with the 1-34, matching it to the original specifications of the Standard Class.

36th National, 1969

The story of the contest at Marfa from June 24 to July 3, 1969, was written by Joe Lincoln. He wrote principally from the pilot's point of view, which required an endless number of pilot interviews after they had completed their flights.

Eighty-two pilots were entered, 70 U.S. pilots and 12 foreign. Of the 82 sailplanes, 60 were of foreign manufacture and 22 were made in the United States.

The weather was typical for Marfa, and a total of 176,569 miles were flown—a new record for a Na-

Marshal Claybourn, competition director for the 1969 National, named to the same position for the first U.S.-conducted WSC in 1970, but a serious illness prevented him from realizing this ambition.

(George Uveges)

tional. On the free distance day there were 6 flights over 500 miles, the best one being 527.3 miles by *Wroblewski.* Fourteen additional flights were over 400 miles, and the day's mileage totaled 27,958 miles. To quote from Joe Lincoln's story:

> George Moffat went into the final day with a lead of 75 points. In this circumstance one would have expected him to fly conservatively, but this is not what he did. He tore around the course at a speed of 69.7 mph and was the first man to land back at Marfa. It was the fastest time of the day, his fourth winning task of the meet! A new U.S. National Champion had been chosen.
>
> Wally Scott did nearly as well, and his speed second best of the day at 68.5 mph, preserved his 2nd place in the final standings. It was an aesthetic ending; with the championship at stake, the two pilots who had dominated the entire contest had come through under immense pressure to prove conclusively that they were indeed the class of the field.
>
> For Rudy Allemann, however, the day was a disappointment. Finishing 45th, he lost 3rd place to John Brittingham by just 10 points. Henry Stouff was the highest finisher of the 9 Std Cl entered.
>
> It was some contest; there may never be another like it.

Marshall Claybourn, Fritz Kahl, the operating crew, and the Marfa supporters put on an excellent contest. The 36th was everything that was expected of it—a truly competitive meet and a good test for the 1970 WSCs.

Directors' Summer Meeting, 1969

At the July 4 meeting in Marfa, the executive director reported that during the first six months of 1969 the SSA had continued to grow at an annual rate of about 1,000 members. There was a 4.3 percent operating surplus for this period, and the reserves were in good position.

As a result of membership pressure for Standard Class recognition, it was agreed that the SSA should advertise for a sponsor of the 1970 Standard Class National. If sufficient interest was shown, consideration would be given to including the top pilots in the seeding lists for future WSCs. The directors also voted to recognize the Standard Class in all future regional contests and to allow retractable gears after 1969 and simple hinged flaps after that date, if approved by the CIVV.

In support of the progress made by the HHSC in establishing a soaring museum at Harris Hill, it was unanimously voted that Harris Hill become the site of the official SSA museum, library, and archives.

Efforts were being made to get the Post Office Department to issue a soaring stamp to commemorate the 1970 WSC.

The officers were all reelected.

Three World Records

Within a period of 23 days, four U.S. pilots set three world records. On July

31 at El Mirage, California, Ross Briegleb and his brother Kenneth set a world record for multiplace speed around a 100-kilometer triangle. The Brieglebs were flying a 2-32 and their speed was 69.97 miles per hour. Then, on August 8, Al Parker, flying his Sisu 1A, beat Wally Scott's goal flight world record of 520.55 miles, with a flight of 570 miles from Odessa to Blanding, Utah. Finally, on August 22, Wally Scott won back the goal flight world record with a flight of 606 miles from Odessa to Gila Bend, Arizona.

The Joy of Soaring

The long-awaited flight training manual finally became a reality in the fall of 1969, when *The Joy of Soaring* was published. It represented a complete SSA effort, with the Publication Committee managing the project, and Carle Conway doing the writing, Gil Parcel the graphics, and the SSA board deciding to publish it. In the foreword Harner Selvidge remarked:

> The title of this book may seem at first glance to be a contradiction, but this is not the case. Proper training and practice are prerequisites for proficiency in any activity, and this is as true for soaring as it is for playing a musical instrument, for example. Gliding is a pleasure from the very start, but the relaxation that comes from flying well and safely adds immeasurably to the enjoyment.
>
> As part of the preparation of this manual, its author visited numerous gliding schools from coast to coast. . . . He soon became aware that different ways of teaching and performing some of the maneuvers in the curriculum were being practiced with apparent success at different schools and clubs. A policy decision had to be made whether to explain all these concepts, or to take a more selective ap-

proach. In order to avoid confusing the student, it was decided to take the latter course.

Particular thanks go to Carle Conway and Gil Parcell, who gave unstintingly of their time and energy for the same purpose.

New Sailplanes

A number of new sailplanes were under development at this time:

CONCEPT 70. Art Zimmerman, a veteran soaring pilot and founder of the Icarus Soaring Club of New Jersey was developing the Concept 70 sailplane of RFP construction for the 1970s.

KASPER BEKAS N. Witold Kasper, who had developed the RKB-1 flying wing sailplane in Canada with S. K. Brochocki, moved to Seattle and was developing the Bekas N Flying Wing.

HP-15. Dick Schreder had competed in his new HP-15 at the Nationals.

MARSKE PIONEER. Jim Marske, who had built the SM-1 Flying Plank, had a new design called the Pioneer for weekend soaring.

Other Activities during 1969

Student Members hit a record high of 1,808, which represented 17.8 percent

Ross Briegleb and David Nees in a 2-32 at El Mirage, California. Ross and his brother Kenneth set a world speed record for the 100-kilometer triangle on July 31, 1969 in a 2-32.

(NSM Collection)

of the total SSA membership of 10,069. Also in 1969, a simplified handicapped system was developed by Dick Mancuso after a thorough study of all sailplanes flying in the United States. "Mr. Purist vs. the Motor Glider" was the title of Bennett Rogers's reply in the October 1969 *Soaring* to a letter to the editor. "Mr. Purist" argued that flying a motorglider is not soaring. However, Rogers pointed out that motorgliders do have a place in the soaring movement.

The First World Championships in the United States, 1970

The SSA was awarded the WSC for 1970 after many years of trying. It was to be held at Marfa, Texas. The Marfa soaring group was eager and had proven itself at two previous Nationals. Thirty-two countries signified their intention to enter about 100 sailplanes.

However, there were some negative factors. Although the Marfa group was able and enthusiastic, the town was small and in the "less endowed"

section of Texas. Financial support from the community was therefore limited. The facilities at this deserted World War II air base might be a disappointment to many of the European contestants, and Marfa was out in the hinterland with little except the WSC to attract spectators to the area. This was also a disadvantage in getting media coverage for the event.

On the other hand, membership support for the $25,000 WSC fund drive was good, and many clubs were turning over their chapter rebates to the fund. A mess hall was to be constructed for the teams and WSC personnel. Many SSA members volunteered their retrieve cars and sailplanes and were willing to act as crew.

The U.S. team pilots were Moffat and Scott in Open Class and A. J. Smith and Allemann in Standard Class.

President's Message

Bernald Smith's editorial in the January 1970 *Soaring* proposed a voluntary flight check:

When is the last time somebody flew in a sailplane with you to observe your techniques?

Fortunately, there still is no FAA ruling that requires further checking. How many of us, though, are mature enough to recognize the value in an individually imposed revalidation process.

Soaring adherents place a very high value on the freedom found in sailplanes, but none any more than someone like myself who lives in the regulated world of airlines and military-reserve aviation. . . . My purpose in suggesting a volunteer program is to prove that we don't need someone outside soaring telling us what to do.

The ABC Flight Training Program

Roy McMaster, the new chairman of the ABC Flight Training Program, reported in the February 1970 *Soaring* that a total of 4,292 badges had been issued since its start in 1962 and that 1,064 badges had been issued in 1969. McMaster noted: "The future of soaring depends upon the efforts of the flight instructor. If he produces competent students who will go on to enjoy safe flying, soaring will grow. These dedicated few are a selected group. . . . They are generous enough to give up much personal enjoyment in solo soaring and competition flying so that others may be initiated into the sport. They get little recognition for their time in the back seat of a 2-22 or 2-33."

The most active instructors and the number of badges issued under each during 1969 were B. Carris, SSS Elmira, 81; N. Nevin, Skysurfing, Hawaii, 77; F. Robinson, Great Western Soaring, Pearblossom, California, 59; Maj. C. Cunningham, Air Force Academy CO, 50; and D. Gustin, HHSC, Elmira, 47.

Directors' Winter Meeting, 1970

With the Marfa WSC approaching and the possibility of two Nationals, much of the meeting at Dallas on January 24–25, 1970, was spent on matters relating to these contests.

Two strong bids had been received for the Standard Class National, one from Pasco, Washington, and the other from Elmira, which was awarded the contest. Considerable discussion centered on whether the top Standard Class finishers would be included in the seeding for the WSC. It was decided that if sufficient support was given to the Standard Class the top finishers would be considered in the seeding.

A study of the membership rates had been made and it was decided to make some changes in order to distribute the costs between the different memberships more fairly.

The directors were divided on whether to subsidize the student members. It was argued that promoting soaring for youth was part of the purpose of the SSA and so should be subsidized to some extent. The executive directors felt that the turnover of student membership was high, but it was decided to continue subsidizing them but to narrow the spread between the actual costs and the student member rate.

The 75 percent increase in student membership rates from $4 to $7 started a steady decline in that type of membership that would continue for years.

The other changes made were to increase the associate member rate to $9 and the business member to $35. The subscription rates for *Soaring* were increased from $7 to $8. The Soaring Association of Canada rate was set at $6, since the magazine was shipped to them in bulk. Advertising rates were increased by 20 percent.

Marshal Claybourn

Claybourn was unable to attend the directors' meeting because he was ill and confined to a hospital in Houston, Texas. He had been fighting leukemia for a number of years, and eight days after the meeting he died.

Claybourn had become the "top" competition director of national soaring contests, having held that position at the 1963, 1965, 1966, 1967, and 1969 Nationals. He had also been scheduled to fill the same role for the 1970 WSC at Marfa. Joe Lincoln's profile of Claybourn noted that "Marshal Claybourn has the soft speech of Texas. In running pilots meetings he is quiet, competent, precise, and knowledgeable. He has enough of the drill sergeant in him to keep things moving and to keep delays from starting."

Claybourn first flew power planes in 1941 and then started soaring in 1951 as a member of the Texas Soaring Association. At that time he was working for Bell Helicopter as a flight test engineer. He studied with Raspet at Mississippi State and then went with Cessna as an aerodynamicist and test pilot. He was one of the founders of the Kansas Soaring Association. He later went with Swearingen Aircraft as an engineering test pilot.

Claybourn had assisted Bill Cleary with Sailplane, Inc., Cleary's commercial operation and Schweizer dealership at Guthrie, Oklahoma, and occasionally got to the SAC plant. On one occasion while he was in Elmira, a Goodyear blimp was at the airport. SAC had arranged a swap of sailplane rides for the blimp crew for blimp rides for SAC's management and SSS key personnel. Claybourn was eager to get a flight in the blimp since it was the only type of aircraft that he had not flown. He ended up getting some dual instruction from the blimp pilot. He was the "complete" aviation enthusiast and had a good understanding of all phases of aviation. He is remembered by the 1-26 Association through its Claybourn Award, given each year for the longest flight in a 1-26. He and two friends had built a 1-26 from a kit and before he died he had earned two Diamonds and had come within a few miles of his third Diamond.

National Soaring Museum

A report on the progress of the NSM appeared in the February 1970 *Soaring*. The museum, which had been started in June of 1969 in the administration building on Harris Hill, was expanding its exhibits.

The HHSC Museum Committee worked with the SSA Liaison Committee headed by Victor Saudek. The Merrill House, a large house at the edge of the Harris Hill Park that was owned by the county, would be a temporary home in which the NSM could grow while it worked to get the support and raise the funds for a new museum. Discussions were under way concerning the possibility of taking over the SSA film library from Walter Hausler and setting up a library and archives.

The 1-26 Sweepstakes

The 1-26 sweepstakes was sponsored by SAC and operated by the 1-26 Association to encourage 1-26 pilots to go cross-country and earn their badges. The contest ran for seven months and there were two classes of pilots: the "pro," a pilot with a Silver "C," and a "Tyro,"—a pilot without a Silver "C."

The prizes were 28 barographs and trophies, two for each SSA region and for eastern and western Canada.

The sweepstakes resulted in many cross-country flights, three of which covered over 300 miles. Harold Eley of Regina, Canada, completed all three Diamonds in a 1-26, and was the second to do so.

The Standard Class Dive-Brake Scandal

The dive-brake scandal came to light in the United States when Graham Thomson wrote Eugen Hanle, owner of Glasflugel, manufacturer of the Standard Libelle, requesting that he sign the SSA form certifying that the Standard-Libelle conforms with the Standard Class air-brake requirement.

Hanle said that the Standard Libelle did not meet the requirements and that the LS-1, Standard Cirrus, and the ASW-15 did not meet it either. He stated that "[the] FAI requirement is nonsense, if the German LFS-requirement, which is accepted by the FAA, only requires a 45° dive."

On May 5 Ivans wrote Pirat Gehriger, Chairman CIVV:

> It has come to my attention that several Standard Class gliders produced in Germany do not carry the vertical dive certification required by the FAI Code, but instead are tested to a rather less rigorous standard, a 45 degree dive. It has been stated further, that such gliders were flown in Poland in 1967.
>
> I intend that SSA will admit as bona fide Standard Class entries at Marfa all such gliders, based upon the precedent of their admission in Poland. If you have advice to the contrary, please let me know at once.

Gehriger replied by cable on May 26th by saying:

> Strongly advise to accept standard class entries without vertical line certification (primo) CIVV is a sporting body interested in effective brakes and not in methods of certification (secundo). Same solution already applied at South Cerney and Leszno (tertio) FAI requirements outdated by acceptance of German LFS Certification Rules by various states. Agree with conclusion of your May 5th letter.

On June 1, Ivans wrote Bernald Smith and other key SSA people:

> Gehriger goes along with the German "FAA" dive brake rules, and under the circumstances I expect that he is forced to.
>
> This leaves us with a very sticky question on how to evaluate homebuilts, HP-15 for example, as entries in our Standard Class Nationals. Also, how to evaluate such non-German Standard Class machines as the Urupema (Brazil), WA-26 (France) in the World Championships.

Ivans said that questions arise such as the following: "a. Why wasn't this discussed at the February 1970, or previous CIVV Meetings? b. What *are* the German dive brake requirements? Why haven't they been broadly disseminated as an acceptable alternative to the very specific test spelled out in the FAI Code? c. If CIVV is 'not interested in methods of certification' why does it spell one out in the Code? Who is to judge what 'effective brakes' are, if no test is to be prescribed? d. Why was there no dissemination of the process whereby 'some solution already applied at South Cerney and Leszno'. I, for one, never heard mention. e. What 'various states' accept the German certification rules?"

On the following day, he also wrote Graham Thomson:

> I am somewhat annoyed with Hanle for the arrogance displayed in his let-

ter to you of May 12th. Specifically, his argument that LFS/FAA approval superseded the rules laid down by CIVV just isn't valid. LFS/FAA would also cheerfully approve a "Standard" Libelle with 20 meter span if it met all other requirements!

I am nearly convinced that *all* of the German manufacturers decided to deliberately ignore the CIVV Air Brakes requirement, call their ships "Standard" nonetheless, and depend upon the number and popularity of ships sold, to bail them out when a confrontation with CIVV appeared imminent.

I am indignant for the Schweizers and others who have in good faith (and no doubt considerable expense) met the CIVV Air Brake requirement, and for all who have purchased "Standard" class gliders from German manufacturers.

SAC had known, since P. A. Schweizer's 1969 trip to Germany, that some Standard Class sailplanes did not meet the dive requirements, but did not realize that this was so widespread. SAC later learned that the British, who had originated the speed-limiting dive brakes, as in the Skylarks,

did not hold the Dart to the CIVV specifications, which required extended vertical dive. Instead, they put the Dart into the start of a vertical dive and then took their hands off the control and let the sailplane go its own way. This was a much less severe dive and was a very practical approach to the problem. The original vertical dive requirements were excessive, whereas the 45-degree dive tests used by the Germans may not have gone far enough, although they have proved to be satisfactory in service.

12th WSC, 1970

Seventy-nine pilots from 25 countries competed in the WSC at Marfa, Texas, from June 21 to July 4, 1970. The entries were almost evenly divided between Open and Standard Class sailplanes. The contest had a good safety record with only one sailplane damaged.

George Moffat, flying the Nimbus, became the world Open Class soaring champion, and Helmut Reichmann of West Germany, flying an LS-1, won

the world Standard Class
championship.

The U.S. team, with Dick Johnson
as captain, did well. In addition to
Moffat's win, Wally Scott finished in
9th position in his ASW-12. In Standard Class, A. J. Smith, flying an LS-1,
finished 7th, and Rudy Allemann,
flying a Standard Libelle, finished 21st.

Ed Butts was competition director,
John Ryan assistant competition director, and Fritz Kahl contest manager, all
of whom contributed to the success of
the competition, which boasted a record 157,301 miles flown (an average
of 221 miles per pilot per day). The
good soaring conditions kept the pilots
and crew happy, and there were no
major complaints.

There were also a number of firsts
at this WSC: Area distance was used
for the first time, and on one of two
such tasks Walter Neubert of West
Germany flew a total of 500 miles.
This WSC marked the start of using
photographs as the only proof of making a turn-point. Another notable feature was that all the competitors had
completed the task of the day on June
25, a 221-mile triangle. The only negative aspect of the meet was that it
ended with a financial deficit and received little publicity nationally.

First Standard Class Nationals, 1970

Forty-three sailplanes were entered in
the first Standard Class Nationals held
at Harris Hill from July 21 to 30, 1970.
Joe Conn, who had competed in Elmira in the 1930s, was competition director and Ned Kelly, HHSC president, was contest manager. George
Moffat, fresh from his victory at
Marfa, flying a Standard Cirrus, became the Standard Class champion.
He won seven of the eight days and

finished with 1,249 points ahead of
second-place finisher, Ted Falk. John
Seymour was third in a Ka-6E, Woody
Woodward was fourth in a Standard
Libelle, and Dr. Wylie Mullen was fifth
in a Standard Cirrus.

Moffat was the only one of the
top 19 pilots on the 1970 WSC seeding
list to compete, which accounted for
the big spread in points. However, the
contest had proven the popularity of
Standard Class.

Dick Wolters, a professional writer
turned competition pilot, did the contest report as a letter to the editor.
This was a new and entertaining twist
in contest write-ups.

Three New World Records

On May 23, Joe Lincoln set a new

SSA president, Bernald S.
Smith, presents a trophy to
the new world soaring
champion, George Moffat, at
the end of the 1970 WSC.
SSA executive secretary,
Lloyd Licher, holds another
trophy. The prototype
Schempp-Hirth Nimbus that
he flew to the championship
is in the background.

(NSM Collection)

Edward Butts, competition director of the Marfa, Texas, World Soaring Championships.

(George Uveges)

world two-place record with a flight of 404.59 miles by flying from Santa Fe, New Mexico, to Salida Colorado, and back. He was flying a 2-32 sailplane and Cris Crowl was the passenger.

On July 26, a spectacular double flight of 716.95 miles (1153.8 kilometers) from Odessa, Texas, to Columbia, Nebraska, set a new world distance record, which was flown by Ben Greene and Wally Scott, each in a Schleicher ASW-12 sailplane. They landed side by side at 8:10 p.m. to jointly claim a new world distance record. They flew separately for most of the flight, but joined up for the last 100 miles.

On August 3, Wally Scott set a world record for single-place out-and-return of 534.38 miles by flying from Odessa to Pampa, Texas, and return. This flight was also made in his ASW-12 sailplane and beat the record that Karl Striedieck had set in Pennsylvania two years before.

These three records tied the United States with Russia at eight world records each.

37th Open Class National, 1970

The meet was held at El Mirage, California, from August 11 to 20, 1970. Gus Briegleb and his two sons, Ross and Ken, all competed, along with 52 other pilots. Ed Butts was competition director and John Williams was contest manager. Going into the last day there were only 158 points between Ross Briegleb in first place flying a Diamant 18, Jerry Robertson in second place flying a Phoebus C, and John Brittingham in third place flying a Cirrus. Ross was able to hold his position and won the Nationals, with Robertson second and Brittingham third. Ross's brother, Ken, flying a Diamant 16.5, finished in eleventh, and Gus finished

thirty-second in a BG-12-16. Doug Lamont's colorful report of the National for the first time was spread over two issues of *Soaring* to allow enough room for a comprehensive story.

Directors' Summer Meeting, 1970

In 1970 the total SSA membership passed the 10,000 mark for the first time. As of June 30 it totaled 10,372, which included 6,793 full, 283 family, 239 life, 48 business, 1,143 associate, 1,860 student, and 6 miscellaneous memberships.

Ivans reported that the CIVV was to review the rules at the November meeting. By a unanimous vote, the directors agreed to instruct the U.S. CIVV delegate to express SSA's indignation over the secret evasion of CIVV specifications on Standard Class dive brakes by European companies. They considered it unfair that U.S. and other manufacturers had met the Standard Class vertical dive requirement, whereas others had failed to do so.

A. J. Smith proposed a sailplane design contest be held to encourage the development of U.S. sailplanes for top competition.

Upon the president's recommendation, the directors decided that top finishers in the 1-26 North American

Joe Lincoln and Cris Crowl get set for a record attempt in the 2-32 Cibola. On May 23, 1970, they set a 404-mile out-and-return world record. (NSM Collection)

championships could qualify for the Open Nationals.

The officers elected for 1971 were Miles Coverdale, president; Marion Griffith, Jr., and J. W. Williams, vice-presidents; Lewis W. Hull, secretary; and T. E. Sharp, treasurer.

Other Developments during 1970

The March and April issues of *Soaring* contained sailplane directories that supplemented the original directory of May 1964. Doug Lamont was named editor of *Soaring* effective with the September issue. Bennett Rogers resigned after three years as editor to resume his career as a journalist.

The Sixth 1-26 North Americans were held at Hobbs, New Mexico, from July 6 to 13. Twenty pilots were entered in the individual category and seven teams of pilots in the team category. A. C. Williams was the individ-

ual champion and the father and son team of W. R. and W. K. Skinner were the team champions.

Neil Armstrong visited the WSC at Marfa as President Richard Nixon's representative. Armstrong was a part owner of a 1-26 and a Libelle, which he got to fly at Marfa.

The "Hang Glider Thing," 1971

"Down Hill Racer," by Jack Lambie, was one of the first articles in *Soaring* (December 1970) on hang gliding. It told about his building an old Chanute-type hang glider at his elementary school with the aid of his sixth- and seventh-grade students. He was more successful than he had been 17 years earlier, when he had built a similar but much heavier Chanute. After considerable flying with his latest version, he concluded: "I've changed my mind about the things. They could have great potential for a whole new sport in the genre of surfing, water skiing, snow skiing, sky diving, or wrestling alligators."

People are attracted to ultralight flying for various reasons: Many want to get closer to basic flight, some want to be able to glide by themselves without the need for a tow, and scientists like the technical challenge. Others like the thrill, and still others see it as an inexpensive alternative to power flying. However, it was not long before it became "the hang glider problem" to the SSA Board of Directors.

Best Competition Pilots of 1970

A tradition was started in the January 1971 *Soaring* when a "double-page spread" included the picture and names of each of the National champions in the Open, Standard, and 1-26 classes, plus the winner of each class of the regional meets. This, in effect, became a "hall of fame" of the best pilots of the previous year.

Directors' Winter Meeting, 1971

At the meeting in Scottsdale, Arizona, on January 23–24, 1971, Licher reported that the total membership was still climbing. Although the number of associate and student members was lower because of the increase in dues, the voting members had grown by almost 1,000.

Because of a small financial loss in 1970 and the increased cost expected in 1971, it was decided to increase member dues from $13 to $15, effective March 15, 1971.

The deficit from the 1970 WSC stood at $12,720 and it was decided to try to raise this amount through another direct-mail general appeal to the membership.

A new policy was adopted whereby the central zone would be the preferred zone for the Nationals every other year.

The SSA decided to allow flaps in SSA-sanctioned contests in 1971, until the CIVV set the policy for the future.

Ben Greene and Wally Scott were presented the Barringer Trophy at a special meeting at the Cosmos Club in Washington, D.C., in July of 1971. Left to right: Ben Greene, Werner von Braun of NASA, SSA President Miles Coverdale, Neil Armstrong of NASA, and Wally Scott.

(NSM Collection)

The availability of the Marfa Airport and the possibility of acquiring it as a national soaring site was considered, and a committee was appointed to study the matter.

The directors agreed to support power sailplane activity, the Power Sailplane Association, and the publication of its newsletter "Motorgliding."

Flight Testing

In the February 1971 *Soaring*, Paul Bikle was acknowledged for his sailplane performance testing and his reports in *Soaring* over the past 18 years. Sailplane performance figures are one of the most popular "hangar flying" subjects among sailplane pilots. Members appreciated having another set of test results to check the claims of manufacturers and of other pilots.

The "Red" Wright Letter

In keeping with the directors' decision, President Coverdale planned to send a letter to the SSA membership requesting donations to pay off the WSC deficit.

"Red" Wright asked if he might send a personal appeal to SSA members. His "open letter" to SSA members gave "The untold story of Marfa and the 1970 WSC" and, explained that many promises of support had not been kept. He asked each member to send in a $5 bill, which, he stated, was "the price of one tow, or two six-paks of beer, or 1 good steak." Coverdale sent Wright's letter with his. The response was excellent. Close to $20,000 was received, which allowed the SSA to write off the deficit. The balance was used to help send the international team to Yugoslavia in 1972.

More Sailplane Classes

Fritz Compton, chairman of the Ad Hoc Committee on Class Competition, prepared a report for the directors. The goal of the committee was that every sailplane should have a competition "home" in which it could effectively and equitably compete. This would require many "homes," or classes, similar to the great number of sailboat classes.

Top: Red Wright, a key figure in Texas soaring, wrote an appeal letter to the SSA membership asking for their donations to cover the 1970 WSC deficit. The appeal went over so well that a good start was made on the team fund for the next WSC.
(NSM Collection)

The key personnel in Schweizer Aircraft Corporations's advertising and promotion program. Left to right: Bill Schweizer, Tony Doherty, Paul A. Schweizer, and Frank Hurtt.
(G. Carlyle Steele)

After four years of growth from 1967 to 1970, during which the SSA membership increased by about 1,200 members a year, growth slackened in 1971, when only 137 new members were enrolled. SAC expanded its cooperative SAC-dealer advertising and promotion program and over the next few years developed a number of methods to increase the response to their ads. They began with a $1 starting kit and later a ride coupon, which enabled the bearer to get a sailplane ride for $5, and a "How to Get Started in Soaring" booklet. At one time the number of inquiries reached over 10,000 a year, which played a significant part in the growth of soaring and the SSA and in building up the SAC and dealer business. SAC and its dealers also continued to support 1-26 regattas and the 1-26 Association.

The report included a list of six basic types of sailplane classes:

1. Unlimited open class

2. Limited span but otherwise unrestricted

3. Limited span formulas (like original Standard Class)

4. Performance handicapped class (performance banding)

5. One design (like Olympia and 1–26)

6. Domestic-origin class (such as an American class).

One of the necessary factors for class flying is that there should be enough sailplanes of a particular type around the country to make class competition practical.

The Schweizer Report

After a lapse of four years, a Schweizer report again appeared in the May 1971 *Soaring*. It noted that four "milestone" sailplanes had been on display at the 1970 annual SAC dealer meeting: the 500th 1-26, the 200th 2-33, the 75th 2-32, and the 50th 1-34. The 1-26 was now all metal (except for the fabric-covered control surfaces), which kept the cost increases to a minimum. A 67-foot version of the 2-32 was built for Joe Lincoln, and it was not long before Lincoln set a new 100-kilometer triangle world record of 74 miles per hour.

SAC hoped to make a top-performance sailplane, but was waiting for the sales potential to build up in order to justify the cost of putting it into production. A total of 250–500 ships over a period of 5 to 10 years would be necessary in order to be able to amortize the development costs.

SAC saw the need to continue to stimulate public interest in soaring and announced that it was to expand its cooperative SAC-dealer advertising and promotional program.

Second Standard Class National, 1971

Thirty-eight pilots entered the Second Standard Class Nationals at Ephrata

Rudy Allemann, winner of the second Standard Class National held at Ephrata, Washington, in 1971. He is shown alongside his Libelle sailplane.

(George Uveges)

Airport, Washington, from June 15 to 24, 1971. Only 5 of the 38 sailplanes were of U.S. manufacture: two 1-34s, the T-6, a Prue Super-Standard, and the Laister Nugget prototype.

The weather was described as a "mixed bag" by Taylor Boyer, who wrote up the contest report for *Soaring*.

The championship was won on the last day by Rudy Allemann. Roy Gimmey, who had been in the lead for the previous three days, failed to complete the last task by a few miles. Allemann won flying a Libelle 301, and Gimmey finished second in a Standard Libelle. Jerry Robertson, also in a Standard Libelle, finished third, Earl Smith was fourth in a Libelle 301, and Bob Moore was fifth in a Phoebus A. Total mileage flown was 52,397 (172 miles per pilot per day).

Everyone was watching the new Laister Nugget that Ross Briegleb was flying. It had been completed just in time to make its first flight at the contest. On the fifth day Briegleb landed in a tall wheat field and damaged the ship, and so was unable to finish the contest.

38th Open Class National, 1971

The 1971 Open National almost did not happen. When no bids for the 1971 open contest were received at the SSA directors' meeting, Dick Schreder called the manager of the Bryan Chamber of Commerce and got his agreement to put in a verbal bid. Bryan received the award. Schreder, with the aid of the Bryan Soaring Club and the Chamber of Commerce, put on an excellent contest in which 65 pilots competed. A. J. Smith won the championship with a 347-point margin. The real battle was for second

place. Dick Johnson, flying his HP-13M, nosed out Ben Greene in his ASW-12 on the last day. R. Chase, in a Cirrus and A. Hurst in a Standard Cirrus finished fourth and fifth. A total of 76,045 miles were flown (146 miles per pilot per day).

The contest report for *Soaring* was written by Gren Seibels, who had competed in the contest. He summarized the contest in a "Retrospective" comment:

> Of the eight contest days, two produced—by Eastern standards—really strong soaring conditions: . . . The remainder ranged from moderate to blah.
>
> Did the big-span ships like the ASW-12 (Smith and Greene) and the 19-meter HP-13M (Johnson) give their pilots a slight extra edge—a few more miles on each glide, to search for lift? Better climb rates in the wobbly 2–300 fpm lift that was par for the meet? Yes, undoubtedly.
>
> I would submit, however, that equipment is by no means the entire Name of the Game. The key factor in any true soaring contest has been, is now, and ever will be—Piloting.

Directors' Summer Meeting, 1971

At the 1971 meeting in Bryan, Ohio, the seeding of Standard Class pilots for the WSC raised some problems among those directors who were still not convinced that the Standard Class had a legitimate place in U.S. soaring. They finally decided that for the 1972 WSC they would use the same seeding method as in the past, but that beginning in 1974 the top 10 finishers from the last two Standard Class Nationals would seed themselves, and at least one would be on the team as the Standard Class pilot.

Bill Allen, SSA's assistant executive director, reported on hang gliding

Karl Striedieck is greeted by his nephew Dan Striedieck just after completing a world out-and-return record of 550 miles in his ASW-15 sailplane.

(Walter Striedieck)

(HG) activity around the country as background for the development of an SSA position on hang gliders. The discussion that followed reflected a complete spectrum of positions, from complete support, to the suggestion that hang gliders go off by themselves to "do their thing." There was general concern, however, that any accidents might be lumped in with FAA glider statistics.

There was also a general feeling that, if SSA was to encompass HG, it would have to be done in hang gliders certified by FAA and flown by certified pilots. It was obvious, however, that many HG proponents did not want any control.

With such diverse views, it was difficult to come up with specific action. It was decided to cease publishing ads for hang gliders in *Soaring* until a decision on HGs was made. Tom

Page volunteered to develop a position paper that the Executive Committee was to approve before it was submitted to *Soaring*.

Tom Page noted that storage space and some archival advice were available from the Northrup Institute of Tehnology.

Details were provided on the progress being made by the NSM, which was in the process of setting up a nonprofit educational corporation that would have on its board three trustees appointed by the SSA. Since the Merrill House had been made available, the NSM had ample space to store its archives. To illustrate the progress of the NSM plans, a scale model of the Harris Hill complex was displayed at the meeting. After some discussion, the board, in a unanimous vote, named A. Hurst, T. Page, and H. Lattimore as trustees of the NSM.

The 1971 officers were reelected for 1972.

Plans for the 1972 WSC

The 13th WSC was to be held in Vrsac, Yugoslavia. The seeded U.S. team pilots were (1) A. J. Smith, (2) G. Moffat, Jr., (3) R. H. Johnson, and (4) B. G. Greene.

FAA Sailplane Airworthiness Requirements

A special committee had been formed to work with the FAA to simplify sailplane type certification requirements. The existing requirements, the "Glider Criteria Handbook" (GCH), had been used by Briegleb, Peterson, Prue, Laister, and Schweizer. Other sailplane designers who had not gotten into the engineering details of the GCH requirements complained that requirements should be simpler. Since they were unfamiliar with the

GCH, they were not able to make specific proposals to FAA on how these regulations should be changed. As a result, FAA moved very slowly in making any changes.

Another Record on the Ridges

Karl Striedieck, flying an ASW-15 sailplane, set a new world out-and-return record of 550 miles. The flight was made on November 8, 1971. Starting from his home field in Port Matilda, Pennsylvania, he flew to a point in Virginia and returned to Port Matilda. He was awarded the Lilienthal medal for this flight.

The Hang Glider Position

It was not easy to put together a position paper based on the lengthy discussion at the director's meeting. After Page submitted several drafts to the members of the executive committee, the paper appeared in the November 1971 *Soaring* under the title "Position Paper: Will the SSA Go Hang?" It reviewed the HG situation, the inherent problems, and the dilemma facing the SSA. It then listed the basic policy and some specific action that SSA should take: "SSA will encourage development of the ultra-light gliders in legal channels provided by the FAA. It will encourage modern design development and safe flight activity in this sector of motorless flight. As a general guide, gliders with a wing loading of less than three pounds per square foot of wing area will be classed as ultra-lights."

The report recommended that the SSA encourage and assist beginners in many ways, accept HG and ULT ads in *Soaring* if plans included instruction in homebuilding under FAA regulations, form an ultralight committee to review plans, consider plans to publish an ASH chapter on ultralights, and, at the proper time, assist with the development of rules and safe practices for SSA sanctioned ULT contests.

Reaction to the Position Paper

Reactions to the paper were mixed. Page and Licher tried to explain their "positions" to the directors. In his memo of November 26 Licher stated:

> I have come to believe that the hang glider "thing" is here to stay, no matter what positions or actions SSA and FAA take, and SSA would be better off to change its position to one of warm helpfulness. This is why I have requested an agenda item on the subject for the Jan 22–23 SSA Board meeting. In the SSA Position Paper, Tom Page uses the sentence "the soaring establishment is sweating over the Hang Glider Thing." Surely, the Paper gives the impression that there is indeed an "Establishment," and it chooses to put down this new area of gliding endeavor, rather than encourage it. Sure, it's fraught with danger, but so is any action-in-a-medium activity. The safety record of conventional sailplane activity is nothing to brag about this year, with a dozen fatalities so far. Any kind of expansion and progress will have its problems, but they should be a challenge, not a curse.

In reply, Page sent a memo to the directors dated December 8, in which he was upset with Licher because he had objected to the position paper after it had been published. His memo included the following comments: "The preliminary draft of the Position Paper was in his (Licher's) hands for comment to the President by about July 29. I am not aware of any objections he raised when the opportunity was open. On the basis of the comments from other responsible officers of SSA, a revised version of the Position Paper was again in his hands by about 29 August, still open to amendment. Still no objections from the Executive Director were heard as the copy went to the Editor of *Soaring*."

Licher replied to this in his memo of December 14: "I regret not having commented on the SSA Position Paper as drafted by Tom. I certainly intended to but time was limited and I would only have repeated the comments I made at the last Directors Meeting, which were not quite in harmony with the position taken by the Board. The main purpose of the Nov 26th letter was to appraise you of the scope of the publicity and activity as it was developing and reiterate my belief that a modification of the SSA position might be called for. I certainly can't evade the content of the SSA Position Paper in my position as Executive Director and have been active in 'enforcing' it for the Society."

Tom Page's willingness to prepare the position paper was a logical thing for him to do, for he was willing to take an unpopular position. He liked to see logical solutions to problems and he was willing to call a "spade a spade." After writing the position paper, he stated: "One reason I volunteered to prepare this Position Paper is

that over ten years, I seemed to have supplied a fair share of the abrasion within the SSA Board which has induced us to deal with some issues which were initially ducked . . . to wit: (1) the Gyros in contests, (2) the drive for cloud flight ratings, (3) the exposure of German manufacturers violation of CIVV standard Class dive brake criterion, and currently, (4) pressure to legalize ballasting that threatens equitable competition."

Other Activities during 1971

"Herold's Hearsay" was a column that Carl Herold wrote for "West Wind," the newsletter of the Pacific Soaring Council. It became so popular that Doug Lamont and B. S. Smith asked Herold to do the monthly columns for *Soaring*. In addition, *Soaring's* front cover for the July 1971 issue was done in four colors for the first time. After one year as editor of the "Safety" column in *Soaring*, Irv Prue asked to be relieved of this responsibility. Stephen Horvath was appointed to replace him.

Air Sailing, Inc., a nonprofit corporation, was formed by a group of Reno and Bay area soaring pilots in January of 1971 to fulfill a need for a soaring facility to service the North California and Nevada areas.

Chapter 11

The Growth of Soaring Continues, 1972–1976

First National Convention, 1972

From 1930 to 1947, the national soaring contests were the main soaring event of the year and Elmira was the mecca for soaring enthusiasts. There they could see sailplanes fly, meet the pilots and other people interested in soaring, and exchange information.

When the Nationals started moving around the country, more people had a chance to see soaring firsthand. In 1969 the SSA membership meeting was expanded and the first award banquet for noncompetition awards was held at the time of the winter directors' meeting.

First Soaring Convention

Marion Griffith conceived the idea of celebrating the 40th anniversary of the SSA with a convention at the time of the winter directors' meeting. Dr. Ed Byars and Bill Holbrook were to put on a soaring symposium, and exhibits of sailplanes and equipment were solicited. Griffith, the general chairman, thought that if 200 people attended, it would work out financially.

Three hundred and fifty-two people registered and the convention was a success. It included a number of exhibits of soaring equipment and a 1-26 exhibited by Southwest Soaring Enterprises. The 1-26 Association and the

SSA business members held meetings, and the NSM displayed a scale model of the proposed museum.

The NSM had a scale model of Harris Hill, including the proposed museum building. The question was how to get it to the convention at minimum cost to the NSM. An arrangement was worked out with Si Gilad, an SSA member and Mohawk Airline pilot from Utica, New York, to fly it from Elmira to Newark, New Jersey, Airport as personal baggage. There he would transfer it to Marion Griffith of Braniff Airlines, who would fly it to Dallas, Texas. This was done and those attending the convention had an opportunity to see the proposed NSM location. After the convention the model was returned the same way. This was a significant contribution by Gilad and Griffith, since the boxed model measured over $3\frac{3}{4} \times 4\frac{1}{2} \times 2$ feet and weighed almost 200 pounds.

The SSA directors were scheduled to meet for Saturday and Sunday mornings so that they could attend the convention meetings. Gren Seibel was the principal speaker at the award banquet at which President Miles Coverdale presented gold medallions to past presidents for their services to the SSA. Now with two Nationals and a soaring convention each year, soaring would get much more exposure as these events moved around the United States.

Walter and Florence Hausler are presented the Eaton Trophy by SSA President Miles Coverdale at the first soaring convention for their 20 years of voluntary work in building up and operating the SSA film library.

(SSA files)

Preparation for Directors' Meeting

It was obvious that the hang gliding problem would be the major topic at the directors' meeting. Page and Licher proposed that the next step would be to petition the FAA to exempt hang gliders from regulations, provided that they stayed below 100 feet, kept 300 feet away from any structure or people, and were not for hire.

In a report of a HG meet, which both Licher and Lamont attended, Lamont wrote: "After observing the highly successful flights of a new tailless bi-plane, at the recent ULT gathering, SSA's MIT-educated director stood momentarily transfixed and murmured to no one in particular, 'that glider could change the course of motorless flying in the U.S.' " It was evident that Licher did not agree with the board and this was the first significant difference that had occurred between them.

Directors' Winter Meeting, 1972

As expected, a great deal of time was spent on the "HG problem" at the January 22–23 meeting in Dallas. Most

directors were reluctant to go ahead with the FAA exemption request since they felt the SSA should not become involved. It was decided that the development board should study the exemption procedure while the position paper was still in effect. Although some concern was expressed over the amount of coverage that ultralights were receiving in *Soaring*, Lamont pointed out that only 7 pages out of 500 had covered this topic in 1971.

At that time confusion had arisen because hang gliders and ultralight sailplanes were lumped together. Efforts were made to clear this up, as the following examples show.

It is easy to become carried away with ultralights and to speculate about the super "windspiels." The possibilities of soaring in what are now unsoarable conditions in sailplanes with lower flying speeds, much lower sinking speeds, and very small turning radii, could open up new areas of soaring. However, to attempt to justify hang gliding by the lofty aims of ultralight sailplanes is not logical and can be misleading.

Some offer ultralights as the answer to low-cost flying. Sailplanes can be built substantially smaller and lighter but probably at higher costs. Aerodynamic improvements can help to offset the unfavorable scale effect, but for the immediate future it is not an area in which production sailplanes are practical.

Those who contend that it is SSA's responsibility to further the hang glider movement should look back to the NGA days when hundreds of primary gliders were crashing all over the United States, and the SSA was formed to stress safety and soaring and to give direction to soaring flight.

Although the directors did not agree on a policy, they did in effect set a "policy" by doing nothing about the movement and letting it go its own way. This approach was later justified when the HG movement developed on its own and the FAI created a separate organization, the CIVL, to cover the foot-launched form of motorless flight.

Another problem for the directors was the loss in student membership during 1971 (from 1,682 to 1,186). The SSA Youth Education Committee recommended that student members be given the right to vote. This plan was referred to committee for consideration.

With the increased use of water ballast to improve high-speed performance in sailplanes, they were now and then loaded beyond their legal maximum weight. It was proposed that a mild exemption for over-gross ballasting be requested from FAA; however, it did not receive much support.

A. J. Smith reported that there were 21 entries in the sailplane design contest, but only $500 had been raised for the prize fund.

The treasurer reported that the SSA was operating at a small loss but had close to $40,000 in reserves. A budget of $270,000 was approved for 1972.

Ray Shamblen, chairman of the Sailplane Census Committee, reported that at the end of 1971 the total sailplane population in the United States totaled 2,313, of which 55 were powered sailplanes. Of this total, 33 percent were multiplace, 29 percent imports, and 14 percent fiberglass construction; 27 percent met the Standard Class requirements. Approximately half of all the sailplanes were built by SAC.

Diamond Badges

By 1971, 1,057 pilots had earned their Diamond badges. Poland was the leader with 215 badges, and the United States was a close second with 213. Next in order were West Germany 200, France 139, Austria 83, Switzerland 24, Great Britain 22, and Canada 15.

CIVV Meetings

CIVV meetings were held in Paris in November and in February. It was decided to approve a moderate "day factor" on a trial basis. A proposal by the West Germans to eliminate cloud flying in WSCs was turned down since the majority felt that this should be decided by the WSC organizers. A proposal to add a motorgliding category to the WSC was delayed until the 1976 WSC. Concern was expressed about the control of water ballast in sailplanes and it was felt that this was the responsibility of WSC stewards.

National Soaring Museum Dedication

After having been operated as a part of the HHSC for four years, the NSM was officially dedicated on May 13. It was in the process of being incorporated as a nonprofit organization under the New York State Educational Department, and the first NSM Board of Trustees meeting was held. Capt. Ralph Barnaby was the dedication speaker.

Smirnoff Sailplane Derby

The Heubling Co., which manufactured Smirnoff vodka, became interested in sponsoring a transcontinental

Tom Beltz, a 20-year-old pilot, won the 1972 Standard Class championship in a Standard Cirrus at Marfa, Texas.

(SSA files)

a wide margin. The derby received good publicity and gave the WSC team fund drive a boost.

Third Standard Class National, 1972

A "full house" of 65 sailplanes had registered for the National in Marfa, Texas, from June 27 to July 6, 1972. Tom Beltz, a 20-year-old from Lehighton, Pennsylvania, won the championship, with W. A. Scott II, Wally Scott's 22-year-old son, second, Allemann third, Gimmey fourth, and Hurst fifth. The new Standard Class trophy, created by Gleb Derujinsky, was awarded for the first time and it was evident that Standard Class competition in the United States had come of age.

13th WSC, 1972

Eighty-nine pilots from 28 countries, including 8 former world champions, competed in this thirteenth WSC, held from July 9 to 23, 1972, in Vrsac, Yugoslavia. The U.S. pilots and their sailplanes were A. J. Smith in Nimbus II and R. Johnson in ASW-17 in the Open Class; and G. Moffat and B. Greene, both in Standard Cirrus, with Standard Class. Paul Bikle was the U.S. team captain.

Poor weather caused many to say that "chance" was a big factor in this WSC. There were 548 out-landings and only 152 completions. There was considerable cloud flying, and a Hungarian pilot crashed to his death in a thunderstorm. A Swedish and a Guernsey pilot collided in a cloud and had to use their parachutes. An accident unrelated to the weather was a collision in which Wolf Mix of Canada died. A truck had suddenly pulled out in front of him as he was landing.

sailplane derby. When it offered to donate $6,000 to the 1972 international team fund, it was given full support. At first, it had hoped that the U.S. team pilots would fly in the derby, but only A. J. Smith was able to do so. Ed Butts was the flight director.

The pilots and sailplanes were Bikle, T-6; R. Briegleb, Kestrel 17; E. Enevoldson, Diamant 18; J. Ryan, Nimbus II; W. Scott, ASW-12; and A. J. Smith, Caproni A-21.

The race consisted of a series of speed tasks to a declared goal along the 2,900-mile path across the country, from Los Angeles to Baltimore, Maryland. One thousand points were given for the best flight of the day and lesser performances were given proportional points. Those who did not make the goal were picked up by trailer and taken to the goal. Wally Scott won by

Goran Ax of Sweden, flying a Nimbus II, was open champion, followed by Matias Witanen of Finland, flying an ASW-17, Stanislav Kluk of Poland, flying a Jantar was 3d, Dick Johnson was 5th, and A. J. Smith 16th.

In the Standard Class, Jan Wroblewski of Poland, flying an Orion, won that championship. For the first time, a Russian did well in a WSC when Eugene Rudensky finished 2d in an ASW-15. Francis Kepka of Poland was 3d in an Orion. Ben Greene was 9th and G. Moffat was 19th.

39th Open Class National, 1972

Of the 53 sailplanes competing in this championship meet at Minden, Nevada, from July 18 to 27, 1972, 11 were Standard Class and only 23 had spans over 15 meters, so it really was not a full-fledged "Open."

Bob Semans, the competition director, called all speed tasks, which tended to favor the smaller ships.

The winner was Ray Gimmey in a Standard Libelle, and the next four pilots, also flying Libelles, were Rudy Allemann, Jack Bamberg, E. D. Smith and Tom Brandes, finishing in that order. After the National, Gimmey said that he did not think the 15-meter Libelles would have done so well if the big ship pilots had not had bad luck or had not made some bad decisions.

Directors' Summer Meeting, 1972

At the July 18 meeting in Minden, Licher reported that the total of all members, as of June 30, stood at 11,270, a gain of 692 over the previous year.

The Development Board proposed

Wallace A. Scott II was second in the 1972 Standard Class championship. He is shown here with his mentor, his father Wally Scott.

(NSM Collection)

an enabling resolution to encourage the formation of national soaring sites. The board was authorized to proceed with negotiations to acquire the Colorado property that had been offered to SSA by John Mattingly. It was proposed that a separate corporation be set up to hold the property.

The election of officers was held and Marion Griffith was elected president, Arthur Hurst and Lawrence Wood vice-presidents, Robert Seamans secretary, and Ted Sharp treasurer.

Ben Shupack

Ben Shupack died in 1972. During World War II Shupack had been the SSA secretary and his home at Utterby Road in Brooklyn, New York, had been the "unofficial" SSA headquarters.

In 1965 Ben Shupack was stricken with a brain tumor and recovered from a major operation, but had difficulty with his sight, speech, and mobility, which he surmounted for seven years in his typical determined way.

Ben was one of the first to install two-way radio in sailplanes, and he worked with Gus Raspet on a number of scientific projects.

Unfortunately, Ben was not a diplomat and he had differences of opinion with many people in soaring. As a result, he gradually drifted away from soaring.

He is remembered for keeping the SSA alive through the World War II period and for helping to develop interest in the technical and scientific side of soaring.

MIT Soaring Association Symposium

Thirty-three papers were presented at the MIT symposium, which ran from October 19 to 22, 1972, and attracted technical people from the soaring world. The high quality of papers left some OSTIV members feeling that such meetings tended to diminish the importance of the biannual OSTIV congress.

World Records

With only five world records, the United States had fallen from its top position to third place behind the USSR, with eight records, and Poland, with seven.

The record category for which there was the most contention in 1972 was the single-place out-and-return record. On September 7, Dick Georgeson of New Zealand set a new record of 623 miles on South Island. On October 7, Karl Striedieck won it back with a flight of 636.9 miles (1,025 kilometers) in his ASW-15. Two days later, Jim Smiley flew the reverse course from Bluefield to Lock Haven and back in his Libelle for a new world record

of 656.6 miles. Six days later, Karl Striedieck won it back by flying 682.6 miles.

Other Activities

Region I Soaring Association (ROSA) held a technical seminar and donated 50 percent of the seminar profits toward the international team fund.

H. Higgins, H. Perl, R. Schreder, E. Schweizer, and F. J. Sweet met with 15 FAA representatives at the FAA headquarters to discuss glider airworthiness regulations. The FAA stated that it was anxious to simplify the glider regulations.

Another Standard Class "Flap," 1973

After 14 years of controversy, the Standard Class was finally accepted in the United States and had become the predominant class. After the 1972 Standard Class Nationals, the only item that remained open was equal status with the "Open" Class in seeding for the WSC team. Equal seeding was later authorized at the directors' meeting at Minden.

At its March 5th, 1971, meeting the CIVV had made what it hoped would be the last Standard Class change for at least 6, and possibly 10, years: approval of simple hinged flaps as an alternate to dive brakes.

From the original concept of "a low-cost, easy-to-fly, club type sailplane," the Standard Class had evolved into a high-performance racing sailplane. It was really an unlimited 15-meter class model, except that camber changing flaps were prohibited. It had become a designer's and builders' class, and as the designers made the sailplanes more sophisticated

Left: Ray Gimmey and his Libelle in which he won the 1972 U.S. Open Class championship at Minden, Nevada.

(George Uveges)

Marion Griffith, SSA president and originator of the SSA soaring conventions.

(SSA files)

and the original restrictions were lifted, the cost steadily increased, and a growing number of Standard Class sailplanes became noncompetitive.

It was assumed in the United States that Standard Class requirements were now "set" and that no more changes would occur for at least six years.

President's Editorial

Marion Griffith took office January 1, 1973, and renewed the practice of having the SSA president write "editorials." He reviewed the most important problems that faced soaring: air space, safety, and the need for greater membership support. One new idea he immediately put into effect was an automatic phone-answering service at the SSA office that permitted the use of taped information about the latest news in the soaring world. He said, "It is my objective to sell soaring in the U.S. in 1973: Its challenge, its beauty, its satisfaction,—will you help?"

The Introductory Ride

An important factor in the expansion of soaring and the SSA over the preceding 15 years was the great increase in the number of "introductory rides." This was an important part of the commercial operators' business, and a good way of recruiting students. These flights were made by commercial glider pilots, who took up a passenger in a two-place sailplane for a 10- to 20-minute flight. The 2-32 made it possible to take two passengers at one time for very little extra cost and increased the profitability.

"Passenger Glider Tourist Attraction," an article by P. W. Herrick in the February 1973 *Soaring*, proposed a 30-place glider. This glider would have to be towed by a DC-3 or equivalent, but Herrick claimed it would be financially feasible.

The *Cleveland Press* reported that an immense catapult-monument had been proposed for the Cleveland lakefront, by A. Geoffrion, designer of World War II cargo gliders for Waco.

The catapult would launch a 14-place glider for a 10-minute flight. Nothing ever came of either of these proposals, which many considered to be "Sunday supplement" features.

Second SSA Convention

The Second SSA Soaring Convention was held in San Antonio, Texas, January 20–21. The early plans for this event did not consider it as a full convention. As plans progressed, A. C. Williams and Carson Gilmer, the organizers, realized it had become just that, since the scheduled events exceeded the activity of the first convention. An exhibit hall, adjacent to the hotel, was used for the exhibition of sailplanes and other sailplane products.

The award banquet had Richard Wolters as principal speaker. One of the awards given was a certificate of appreciation to Bill and Alice Fuchs for the completion of the *American Soaring Handbook*.

Directors' Winter Meeting, 1973

The treasurer reported to the directors meeting in San Antonio on January 19–21, 1973, that operations showed a 5.6 percent surplus and that the reserves had increased about 20 percent. The executive director reported that the membership had grown by 790 members over the last year and was now at 11,656.

The SSA Development Board reported that it was not feasible to establish a new corporation to accept the Colorado land that had been offered to SSA. Because of the potential benefits to SSA, a further study on means of acquiring land was authorized.

Efforts to raise funds to pay for the perpetual U.S. National Standard

Class Trophy had not been very successful, and an effort was to be made to get the Standard Class pilots to contribute.

It was agreed that, in the U.S. Standard Class competitions, sailplanes must conform to the CIVV definition, but that sailplanes with both flaps and dive brakes could enter only if the flap setting was fixed prior to the first contest flight. A seal was to be added to ensure that the flaps were not used.

FAA had announced that HG operations would be exempt from its regulations; but the SSA expressed concern over the apparent lack of self-regulation.

CIVV Spring Meeting

At the spring meeting in Paris, the CIVV, responding to some pressure for change, proposed that the only restriction on the Standard Class be the 15-meter span. The concern of some of the CIVV members was that the flap would be used for other purposes, such as improving circling and high-speed performance.

The proposal included a provision to "freeze" the existing Standard Class definition at its 1972 level, that is, retractable wheel, disposible ballast, but no flaps. Championships would then be held in three world classes: Open, 15-Meter, and the 1972 Standard Class. A final decision on this was to be made after the 1974 WSC.

The CIVV committee claimed that these changes were justified because it would help to preserve the investment of present Standard Class owners for a reasonable period. Ignored were the great number of sailplanes that had already been made obsolete by permitting retractable gear and water ballast, and the four U.S. manufacturers and one each in Finland and Germany who had gone ahead in good faith and installed flaps at considerable cost.

This proposal raised a furor among the sailplane manufacturers in the United States. Their flapped sailplanes would not be competitive in an unlimited 15-meter class, since recent new developments in airfoils using variable camber flaps could substantially increase performance and give the Europeans another chance to move ahead.

Parker Leonard, 1902–1973

Parker Leonard, who had held the office of SSA president longer than anyone else, died on March 16, 1973. He began his gliding by flying a primary that he had built in the early 1930s, after he had seen one fly at Cape Cod. Leonard designed and built an intermediate two-place wooden training sailplane that became known as the Parker Box because of its rectangular appearance.

He was one of the first instructors in the EASC glider training school. He then worked with the Gould Aeronautical Division of Pratt-Read and aided in the design and construction of the Pratt-Read trainer. His next position was with the Ludington-Griswold Co. and he worked on various aeronautical developments. A prophetic article by Leonard had appeared in the November-December 1944 *Soaring* in which he proposed a one-design class sailplane. His son-in-law, Paul B. MacCready, said that "His life was varied, full and happy. He gave much to soaring and received much in return."

Another World Out-and-Return Record

Bill Holbrook broke Striedieck's record on May 4, 1973. Starting out from

A letter from SAC to Marion Griffith was typical of the objection to the change. Quotations from this letter follow:

We here at SAC are very strongly against the German proposal to freeze the Standard Class as it now is except to delete the provisional allowance of flaps, and to create a new 15 meter class with limits on wing span only.

It appears to us that now that the Europeans are having difficulties in adopting landing flaps on their flexible fiber glass structure, and due to the general European aversion to landing flaps, they are against having them permitted.

Since the requirements for terminal brakes was withdrawn (another case of European one-upsmanship) it has opened the way for landing flaps. Previously to this, a flap was not a practical answer to the terminal brake requirements. Under the new requirements, the simple hinged flap has a definite place and has some definite advantages over the dive brakes.

. . . it is hereby proposed that the SSA take a very strong and definite stand to keep the Standard Class requirements as they are for the 1974 Internationals and freeze it at this point.

. . . the idea of the 15 meter class comes much too late, and if permitted, would obsolete all these new American designs and provide another opportunity for the Europeans to gain another advantage over us by having a clear shot at the unlimited 15-meter class.

Lock Haven Airport, he flew to Hansonville, Virginia, and return to Lock Haven, a distance of 782 miles, for a new world record. He was flying a Libelle and averaged over 70 miles per hour on the flight.

Second Annual Smirnoff Derby

Wally Scott was to defend his title against a new group of pilots in the 1973 Smirnoff Derby. Included were world Open champion Goran Ax of Sweden, U.S. Open champion Ray Gimmey, former U.S. Open champion John Ryan, Woodson K. Woods, and Betsy Howell, the first woman to fly in the derby. Poor weather made it necessary to trailer the sailplanes on 4 of the 12 legs. Ax came first, winning three days; Ryan second, winning one day; Scott third, winning one day; Ray Gimmey fourth, winning two days; Woods fifth, winning one day; and Howell sixth. The Smirnoff Company

Bill Holbrook tells about setting a new world record at an NSM Hall of Fame banquet. On May 4, 1973, he made a flight of 782 miles from Lock Haven, Pennsylvania, to Hansonville, Virginia, and return.

(NSM Collection)

again made a cash contribution of $6,000 to the SSA international team fund.

FAA-SSA Meeting

Four FAA representatives were present at a meeting on gliders and motorglider regulations that was held during the NSM spring soaring weekend. E. Schweizer and F. J. Sweet had organized the meeting, which covered various phases of sailplane regulations. The item that caused the most controversy was FAA's position on motorgliders. It considered them to be self-launching sailplanes (SLS) and so recommended that the fuel should be limited to takeoff and climb to 4,000 feet only. In the FAA view, the capability for air retrieves, power "saves," or dual training would make it an airplane and subject it to these requirements. This view was objected to by the majority of the group, and the

FAA said that the notice of proposed rule making (NPRM) could still be modified.

Sailplane Developments

The steady growth of soaring in the United States had encouraged U.S. manufacturers to go ahead with new designs.

The Concept 70 was now in production and seven had been delivered.

The Laister Nugget, a Standard Class sailplane, was being put into production and was in the process of getting its ATC.

The Mescalero, a new design by George Applebay of Alberquerque, New Mexico, was under construction and the prototype was to be ready in early 1974. It was a large 69-foot span sailplane with an aspect ratio of 33 to 1.

The Javelin was the result of six years of work by Max Peterson, a California aero engineer. He announced in the June 1973 *Soaring* that it had received its ATC.

The HP-17 was Schreder's latest, an all-metal Standard Class sailplane, except for the foam ribs bonded to the structure. He was rushing to complete it so he could compete in the Standard Class Nationals.

Robert Lamson, a former experimental test pilot for Boeing and long-time soaring enthusiast, reported on his *Alcor* project in the November 1973 *Soaring:* "The *Alcor* design has proven to be workable and test results to date are gratifying. The sailplane should be an excellent test bed for the interesting work ahead."

1-26 Championships, 1973

Forty-six sailplanes were entered in the eighth 1-26 National held at the Black

Forest Glider Port in Colorado Springs, June 20–27, 1973. Mike Moore of "Wave Flights" competed in the contest and wrote the contest report for September 1973 *Soaring*. He commented: "The 1-26 contest has moved into the big time. It's still a heck of a fun contest, but the competition has become fierce. Everyone came to fly hard and to win. When the dust settled, 46 sailplanes had flown 33,640 miles during the seven days of the contest." This was an average distance of almost 105 miles per pilot per day. The contest outcome was in doubt until the last day, when Ted Teach of Springfield, Ohio, won the championship.

John Brittingham from the Colorado Springs area, a regular competitor in 1-26 championships, was competing in the Standard Class Nationals in Chester, held at the same time. He called each night to compare results with the Chester flights. On June 24 both contests had a speed event and

Dave Johnson, the day's winner, reached a speed of 55.6 miles per hour, whereas Paul Bikle the winner at Chester, flying a Nugget, reached only 42.3 miles per hour. As a result, there was a lot of ribbing about the relative merits of the 1-26s and the Standard Class sailplanes and of the eastern and western soaring conditions.

Fourth Standard Class National, 1973

Fifty-six pilots were entered in the Fourth Standard Class National. The first four days of the contest were "no contest" owing to rainy weather. Sam Francis, the competition director, was concerned whether they would even have the four contest days needed to make it an official National. The weather finally became flyable on the fifth day and five tasks were completed in succession.

Karl Striedieck was the winner and showed that he could fly thermals as well as the ridges! Moffat and Tom

A Concept 70 developed and produced by Art Zimmerman getting ready for an early morning takeoff.

(Michael T. Dial)

The Javelin, a single-place all-metal sailplane designed, built, and certified by the Peterson Sailplane Corp., in flight over some unhospitable California countryside.
(Peterson Sailplane Corp.)

Beltz were a close second and third, and only 232 points separated the next seven pilots.

40th Open Class National, 1973

Seventy pilots competed in the "open" meet at Liberal, Kansas, from July 24 to August 2, 1973. The weather was challenging, owing to the overbuilding cumulus clouds and resulting thunderstorms, which were not typical for Kansas at that time of the year.

Unlike the previous Open Nationals, this one ended with the big ships taking over. The highest 15-meter finisher was Walt Cannon, who came 15th in a Libelle. The separation between the Open and Standard Class ships was obviously growing. George Moffat was the winner, and Johnson and Greene were 2d and 3d—all flying ASW-17s. Wally Scott was 4th in an ASW-12 and Tom Brandes 5th in a 604.

Directors' Summer Meeting, 1973

At the August 3 meeting in Liberal, the executive directors reported a new all-time high of 12,174 members as of June 30, and the treasurer reported that the SSA was in good financial condition.

A resolution was passed to have the SSA representative on the CIVV strongly protest the consideration of the proposed changes to the Standard Class and to recommend that they be withdrawn.

It was announced that the FAA was exempting gliders from carrying transponders below 18,000 feet beginning in July 1974.

The sailplanes entered in the sailplane design competition were to be flight-evaluated at El Mirage in November. The funds raised to date were to be used for the expenses of running tests.

After a lengthy discussion, the

HG position paper remained unchanged, and the directors decided that *Soaring* should carry a general disclaimer about products advertised therein, so that there would be no implication of endorsement by SSA. It was noted that FAI soaring badges could be earned using hang gliders.

In view of the difficulty of raising funds for the Standard Class Trophy, it was voted that a surcharge on entry fees be introduced at the Standard Class National until the trophy was paid for and a $5,000 fund established.

The Marfa Chamber of Commerce had offered to lease property on the Marfa Municipal Airport to SSA for a nominal fee.

All 1973 officers were reelected for 1974.

First Woman's World Soaring Championship, 1973

The first woman's WSC was held at Leszno, Poland, June 21 to July 8, 1973, with 21 pilots from 13 countries, competing.

Pelagia Majewska of Poland was the winner and Sue Martin of Australia finished 2d. The U.S. entrants, Hetty Freese and Brit Floden finished 13th and 20th. All pilots flew the Polish Pirat sailplane in this one-design-class event.

Schweizer Aircraft Corporation

The SAC announced that it had delivered its 1,500th sailplane. Its report in the September *Soaring* noted:

> A new Standard Class competition sailplane is scheduled to join the family of Schweizer sailplanes. It will be known as the Schweizer 1-35. The pro-

totype was started late last year and flown in April. After 50 hours of flying and many comparison flights with current European fiberglass ships, it was decided, on May 10th, to put this sailplane into production.

> One of the most favorable factors for American sailplane manufacturers is the drastic increase in price of the European sailplanes over the last year. This has been primarily due to the devaluation of the dollar.

> Our goals are to get the FAA Type Certificate for the 1-35 before the end of the year and have the ship in production by early next spring.

National Soaring Museum

In 1973, an anonymous donor contributed $42,000 in stock to the NSM, to bring the fund total to over $70,000. It was decided to hire a museum director and Liam English of Amherst, Massachusetts, a trained historian, a soaring pilot, and sailplane owner, was chosen. Up to that time the museum had had only a part-time employee, Shirley Sliwa. At the spring session on May 11–13 the museum had its annual meeting and sponsored a World War II glider symposium that attracted many of those who had been active in military gliding during the war.

Preparation for Fourteenth WSC in Australia

Plans were well along for sending a team to the WSC to be held in Waikerie January 12–27, 1974. The fund drive had raised over $36,000, very close to what was needed. The seeded pilots were George Moffat and Dick Johnson in the Open Class, and Tom Beltz and Ben Greene in the Standard Class. Jim Herman was team captain.

The fuel shortage first hit in Colorado in June of 1973. At that time, P. A. and Ginny Schweizer were taking a 1-26 to the North American championships at Black Forest. Approaching Denver from the northeast, they planned to get gas when they reached the outskirts of Denver, but all the gas stations they went by were closed that evening. As they drove through Denver they could not find any open, and since their fuel indicator had been at "empty" for some time, they phoned the police. Directions were given to a gas station, but when they got there it too was closed. As they were about to call the police again, a "hippy" drove up and asked what they had attached to the car. An explanation was given and he then asked why they were at the closed gas station and they told him of their gas problem. He mentioned the gas shortage and said he had a can of gas in his car which they could have. After making the transfer, he refused payment for the gas but asked more questions about soaring. They suggested that he visit the Black Forest Gliderport and take an introductory ride. They later learned that the "good Samaritan" had come to the gliderport and taken a flight, and they hoped that he became "hooked" on soaring.

mittee members seeking to outlaw flaps in Std Cl.

Oral arguments included statements that flapped, no-airbrake gliders are likely to be dangerous and difficult to land, except by competition-level pilots. . . . Robert Buck countered this argument with a very persuasive description of the approach and landing qualities of flapped gliders, including the new Schweizer 1-35. . . . President Gehriger stated that this CIVV rule. . .does not prohibit the use of these [simple] flaps for improving circling or running performance.

The fact that an unopposed consensus was reached. . .can only be regarded as remarkable, in view of the wide initial divergence of views.

Helen Dick at one time held the U.S. national women's records for distance, goal and out-and-return flights. She was awarded the Eaton Trophy in 1972 for her contributions to soaring.

(George Uveges)

CIVV Meeting

The CIVV meeting took place in Paris on October 25, 1973. Bill Ivans reported the results in the January 1974 *Soaring*:

> It was established as a consensus that the 1971 decision of the CIVV—to permit flaps as an alternative to airbrakes on Standard Class sailplanes would stand at least through 1977.
>
> Written arguments had been circulated prior to the meeting by the English, W. Germans and French com-

Other Activities during 1973

R. E. Franklin, designer of the famous utility glider, died during the year.

Don Monroe, SSA assistant executive director, began to edit *Motorgliding* on a volunteer basis.

Ray Shamblen, SSA sailplane census taker, reported that there were 2,459 sailplanes in the United States, 200 of which were World War II gliders, 336 FRP sailplanes, and 451 1-26s.

Roy McMaster, Flight Training Committee chrmn, reported that 1,546 badges were earned in 1972, a new record; John McMurty of the USAF Academy was named top noncommercial instructor, with 29 badges, and Bernie Carris of the SSS became the top commercial instructor, with 185 badges.

The NSM held its first Barnaby Lecture during the year. The event took place in Philadelphia, and Captain Barnaby appropriately gave the first lecture. This has become an annual affair at which a noted soaring personality delivers the lecture.

Helen Dick won the Eaton Award for 1972, and Bertha Ryan was inducted into the Soaring Hall of Fame in 1973.

The Fuel Crisis, 1974

The fuel crisis that had developed during the last half of 1973 and the proposed National Energy Emergency Act that called for a 50 percent cutback in fuel for personal, pleasure, and instruction flying would have serious effects on soaring. The SSA had urged members, clubs, and commercial operators to contact their Congressmen to urge them to vote for the Goldwater-Rooney Amendment, which would reduce the cutback for aviation fuel. Soaring people felt it would not only restrict soaring but also limit the number of contestants who would compete in the regional and national contests.

FAA Award

Bernie Carris, chief instructor at SSS, guest columnist for the "Safety Corner" in the January 1974 *Soaring*, re-

ported that the Schweizer Soaring School had been awarded an FAA Plaque of Commendation in 1973 for having completed 100,000 flights without a serious accident since its start in 1946. He stated: "Disciplined flying and strong emphasis on pattern flying were the important factors that contributed to this safety record."

14th WSC, 1974

Twenty-eight Open Class and 39 Standard Class pilots competed in the 1974 WSC held in Waikerie, Australia, from January 12 to 27. George Moffat won the Open Class championship in a Numbus II, B. Zegel of Belgium was second in a 604, and H. W. Grosse of West Germany third in an ASW-17. Dick Johnson finished eighth in an ASW-17. A Haemmerie of Austria won the 19-meter cup.

The Standard Class was much more competitive. By the last day, there were five pilots with a good chance of winning the championships. However, Helmut Reichmann of West Germany won out in a flapped LS-2, I. Renner of Australia in a Cirrus was 29 points behind Reichmann. Ben Greene finished in 9th place in a Cirrus and Tom Beltz finished 17th, also in a Cirrus.

A comprehensive report of the WSC by Sylvia Colton and Tom Page appeared in the April 1974 *Soaring*. Some of the highlights were an Open Class 440-mile triangle, the longest speed task ever set in WSC, which a number of pilots completed, an Open Class 500-kilometer triangle in which the top three finishers exceeded the world record. The winner, C. Ax, averaged 87 miles per hour. The championships required a number of tough decisions by the WSC competition di-

Bertha Ryan at a soaring contest. Ryan was inducted into the SSA Hall of Fame for her many years of supporting soaring and the SSA and for carrying out the FAI homologation of records for the SSA.

(Sandor Aldott)

Scene showing a Polish *Jantar* sailplane passing over the finish line at WSC in Australia.

(Australian Information Service)

rector and the jury. The greatest concern was how to prevent sailplanes from flying above their legal gross weight. The threat of using scales and the moderate soaring conditions prevented a showdown on this point.

Colton and Page summed up the WSC by saying "Waikerie had been best organized, safest, and the longest soaring Championships ever."

Third Soaring Convention, 1974

The Third Soaring Convention was sponsored by the Mid-Georgia Soaring Association with John Karlovich as convention chairman. It included a Byars-Holbrook soaring symposium, a sailplane exhibit, and meetings of various soaring organizations, including the SSA business members, SSA directors, NSM Board of Trustees, and the 1-26 Association.

The symposium featured a "critique" of the 14th WSC by the four U.S. team pilots who had just re-

turned from Australia, and George Moffat was the main speaker at the award banquet.

The convention was a success and the "profits" were turned over to the SSA to be used to pay off the balance of the cost of the Standard Class Trophy. The amount remaining was to be used as a start-up fund for future conventions.

Directors' Winter Meeting, 1974

In order to continue to operate during the fuel crisis, the directors meeting in Atlanta, Georgia, on February 23–24 decided to eliminate free distance tasks and encourage tasks that minimize the retrieves. Relights after retrieves from off-field landings were eliminated, and policy was set to handle the early ending of a contest because of a lack of fuel. The use of ground towing was encouraged, particularly for training.

The SSA had ended 1973 with a "profit" of $16,000, but there was concern that rising inflation would mean higher operating costs in 1974. Licher had recommended a 10–20 percent increase in SSA employee wages, and it was obvious that the society would have to grow at a faster rate if it was to avoid a dues increase.

The commercial operators felt that a dues increase would discourage new people from taking up soaring. They argued that the SSA should be more aggressive in going out for new members. Just before the SSA directors' meeting, the commercial operators had pledged about $8,000 to SSA for an aggressive cooperative advertising program to get more people into soaring and the SSA. They planned to use the theme "Fuel-Free Soaring" in their ads. They also kept pushing for a 15-minute film that could be used to attract people to soaring.

Marion Griffith, SSA president, was concerned about the organization's promotion and public relations efforts. He noted that $1,500 of the promotional budget for 1973 was unspent, even though SSA expenses were below budget. Lloyd Licher and his assistant, Don Monroe, did not seem to be promotional-minded and they neither saw the point of announcing the Atlanta convention on the phone-recording device, after Griffith had suggested it several times. Griffith was looking for directors' reactions to the proposal for putting Licher and Monroe on a commission instead of raising salaries.

The NSM report listed some recent developments: The New York Council for the Arts had approved a grant of $7,500, the IRS had approved tax-deductible contributions for NSM, and a $10,000 grant had been received from the Urban Development Corp. for a feasibility study. Good progress was being made—the NSM had over

8,000 visitors in 1973 and the film library had rented out 430 films that year. There was much discussion on how SSA should support the NSM, and it was agreed that this should be referred to the Long-Range Planning Committee (LRPC) for further study.

Chairman A. J. Smith recommended that the sailplane design competition be discontinued because after four years it had not produced any designs for evaluation tests. The C-70, which had not been designed and built for the competition, was the only sailplane close to being ready for evaluation. The other U.S. manufacturers apparently felt, as SAC did, that the small prize fund and the extra work and cost of competing in the competition did not warrant entering. The board voted to give special recognition to Art Zimmerman and the Berkshire Manufacturing Co. for developing the C-70. The design competition had been a disappointment, but the committee would continue to evaluate sailplanes in cooperation with NASA.

At a previous meeting of the NSM Board of Trustees, it was agreed that the NSM and SSA should work closer together. Various ways of doing this were discussed, including the possibility of opening an eastern SSA office at the NSM. It was generally felt that the NSM should establish itself and prove its value to the SSA, whereupon a working agreement could be made.

Because there was considerable pressure to establish a category for woman's state records, it was decided to do so in four categories: distance, altitude gained, absolute altitude, and one-speed triangle.

Art Zimmerman

Art Zimmermann, a dedicated soaring enthusiast, died of cancer on April 15,

1974. He had formed the Icarus Soaring Club in 1960 and had operated a sailplane repair service for many years. He gave up a good industrial position when he went full-time on the C-70 project in 1970. He also took the time to be the sailplane repair specialist for the 1972 international team.

Third Annual Smirnoff Derby, 1974

Seven pilots were entered in the Third Smirnoff Derby. It started at the Whiteman Airpark in Los Angeles and finished at Dulles Airport near Washington, D.C. The pilots and sailplanes were as follows: Ken Briegleb, Kestrel; Danny Pierson, Diamant 18; Ross Briegleb, Concept 70; Richard Schreder, RS-15; Bill Holbrook, Libelle; Karl Striedieck, ASW-15; and Hannes Linke, Kestrel 17.

Karl Striedieck commented that a new task each day coupled with a wide spectrum of weather and geography was a true challenge. Bill Holbrook won the derby with 7,881 points, Linke was a close second with 7,836, and Ken Briegleb was third with 7,775 points.

The Bowers Bantam

Pete Bowers reported on his new homebuilt Bantam sailplane in the June 1974 *Soaring*. When the Australian Gliding Federation design contest for a 13-meter sailplane was announced, this was the incentive that he needed to redesign his half-completed Bantam into the Bantam II. Bowers states:

> At the present time, the world soaring movement seems to be caught in a performance race—new models are continually appearing that have the edge on last year's models, and the

prices go up accordingly. This is tending to make soaring a sport for a very prosperous elite—something like the American's sailboating.

> We have plenty of evidence of a reaction to this trend in the current hang gliding boom. . . . While not an actual rebellion against high cost and elitism, it does prove conclusively that the simple achievement of soaring flight, not cross-country performance, is the primary goal of the grass-root flier.

> What is needed, I feel, is a new design in the utility performance range that will, through structured simplicity and low cost, be able to increase activity in this area.

41st Open Class National, 1974

The Adrian, Michigan, Soaring Club sponsored the 41st National held from July 2 to 11, 1974. Of the 46 pilots competing, Dick Johnson, who had not won a National since 1964, was the sentimental favorite. He was in first place at the start of the last day's task by a thin margin over Ben Greene, but Greene managed to go 3 miles an hour faster and won the championship, with Johnson in 2d place. Both were flying ASW-17s. Bob Chase, in a Nimbus was 3d; Dick Butler, in an ASW-12, was 4th; and A. J. Smith, also in an ASW-12, was 5th. The first 15 sailplanes were all "open" large-span ships, with the highest Standard Class entry, Herb Mozer, in 18th place. This was more evidence of the performance separation between the two classes.

Fifth Standard Class National, 1974

The soaring conditions were excellent for the meet at Hobbs, New Mexico, from July 16 to 25. Sixty eager Standard Class pilots set a new record of total miles flown in a National, 127,735.1 miles, which averaged out to 236.5 miles per day per pilot. Speeds on the tasks were phenomenal, with Tom Beltz turning in the fastest time of 91.89 miles per hour on a 245.6-mile triangle. Part of the reason for such good speeds in Standard Class sailplanes was that many sailplanes were illegally overloaded, some with cockpit ballast. Wally Scott wrote a letter to the editor of *Soaring* entitled "Better than a Pine Box." He was not flying in the contest but made several visits there and was very upset with what he saw:

> Imagine how appalling it was to find that many of the gliders at, or in excess of, 9#/sq/ft/wing loadings. Thirty gallons of water ballast tanks were not unusual and many of the contestants were loading four, six, or eight 25# bags of shot into their cockpit. . . . Man this is as illegal as hell and utterly ridiculous. . . . I feel we should strongly protest such antics.
>
> So, fellows, we'd better get smart and use some of our talents toward self-regulation and enforcement instead of "throttle bending."

In forwarding a copy of Wally Scott's letter to Tom Page, Licher had addressed it to Tom Page, Chairman SSA Committee for Exposing Things for the Directors to Sweep under the Rug. Page had developed a reputation for bringing before the board situations that needed attention but were difficult to handle. Usually the board found solutions that were different from Page's direct approach. Page's proposals were always well worked out and tried to cover all eventualities, but as a result they tended to be long and complicated. The directors often decided that other action, or no action at all, was required, which accounted for the "sweeping under the rug"

claim. In some cases, like the prohibition of gyros and the weighing of sailplanes, they were later approved, even though SSA had ruled against them at the start.

Wally's letter went on to say that Dick Johnson, flying a PIK-20, who won the contest "did it without having to resort to lead shot." Tom Beltz, in a Cirrus, was a close second; John Bird, also in a Cirrus, was third; Ross Briegleb, in a Nugget, was fourth; and Ray Gimmey, in a Libelle, was fifth. Hal Lattimore was the competition director and Jack Gomez contest manager.

Directors's Summer Meeting, 1974

After being under consideration since 1972, the SSA bylaws were amended to add two new classes of membership: affiliates and branches. This was to encourage other soaring-oriented organizations to affiliate with the SSA. Griffith cited this as a milestone action and expressed his desire that the NSM would apply for affiliate status.

A proposal by Gunter Voltz, chairman of the SSA Youth Education Committee, recommended giving student members voting privileges. It failed by a few votes.

David Scott was chosen to be SSA's Washington, D.C., watchdog and was asked to report on any activity that could affect soaring or the SSA. Scott, who was not a registered lobbyist, performed the same service for the EAA and wrote a monthly report for EAA's *Sport Flying* magazine.

A new slate of officers was elected: Lawrence Wood, president; Samuel A. Francis and Robert L. Semans, vice-presidents; R. E. Schreder, secretary; and T. E. Sharp, treasurer.

Larry Wood, the president-elect, along with some other directors and many commercial operators, was concerned about the direction in which the SSA was going. They all felt that the SSA was not reaching out for new members and new opportunities to further soaring as it should. They also feared that increasing membership dues, to take care of the fast growing inflation, would seriously hold back the growth of SSA. Some felt that the society was becoming an "exclusive club" and that it was not fulfilling its obligation to promote soaring in all its phases. Woods asked various directors what needed to be done.

Two World Records

Ken Briegleb set a new world record for speed around a 100-kilometer triangle in his Kestrel 17 on July 18. His speed of 102.7 miles per hour was the first world record to exceed 100 miles per hour. Briegleb lived near El Mirage, where the Kestrel was based, and whenever the weather looked promising he was able to give it a try. On the same day and on the same course, Mrs. Lee Tweed, in another

Kestrel, set a woman's world record for the 100-kilometer triangle with a speed of 76.9 miles per hour. She worked only one thermal on the course.

The Sailplane Directory

The August 1974 *Soaring* was a sailplane directory, edited by Bennett Rogers. It listed sailplanes that were not included in the previous two directories of May 1964 and March-April 1970 issues of *Soaring*.

Air Cadet League of Canada

SAC had been supplying training gliders to the Air Cadet League of Canada (ACLC) for a number of years. The ACLC is a civilian nonprofit corporation that conducts a national youth program administered by Canadian military forces. Its purpose is to expose young people to aviation and to motivate them to go into the Air Force, air lines, or commercial aviation. In order to admit the maximum number of young people, the cadets are brought up only to solo at their summer encampments. In order to encourage soaring, as well as to show SAC's appreciation for the sailplane business, SAC gives five soaring scholarships at the SSS for the best cadet at each of the five summer encampments. They usually end up with a "C" soaring award and return to Canada enthusiastic soaring pilots.

Vintage Sailplane Association

Jan Scott wrote an article in the March 1974 *Soaring* about restoring and flying antique sailplanes and encouraged others to become involved. The NSM sponsored a vintage sailplane regatta

World champions: Helmut Reichmann, Standard Class; George Moffat, Open Class; and Andreas Haemmerle, 19-meter cup winner.

(River News)

over the Labor Day weekend at Harris Hill. Seven vintage sailplanes were at the regatta, two of which were from the NSM collection: the Elmira 1930 Primary that Gus Scheurer had restored and the Minimoa that Dick du Point had flown.

The idea of a Vintage Soaring Association (VSA) was proposed at a meeting and a good number of those present donated $5 to get the organization started. Geoffrey Steele was elected provisional president, and the NSM was to be the temporary home of the VSA.

Second International Symposium on the Technology and Science of Low-Speed and Motorless Flight

The second "MIT" symposium was sponsored by the AIAA, MIT, and SSA and held at MIT from September 11 to 13. Jim Nash-Weber was the chairman. An overview of the symposium by John McMasters and Paul MacCready, Jr., in the December 1974 *Soaring* noted:

The 47 papers and associated panel discussions covered sailplane aerodynamics, flight testing, structural, flight-path optimization, instrumentation, and meteorology. Mostly the session focused on matters related to high performance sailplanes, but there were also sessions on man-powered aircraft and ultralight gliders. Lack of travel funding for this year's conference resulted in fewer visitors from overseas.

To generalize the tone of the meeting in comparison to the prior one, it can be said that it emphasized the professional side of the field and the advance of technology—but the authors of this article were hard pressed to identify any new breakthrough.

Contests during the Energy Crisis

Marion Griffith commented about the fuel shortage in *Soaring:* "It seems appropriate to express my pleasure and admiration of the Board's position regarding the 1974 contests and the energy shortage. . . . The approach taken by the Contest Board was a cautious one. . . . With possible courses of action ranging from total cancellation of

Kenny Briegleb, who set the 100-kilometer triangle world record in a Kestrel 17 on July 18, 1974, from El Mirage, California Gliderport.

(George Uveges)

Leila Tweed, who set the 100-kilometer triangle women's world record in a Kestrel 17 on July 18, 1974, from El Mirage Gliderport.

(George Uveges)

contests to no changes at all, it appears the Contest Board, supported by the Directors at Atlanta, has selected exactly the best course of action."

CIVV Meeting

The CIVV meeting was held in Paris on October 4, 1974. A decision was made to permit linking of flaps and ailerons for Standard Class planes entered in the WSC's after 1977. Two new world speed record categories were established for a speed around a 750-kilometer triangle and speed around a 1,000-kilometer triangle. The CIVV also wrestled with the problem of hang gliders (HGs) and ultralights, but no conclusions were reached as to how to accommodate them.

Other Activities during 1974

In order to reduce accidents, the FAA announced that, beginning in November 1974, all pilots would be required to take a biennial flight review.

Two famous soaring personalities died during 1974—Dr. Karl Lange, who was very active at the early soaring contests at Elmira, and Mike Stroukoff, famous architect and glider and airplane designer who gave the Stroukoff Trophy to SSA.

A Three-Class World Championship, 1975

There had been little activity on Standard Class requirements since the fall of 1973. The only change was the decision to permit the interconnection of flaps and ailerons after 1977, which would give the flapped airplanes some advantage over those equipped with dive brakes. In view of this and the fact that the existing (1974) require-

ments were only guaranteed until 1977, it appeared likely that another effort would be made to change the class requirements at the coming CIVV meeting in March. The four U.S. manufacturers of Standard Class sailplanes were in production after having spent considerable funds in approving, tooling up, and getting production going and they hoped that the rules would not be changed so that their sailplanes would be successful financially.

Griffith's Remarks

Marion S. Griffith commented on his two years as SSA president in the January 1975 *Soaring:* "The backbone of SSA is the members who do something, not just talk about it—chapters, clubs, and groups all around the country who take the initiative, plan, accomplish, and soar. I am more convinced than ever that soaring and SSA have a proper place in the lives of people interested in challenge."

Contest Entry Priority

The new pilot entry priority list for the two national soaring contests totaled about 300 names. The list was necessary because the directors had limited the number of entrants in a National to 60 U.S. pilots, and to a maximum of 65 pilots in Regionals.

Fourth National Convention, 1975

The Fourth National Soaring Convention at San Francisco from January 30 to February 2 set a registration record. Excellent press and TV coverage resulted in good publicity and a significant number of walk-in spectators. B. S. Smith was the convention chairman and Nancy Davis his assistant.

Stan Hall was in charge of the technical sessions, which included reports on the Nugget, HP-10, and the 1-35 given by Jack and Bill Laister, Dick Schreder, and Paul A. Schweizer.

The 1-35 Report pointed out the many problems that SAC had had in obtaining FAA approval. In particular, it had been necessary to run a great number of loading conditions through stress analysis and static and flight tests as there were so many different combinations of flap positions—center of gravity locations and water ballast amounts.

As the FAA did not have any loading for "T" tails, this had to be developed by NASA. Because the FAA and NASA test pilots had no experience flying high-performance sailplanes, SAC had to check them out for the flight tests.

There were some humorous requirements. The FAA considered it necessary to demonstrate that the 1-35 met the noise abatement standards required by the Environmental Protection Agency. One FAA representative wanted to know what was to be done with the water that was drained from the airspeed indicator and he also wanted to know what was going to be done about smoking, and gave SAC the option of either putting in an ash tray or a No Smoking sign.

Seven sailplanes were on exhibit in the convention ballroom, along with a scale model of the proposed NSM building designed by Eliot Noyes. The SSA noncompetition awards were given out and the speaker was astronaut Henry Hartsfield, who was scheduled to fly the space shuttle.

Directors' Winter Meeting, 1975

The winter meeting was held in San Francisco on February 1–2, 1975. The 1974 $7,000 loss plus the increase in inflation made a dues increase likely, but many directors felt that the SSA had to change its ways in order to achieve its overall aims. Some hoped that, by increasing membership and economizing in some areas, a dues increase could be delayed. The meeting had to go into an extra session because of the time spent on this matter. It was finally agreed to increase the membership rates, provided that the president and Executive Committee came up with a plan for adding a key person to handle promotion and public relations and to improve the growth rate of SSA and the services to its members. The new rates were to be as follows: member, $20; associate member, $12; student member, $10; family membership, $7; business membership, $45; industrial membership, $65; life membership, $250.

The second controversial item was the matter of how to limit ballast used in sailplanes. Tom Page suggested re-

Lawrence "Larry" Wood, SSA president and Donald Hamilton, former SSA director, at the 1975 NSM spring reception at the Harris Hill administration building.

(NSM Collection)

Ivans had asked manufacturers for information on (1) their production plans for Standard Class sailplanes, (2) the money spent on design, certification, and setting up production, (3) the relative complexity of flaps vs. dive brakes, and (4) pilots' reactions to Standard Class sailplanes with and without flaps.

SAC indicated that (1) it had a backlog up to ship no. 100 and that it had already produced 20, (2) that it had expended almost $500,000 on the engineering, prototype, testing, tooling, and putting the 1-35 into production, (3) that the BGA estimate of a 20 percent increase in the cost for flap was very high and should be more like 5 percent, and (4) that the pilot reaction to the 1-35 flap had been enthusiastic.

SAC also remarked that the BGA statement that flaps should be forbidden since the Standard Class should remain a cheap and simple sailplane, was beside the point as this objective had been abandoned 15 years before.

stricting the gross weight of sailplanes in SSA-sanctioned contests to ensure equity of competition. The majority felt that the SSA should not try to administer FARs and so the policy became that SSA has no powers in this regard and that it should only exert pressure in matters pertaining to compliance, in terms of sportsmanship.

Among the other items covered, the directors approved the use of interconnecting flaps and ailerons for the Standard Class National beginning in 1975, agreed that the top 10 percent finishing in the 1-26 North American would be seeded in Category II for national qualifications, gave student members voting rights, and named the NSM the 1st affiliate of the SSA. However, a step backward was taken when directors voted that a prize no longer be awarded in national and regional contests to the pilot with the best score in a U.S.-built sailplane.

Preparation for the CIVV Meeting

In a report to the CIVV, Ann Welch and the BGA proposed to create three classes and to force flapped sailplanes to fly in the unrestricted 15-Meter

Class. Ivans wrote the U.S. sailplane manufacturers to ask them for support, in order to be able to oppose this proposal. He also named Dick Johnson to report on the PIK-20 flaps, hoping to counteract Reichmann's derogatory remarks about the flaps on the LS-1.

The CIVV Report

The May 1975 *Soaring* reported on the CIVV meeting held in Paris on March 14–15 (Robert Buck was the U.S. representative in place of W. S. Ivans, who was unable to attend because of illness):

> Bob Buck reported on subjects which have been under consideration by the CIVV for a number of years:
> 1. Redefinition of World Championship Classes.
>   a. After December 31, 1977, there will be three classes in a World Championships:
>   1. OPEN CLASS (with World Cup for best 19 m performance).
>   2. 15 METER CLASS, no restrictions except span.
>   3. 15 Meter RESTRICTED CLASS, which is the 1972 definition Standard Class (no flaps; ballast OK; retractable wheel OK). CLUB GLIDER sub-class is to be established, with a World Cup for best performance. It will have a 15 meter span limit; other limitations will be provided by CIVV after the national aero club recommendations.
>   b. The 1976 World Championships will have Class definitions as at Waikerie in 1974: Open Class (with 19 meter Cup) and Standard Class (flaps permitted as alternative to dive brakes).

Ivans commented:

> These are far-reaching decisions indeed. The Class "home" for gliders such as the 1-35, Nugget, HP-15, -16, -18, PIK-20, etc. will shift after the 1976 Championships to the 15 Meter (unrestricted) Class.

The advent of a 15 Meter Club Glider sub-class represents an attempt to return to the concept of a simple, inexpensive, durable glider still suitable for competition. Whether any such design can remain inexpensive and still be capable of winning world competition is open to serious doubt. Room must be found in our U.S. competition structure to accommodate the new Class(es).

Debate revealed a very strong "anti-flap" sentiment on the part of England, Germany, Belgium, Sweden . . . with only Finland, Holland, and Italy supporting the U.S. position favoring flaps. A U.S. proposal to use 1974 (Waikerie) Standard Class rules as definition for "new" 15 Meter Restricted Class was voted down 7 to 13.

10,000th Active SSA Member

An indication of SSA's growth was the announcement that Edward Warmoth of Sacramento, California, became the 10,000th active member. The total SSA membership was 13,567 at that time. *Soaring* noted: "Licher was so delighted that he made a special announcement for the SSA telephone news tape and treated the office staff to ice cream."

National Soaring Week

The SSA designated June 30 to July 6, 1975, the first National Soaring Week to help call attention to soaring. Schools and clubs were encouraged to publicize this affair and to plan special events at their sites.

The CIVL

At its February 1975 meeting, the CIVV recommended to the FAI that a special commission be set up to handle hang gliding. As a result, an organizational meeting was set up by Ann Welch in June to establish the CIVL. Thirteen countries sent delegates. After a long debate, they agreed to define a hang glider as "A heavier-than-air, fixed wing glider capable of being carried, foot launched, and landed solely by the energy and use of the pilots legs." This statement now "legally" separated hang gliders from sailplanes and justified the position that the SSA directors had taken.

J. C. Lincoln

His many friends and the soaring world were saddened to hear of the death of Joe Lincoln on May 19, 1975, from an inoperable brain tumor. He is an important part of American soaring history. He left behind an outstanding flying record as well as many books and articles on soaring that gave enjoyment to many soaring enthusiasts. Lincoln was a staunch supporter of the SSA and NSM, and his generous gift

---

The Schweizers had known Joe for almost 20 years, ever since he had replaced his Baby Albatross with a 1-23D that he named Cirro-Q. *He visited Elmira many times in connection with his various soaring activities, which included flying in the 1957 Nationals, picking up his 2-32 (which he named* Cibola), *and then arranging for special long wings for his 2-32. His great desire to extend soaring records led him to make many noteworthy record flights.*

Joe was fun to be with and he had a great sense of humor. When something really tickled him, he would explode into a loud burst of laughter that could be heard all over. He was reluctant to leave a friendly conversation on soaring and would shake hands a number of times before he could finally break away. He was also a generous person, and his contributions to the NSM made it possible to hire a director and to start on a new building.

Many soaring friends from around the United States were part of the large assembly that attended his funeral service, at which his coffin was draped with the SSA flag.

Joe Lincoln at the 1970 WSC at Marfa, Texas, where he wrote the official SSA report for *Soaring*. He was awarded the Eaton Trophy for 1975 posthumously, in recognition of his great support of soaring in the United States.

(NSM Collection)

in 1974 enabled the NSM to hire a director and to proceed with its building plans. Joe's wife, Dorothy, had a memorial booklet published entitled "Reflections of Joseph C. Lincoln," which included quotations from the book that he was working on at the time of his death and some of the ideas that guided him through life and endeared him to so many people.

Fourth Smirnoff Derby, 1975

The 1975 Smirnoff Derby entrants looked like a page from a who's who of soaring: There were three world champions (Ralph Hossinger of Argentina in a Cirrus, George Moffat of the United States in a PIK-20, and Helmuth Reichmann of West Germany in a PIK-20) plus a U.S. national champion (Karl Striedieck in an ASW-15) and a Smirnoff defending champion (Bill Holbrook in a 1-35).

The weather was good for the first third of the course, but the central part of the country was wet and so Ed Butts, derby director, had contestants trailer their sailplanes from Dallas,

Texas, to St. Louis, Missouri. The weather in the East was not very good either, and the derby ended at La-trobe, Pennsylvania. Moffat came first with 6,681 points, Reichmann second with 6,298 points and Hossinger third with 5,752 points.

Sixth Standard Class Nationals, 1975

Fifty-nine pilots entered the Standard Class National at Minden, Nevada, July 1–10, 1975. The contest was plagued with unpredictable weather, which made setting tasks very difficult and increased the "luck factor." There was great interest in seeing how the new breed of flapped sailplanes (the six PIK-20s, four 1-35s, three Nuggets, one HP-18, and one C-70) would compare with the German sailplanes. Ross Briegleb, who flew a Nugget, was able to overtake Tom Beltz in a PIK-20 on the last day to win the championship. Ray Gimmey was 3d in a Nugget, Bob Klemmedson was 4th in a Cirrus, and Ted Grabowsky was 5th in a PIK-20. Las Horvath, flying his first National in a 1-35, was 8th and made the fastest speed of the contest in winning a 260-mile triangle. Schreder's new HP-18 was not contest-ready and he finished in 41st place. The C-70, flown by Dick Crosse, came in 42d.

Moffat noted that seven pilots who had won 22 national and international contests had finished in a wide range of positions, from first to forty-first, and that this was due to the changeable weather and "overtasking." Moffat, A. J. Smith and Dick Johnson, all in PIK-20s, had finished 11th, 13th, and 18th, respectively.

Carl Herold, the contest director, agreed with George Moffat: "Speed Tasks were selected conservatively with an eye to minimizing local pilot advantage. Each day the weather changes wiped out the conservative factor of the task and 'overtasking' appeared to be the result.''

42d Open Class National, 1975

After the very successful Standard Class National at Hobbs in 1974, the Open pilots were expecting super performances, when they got their Nimbus IIs, ASW-17s, 604s, and other sailplanes loaded with water and ready to go at the meet in Hobbs, from July 14 to 24.

They were in for a disappointment, however. The 42d National had the worst weather that Hobbs had experienced in many a year. For awhile, Hal Lattimore, the competition director, thought that participants would not even get in the four contest days needed to make it a championship.

Thirty-nine of the 64 sailplanes entered were Open sailplanes. There were 6 contest days out of the 10 scheduled and the tasks were very modest compared with 1974. The completions averaged below 50 percent. On the day next to last only 11 sailplanes made it back.

Dick Johnson, in his Nimbus II, was in first place from the third day on and was able to withstand a last day charge by Dick Butler to win the championships. Butler finished second in his 604, Wally Scott was third in his ASW-12, E. D. Welch was fourth in an ASW-17, and Brian Utley was fifth in a Nimbus II.

Directors' Summer Meeting, 1975

The directors' meeting on July 25, 1975, in Hobbs was sparked by a spirited debate on the new CIVV classes. Directors were pressured to outlaw flaps in the Standard Class by many owners of nonflapped sailplanes in the United States, which were estimated to number about 300, alongside only about 35 flapped Standard Class sailplanes. It was a losing battle for the U.S. manufacturers. The majority agreed that the SSA should follow the CIVV plan of three classes. It was also decided that sailplanes with both flaps and dive brakes could enter in the Standard Class if the flaps were sealed.

The SSA was the beneficiary of Joe Lincoln's sailplanes and equipment. Included were a Nimbus II, a 1-23D, a 2-32, and a set of longwings for a 2-32, all to be sold by bid.

This was a great blow to P. A. Schweizer, who had preached safety in soaring for many years. He looked into the possible reasons for the accident in the hope that something could be learned from it.

One lesson was that if his shoulder harness had been tight he would have merely limped away from the accident. Ginny had reminded him to tighten his harness as she shut the canopy. The ''hookup boy'' wanted to get the ring in the tow hook and the starter was eager to wave him off. Because of this, he forgot to tighten his shoulder harness. In the crash, the combination of the loose harness and the resulting stretch from the high ''G'' load caused his head to hit the instrument panel.

He also concluded that the accident was due to a combination of very hot weather, dehydration, and fatigue. After about six hours of difficult flying and not having used any water in his thermos bottle, he had set up a pattern to land in a cotton field, but could not remember anything further.

Looking back, he recalled the very busy week before, when Ginny and he had left for Texas. After a two-day drive, they were immediately involved in the ''pre-contest whirl'' and practice tasks. After the second day's task, Paul and Ginny drove to Dallas to visit Ginny's girlhood friend. They returned after 2 a.m. and then got up early, expecting a distance task that day.

From this, it's obvious that pilots have to be concerned about their physical condition when they fly, particularly if (1) it's a hot day, (2) they are participating in a competition, and (3) they are older.

There was an extended discussion about the relationship between commercial operators and the SSA. It was pointed out that about 80 percent of the U.S. glider activity was carried out by the COs and that they accounted for many of the new SSA members. Thus it was decided to have a regular agenda item for CO-SSA matters at future directors' meetings.

Bill Cleary's ad hoc development committee was to develop the promotion manager job description.

All officers were reelected for 1976.

1-26 Championships, 1975

The 10th 1-26 National was held at Southwest Soaring operation at Caddo Mills, Texas, from August 6 to 13. Thirty-seven 1-26s were entered.

On the third day, a prescribed area distance task, the very hot weather and the length of the task had an adverse effect on some of the pilots. P. A. Schweizer had the misfortune of having an accident, his first in his 45 years of flying. After six days of competition, Harry Baldwin was again

the winner, with Ted Teach close behind. T. Cooper was third, Tom Knauff fourth, and C. Lind fifth.

Two New World Records

On March 5, Babbs Nutt and Hanna Duncan set a world's women's absolute altitude record of 35,463 feet in a 2-32 sailplane at Colorado Springs. On July 26, Edward Minghelli and Bob Gravance set a world's two-place out-and-return record of 466.84 miles in a Prue IIA sailplane in California. As a result, the United States was now tied with Poland at eight world records each. The USSR was third with seven, and West Germany was next with five.

The 1976 U.S. WSC Team

The 1976 WSC team included Dick Johnson, Dick Butler in the Open Class, and Tom Beltz and Ross Briegleb in the Standard Class. Many questioned why George Moffat was not on the team, since they felt that a current world champion should automatically defend his title, even though CIVV rules contain no provision for this. A review committee considered the seeding proper. George Moffat had been seeded fourth in the Open Class and fifth in the Standard Class.

Sailplane Developments

Concept Sailplanes, Inc., resumed production of the Concept C-70 sailplane, with Bryan Evans as general manager.

Dan Summer's "Mescalero" story in the March 1975 *Soaring* told how the sailplane design competition got George Applebay started.

Stan Hall described his Vector I, an ultralight sailplane with foot-launching potential, which he had

Ross Briegleb (left) and crew prepare the Laister Nuggett for a contest flight at the second Standard Class nationals at Ephrata, Washington.
(Paul Einarsen)

Top: Babbs Nutt (right) and Hanna Duncan in Wave Flights 2-32, in which they set a new world women's two-place altitude record.
(Chinook Graphic)

Edward Minghelli, builder of the Prue IIA in which he set a world two-place out-and-return record with Bob Gravance.
(George Uveges)

tested using auto tow. In the June 1975 *Soaring* John McMasters reported on recent development in ultralights.

Other Happenings during 1975

At the end of 1975, the United States, with 304 three-diamond pilots, was still in second place in the number of Diamond awards won. West Germany was first with 350, followed by Poland with 296, France with 189, and Austria with 112.

The Second World Women's Soaring Championship was held in Leszno, Poland, and Britt Floden and Erica Scurr represented the United States. Three Polish pilots won. Scurr came in 19th and Floden 21st.

Charles Abel, the real pusher behind the Smithsonian plaques, died during 1975.

Lloyd Licher Resigns, 1976

In 1976 Lloyd Licher was beginning his twentieth year as executive director. During that time the SSA had grown from about 1,000 members to over 13,000. Licher had operated the SSA on a low-cost "austerity" basis and was assisted by a loyal group of handpicked employees. His relations with the officers and directors were generally good. About the only problems he had occurred in the early years when he had trouble getting *Soaring* out on time, and so did not have the time to maintain good communications with the members.

After 15 years, however, differences started to develop, beginning with the hang glider controversy. Licher disagreed with the directors' policy, or, as he felt, their lack of a policy. Some directors were disturbed when he became personally involved with hang glider activities, but recognized that he had the right to do so on his own time.

Licher was such a highly principled person that it bothered him when the board did not face up to a problem, and on a number of occasions he felt that they were "sweeping it under the rug." There were also differences over promotion and public relations and some were disappointed by his lack of enthusiasm for the advertising program financed by commercial operators.

When inflation pushed up operating costs, and Licher recommended employee wage increases, it looked as though membership dues would have to be increased substantially. Many felt that this would discourage memberships. This problem came to a head at the San Francisco meeting, when the directors approved the rate increases providing that a promotion person would be hired to help SSA grow. Although a serious difference had not developed between Licher and the directors, they were drifting apart!

Directors' Winter Meeting, 1976

At the meeting in Denver on February 6–8, 1976, the directors reviewed the controversy that had arisen because Moffat had not been selected for the 1976 WSC team. The directors felt that the SSA seeding was properly carried out and so should not be changed.

However, the board did direct Ivans to ask the CIVV to allow present world champions to fly in the WSC without reducing the number of pilots on his country's team.

One of the most heated discussions at an SSA directors' meeting arose over the proposal to permit the current flapped sailplane designs that were flown in 1975 to fly in the U.S. Standard Class championships under a grandfather clause. This vote failed 10 to 13. The directors then voted unanimously to permit flaps in the competition if they were used only for safety purposes and an approved timing device was used to limit the use of flaps to five minutes.

It was decided to sanction Sportsman Class competition as an adjunct to the 1976 regional championships, providing it did not interfere with the number of entries and starting times.

A Polish sailplane manufacturer offered the use of two Standard Jantars and two Open Jantars for the 1976 WSC. Although this generous offer would reduce the team costs, the directors felt that the pilot should make his own decision as to what he would fly.

Fifth Annual SSA Soaring Convention, 1976

The April 1976 issue of *Soaring* stated:

> They transformed Denver's Regency Tower complex into a soaring mini-metropolis. For five days the facility buzzed with meetings, lectures, discussions, hangar flying and sailplane ogling.
>
> In addition to the sessions, displays, and Director's meeting, it was possible for the peripatetic enthusiast to eavesdrop on the activities of the 1-26 Association, the Commercial and Business Members, the Women Soaring Pilots, the National Soaring Mu-

seum Trustees, the SSA State Governors. . . . Another attraction was a showing of the new SSA film, "The Joy of Soaring."

Hall of Fame Moves to NSM

In 1975 the directors decided that the NSM should take over the Soaring Hall of Fame. The SSA directors would still select candidates for the Hall of Fame, but they would be awarded each year at the time of the spring NSM Hall of Fame weekend. The first to be inducted at the NSM Hall of Fame weekend in 1976 were Gus Scheurer and Tom Page, which brought the total in the Hall of Fame to 55.

CIVV Report

At the March 5 meeting of the CIVV, F. Weinholtz of West Germany recommended that current FAI world champions be automatically invited to defend their title and the United States endorsed this recommendation. However, the majority of the members were strongly opposed, since they believed that it would favor the home country of the current champions.

A club class was discussed at length and it was agreed that further details were to be developed by the Club Class Committee headed by P. Oberg of Sweden.

P. Weishaupt of Denmark led a discussion on the progress of motorglider competition. The consensus favored the continuing development of tasks in which the motor could be used during the course of the task, instead of restricting its use for just self-launching and for "getting home."

Bill Ivans was unanimously

elected president of the CIVV by the 26 representatives of the national soaring clubs to replace Pirat Gehriger, who had been elected vice-president of the FAI.

New World Out-and-Return Record

Karl Striedieck and Roy McMaster teamed up to set a new out-and-return record of 807 miles in an ASW-17 and a Standard Class Cirrus, by making the round-trip between Lock Haven, Pennsylvania, and Mendota, Virginia, on March 17, 1976. The flight was made in weather that froze their drinking water and the Cirrus's untreated ballast water. On the way down, they had to contend with snow, low clouds, and quartering head winds, and on the way back they reached a speed of 100 miles an hour and registered $+5$ and -6 on their g-meters. They were subjected to a physical pounding as they skimmed the ridges. McMaster's flight also set a U.S. Standard Class national record.

Sailplane Developments

"Building the HP-18" was the title of a six-part article in *Soaring* by Dick Schreder. The comments on the SSA members' renewal forms showed that homebuilding was the main topic of interest to readers of *Soaring*. Schreder's series explained how to build the 15-Meter Class HP-18. He cautioned the readers that these articles were not a complete, all-inclusive, step by step manual, but that they would give the reader better understanding of what such a project entails.

The Spirit of '76 version of the 2-33 was produced to celebrate the bicentenial. It was finished in a red, white, and blue with stars and stripes on its wings and tail surfaces. Many commercial operators used these 2-33s to feature bicentennial introductory rides.

American Eaglet was the name of Larry Haig's 150-pound self-launching glider, which was to be made available as a homebuilt kit sailplane.

The J-4 Javalin was put into production by the Peterson Sailplane Division of the Poly Industries, Inc. It was announced in a two-page color ad in the April '76 issue of *Soaring* and listed five U.S. distributors.

The Zuni, a new 15-Meter Class fiberglass sailplane was announced in the April '76 *Soaring*. The design was by George Appelbay, who had developed the Mescalero. The Zuni incorporated the latest Wortmann airfoil and used flaps with aileron interconnect. It first flew on November 18.

The Soaring Star, a high-performance two-place airplane—was announced at a press party by Ted Smith, noted designer of the Aerostar and Aero Commander airplanes. A mock-up of this all-metal sailplane was on display and the prototype was being built.

Director of Development

President Wood announced that Sunny Vegso would be SSA's first director of development. She was chosen after a lengthy search. Among her responsibilities were the development, guidance, and implementation of programs designed to broaden interest, strengthen the meaning of SSA membership, enlarge the membership, and bring it closer together.

First Soaring Flight over 1,000 Miles

Karl Striedieck, who had held the World out-and-return record five times

in the last eight years, usually declared a turn-point that was just sufficient to establish a new mark. This time he chose a turn-point that would give him a flight in excess of 1,000 miles. On May 19, 1976 he started at 5:35 a.m., and flew his ASW-17 from Lock Haven to a point east of Oak Ridge, Tennessee, and back to Lock Haven, Pennsylvania. He landed at 7 p.m.—a 1,015-mile flight in 13½ hours.

Reflecting on the flight, he noted, "This sort of ridge running is very demanding physically, exhausting mentally and is hazardous. Rarely are you one minute from landing if your ridge lift quits. . . . Rarely, also are you above a safe landing field. . . . and then there are those blasted snow showers. . . . But, as long as I fly, I'll still soar down the Appalachian Expressway because it's beautiful and exciting and scary and sensational and if the eagles do it—its got to be right!" Unfortunately, because his turn-pont picture was not up to specification, the flight was not accepted as a record by the FAI.

Wally Scott Wins Smirnoff Derby, 1976

Wally Scott, Sr., flying a 1-35, nosed out Dan Pierson in a Laister Nugget to win the 1976 Smirnoff Derby. Because of poor weather only 6 completed the 10 daily tasks, and so it really became a distance contest. The top finishers were (1) Scott, 6,776 in a 1-35; (2) Pierson, 6,590 in a Nugget, and (3) R. Allemann, 6,312 in a Libelle.

15th WSC, 1976

Thirty-nine Open and 46 Standard Class pilots were entered in the 15th WSC at Rayskala, Finland. The poor weather caused 313 outlandings from

the 590 contest launches. Dick Butler was the only one whose sailplane sustained major damage. Volunteer help from other teams enabled the U.S. team to get his 604 flying again without his losing a day.

George Lee of Great Britain, flying an ASW-17, was the Open champion by a good margin. J. Ziobro and H. Masyczynski of Poland finished second and third, both flying Jantar IIs. K. Holighaus of West Germany was fourth in a Nimbus II, and Dick Butler of the United States was fifth. Dick Johnson was close behind in seventh place in a Jantar. I. Hahner of Hungary won the 19-meter world cup.

Ingo Renner of Australia was 1st in the Standard Class. Karlson of Sweden was 2d and G. Burton of Great Britain was 3d, all flying PIK-20s. Tom Beltz of the United States was 5th in a PIK-20B. Ross Briegleb of the United States was 27th in a Standard Jantar.

Billy Hill flying his Zuni over the Black Forest Gliderport.
(Jim Foreman)

Top: Al Leffler won the 1976 National Open flying a Nimbus at El Mirage, California. He is shown here getting into a Cirrus sailplane at a previous contest, with parasol ready to ward off the sun.

(George Uveges)

Joe Emmons, winner of the first 15-Meter National at Bryan, Ohio, in July of 1976. He flew a Libelle 301.

(George Uveges)

First 15-Meter Class National, 1976

Fifty-four 15-meter sailplanes entered the first 15-Meter National held in Bryan, Ohio, from June 29 to July 9, 1976. Hal Lattimore was competition director and Neal Ridenour operations director. Nine days of soarable weather with eight triangles and one goal-and-return flight made this a good contest. Joe Emons narrowly beat out John Bryd, both flying H-301 Libelles. Woody Woodward, flying a PIK 20 was third; Herb Mozer, flying an ASW-19, was fourth; and Las Horvath in a 1-35 was fifth. The principal sailplanes entered included 16 Libelles, 14 PIK 20s, 7 1-35s, 3 Nuggets, and 1 Concept 70. The 15-Meter Class in the United States had arrived.

Seventh Standard Class National, 1976

A "full house" of 65 pilots competed in the Standard Class National held in Hutchinson, Kansas, July 13–22. Despite very windy weather and chopped uplift, competition was possible on 8 of the 10 days. Ray Gimmey, flying a Standard Libelle, was the winner, Tom Hanson in an ASW-19 was second, Carson Gilmer in an ASW-15 was third, Herb Mozer was fourth in an ASW-19, and Carl Koenig was fifth in a Cirrus.

43d Open Class National, 1976

Thirty-six "open" sailplanes joined by eight 15-meter sailplanes, competed in the Open Nationals. Allen Leffler, flying a Nimbus II, won the championship. Tom Brandes in a 604 was second, J. Baird in a Nimbus II was third, B. Utley in a Nimbus II was fourth, and A. J. Smith in a 604 was fifth. A cold air mass that dominated the contest area for the duration of the meet

There was some disappointment that Briegleb did not fly a Nugget.

Tom Page reported in *Soaring* that the only important technical improvement was the use of carbon filaments in the spars of the PIK-20B. The WSC contest officials attempted to control flying weight by running last-minute weighing-in of a sampling of sailplanes before each task. Again the weather was not strong enough to make it worthwhile to risk flying overweight.

did not give the strong soaring conditions usually experienced at El Mirage.

Directors' Summer Meeting, 1976

All the SSA directors were present at the August 13–14 meeting in Victorville, California, except Larry Wood, who was out of the country. Sam Francis chaired the meeting. With the 37 items on the agenda, the meeting ran for two days, the first time that this had happened at a summer meeting.

Licher reported that the membership had shown a slight loss in the first six months of 1976 owing to the dues increase of 1975. This concerned the directors.

Sunny Vegso made her first director of development report, beginning with her strategy to increase and improve the service to the present membership and then her plan to increase the membership. She introduced a representative of the Jeppesson-Sanderson Co. who made a proposal of a $250,000 audiovisual sailplane ground school course, similar to what Beech, Cessna and Piper use. The directors authorized Vegso to cover $50,000 of the cost, if the balance of the support could be raised from outside the SSA.

The matter of safety was given considerable attention as a result of the increased number of accidents during the last year. A Flight Training and Safety Board was created to concentrate on safety and training. The former Education and Training Board was renamed the Member Relation Board and it was to include club/chapter liaison, powered sailplanes, ultralights, business members, commercial operators, youth education, and the National Soaring Museum.

The board adopted a policy of supporting Sports Class to encourage competition in all types of sailplanes. It also gave the older Standard Class sailplanes a class in which they could compete. Medallions would be awarded and *Soaring* would cover these contests.

Sterling Starr was named chairman of the Contest Committee and Robert N. Buck was appointed the SSA delegate to the CIVV.

Because Rhodesia was excluded from the 1976 WSC by the Finnish government, the SSA board unanimously voted to adopt a resolution that "the SSA Board of Directors reaffirms its belief that all FAI member countries should be accepted into the world soaring competition without any discrimination of any kind."

An extended executive session was held during which the new director of development position and the executive director position were reviewed. Bill Cleary and Sam Francis had worked with Licher for the past six months on the development position, and with Sunny Vegso. They reported that the change did not seem to be accepted by Licher and that the morale in the SSA office was low owing to this change and to other factors.

At the same time, the presentation that Vegso had made to the directors at the meeting convinced many directors of the benefit of having someone working on development. Many felt that more progressive management was necessary, if the SSA was to grow at an increased rate. Licher had carried out the SSA operation on a very frugal basis, which was necessary at the start, but some questioned whether he could adapt to the new type of operation that was needed to develop the SSA to its full potential.

The directors were reluctant to change something that had worked for 19 years, particularly since Licher was a dedicated person and had the best

P. A. Schweizer had known Licher since the early 1950s, when he came to Harris Hill as a member of the MIT Glider Club. Licher became executive director and Schweizer was elected president of SSA at the same meeting, and they worked closely together in the transfer of the SSA offices from Elmira, New York, to Santa Monica, California. Although they frequently exchanged letters and occasional phone calls, their future contacts were mainly at the director's meetings, contests, and soaring conventions.

As SAC developed its dealer program, Schweizer occasionally got the impression that Licher had some reservations about the propriety of trying to make money from soaring. Time has shown that commercial operations have played an important part in the growth of soaring and the SSA, also, that unless a large enough market is developed, principally by the commercial operators, it cannot support a sailplane industry. Unfortunately, some soaring people still do not understand the difficult economic and business problems of producing sailplanes in the United States and the need for commercial operators to assist in promoting soaring.

In spite of some differences, P. A. Schweizer and Licher understood each other and they worked together effectively while Licher was executive director.

interest of the SSA at heart. After a long and agonizing discussion, the board finally voted for a change, and the Executive Committee was authorized to work out the matter with Licher.

The officers elected for 1977 were William B. Cleary, president; Samuel A. Francis, vice-president; Brian Utley, vice-president; Richard E. Schreder, secretary; and T. E. Sharp, treasurer.

Lloyd Licher

Shortly after the directors' meeting, Licher resigned, effective September 15. In his resignation letter of August 14, he stated: "It is best that I pursue other business and professional interest at this time." He closed his letter by saying: "It has certainly been a pleasure and an honor to have helped conduct the affairs of the Society and contribute to its growth over the years. Many of the finest people I have come to know are SSA members and directors, and I hold them in high esteem. May SSA continue to grow and prosper as you and the other directors desire."

Bennett Rogers, former editor of *Soaring* wrote a tribute to Licher in the October 1976 *Soaring* that echoed the feelings of many SSA members, particularly those who had worked with him.

> Now that Lloyd is actually departing after almost two decades of dedicated service to the soaring community, it seems appropriate to do a little looking back and summing up of what this remarkable person has meant to all of us.
>
> When Lloyd became SSA's first and only paid employee . . . , he truly felt it a privilege to be able to spend almost his entire waking existence working at a job that paid substantially less than what he had previously earned.
>
> I doubt anyone really knows how hard and long he and his wife, Rose Marie, labored in those early years. As an example, Lloyd was not only handling his current executive duties but was also single-handedly putting out *Soaring* magazine.
>
> His dedication and self-discipline were all the more amazing in that they were in no way fueled by ego or personal ambition. . . . There was simply no guile to the man whatsoever. He never shaded the truth, covered up a mistake, paid an insincere compliment, took credit for someone else's thought or action; he had an unwavering integrity.
>
> The final measure of Lloyd's contribution is that the Society can now survive and continue to prosper without him.

The President's Message

In his last message as president in the December '76 *Soaring*, Larry Wood

John Williams, who had pioneered soaring in the Elsinore area in the 1940s, and then in San Diego, was killed in a tragic midair collision. A Region 12 director, he also helped to organize the California Competition Club.

John Williams was awarded the Eaton Memorial Trophy posthumously for 1976. He was a regional director and one of the organizers of the California Competition Club.

(George Uveges)

commented: "Let's look forward and realize, too, that the SSA is poised for a new and bigger step into the coming months and years. We continue to exercise the search for modern techniques to aid our staff and improve liaison with our membership.

Other Happenings during 1976

After an 18-month lapse, the "Herold Hearsay" column returned to *Soaring* in the August 1976 issue with its main subject, sportsman competition and handicapping. In the November 1976 *Soaring* Sunny Vegso proposed a new SSA insignia or logo in her column "The Sunny Side." In the December 1976 *Soaring* the HHSC's Junior Program was featured in an article by David Sliwa, who noted that it is not a matter of doing it for the young people, but rather making it possible for them to be able to do it for themselves.

Chapter 12

The Adjustment Period, 1977–1979

A New Executive Director, 1977

The transition from the past method of operating to a new and more progressive management was not an easy one and would take time. It was important to find a capable executive director who could carry out the change and at the same time help SSA to grow at a faster rate and to promote all phases of soaring.

The Executive Committee was looking for someone with business management experience who "was on the way up." They realized that a manager of this type might stay only a few years, but it would be worthwhile if he were effective. The committee's goal was to have a new executive director chosen in time for the winter directors' meeting in Tuscon, Arizona.

Looking Ahead to the Year 2000

Comments on a membership renewal blank by Val Brain were forwarded to Bernald Smith, chairman of the Development Committee. Smith was so impressed with Brain's comments that he asked him to plan a series of articles starting in the January 1977 *Soaring* that looked ahead to the year 2000. Brain wrote the first of the series, which was entitled "The Next 25 Years—An Overview." John J. MacMaster and Jim Nash-Webber looked ahead to the technical development in

"Some Technical Extrapolations," Jack Green wrote about the 1-26 and the future of one design class soaring in "Immortality in Its Time," and Bruce Carmichael's "On Predicting the Future of Soaring Flight" included 10 predictions. From their forecasts it was clear that soaring in 1977 was far from being at the end of its development.

CIVV Report

Bob Buck reported in the January '77 *Soaring* that at the last CIVV meeting the Club Class was changed from creating specifications for a new class to one that encouraged competition for gliders that were not competitive in the present classes. It was recommended that these gliders be divided into performance classes, or be used with handicaps, so that fair competition would ensue. Sweden was planning a European Club Class Contest in 1979.

Soaring Convention, 1977

The Tuscon Soaring Club put on the largest convention to date on February 2–6, 1977, in Tucson, Arizona, with over 1,000 members registered. The exhibit hall had 18 sailplanes, 3 motorgliders, 3 trailers on display, and 25 booths. The convention featured a full schedule of meetings and technical sessions throughout the three-day period. It was a financial success generating over $2,000 in contributions to various soaring causes and approximately $4,000 for the TSC.

Directors' Winter Meeting, 1977

At the February 4–5, 1977, meeting in Tucson, President Cleary introduced Forrest Blossom, the Search Committee's choice for the position of executive director. Cleary said Blossom had had a great deal of experience in the management techniques SSA needed. He had also been involved in pilot training as a flight instructor and in soaring as a Cirrus and Libelle pilot for a number of years. Best of all, he was enthusiastic about soaring and the SSA. At an executive session of the board, he was approved as the executive director.

The officers reported that membership was at an all-time high of 14,119, and at end of 1977 there was a $1,000 surplus.

Sunny Vegso, director of development, reported on her activities during the preceding six months and her plans for SSA. The directors were impressed with many of the projects that were under way, or in the planning stages, but there was strong opposition to her proposed change of the SSA emblem. She did not realize how "attached" many SSA members were to the SSA emblem. An ad hoc committee was therefore set up to make recommendations. At the next day's meeting the committee recommended that this proposed change by tabled.

Vegso announced that there was a very good response to the proposed ground school course. The directors authorized up to $20,000 for work on this first phase, which would proceed

under SSA supervision and be carried out by a professional writer.

A proposed $36,000 advertising program in *Reader's Digest* had been submitted by the Lawrence and Lierle Agency. The COs pledged $13,000 toward this program on the basis of $50 for each sailplane that they operated and requested financial help from SSA for this program. It was turned down because of the extra costs of developing the ground school course, the increased costs of the director of developments program, and the deficit budget forecast for 1977.

Sterling Starr reported that the Contest Board was dedicated to fostering and stimulating Sport Class competition and that Sport Class rules were being drafted by Harry Baldwin. He also reported on a number of policy changes, including the elimination of free distance from available task options for national and regional meets and the entry requirement of Category IV seeding or better for the Nationals.

Motorgliding has been discontinued and the Publication Board was asked to submit a plan for its future. *Technical Soaring*, with a circulation of 450, was being published regularly and edited by Bernie Paiewonsky and produced by Rose Marie Licher.

After a discussion of the newstand sales of *Soaring*, Editor Doug Lamont said that there were a large number of enthusiasts who wanted to soar but could not afford it. He urged that more attention be given to low-cost soaring.

Jim Short, chairman of the Commercial Operators Committee, said that the COs made the following recommendations: Continue with the director of development, start an SSA instructor safety newsletter, Insert an updated training reference list in all future *Joy of Soaring*, use "in-house" updating of instructors rather than regulatory changes and recommend that a national soaring week be held every June.

1,000-Mile World Record

Karl Striedieck had run into problems in trying to get his 1,000-mile out-and-return flight of last May approved as a record. On May 9, 1977, conditions were suitable and Striedieck decided to try again. He took off from his strip at 5:52 a.m. in his ASW-17 and went through the gate at Lock Haven at 6:07 a.m. He had a quartering tail wind on the way down to the turn-point. This enabled him to average almost 130 miles an hour for the first 420 miles. The next 80 miles were more difficult owing to weaker conditions. After taking two pictures at the turn-point, he had to fly against a headwind all the way back. It was tough going, but he finally got back to Lock Haven at 8:10 p.m., with a total flying time of 14 hours, 18 minutes. This time, the record was approved.

Sixth Smirnoff Derby, 1977

The 1977 Smirnoff Derby of May 3–20, 1977, included an outstanding group of soaring pilots: Wally Scott, 1976 Derby winner (1-35); George Lee of Great Britain, world Open champion 1976 (PIK-20B); Ingo Renner, Australia, world Standard Class champion, Modified (301 Libelle); Al Leffler, U.S. national Unlimited champion (PIK-20B); and George Moffat, world Open champion in 1970 and 1974 (PIK-20B). Hannes Linke was the contest flight director. Ingo Renner won the derby by 548 points, and 8 of the 10 days. Lee and Scott had their own contest for second place until the last day,

Eric Herbert Mozer, winner of the 1977 Standard Class National at Ionia, Michigan, with his brother and crew-chief Peter. Their father Rudy has been very active in soaring since the 1950s and two other brothers, Norman and Richard, are also soaring pilots.

(Rudy Mozer)

when Scott had to make an out-landing. The final standings were Renner 9,785, Lee 9,137, Scott 8,568, Moffat 8,290, and Leffler 7,388.

Eighth Standard Class National, 1977

Only 45 Standard Class pilots entered the Eighth Standard Class National at Ionia, Michigan, on June 21–30, 1977. This was a big drop from the previous National at Hutchinson.

Going into what proved to be the last day, Karl Striedieck was in first place, Roy McMaster in second and Herb Mozer in seventh. By the end of this last day Herb Mozer was on top, closely followed by Karl Striedieck and Roy McMaster. Mozer and Striedieck flew ASW-19s and MacMaster a Cirrus. Rudy Mozer, Herb's father, finished in fourth place in an LS-1 and Bill Snead was fifth in a Libelle. Johann Kuhn was competition director and Jerry Benz was contest manager.

1-26 Championships, 1977

Fifty-four 1-26s and 76 pilots were entered in the 1-26 North American held on June 22–29, 1977, in Colorado Springs. Sixteen of the 1-26s were

Dick Butler, winner of the 1977 National Open held at Caddo Mills, Texas.

(George Uveges)

flown by 37 team pilots. This was the largest North American held to date and was evidence of the growing interest in one-design class flying.

The top five finishers were Harry Senn, Dick Mockler, Tom Knauff, Dave Johnson, and Gary Knapp. The team champions were Mike Jensen and Nels Johnson (Dick's son).

Before the start of the award banquet, all the pilots lifted Harry Senn, seated in his 1-26, over their heads in a symbol of victory.

Second 15-Meter Class National, 1977

The NSF and the Hobbs Soaring Society sponsored the second 15-meter Nationals at Hobbs, New Mexico, with 64 pilots entered. Hal Lattimore was competition director and Jack Gomez contest manager.

Overall, the weather was good, with nine contest days. All the tasks were speed triangles, the longest being 352.24 miles. Best speed was 79.45 miles per hour, made by Ed Byars in a PIK-20 on a 317-mile triangle.

Karl Striedieck, flying a 15-meter version of his ASW-17, held the lead throughout the contest and became the 15-meter champion. Ben Greene and Herb Mozer both in LS-3s, finished second and third. Dick Johnson in a PIK-20B was fourth and Wally Scott in a 1-35 was fifth.

Personnel Changes

As might be expected with a new director, a number of SSA personnel changes occurred in 1977. In April, Don Monroe, SSA operation officer, resigned. He had been assistant executive director for 3½ years and was acting executive director for the five-

month period after Lloyd Licher had resigned. In addition to his administrative duties, he had published *Motorgliding* and done photographic work for *Soaring* on his own time.

A short time later, Sunny Vegso resigned to take a new position with a real estate firm. Penny Maines, Assistant to Forrest Blossom, assumed most of the promotion and membership service responsibilities.

In August, John Dezzutti was hired as operations manager. Dezzutti had professional management experience, was a soaring enthusiast, and a rated commercial glider and power pilot.

44th Open Class National, 1977

All the 39 sailplanes entered in the 44th Nationals (August 2–11) at Caddo Mills, Texas, were long-spanned sailplanes, except for an HP-14 and a 301 Libelle. This was the highest concentration of Open sailplanes in an unlimited class National. The weather was excellent, with nine contest days, and a 92.4 percent completion rate was achieved with only 25 out-landings. The top 14 pilots had no out-landings and the next 9 pilots had only one. Competition director, Hal Lattimore, called all triangle speed tasks. Dick Butler won the championship in his 604, Dick Johnson was second in a Nimbus II. L. Horvath came third in a Jantar 2A, A. J. Smith fourth in a 604, George Moffat fifth in a Jantar 2A.

Directors' Summer Meeting, 1977

At the meeting in Greenville, Texas, on August 12, the executive director reported that the membership had grown by 1,235 since July, 1976, that SSA was strong financially, and that an 11 percent annual growth in membership would be necessary if dues increases were to be avoided.

The life member rate was increased from $250 to $300, which would enable the trust fund earnings to cover the life member service costs.

The board felt that more time was needed to prepare for the conventions and it was decided to select them three years in advance. Chicago was chosen for 1979 and Seattle for 1980.

Three major programs were approved that would improve the quality of service to members: (1) Jeppesen-Sanderson, Inc. would prepare a ground school course for sailplane training; (2) the SSA's membership records would be shifted to electronic data processing; and (3) B. S. Smith proposed the Hull and Liability Insurance Program for SSA members, which was approved pending a final review of the details by the Executive Committee.

The board approved the establishment of a "1982 Committee," since 1982 would be the 50th anniversary of

the SSA. The 1977 officers were re-elected for 1978.

Executive Director's Performance

After six months in office, Blossom had made a number of positive changes, and the directors were much better informed through more frequent reports. He requested that all reports for the directors' meetings by the officers, directors, board chairmen and committees be in the SSA office at least a month in advance so that they could be arranged in a special notebook and then be sent to the directors a few weeks before the meeting.

Blossom had taken a number of trips around the country to become acquainted with the various soaring groups, and he spent some time in Washington, D.C., to meet key people in the FAA and other government agencies that SSA had to deal with.

Sailplane Developments

Progress on the Zuni, the second all-fiberglass sailplane to be put into production in the United States was reported in Alcide Santilli's story in the February 1977 *Soaring*. George Applebay had developed it with some assistance from Harlan Ross. It was being built by AERO TEK, which had received a $200,000 grant from the New Mexico Development Agency.

The Cloudster, a motorglider built by T. Claude Ryan's Ryson Aviation Corp., was being tested in early 1977. It had all-metal construction and was equipped with a 100-horsepower aircraft engine. In the July issue, Doug Lamont wrote about a flight that he made with Ray Cote, Ryson test pilot. Lamont was picked up by Cote at the

Hall of Fame members during induction of Harner Selvedge and Robert Stanley. Bottom, left to right: Gus Scheurer, Harner Selvidge, Robert Stanley, and Capt. R. S. Barnaby; Top: F. J. Sweet, S. W. Smith, A. J. Smith, V. M. Schweizer, W. Holbrook, R. Schreder, and P. A. Schweizer.

(NSM Collection)

Santa Monica Airport and after a 4-hour, 16-minute flight, which included much wave soaring, they landed at Minden, Nevada, having used less than 8 gallons of fuel.

SAC reported on the delivery of the 500th 2-33 and the new Club 35, a reduced-price 1-35 made possible by eliminating the retractable gear and by incorporating other simplifications.

NSM Construction Begins

A fire on January 19, 1977, destroyed the historic Harris Hill administration building, where some of the NSM exhibits were located. The NSM Board of Trustees, who had been working for a number of years toward getting a permanent building, pledged $105,000 at the meeting at the Tucson, Arizona, convention. This, plus the $87,000 insurance payment for the administration building, was the start of a successful building fund drive. By the summer, $500,000 had been raised and a 16,000 square-foot building was started in August. Eliot Noyes and Associates were the architects.

Dick Johnson's Flight Test Evaluations

Dick Johnson, who had started performance flight testing of sailplanes while he was a student under Gus Raspet of Mississippi State, had continued to test them near his home in Dallas. He wrote up his reports for *Soaring* and they became one of the magazine's popular features. He was fortunate that that part of Texas was very flat and ideal for testing. This enabled him to get fairly accurate results, although he occasionally heard from unhappy designers, who felt that he had underrated their sailplane.

Paul MacCready's Gossamer Condor Wins Kremer Prize

MacCready and his associates, including a number of soaring pilots, developed a very light 96-foot-span Gossamer Condor, which looked somewhat like a large model hang glider. It won the Kremer Prize on August 23, 1977, when the pilot and "power plant," Bryan Allen, flew the required course in California.

For the first time, there would be three classes in the WSC, and so a two-stage seeding process was required. The pilots and class in the order in which they were chosen were Dick Butler, Open Class; Karl Striedieck, 15-Meter Class; Herb Mozer, Standard Class; and Dick Johnson, Open Class.

Other Happenings during 1977

A number of soaring pioneers died during 1977: Larry Lawrence and F. K. "Bud" Iszard, both founders of the SSA; Bob Stanley, former president of SSA, who lost his life in an airplane accident soon after he had been inducted into the Soaring Hall of Fame; Eliot Noyes, whose last activity was designing the NSM building on Harris Hill; Harlan C. Ross, who had started working on sailplanes with Hawley Bowlus in 1930; Roy Schlemeyer of Odessa, Texas; who had still been instructing in gliders at the age of 81; and Ted Smith, who died a few months after announcing his new two-place sailplane design.

The Third Women's International Gliding Competition was held at Oerlinghausen, Germany. Pelagia Majewska of Poland was the winner, and Judy Silverman and Alberta Stirling of the United States finished 15th and 17th.

SSA Goes to Washington, D.C., 1978

In the past, SSA's contacts with the FAA, NAA, and other government agencies in Washington were usually made through volunteer SSA members from the Washington area. Licher seldom traveled there, so it was usually up to members like Floyd Sweet, Bob Ball, and others in the Washington area to make these contacts. This worked out quite well in the early years, but with the advent of greater air space controls, it became a more complicated matter. John Ryan started the trend of more frequent SSA visits to the FAA in the 1960s.

At the start of 1978, there were a number of proposed FAA rule changes that could seriously affect soaring: (1) The R2508 Enhancement Plan, would require transponders and 720 channel transceivers on all aircraft, including gliders, in order to fly over some areas of California and Nevada; (2) the FAA Eastern Region ruled that tow pilots had to have commercial licenses. (3) The FAA proposed that medical examinations be required for glider pilots; (4) new glider airworthiness regulations were needed that would be simpler and that would reduce the cost of certification, and the same requirements needed to be applied to imported sailplanes as domestic sailplanes.

Since the first three changes could be quite disruptive to U.S. soaring, the SSA was anxious to resolve these problems. SSA representatives thus had to make many more trips to Washington.

It was a fortuitous decision that set the convention in Washington for that time. The SSA worked with the Middle-Atlantic Soaring Association (MASA) to use the convention as a means of exposing soaring and the SSA to the FAA.

Motorgliding

Motorgliding was added to the masthead of *Soaring* in the January 1978 issue, since there was not enough inter-

est, with only about 100 motorgliders in the country, to support a separate publication. Articles and reports on motorgliding would be included in *Soaring* as development and readers interest warranted.

National Soaring Foundation

President Cleary reported on the National Soaring Foundation (NSF) that was organized in 1976. The main purpose of this organization was to establish a national soaring site at Hobbs, New Mexico, to promote regional, national, and international contests there.

Youth Training Activities

A CAP glider encampment was held at Red Oak, Iowa, by the Iowa Wing of the CAP and the Central Iowa Soaring Society. Cadets were trained up to the solo level at the cost of only $95 each. A similar program was carried out in 1977 at the Santa Fe Community College in Gainsville, Florida. It was felt that this same plan could be used for Explorer Scout Units and other youth groups around the country. A report on the Air Cadet League of Canada youth program described how it had grown to the point where 40,000 training flights had been made in 1977.

Seventh SSA Soaring Convention, 1978

The seventh convention was held from February 9 to 12, 1978, in Washington, D.C., on the 40th anniversary of the first National Gliding and Soaring Convention. Only 68 SSA members attended that first meeting, which amounted to 6.8 percent of the SSA members at that time. The 1,100 members attending the 1978 convention represented 7.6 percent of the 1978 membership.

The convention featured special visits to the National Air and Space Museum and to the Silver Hill Restoration Facilities. A record number of sailplanes were on exhibit, and for the first time a club-management forum was held and attempts were made to attend to the needs of the "little guys."

The award banquet was the largest one yet and the featured speaker was Clark Onstad, general counselor for the FAA, who substituted for FAA administrator Langhorne Bond. Onstad expressed FAA's desire to help soaring, and announced that the Eastern Region decision on tow plane pilots was reversed so that properly qualified private pilots could continue towing in clubs. Joe Engle, the pilot on the first glider flight of the space shuttle, accepted an SSA Exceptional

Achievement Award for the crew. It was a gala banquet and the only somber note was the news that Philip Wills, the famous English soaring personality, had died a few days before.

Directors' Winter Meeting, 1978

At the February 11–12, 1978, meeting in Washington, D.C., the executive director reported that the SSA had ended the year "with $11,000 in the black" and that 860 members had been added during 1977. Since the life memberships fund was not earning enough to cover the service costs, it was voted that an actuarial study be made of life members. In addition, it was agreed that associate members' dues should increase from $12 to $14 per year and that the business and industrial members be combined into a single business membership.

The bylaws were changed to call for divisions instead of branches. It was decided that the 1-26 Association should have 67 percent SSA members and that the percentage for other new divisions would be negotiated starting from 67 percent, with the aim of making it as close to 100 percent as was fair for both groups. The 1-26 Association was then approved as the first division of the SSA.

It was decided to reinstate the Youth Education Committee as part of the Member Relations Board.

The Commercial Operators and Business Members Committee proposed to provide $15,000 to enable the SSA to promote the sport of soaring, with SSA matching CO's contributions up to $5,000 on a one-for-two basis.

The board accepted the resignation of Jim Nash-Webber, the chairman of the SSA Technical Board. In his final report he expressed his dissatisfaction

with the status of the FAA sailplane airworthiness regulations. He felt that the SSA should recommend that the FAA accept the revised OSTIV regulations or the joint aircraft regulations (JAR).

P. A. Schweizer said that SAC was in favor of using the present regulations as a basis for developing new regulations, since they had been used successfully and would minimize the shock of new regulations. Sam Francis reported that he and Blossom had met with the FAA administrator, Langhorne Bond, and that he wanted a solid stand from the SSA, not one from the manufacturers and one from the Technical Board. The Technical Committee was instructed to set up a certification committee and to investigate funding possibilities for carrying out a study on new regulations.

The Technical Board chairman, executive director, and most of the directors were not familiar with the FAA airworthiness requirements or the detailed process of getting a sailplane certified by the FAA. They had the feeling that the present regulations were holding back sailplane development and manufacture in the United States and that new regulations were the answer to the problem. The OSTIV regulations, however, were more complex than the present regulations, and the JAR regulations were only being developed.

SAC was the only sailplane manufacturer that had regularly used the FAA airworthiness regulations, having put nine basic sailplane types through the certification process. Although the present regulations had some limitations, they were usable and had also been successfully used by Laister, Peterson, Prue, and Briegleb. SAC was concerned that new regulations would take a long time to develop and prove

A Woodstock all-wood home-built sailplane designed by Jim Maupin. He said that a couple of determined teenagers could build it "in a year's time."

(George Uveges)

out and that "the cure might be worse than the disease." SAC had enough problems trying to stay in the sailplane business without having new un-proven regulations to contend with. Since SAC was the only ones getting sailplanes approved at that time, it would be the one subjected to the lengthy proving out process of getting new regulations to work. Conse-quently, SAC felt that the practical way was to update and simplify the present regulations.

SSA Airspace Activity

The executive director and some SSA members met with the FAA a number of times to attempt to reduce the im-pact of the R2508 Enhancement Plan. They were able to get FAA to down-grade their radio requirements from 720 channels to one channel (123.3). To ascertain the tracking capabilities of sailplanes by radar, two days of tests were carried out by Carl Herold, Harry Combs, Bob Hoey, Bud Yenney, and Duane Russel.

National Geographic *Article*

An article in the March 1978 issue of *National Geographic* by Karl Striedieck told of his 1,115-mile world record flight. The *Geographic* did its usually fine job with the photos and art work in the article.

The SSA Vacation Derby

The SSA proposed to run a series of Traveling Vacation Derbys for soaring pilots, using a different soaring center as a goal for each day. The "proto-type" derby was run from April 23 to May 5, starting at Bermuda High Soar-ing in Chester, South Carolina, and the plan was to visit 11 soaring centers on the way north to Yankee Aviation in Warren, Vermont. This was not to be a high-level competition event, but a fun vacation tour. It would provide SSA members an opportunity to visit other gliderports, meet new soaring friends, and at the same time get XC experience over new territory. None of

the group that started completed the course, but, John Dezzutti, the operations manager, said that "all those involved reported they had great fun. Group cross-country is catching on"!

Sailplane Developments

The Woodstock, a simple low-cost wooden sailplane, was designed by Jim Maupin, a craft that "a couple of determined teenagers with very little experience in woodwork, and $750 each could build and instrument Woodstock in a years spare time."

The MONERAI, a simple, kit-built, intermediate all-metal sailplane was first shown at the Washington convention.

The AMERICAN EAGLE was also aimed at this same market. Its novelty was its self-launching feature, a small engine mounted in the aft section of its Baby Bowlus pod.

Al Backstrom's latest PLANK was an intermediate self-launching sailplane and was based on his successful Flying Plank design.

Zuni sailplane production resumed when Applebay Sailplanes was formed. Aerotek had gone bankrupt after a 2 million dollar suit had been filed as a result of an accident in 1977.

SAC announced its two thousandth sailplane in the June 1978 *Soaring*. The ad used a poster by Frank Hurtt of the 15 most popular Schweizer sailplane types. It was also announced that a second generation of Schweizer's were now active at SAC: Ernie's son Leslie, and Bill's sons Stuart and Paul H. All were aeronautical engineers and soaring pilots, and were being groomed to take over the company and to "continue the tradition of producing quality sailplanes, aircraft, aircraft components and light metal structures."

Seventh Smirnoff Derby, 1978

This was really a 15-meter class derby since Karl Striedieck, Wally Scott, Rudy Mozer, and Herb Mozer all flew

Two generations of Schweizers and the 2,000th Schweizer sailplane, a 1-35. Left to right: Leslie E. (Ernie's son), W. Stuart and Paul H. (Bill's sons), and Ernie, Paul A., and Bill Schweizer.

(Schweizer Aircraft Corporation)

Laszlo Horvath, winner of the 1978 15-Meter National at Marana, Arizona, in as AS-W-19 sailplane, was in first place for the entire contest.
(SSA files)

ASW-20s and Ingo Renner flew a Mosquito. The third day's task, a 267-mile flight from Los Cruces to Odessa, Texas, proved to be the outstanding day. All five pilots made the goal and the fastest had a speed of 94 miles per hour. The race had to end at St. Louis because of the bad weather on the last four days, which required trailering to Washington, D.C. Karl Striedieck was the winner, leading Wally Scott by 768 points. Renner was third, Herb Mozer fourth, and Rudy Mozer fifth.

Third 15-Meter Class National, 1978

A full house of 65 sailplanes were entered in the third 15-meter National held at Ephrata, Washington, June 20–29, and sponsored by the Seattle Glider Council. Speed-limiting start gate rules were used for the first time at a nationals meet.

Moffat was back at top form in his ASW-20 and won six of the eight days and was in first place during the entire meet, finishing 444 points ahead of Brian Utley, also in a ASW-20. Roger Frank and Wodson Woods finished

third and fourth, both flying the new Mosquito.

Directors' Summer Meeting, 1978

The executive director reported at the June 30 meeting in Ephrata that SSA now had over 15,100 members and that by the end of May it had a new positive balance of over $35,000 in addition to reserves of approximately $131,000.

It was agreed to eliminate the $3 chapter rebate for life memberships in order to avoid having to raise the rate.

The board had received bids from Ephrata and Reno, Nevada, to host the 1981 WSC. It was decided to submit the Reno proposal.

The possibility of having a soaring event to tie in with the 1984 Olympics was to be investigated by Don Knypstra.

Officers elected for 1979 were Bryan Utley, president; Bob Kramer, vice-president; Woody Woodward, vice-president; Richard Schreder, secretary; and Ted Sharp, treasurer.

1-26 Championships, 1978

Forty-one 1-26s showed up at Hobbs, New Mexico, for the 13th championships, June 23 to 30. The best flight on the free distance day was 337.4 miles by Harry Baldwin. Scott Imlay from Seattle was the winner, beating out Harry Baldwin by 27 points. Charles Shaw was third and the best team was Marvin Willis and Tommy Thomason.

Ninth Standard Class National, 1978

Excellent weather prevailed at the championships in Tucson from July 4 to 13. There were eight contest days, a rest day, and a day that was scrubbed owing to incorrect turn-point information. Forty-seven Standard Class ships were entered in this contest sponsored by the Arizona Soaring Association and the Tucson Soaring Club. Las Horvath, flying a ASW-19, won four days and was in first place for the entire meet. Woody Woodward was second in a ASW-20, and Chris Woods third in a H301 Libelle. All the tasks were triangles.

16th WSC, 1978

The former U.S. Strategic Air Force base at Chateauroux in the central part of France was the site of the 16th WSC, July 15–30, 1978. Twenty-three countries entered 24 Open Class ships, 32 15-Meter Class, and 23 Standard Class sailplanes. There were no entries from the iron curtain countries since they were boycotting the WSC because South Africa had entered. The tasks chosen were much longer than the usual U.S. tasks and emphasized distance flying rather than speed. An unusual experience for many pilots was flying the pyro-thermals formed from the farmers burning their wheat stubble!

The most competitive class was the 15-meter in which Reichmann, flying the SB-11, a variable geometry sailplane reported to have cost $250,000, nosed out Karl Striedieck in a ASW-20 by 44 points. Gordon Ax of Sweden was third in an ASW-20.

In the Open Class, George Lee of Great Britain, flying an ASW-17, became the world Open Class champion, beating out Brundo Gantebrink of West Germany, who was flying a Nimbus. Francois Henry of France, also flying a Nimbus, was 3d. Dick Johnson in a Jantar finished 6th, and Dick Butler in his 604 finished 12th.

The Standard Class was won by Selen of Holland in a ASW-19. Briglidori of Italy was 2d, Recule of France was 3d, both in Cirruses, and Herb Mozer was 8th, flying an ASW-19.

SSA President William Cleary congratulates Bernald S. Smith, NSM president, at the opening of the NSM building on Harris Hill. Left to right: William English, director of the NSM, Cleary, Smith, and Vic Powell, executive director of the National Aeronautics Association.

(Wesley Buth, NSM Collection)

45th Open Class National, 1978

Only 20 sailplanes were entered in the meet at Chester, South Carolina, from August 1 to 10, the lowest total number since 1938. This was partly due to the fact that the WSC going on in France at the same time and to the "soft" weather expected around Chester in August. The weather was bad and there were only five contest days. The longest task was a 138-mile triangle, and the fastest speed was 58 miles per hour. A fatal accident occurred on the last day when Norman Hunter, making an off-field landing, hooked a wing of his Nimbus in a pecan tree.

A. J. Smith, flying a 604, was the winner, finishing 42 points ahead of Sherman Griffith in a Nimbus. Ben Greene was third in an ASW-17.

Sports Class Meets Become Popular

There were 10 Sports Class contests held in 1978 in addition to the 4 national and 12 regional meets, and an array of other contests such as the Little Guys Meet, Soaring Fiesta, Soaring Safari, numerous fun meets, soaring camps, and four 1-26 Regattas. This increase in the number of smaller and less formal contests made it possible for more pilots to engage in friendly competition that suited their sailplanes, flying experience, and their wallets.

The largest was the Western Region Sports Class Contest held at El Mirage, which involved 57 pilots and sailplanes. It featured a pilot's choice of speed tasks using some of the 90 turn-points. Carl Herold's handicap factors were used to set the distance to be flown and to determine the speed points for each type of sailplane. The mix of sailplanes in the final standing showed that it was successful when

the top 10 included two 1-26s and a BG-12.

The New National Soaring Museum Building

The official opening of the NSM building took place on September 9, 1978, with Bernald S. Smith, NSM president, presiding. The 16,000-square-foot $500,000 building is located on the site of the old Harris Hill administration building. The exhibits in the museum include Dick du Pont's Bowlus-du Pont Albatross, the Sisu, and a restoration of a primary that Floyd Sweet and some Elmira friends had built in 1930.

At the NSM trustee meeting, Jack Baugh was elected the new president. That evening the Hall of Fame banquet honored Barney Wiggin and Steve Bennis as the two latest inductees.

Eliot Noyes, the architect of the museum building, gained fame as the designer of the first postwar IBM typewriter. He worked with IBM, Westinghouse, and Mobil in architecture and industrial design and arranged for the famous sculptor Isamu Nagouchi to design and make the Barringer trophy. Noyes's interest in and enthusiasm for soaring continued and he encouraged many others to take it up, including his sons and Tom Watson, Jr. He designed the National Soaring Museum building at Harris Hill just before his death in 1977.

The SSA President's Report

President Bill Cleary's report to the membership in the September 1978 *Soaring* noted:

> We discussed the management demand and supervision required in

overseeing a budget of more than $600,000, and your outgoing officers felt that continued relatively close surveillance by the President and the Executive Committee was advisable, but that the cost of such surveillance was a considerable burden on those who had been elected to do those jobs. Accordingly, the Directors voted the sum of $5,000 to be used to partially reimburse members of the Executive Committee for the cost of attending those meetings with the SSA staff held between the dates of the regular Directors' meetings.

We have many members who would make fine directors, but who can't afford to make the financial sacrifice to serve. Some regions have fundraising projects to provide money to help their Director cover his or her SSA expenses, and I'd like to see that practice expanded.

Soaring to Win

George Moffat's new column in the November *Soaring* was entitled "Needed Weekend Contest Flying." He began this series by remarking,

> If contests are good, fun, and educational, why do only about 350 out of some 10,000 U.S. pilots compete each year? The answer seems simple to me. Almost the only contests available are Regionals and Nationals and both have grown large, complex, time-consuming, and expensive. Furthermore, the vast majority of the contests are tightly packed between June 1 and Labor Day. This leaves nine months with nothing much going on.
>
> With the cost of a competitive glass ship, instrumented, trailered, and ready to aviate in the $20–35,000 range, small wonder that contest flying as it exists today is getting to look more and more like a well-to-do man's sport.
>
> What we need is many more informal contests at the club level. What

keeps interest high in sailing racing isn't the America's Cup or the Bermuda Race, it's the club-level, Saturday-and-Sunday series held every weekend throughout the season. This sort of thing is what we need to develop in soaring.

Other Happenings during 1978

John Lee was hired as the new administrative assistant for promotion and development.

The Air and Space Museum opened its *Flying for Fun* Gallery in June. Al Parker's Sisu 1A and the 1-35 that Wally Scott used to win the 1976 Smirnoff Derby, were exhibited along with hang gliders, kites, and boomerangs.

Charles Glattly of Reno, Nevada, SSA general council, died during 1978. He was very active in the Nevada Soaring Association and had helped form Air Sailing.

Jo Ann Shaw became the first woman to win three Diamonds in a 1-26 sailplane. She joined 11 others in this select group.

Bryan Utley, three-term SSA president (1979–81) at the podium during the 1980 convention in Seattle. The official SSA flag is in the background, and the Barringer Trophy in the foreground.
(Norm Dalke)

The Air Space Grab, 1979

The San Diego midair collision in the fall of 1978 created a great deal of public pressure on the FAA. On December 27 FAA administrator Langhorne Bond outlined a "Wide Range Air Safety Program Designed to Provide Increased Protection against Mid-Air Collisions at Commercial Airports." On January 4, the FAA issued its Notice of Proposed Rule Making (NPRM) that proposed to lower the controlled air space from 18,000 feet to 10,000 feet in the West and 12,500 feet in the rest of the country. Another NPRM to be issued at a later date would require encoding altimeters and transponders for 166 areas in the United States.

If approved, these new regulations would greatly restrict sailplane operation. They would include (1) termination of as many as 30 existing glider operators as a result of proposed terminal control areas (TCAs), (2) substantial curtailment of activities at approximately 15 glider operators owing to the addition of these TCAs, (3) required notification to FAA Air Traffic Control every time a sailplane planned to fly above 10,000 feet or 12,500 feet, depending on the location. The SSA recognized the seriousness of these proposals and the Executive Committee, executive director, and the Air Space Committee met in Chicago to prepare for the coming SSA directors' meeting.

The President's Message

In the January *Soaring*, Brian Utley, the new SSA president, started his term with the message: "At the last Executive Committee meeting we reviewed the accident record for 1978. The number of accidents and the serious injuries or fatalities is a great concern to us. . . . A meeting was held with Don Slotten who is Chairman of the Flight Training and Safety Board. . . . Don was asked to form a committee to review our current training programs and environment to determine whether any particular action or program should be undertaken by the Society beyond those currently in place."

Doug Lamont's Centennial Issue

The January 1979 issue of *Soaring* was the 100th issue edited by Doug Lamont. In a tribute to Lamont, Bernald Smith, SSA Publication Board chairman, said: "There's hardly any way to adequately describe Doug's devotion to *Soaring* and soaring. He does it best himself, I think, if you read his material. His love for the people and the sport is untrammelled. The man's dedication to serve the varying reader interests in technical, beginner flight, or contest stories, and everything else, with the limited budget and time constraints of a small staff are monumental."

Eighth National Convention, 1979

The Chicagoland Glider Council sponsored the Eighth Soaring Convention held January 31 to February 4, 1979. In spite of the great amount of snow in Chicago, there was a good turnout.

Fifteen sailplanes and two airplanes were on display and 23 booths were located in the large exhibit hall adjacent to the hotel. The convention included technical sessions and other associated meetings. The award banquet featured an advance showing of the new Disney film "Sky Trap," in which gliders played an important part. Paul Poberezney, president of the EAA and Charles Spencer of the

AOPA were guests at the banquet. They were to have special meetings with the SSA Executive Committee and members of the government Liaison Board on the air space problem.

Directors' Winter Meeting, 1979

At the February 3–4 meeting in Chicago it was announced that the SSA had grown by 634 members during 1978 and the financial condition was sound, with reserves of $141,800. Carl Herold was elected vice-president to replace Bob Kramer, who had resigned. John Lee was named the new administrative assistant for promotion and development.

The board approved an agreement with the Vintage Soaring Association (VSA) making it a division of the SSA.

Liam English reported that the NSM, after ten years in existence, was now housed in a $500,000 permanent facility.

The board accepted Richard Wolters's gift of publication rights of his book *Once Upon a Thermal*.

The board also approved the plan to bid at the coming CIVV meeting for the WSC for 1981, to be held at Stead Airport near Reno, Nevada.

Jim Haynes, chairman of the government Liaison Board, read a response to the NPRM that had been prepared by the Executive Committee and the executive director. This generated considerable discussion, and later in the meeting a revised version was reviewed and approved as SSA's official position on the NPRM.

The matter of FAA glider airworthiness requirements was discussed by Bob Lamson in his technical report. He proposed that SSA advise the FAA that they approved the JARs. P. A. Schweizer noted that SAC had not yet seen a draft of the JARs and understood that they were not in final form. He therefore recommended that blanket approval should not be given to them. Utley expressed concern over the lack of a unified position on JARs and instructed Lamson, Sweet, and Schweizer to come up with a position paper for the board's consideration before the conclusion of the meeting.

The position paper was presented by Sweet later in the meeting and read as follows:

> The SSA has reviewed the matter of Federal Airworthiness Requirements for Sailplanes and Self-launching Sailplanes. It finds that American designers and manufacturers are disadvantaged by the existing dual standards— one for American aircraft and another for foreign aircraft. Further, the lack of a formalized set of American requirements results in conflicting interpretations within the U.S. Therefore, after due deliberations, the SSA Board recommends that the FAA be requested to adopt the JARs for Sailplanes and Motorgliders which are being adopted by the European Aircraft Consortium Countries, as the SSA/Industry agreed course of action. It is assumed that the adoption procedure would follow the NPRM process.

This was acceptable to the U.S. manufacturers, since they would have the opportunity to comment once the NPRM was issued.

A New World Record

On February 14, 1979, Sabrina Jackintell set a net woman's absolute altitude record of 41,460 feet at Colorado Springs. She flew an Astir sailplane and was the first woman to qualify for the Symons Wave Memorial Triple Lennie. She described the flight in the May 1979 *Soaring:*

The CIVV Report

Bill Cleary brought SSA's bid for the 1981 WSC to the CIVV meeting in March. The other bidders were West Germany and Great Britain. The first ballot ended in a 13–13 tie between the United States and West Germany, with Great Britain in third place with 2 votes. On the second ballot West Germany won by a vote of 15 to 13. The 1981 WSC would be held at the Paderborn-Haxterburg Airfield.

It was announced that the First European Club type championships would be held in Orebro, Sweden, June 14–23, 1979, and that a new record category was established for speeds around a triangle of at least 1,250 kilometers.

Sabrina Jackentell in her Astir sailplane in which she established a women's world absolute altitude record after a start from the Black Forest Gliderport. She was the first woman to qualify for the 3 Lennie pin.

(Jim Foreman)

At 40,000 feet I felt so far up, distant. There was an almost tearful joy at finally seeing 40,000 on the altimeter after so many tries. I wished everyone could see that, wanted to share it. . . . Couldn't resist a small chandelle at the top before saying good-bye and starting down.

Afterward, even now, I have a strong need to share the positive feeling of achievement and joy that came from that flight, especially with people who can understand, who know.

House Aviation Subcommittee Hearing on the Air Space NPRM

The SSA attended a congressional hearing in Washington, D.C., March 20–21, 1979, on the proposed "Airspace NPRM." SSA had seven representatives present and they joined many other flying organizations in objecting to the proposed changes. A report on this hearing in the May 1979 Soaring encouraged members to write their government representatives. Up to that time the letter-writing effort to the FAA had resulted in the greatest number of letters ever received by the FAA, which were almost 100 percent against the change.

Soaring in the 1984 Olympics

A letter to the editor in the January 1979 Soaring by George Vakkur opposed the idea of having soaring in the Olympics, owing to the international politics involved and the amateur standards question. Don Knypstra, who had been authorized by the SSA Board of Directors to look into this matter, replied in the March 1979 Soaring. He felt that although there were problems involved, the U.S. soaring movement would benefit from having participants in the Olympics.

The Third International Symposium on the Science and Technology of Low-Speed and Motorless Flight

The NASA and the SSA jointly sponsored this symposium, which was held at NASA'S Langley Research Center in Hampton, Virginia, March 29–31, 1979. There were 260 registrants. Twenty-six speakers gave papers on low-speed aerodynamics, structures and materials, optimal flight techniques, advanced instrumentation, ultralight sailplanes and HGs, and power sailplanes. The general chairman was Perry Hanson of NASA, and Oran Nicks, deputy director of NASA, gave the welcoming address. The proceedings of the symposium were made available in a 600-page publication. Wolf Elber, also of NASA, commented on the symposium in the June 1979 *Soaring:* "The Conference seemed to have something for everybody."

The Aero Club Albatross

The Aero Club Albatross (ACA) celebrated its 50th anniversary on April 7, 1979. Gus Scheurer, the founder and honorary president, and five other original members were present. The ACA was the oldest continuously operating soaring club in the United States, and Scheurer was given a special New Jersey license plate for his car with the number ACA 50. Scheurer had started soaring in the early 1920s in Germany and came to the United States in the middle 1920s. He formed the ACA a few years later. Since his retirement he had restored a 1-19, a primary and a Herring-Chanute for the NSM.

Two More World Records

On the same day, a good ridge wind was blowing and Doris Grove, starting from Ridge Soaring in a ASW-19, made an out-and-return world record by flying to Mountain Grove, 227 miles south and back to Ridge Soaring

for a distance of 454.4 miles. On the same day, Hanna Reitsch of West Germany, in a borrowed ASW-20, starting from Karl Striedieck's field a few miles southwest of Ridge Soaring, flew north to Lock Haven as the starting point in her proposed flight. Karl Striedieck, L. Roy McMaster, and Will Schuemann flew along on the trip. She was able to complete the flight, which exceeded Doris Grove's distance, but her barograph did not work, so the flight could not be considered, even though her three companions could vouch for the turn-point at Mountain Grove.

At the same time, Tom Knauff, with Robert Tawse as copilot, flew a two-place Lark for a new world multiplace out-and-return record to Sweet Springs and back, a distance of 515.5 miles.

In her pilot description document required for FAI record claims, Doris Grove said of her trip from the turn-point, "At Cumberland, my thoughts were 'Oh gee, if I land, the retrieve won't be too long now.' I was able to thermal across Bedford (Gap) and decided to slow down and be conservative since it looked like I was going to make it."

Gus Scheurer in the "Elmira" primary at a Vintage Soaring Association regatta at Harris Hill. He restored this first glider of the Elmira Glider Club for the NSM and before turning it over to them he gave it a test flight.

(Dick Hosenfeld)

Dave Culpeper of Monroe, Georgia, the 1979 Standard Class champion, in his LS-3 sailplane.

(David G. Culpepper)

46th Open Class National, 1979

The 29 open sailplanes entered at this 46th championship, June 19–28 at Minden, Nevada, numbered almost 2½ times those entered at Chester the year before. The balance of the 66 sailplanes entered were 15-meter sailplanes. An indication of how good the conditions were was Dick Butler's record of 92.44 miles an hour on a 347.3-mile task, the fastest speed task ever flown in a U.S. National. This helped Butler, who won three of the eight days, to win the championships in his 604 sailplane. Laszlo Horvath was second in a Nimbus II and A. J. Smith was third in a 604. There were 10 former champions entered, with 8 finishing in the top 10; Dick Johnson was fourth and George Moffat fifth.

Fourth 15-Meter Class National, 1979

Fifty-eight pilots, including 7 former national champions, competed in the fourth 15-meter championships, July 3–12, at Adrian, Michigan. Competition director, Hal Lattimore, called three out-and-return and five triangle tasks. Eric Mozer was able to win three days, which enabled him to win the championships in his ASW-20. A. J. Smith, who was flying a Mos-

quito, finished second, only 18 points behind. Ben Greene, flying an ASW-20 was third, Joe Emons in a 301B Libelle was fourth, and Karl Striedieck was fifth in an ASW-20. Uncertain weather resulted in a lot of "Gaggle" flying and a midair collision occurred, but fortunately both pilots landed safely.

Second SSA Vacation Derby, 1979

The 1979 derby started at Hobbs, New Mexico, with Hutchinson, Kansas, as its ultimate goal. Intermediate stops were at Amarillo, Texas, and Liberal, Kansas. Twelve sailplanes were entered. Mahlon Weir, who was there with a RS-5b Sperber motorglider, acted as "Mother Goose" for the less experienced pilots. The only pilot to make the complete course was Ed Kilbourne, who was flying a "vintage" Ka-6. Beside giving the contestants some good experience in cross-country flying over new territory, the derby featured a "cookout" by the local soaring club at every stop.

10th Standard Class National, 1979

The usual August weather of hazy and sultry days made soaring competition possible on only 5 of the 10 days at the July 17–26 meet in Hutchinson, Kansas. The longest flight was a 165-mile triangle. These conditions suited Justin Wills of Great Britain, the son of Philip Wills, who earned the most points, flying a Mosquito. Dave Culpepper, flying a LS-3, was the Standard Class champion, finishing next to Wills. A. J. Smith was second in his Hornet and Ben Greene third in an ASW-20.

Directors' Summer Meeting, 1979

At the July 27 meeting in Hutchinson,

the executive director reported that the membership stood at 15,620, an all-time high. Although revenues were up to expectations, the increased cost in presenting the case against the FAA air space proposal, plus the higher inflation-related costs of *Soaring* and other services to the members made a dues increase necessary. The active membership was raised from $20 to $23 a year (or $42 for two years), and the business membership from $45 to $60.

It was reported that many groups around the country were voicing objections to the new air space proposal, but that activity on these changes was now "on hold" since the FAA was involved in investigating the Chicago DC-10 accident.

The board authorized a feasibility study on using motorgliders as a training vehicle, providing that the FAA would permit the use of experimental motorgliders for such courses.

The board approved an allocation of $1,823 to the NSM for purchasing files to store the SSA archives that were shipped there in 1977.

Bernald S. Smith reported that the SSA hull and liability insurance plans were now being underwritten by the American Home Insurance Company.

The present officers were reelected.

1-26 Championships, 1979

Tom Cooper's story of the 1-26 National, was preceded with the following comment: "To many sailplane pilots the Schweizer 1-26 is just a stepping stone between dual trainer and glass. But, to a growing number of others the 1-26 is a formula racing machine and the only sailplane that offers true one-design competition. This year's contest proved once again that for tough, high-caliber competi-

tion in the air, coupled with a warm sense of communicaty and friendship on the ground, a soaring pilot and crew need look no further than the 1-26 Championships."

The championship was held at El Mirage, California, with Ross Briegleb as competition director. There were only 27 1-26s entered, since many of the regular 1-26 competitors from the East and Midwest decided to pass this one up because of the fuel shortage. Bob Gravance, who usually flew an ASW-12, won over 1978 Champion Scott Imaly by a mere 13 points. Tom Cooper was third, nosing out Harry Baldwin. The team champions were Jim Gallacher and Jess Green.

Gossamer Albatross

U.S. soaring enthusiasts had been following Paul MacCready's efforts to build an MPA that would fly the English Channel. They were particularly interested because this craft might have some fallout for ultralight sailplanes. Jack Lambie, who was part of the effort, wrote a report of the sensational flight over the Channel for the August 1979 *Soaring*.

First Homebuilders Workshop

John Lee, SSA's director of development, organized a successful homebuilders workshop at the NSM over the Labor Day weekend. There were 217 registered for the workshop. At the same time, the VSA held a regatta with 12 vintage sailplanes entered. The workshop brought together homebuilders from all over the country. At an open session, Lee discussed the possibility of a sailplane homebuilders association and considerable interest was shown. Bob Smith of Pascagoula,

Gus and Anne Briegleb in December of 1962, the "team" that ran the El Mirage Gliderport for many years, and the parents of two famous soaring pilots, Ross and Ken Briegleb.

(George Uveges)

Mississippi, was named chairman of the Steering Committee, and 11 members chosen from those present were asked to come up with proposed plans.

Washington Update

In the "SSA in Action" column in the November 1979 *Soaring*, Blossom reported on the status of the air space proposal: "Langhorne Bond has made public his decision to withdraw NPRM 78-19 from further consideration. This marks a significant victory by the SSA membership and the general aviation community. Mr. Bond noted that the SSA and the EAA were the only organizations represented at every meeting dealing with the NPRM and the 44 proposed TCAs. However, as the saying goes, we have only won the battle, not the war."

Other Activity

Charles. H. Gale, one of the founders of SSA and editor of the early SSA Gliding & Soaring bulletin, died in 1979.

Sierra Soaring Seminar, principally for women soaring pilots, was held at

Skylark North, Tehacapi, California, August 18–21. Doris Grove, Sabrina Jackintell, Erica Scurr, and Nancy Lee Evans were the featured speakers.

Anne Briegleb, wife of Gus, who supported him in his many soaring endeavors, died in 1979. Their many friends established a memorial by having the historic Briegleb sailplane *67 Charlie* on exhibit at the Fox Field Air Museum in Antelope Valley.

The 700th, and last, 1-26 was completed by the end of 1979. The 1-26 had been in production for 25 years and the last 20 were known as silver anniversary models.

Jean Doty of Phoenix, Arizona, who had spent more than seven years putting together the *Soaring* magazine indexes that covered the years from 1937 to 1977, also died in 1979.

Chapter 13

50-Year Anniversaries

The 50th Anniversary of the First National Soaring Contest, 1980

Early in 1980 plans were formulated to celebrate the 50th anniversary of the first National Soaring Contest. Many celebrations would highlight the impressive growth and improved performance of these contests, from the small beginning in 1930, in Elmira, New York, to the present—now there are four national, 12 regional, and many other contests each year in the United States. These celebrations would also recognize the many soaring advocates who made this growth possible.

The Elmira area would also celebrate the 50 years of community support for soaring that had begun in 1930, when the Elmira Association of Commerce and the Chemung County Board of Supervisors had welcomed the first soaring pilots to Elmira. The success of the first National convinced them that soaring had a future and encouraged them to continue supporting it for over 50 years.

Sports Class and Handicapping

With the steady improvement in the three WSC class sailplanes, a growing number of sailplanes were no longer competitive. As a result, attention turned to a Sport Class, in which these sailplanes could fly under a handicap system. In 1966 Carl Herold had developed his CH-66 handicap system in which each sailplane could fly under a handicap system. In Herold's system, each sailplane performance is leveled out by using a factor. Herold reviews his handicap factors each year on the basis of new information from competition experience, flight testing, or other sources. His reply to a criticism in the *Soaring* mail column in the January 1980 *Soaring* noted: "It is not my intent to give all pilots an equal chance of winning a contest. It is my intention to give all sailplanes a more fair competitive chance when their performance is averaged over the duration of the contest. On many days the handicap can be unfair to all but the winner. You have to accept this with a handicap, no matter how sophisticated. To date, however, the growing contest results show only the better pilots win whether flying a *1-26* or a *Nimbus*."

Moffat Comments on U.S. Sailplanes

In his column "Soaring to Win" in the January 1980 *Soaring*, Moffat made some observations on the U.S. sailplane situation:

> Arthur Zimmerman brought out the *C-70*, a thoroughly competitive ship in its day which, suffering from few orders and slow development, never really got off the ground before the

death of its designer. The *Zuni* project started by George Applebay, has had the same kind of growing problems and also a similar share of plain bad luck. Both ships suffer from the very slow start-up time brought about by involved FAA regulations. The result is that a new ship such as the *Zuni* or *Schweizer 1-35* may be totally competitive when the design is finalized but already out-built before any significant number get into the hands of customers years later. Schweizer estimated half a million dollars to certify the 1-35. Klaus Holighaus estimated $10–15,000 to certify a German ship with correspondingly shorter time. Is it any wonder the United States has lagged in development?

On the other end of the performance spectrum . . . the crying need [is] for a good, light, fairly inexpensive, one-design ship in the 30:1 performance range. Not all of us are going to be able to afford the $50,000+ that a 15 Meter ship will be likely to cost by the mid 1980's. The boating world has shown us that the best racing is often in the inexpensive 14' Lazers, not the exotic, million-dollar America's Cup boats.

Although the increase in the value of the dollar and the resulting decrease in European sailplane costs in the early 1980s left Moffat's $50,000 prediction unrealized, his point remained valid!

1980 Soaring Convention

Over 1,000 delegates attended the convention in Seattle, February 27 to March 2, 1980, which was sponsored by the Seattle Glider Council with Marion Barritt and Ron Ferguson as cochairmen.

One feature of the convention was the first FAA-approved SSA glider flight instructor revalidation clinic.

Thirty-three instructors attended this clinic, which was produced by Mike Moore, chairman of the Flight Training and Safety Board, and Steve Brown. An exhibit of 17 sailplanes was held in the large Seattle Center exhibit hall, with 49 booths lined around the periphery of the main hall.

There were the usual meetings of soaring associations, affiliates, and divisions. An unscheduled but well-attended meeting was held on motorgliding. The award banquet featured Ann Welch of England, who reminisced about "A Life in Aviation."

Directors' Winter Meeting, 1980

At its March 1–2 meeting in Seattle, the Board authorized a six-month motorglider study to evaluate the feasibility of using motorgliding in the United States as glider pilot training vehicles. Southwest Soaring in Caddo Mills, Texas, and the Schweizer Soaring School in Elmira, New York, were selected as the commercial operators to conduct the study.

The Colorado Soaring Association offered to turn over the administration of the Kolstad youth award to the SSA.

Dick Schreder was selected as the chairman of the committee for the celebration of the 50th Anniversary of SSA.

The formation of regional soaring organizations was discussed, and Jon Mead and Ron Ferguson were to prepare recommendations.

B. S. Smith reported that the Wyatt Agency, which administered the SSA insurance program, had issued over 2,000 policies and the rates had not changed in three years.

The board discussed the controversy that had developed when a for-

eign sailplane designer felt that an article on flight tests in *Soaring* did not
rate his sailplanes high enough. The
board decided that in the future it
would put a disclaimer at the end of
any performance-testing article in
Soaring.

Because the differences in performances between top sailplanes in a
class are very small, test flights must
be done very carefully and in stable
air. Any movement of the air or unnecessary movement of the controls
can affect the results. Also, the vari-
ation between the test sailplane and
others of the same type often can
cause different results among different
test groups. For this reason, the SSA
directors decided that a disclaimer
would be appropriate.

SAC did a great deal of performance testing of its own, but having
to run these tests above the rolling
800-foot-high hills over western New
York State was difficult because of the
lack of stable air. SAC had to rely on
comparison testing, using a proven
"trial horse" sailplane to fly with the
sailplane being tested. Although this
method has its limitations, it does provide useful information. For these reasons, SAC never went public with its
test results, except in projecting the
expected performance of its sailplanes.

Forrest Blossom

Forrest Blossom was not able to attend
the SSA directors' meeting in Seattle
because of ill health. In the spring of
1979, during the high activity on the
air space matter, he had to undergo
neural surgery.

He did return for a while, but one
week after the Seattle meeting, Bryan
Utley informed the directors that Blossom had resigned.

Blossom had made a good start in
developing the SSA into a more busi-
ness-like organization with improved
services to the membership. During
the air space crisis in 1979, he played a
key role by coordinating SSA's effort
with the AOPA and the EAA in carrying the fight to Congress and the FAA.

Blossom had the unpopular job of
changing SSA personnel, as well as
practices that had been in place for
many years. Utley noted, however,
that "Forrest Blossom's contributions
to the Society have been most appreciated and it is with profound sadness
that we report that his health will not
allow him to continue his service as
Executive Director."

Sailplane Development

Applebay Sailplanes announced the
Zuni II in *Soaring*. This was developed
from the Zuni with the assistance of
Devore Aviation and the Los Alomos
Scientific Laboratories.

Jack Laister reported on the costs
of certifying sailplanes and the time
and cost involved in meeting the terminal velocity limiting dive brakes requirement for the Standard Class.
After an expensive 60-day proving period of the brakes, he was advised that
the FAI had simplified these
requirements.

SAC announced the Sprite (the
1-36), a 14-meter sailplane for recreational flying, in its ad in the March
1980 *Soaring*. With the 1-26 now out of
production, it hoped that the Sprite
would become the basis for another
competition class.

Al Backstrom's article in the June
1980 *Soaring* proposed two classes of
small sailplanes: the 8^2 Submidget,
8-meter (26.4 foot) span and 8-meter-
square (86.12-square-foot) area, and
the 10^2 Midget, 10-meter (32.81 foot)

span and 10-meter-square (107.65-square-foot) area. He closes by saying: "Remember, Small can be beautiful."

As sailplanes get smaller, however, you run into increasing problems of "scale effect." For this reason, most small sailplanes of the past were not successful, particularly if they were flown by the average pilot. A number of basic factors work against the designer here. The weight and size of the pilot, instruments, equipment, and other standard items all become proportionally heavier and larger. The adverse effect of smaller Reynolds numbers called "scale effect" becomes larger as the sailplanes become smaller. The fuselage size must remain the same unless it is designed for smaller pilots. The net result is that a small sailplane usually becomes a "hot ship" that requires experienced pilots, if it is to stay in the air in light conditions. It is recognized that new aerodynamics and new materials can offset some of these factors, but they will not, for some time at least, be the low-cost answer that prompts many to consider going "small."

A U.S. Akaflieg

Sailplane development in the United States has been limited by the high cost of doing research work and the fact that the sailplane market is too small to support such research. In Germany much of the sailplane development is carried out by "Akaflieg groups," which consist of students supported by university staff who undertake the research, design, and construction of projects. This was the way that the present leading German designers got their start.

The few U.S. sailplane manufacturers, although not able financially to do research themselves, do benefit from the research and development carried out by other companies that can be applied to sailplanes. However it still takes many years to get new material or new design concepts accepted by the FAA for production sailplanes.

The first Akaflieg effort in the United States was started by Rensselaer Polytechnic Institute in Troy, New York, in 1978. Gunther Helwig, a graduate of Darmstadt who had been working on a variable geometry sailplane, was chosen for the job as research assistant. He would head a composite material project using a glider as a test bed and help RPI build up a composite lab to attract students and to help the institute complete a contract commitment with NASA. The first project was the RP-1, an intermediate performance ultralight sailplane. If Akaflieg projects could be expanded to other universities, it could have a favorable effect on sailplane development in the United States.

The RPI Akaflieg program was assisted by Dr. Francis Bundy of the nearby Mohawk Soaring Club. Bundy, an experienced soaring pilot with three Diamonds, test-flew the RP-1. Progress on the more advanced RP-2 slowed down when Helwig left the project. Although no additional Akafliegs were formed, other university groups in the United States were involved in soaring, the most active being the group at MIT.

The Women's Record Controversy

On March 11, 1980, Doris Grove made the first 1,000-kilometer soaring flight by a woman. She flew out-and-return from Ridge Soaring Gliderport to Bluefield, Virginia (622 miles, 1,001 kilometers) in her ASW-19 for a new world record. Karl Striedieck was flying the ridges at the same time and they saw each other and talked by radio a number of times during the day.

Twenty-five days later, Cornelia Yoder became the second woman to fly over 1,000 kilometers. She flew her ASW-19 from Port Matilda, Pennsylvania, to Tazewell, Virginia, and return to claim a new world record of 637 miles (1,025 kilometers). Striedieck was also flying that day and they observed each other and had radio contact a number of times.

A letter to the Editor in the July, 1980 *Soaring* raised some questions about the propriety of receiving assistance during some of the record soaring flights that were made along the ridges over the last few years. In answer to this letter Karl Striedieck wrote:

> First, my involvement in the successful flights of Hanna Reitsch, Doris Grove and Cornelia Yoder was identical in all respects. . . . The truth is that my radio comments, time spent out front, and moral support was the same for

all three of these excellent pilots.

> Did my presence make a difference as to whether or not these flights would have been successful? I think not. The weather made all three "cake missions" as a fighter jockey might say.

In the same issue, CIVV President Bill Ivans commented: "I am aware of no rule within either CIVV or FAI which prohibits help on record flights. Record claims are therefore, not compromised by help which may have been accepted during the course of the flight."

National Soaring Centers

A concern was developing among soaring enthusiasts about where soaring would be done in the future. Some groups have taken steps to acquire sites, such as Air Sailing in Nevada and National Soaring Foundation in Hobbs, New Mexico. El Mirage, California, Gliderport, which had been used for soaring since Briegleb purchased the airport shortly after World

Cornelia Yoder with the ASW19 that she flew to a new women's world out-and-return record of 637 miles on April 5, 1980.

(Robert Lerner)

A revolving stainless steel sculpture commemorating 75 years of the Rotary Club in Elmira and the 50th anniversary of the first soaring contest. The sculpture was designed by Ernest Schweizer and built by volunteer gliding enthusiasts and Rotarians.

(Tony Fusare)

at least 90 percent of his total. Soaring lost two well-known pilots during the contest. Joe Beardon of Cincinnati, Ohio, crashed on the last leg of a task and was killed, and Joe Giltner of Chester, South Carolina, who had been hospitalized after a task, died a few days later because of a heart condition.

11th Standard Class National, 1980

This National, held at Harris Hill, July 1–10, 1980, commemorated the 50th Anniversary of the First National Soaring Contest. Fifty-five pilots entered this meet. Karl Striedieck, flying an ASW-20, won the first day and stayed in first position for the entire meet. Roy McMaster was second in an ASW-20, Las Horvath third in an ASW-20, Michael Opitz was fourth in an ASW-19, and David Welles fifth in a 1-35. At the award breakfast, a special Steuben crystal eagle was presented to Stanley Smith for his many years of competitive flying. A special prize was also given to Doug Jacobs for gallantry, as he had landed to aid Bruce Dyson, who had crashed while attempting to make an out-landing during a task.

Celebrating the 50th Anniversary

The celebration started with a NSM exhibition featuring the first National and included a Franklin Utility glider. Before the contest, the Elmira Rotary Club dedicated a revolving soaring sculpture, by Ernie Schweizer, that commemorated the 75th anniversary of Rotary and the 50th anniversary of soaring in the Elmira area. This stainless steel structure, with two rotating sailplanes, is mounted in downtown Riverside Park in Elmira.

A community soaring banquet

War II, was now owned by a liquidating trust, and an effort was under way to purchase the land so that its future for soaring could be ensured. It was clear that this would become a matter of increasing importance.

Fifth 15-Meter Class National, 1980

Sixty-seven (67) pilots were entered in the Fifth 15-Meter Championships, June 17–26, at Springfield, Ohio. Wally Scott was leading the field at the start of the last day, but Karl Striedieck, who had been in first place on five days, won the final day and the championship. Ray Gimmey was second, Tom Beltz was third, Wally Scott was fourth, and Ben Greene was fifth—all flying ASW-20s. It was a very competitive contest with the next four pilots finishing within 132 points of Striedieck and 19 pilots finishing with was held at the Elmira Campus Center the Sunday before the start of the 11th National. Arthur Godfrey, who had started his flying career by flying a primary glider in the early 1930s, was the speaker of the evening, and Eddie Mooers, who had supported soaring in the area since its start, was also honored.

On July 2, Stan Smith and Floyd Sweet flew an official airmail flight from Harris Hill to the Chemung County Airport. The Elmira Stamp Club had sponsored this flight and arranged with the U.S. Postal Service to set up a special post office on Harris Hill to cancel these letters with a special pictorial canceler.

On October 4, Wolf Hirth's famous 1930 soaring flight was reenacted with flights to Apalachin and landing at the Tri-Cities Airport, where a dinner commemorated the flight.

Directors' Summer Meeting, 1980

At the July 11 meeting in Elmira, John Dezzutti was appointed executive director after having served almost six months as acting director.

The president projected that if no actions were taken, the yearly deficit could reach $80,000 in the face of the energy shortage and spiraling inflation. The Executive Committee had decided that immediate action was needed—very tight controls would be required on all costs, all unnecessary costs would have to be reduced, and dues would have to go up.

Many expressed concern that another dues increase would discourage new members and keep present members from renewing. However, it was pointed out that in spite of the increase in member and business member dues in 1979, the membership had

continued to grow. The board therefore approved the following increases: members to $28 ($52 for two years), student members to $18, family members to $14, life members to $450, and business members to $100. In an effort to prevent newer members from transferring to associate membership, it was restricted to present associate members, or to those who had been a member for five consecutive previous years. This regulation was passed, even though it would eliminate a membership category for those who were not active in soaring but wanted to be kept informed by reading *Soaring*.

It was also decided to eliminate the position of promotion director, even though some felt that more promotion was needed rather than less.

The same officers were reelected.

47th Open Class National, 1980

Ten former national champions were among the 49 pilots entered in the 1980 Open at Hobbs, New Mexico, July 15–24. The contest started on a sad note when Mahlon Weir was killed in a crash shortly after taking off in his ASW-20. He had been the "court jester" at contests and his smiling face, his enthusiasm, and funny hats would be missed.

For the first time in competition soaring history, three pilots topped 100 miles per hour during practice day tasks. Dick Butler (604), George Moffat (Jantar 2A), and Gary Hagemeister (Nimbus II) recorded 107.67 miles per hour, 102.58 miles per hour, and 101.67 miles per hour, respectively, around a 127.3-mile triangle.

Hal Lattimore, the competition director, called all speed tasks. The "big ships" dominated this national, and

Butler won the first day and kept the lead for the entire contest. A last-day charge by Moffat, whose 90.81 winning speed brought him within 27 points of Butler, put him in second place. Las Horvath was third in a Nimbus II, Striedieck was fourth and Greene fifth in ASW-17s.

Second Homebuilders Workshop, 1980

The details of the homebuilt sailplane design contest were announced at the workshop held at Harris Hill, August 30 to September 1, 1980. The rules stated that "the Design Competition is aimed at providing a low cost, easy-to-build, safe sailplane which is easy to fly and fun to soar. A self-launching capability is considered to be highly desirable as a means of making soaring accessible and affordable to the majority of the participants. . . . A flyoff and evaluation would occur during the summer of 1982." The workshop included many lectures, demon-

strations, and discussions on the formation of a sailplane homebuilders association. The keynote address at the banquet by John McMasters was entitled "Those Who Have Imagination without Learning Have Wings But No Feet."

National Soaring Museum

The NSM director, Liam English, resigned at the end of 1979 and Shirley Sliwa was named acting director. At the annual trustees' meeting in May 1980 she was named director. A $200,000 fund drive for the Phase II Development Program was launched.

Preparation for the WSC

Bill Cleary was named to head a $60,000 fund drive to send a team to the 1981 WSC at Paderborn, West Germany. The Heubling Corp. donated to the SSA the 1-35 in which Wally Scott had won the Smirnoff Derby in 1976. It had been on exhibit in the Air and Space Museum, but now was to be used as the prize for a fund-raising raffle among the SSA membership.

The four pilots chosen by the seeding committee were Karl Striedieck, Dick Butler, Ray Gimmey, and Ben Greene. The team captain was John Brittingham and the team manager Rudy Mozer.

Other Happenings during 1980

Soaring lost five well-known soaring pilots during 1980, all as a result of natural causes: Si Gilad, Harold Jensen, Al Parker, Ray Parker, and Wally Wiberg. Alcidi Santilli and Sterling Starr were inducted into the Soaring Hall of Fame during 1980.

The contestant and the competition director, George Moffat and Judge "Hal" Lattimore, discussing a contest rule at a national contest.
(Rathbun, NSM Collection)

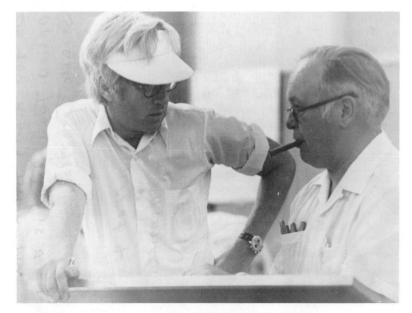

Reverse Growth, 1981

The SSA had grown at a steady rate of about 4 percent a year, from 1,137 members in 1957 to 16,121 members by the end of 1980. This represented an average increase of 650 members a year. The growth started to decline at the end of 1980 and in 1981 it assumed a negative value in excess of 2 percent, which was to continue for a number of years. Along with this came a reduction in soaring activity and the number of commercial operators, and the number of students turned out by the COs.

The main reasons for this reversal in growth of the SSA were rapidly increasing inflation, a general decline in the economy, and the large increase in SSA dues. It was evident that soaring had a cost problem and something would have to be done to get soaring growing again.

Ninth Soaring Convention, 1981

About 700 members attended this convention, in Phoenix from January 14 to 18, 1981, which was sponsored by the Arizona Soaring Association. It followed generally the pattern set by previous conventions and included a sailplane and supplier exhibition at the Phoenix Civic Plaza and an awards banquet, which featured Astronaut Ron Evans. On Saturday afternoon most of the convention delegates, except the SSA directors who were busy at their meeting, attended the production "Wings of Dreams and Flying Machines," which took place at the Gammage Auditorium. Ernest Gann, the famous author, Paul MacCready, George Moffat, and Chauncy Dunn (balloonist), with Gren Seibel as master of ceremonies, presented a flying spectacular of lectures and films. Flight

Another aspect of this decline was the smaller number of two-place training gliders being delivered. The sales of the 2-33, which most COs and clubs used for training had decreased. Its production had started in 1967 and in the 14 years up to the end of 1980, 575 had been built, which represented an average of 40 sailplanes per year. The highest sales were 66 in 1968 and 56 in 1974. The market decline began in 1977, and it tapered down to only 9 in 1980, and only 4 in 1981. The increase in imports of higher-performance two-place sailplanes from Europe, which would be used mainly for advanced training, transition to high-performance single-place sailplanes, and for passenger rides, further lightened the requirement for 2-33s.

Floyd J. Sweet presents some historic sailplane material to Shirley Sliwa, director of the National Soaring Museum.
(Frances Sweet)

sessions on Sunday at Turf and Estrella Gliderport rounded out the convention.

Directors' Winter Meeting, 1981

A deficit of $17,586 was reported for 1980 at the Phoenix meeting of January 17, 1981. The membership had grown at a slower rate for the first 10 months and then started to decrease in November when the effect of the dues increases became more pronounced.

B. S. Smith reported that the hull and liability insurance experience during 1980 showed a 125 percent loss ratio. After three years at the same rates, an increase was necessary and the poor experience emphasized the need for improving flying safety.

It was voted to permit contest entry fees to go up to $350 for Nationals and $185 for Regionals, with sanction fees set at $20 per pilot entered.

The SSA agreed to sponsor an undergraduate student sailplane design contest in cooperation with the AIAA. A fund of $2,500 was approved for this competition.

Plans for the 50th anniversary of SSA were discussed and the May 1982 issue of *Soaring* would be a special anniversary issue.

Freedom Wings, a disabled pilots' association, applied to SSA for affiliation.

New FAA Airworthiness Requirements

On October 14, 1980, the FAA issued an NPRM that proposed to use the JARs as the new airworthiness requirements for sailplanes and motorgliders.

At the soaring convention, Craig Beard, director of the FAA's Office of Airworthiness, announced the publication of Advisory Circular AC 21.23-1, which formally adopted the JARs as an acceptable equivalent standard for the type certification of sailplanes and motorgliders. This was primarily the result of the effort of Nelson Shapter, chairman of SSA's Airworthiness Technical Standards Committee.

Instead of using only the unproven JARs, the FAA advisory circular permitted three alternative methods: the new JAR 22, the appropriate requirements from Part FAR 23, and the old Basic Glider Criteria Handbook. This was an excellent solution to the problem, but it was regrettable that the sale of U.S. sailplanes was so small that few manufacturers would have their sailplanes certified.

The effort to get legal glider regulations began in 1960, but very little was done until the February 1978 directors' meeting. The FAA administrators were looking for a common stand on the regulations, and FAA's Clark Onstad proposed that an FAA hearing with SSA and the glider manufacturers be held to obtain specific recommendations, rather than generalizations.

Some SSA key personnel thought naively that the glider manufacturers should not be involved in these negotiations, whereas the glider manufacturers were the only ones who could make the specific recommendations that the FAA wanted. At the Chicago directors' meeting, efforts were made to get the board to approve the acceptance of the JARs, which were still being developed in Europe. The board finally accepted them when it was agreed that the manufacturers would have the opportunity to comment on them.

Alcidi Santilli (left) and Sterling Starr after being inducted into the SSA Soaring Hall of Fame at the 1980 ceremonies. Santilli began his soaring activities at the early contests at Elmira, New York. Sterling Starr became active after World War II and was SSA president in 1967 and 1968.

(NSM Collection)

The JARs were available in late 1980 and an NPRM was issued shortly thereafter. During this three-year period the proposed SSA glider manufacturers' hearing was never held, and, as John Dezzutti later pointed out, "They [the glider manufacturers] were left out of the loop." It was evident that SAC's past position on the regulations and its comments on the NPRM were factors that influenced the FAA's decision to provide for three methods of certifying gliders instead of just the unproven JARs. This was a plus factor for all U.S. glider manufacturers, but unfortunately few were still active.

The SSA Motorglider Evaluation Tests

The evaluation of motorgliders for training, which was carried out as an SSA-FAA project, showed that motorgliders could be effectively used as part of a sailplane training program. It was not clear, however, how the costs compared in view of the short programs carried out and the use of rented equipment. Derek Piggot, who had accumulated some 2,000 hours of instructing in motorgliders at Lasham, England, ran the program at Southwest Soaring Enterprises in Caddo Mills, Texas. He reported on their program in the April 1981 *Soaring.* He was very enthusiastic about the results from a training point of view, but did not get into the details of the costs.

The Schweizer Soaring School program was supervised by Jim Short, who remarked in his final report to the SSA:

We feel that the FAA/SSA experiment has been a success . . . that motorglider training is practical and safe. . . . We see no need to make any major changes in published motorglider cur-

riculums. We recognize the need for these to evolve with the individual operator. . . . We would support the continued use of motorgliders in the U.S. soaring schools, either on an experimental basis or on an unrestricted basis. At the current time, we are not too certain of the economic viability of operating motorgliders in the United States for the following reasons:
1. Their cost–2. Customer reluctance–3. Conflict between aircraft and staff usage in the existing pure sailplane/towplane schools.

The SSS, where most students come for a period of a week or two, found that some students felt that they had come for a sailplane course and as a result were not interested in doing part of it in the motorglider. Staff and operating problems had to be worked out, and often the easy way was to do it the old way. Thus, the amount of motorglider use was not as high as expected.

The difference between the two test results were no doubt affected by the fact that Derek Piggot was an instructor with a great deal of motorglid-

Doug and Lianna Lamont, editor and production manager of *Soaring* magazine, were awarded the Eaton Memorial Trophy for 1980.

(NSM Collection)

ing experience, whereas Bernie Carris, SSS chief instructor, and his staff were new to motorgliding, although they were ready to give it a try. An important question at SAC was the cost factor, whether there was a cost advantage in using the motorgliders. The one point that all agreed on was that motorglider training could be carried out with a minimum of staff and that it would be an ideal way to provide introductory flights and to conduct training and soaring at nearby nonglider airports.

SSS used the Fournier RF-5B tandem motorglider, while Southwest Soaring Enterprises used a Scheibe SF-25E Super Falke side-by-side for the first half of the six-month trial and a Sportavia RF-5 Sperber for the balance of the period.

17th WSC, 1981

Eighty-one pilots from 25 nations competed in the 17th WSC at Paderborn, West Germany, May 24 to June 7, 1981. Six nations (Australia, Bulgaria, Czechoslovakia, Hungary, the USSR, and Yugoslavia) withdrew before the contest started because a South African team was entered. The Polish government permitted members of the Polish team to compete as individuals under the FAI flag. Dick Butler flew a modified 23-meter ASW-17 in the Open Class, Karl Striedieck and Ray Gimmey flew ASW-20s in the 15-Meter Class, and Ben Greene flew an LS-4 in the Standard Class.

The weak thermals, low clouds, and soft conditions on the first three days proved to be the undoing of the U.S. team. The Open Class was mainly a contest between George Lee of Great Britain and Klaus Holighaus of West Germany. On the last day, Lee nosed out Holighaus and became the

first pilot in history to win three world championships in a row. Holighaus finished 2d and Gantenbrink of West Germany was 3d, all flying the new Nimbus III. Butler was the only one to complete the last day's task, but only finished in 7th place.

Goran Ax and Ake Pettersson, both of Sweden flying ASW-20s, finished 1st and 2d in the 15-Meter Class, and Pare of the Netherlands was 3d in the Ventus B. Striedieck won the last day and finished 16th, and Gimmey was 27th.

In the Standard Class the first three finishers were Schroeder of France, Kristiansen of Norway, and Chenevay of France, all flying LS-4s. Greene finished in 24th position.

This was the poorest U.S. team showing in a WSC, and John Brittingham made the following comments in his report to the directors: "So what went wrong? WEATHER, WEATHER, WEATHER, and perhaps scoring. The weather was cold, wet, and generally very weak. They set tasks and flew on days that we wouldn't have opened the hangar doors here. . . . We just didn't realize that they would set tasks in that kind of weather. . . . The peak was reached when the open class had an official contest day with the winner getting 0 points, Dick Butler was second that day, just 30 seconds behind the winner, also with 0 points. . . . *Perhaps our policy of trying for a high percentage of completions and not flying in very chancy weather handicaps our pilots in championships such as this one.*"

The First Soaring Landmark

The dedication of the first soaring landmark took place at Corn Hill, Cape Cod, Massachusetts, on June 12, 1981. The bronze plaque commemorated the first U.S. "C" award earned

by Ralph S. Barnaby, on August 18, 1929, which beat Orvill Wright's record. Jon Mead, SSA regional director for the New England Area, carried special airmail letters commemorating the event and landed on the beach below Corn Hill.

The National Soaring Museum National Landmark Program, with Wally Setz as chairman, plans to dedicate plaques at locations at which historic soaring events have taken place.

48th Open Class National, 1981

The contest was held from June 16 to 25, 1981, at J. W. Benz Soaring, a commercial operation located at the Ionia Airport in Michigan. Johan Kuhn was competition director and Jerry Benz was the operation manager. Only 30 pilots were entered since the WSC was being held almost the same time in West Germany and the site was not noted for particularly strong conditions, which make competition with open ships so rewarding.

The average task was 143 miles and the best winning speeds were in the range of 40 to 60 miles per hour. Dick Johnson, flying a Nimbus II, won the championships with Sherman Griffith second in an ASW-17. His father, Marion Griffith, Jr., was third in a 604, Jim Gallaway was fourth in a Jantar 2A, and Ron Tabery was fifth in an ASW-12.

Sixth 15-Meter Class National, 1981

Eight former, or present, champions were among the 65 pilots who entered 15-Meter National at Minden, Nevada, June 30 to July 9, 1981. The entry list included Klaus Holighaus of West Germany, who was competing in his new Ventus 15-meter sailplane. Under excellent weather conditions, the task distance averaged 295 miles, the longest being 455 miles. The winning task speed ranged from 92.98 to 56.77 miles per hour. The slowest was on the day that only two pilots, Gimmey and Briegleb, completed the task.

The scene at the typical "fiberglass forest" at a national contest.

(Gren Seibles)

K. Holighaus was first and Ray Gimmey second. Gimmey and the next six finishers all flew ASW-20s. Leffler came third, Cannon fourth, Cris Woods fifth, and Roy McMaster sixth.

John Joss's report for the October 1981 *Soaring* concluded: "Whatever those numbers 'prove,' there are other answers buried in the heart of soaring itself that explain why we fly and who 'wins.' The effects are repeated tens of thousands of times in contests, in cross-country and badge flying, in the smallest increment of skill we gain day by day. The winners and achievers in soaring rely on the same attributes as the winners and achievers in life: they perceive and accept a goal, they work tirelessly at it, they submit stoically in interim defeat and set it aside as irrelevant, they husband their resources and make the most of their skills— emotional, intellectual, physical. And they rarely give up."

Directors' Summer Meeting, 1981

At the July 9 meeting in Carson City, Nevada, President Utley announced that a 20–25 percent dues increase might be necessary by 1983, even though May had ended with a surplus. SSA membership was still decreasing—there had already been a loss of 274 members since the first of the year.

The raffle of the Smirnoff 1-35 had been very successful in raising funds for the international team. Red Wright's "open letter" to the membership again did the job. After the team expenses had been paid, there was a surplus of $35,000 that would be invested and used for the next team effort.

The Santa Monica Airport authorities had given the SSA a notice that it would not renew its office lease. A study was being made on a temporary relocation of the office, in the event that this might become necessary. At the same time, a Relocation Committee was investigating the possibility of a permanent home for the SSA.

Don Slotten had resigned from his position as chairman of the Safety and Training Board and Gene Hammond was named his successor.

Marion Barritt was assigned to establish guidelines for convention sponsors so that they would have a better chance of doing the job well and not end up with a financial loss.

A $100 prize was to be given each year by SSA for the best model sailplane soaring flight at the AMA National Model Meet.

The new officers for 1982 were Carl Herold, president; A. C. Williams, vice-president; Ed Sessions, vice-president; Ted Sharp, treasurer; and Dick Schreder, secretary.

Standard Class National, 1981

The National Soaring Foundation dedicated its new hangar to the memory of Mahlon Weir before the start of the meet. The "nonoptimum" weather still made possible nine contest days. The largest task was 333 miles, and the fastest winning speed ranged from 75.31 to 48.81 miles per hour, but was not up to Hobbs standards. Nonetheless, it was a competitive event, with 61 pilots entered, 14 of whom finished within 10 percent of the winners. The real competition was between Karl Striedieck and Tom Beltz, both flying ASW-19s. Striedieck finally won with a 54-point margin over Beltz.

Jim Smiley and Mike Opitz finished third and fourth, also flying ASW-19s. Doug Jacobs, a fast-improving pilot, finished in fifth place in an

LS-4. Alcide Santilli reported in the November 1981 *Soaring* that 107,600 task miles had been flown. He commented: "Fate held the choice of the winners in reserve until the last."

1-26 Championships, 1981

Fourteen of the 1-26s entered in the August 2–10, 1981, meet at the USAF Academy in Colorado were flown by teams of two pilots, for a total of 52 pilots. A number of the teams were from the AFA, which has an effective glider-training program for the cadets. The Connor father-son team scored the most points and were named the team champions; Dave Mockler won the individual championship. John Brittingham was the competition director and Jim Foreman the contest manager. Foreman's report for the November 1981 *Soaring* concluded: "The 1-26 Championships at the Academy was a trial balloon to see if it would be possible to hold a soaring contest with civilian pilots in harmony with a military environment. Not only did it prove possible but it worked so well that we may see more such contests in the years to come. The Air Force had a beautiful facility and were gracious hosts."

Homebuilders Workshop

In 1981 two homebuilders workshops were held over Labor Day weekend, one at Fantasy Haven in Tehachapi, California, for the western half of the United States, and the other at Harris Hill, the eastern half. Strong SSA support continued, with staff members Nancy Evans assisting at the Tehachapi event and Cindy Brinker at Harris Hill. Attendance at these two events, plus the homebuilders session at the EAA fly-in at Oshkosh was estimated

to be over 600. Further steps were taken to get the Sailplane Homebuilder Association organized. It was announced that 18 entrants had been accepted in the design contest.

Sailplane Developments during 1981

The Monarch ultralight sailplane, the latest of Jim Marske's line of flying-wing designs, was described in the December 1981 *Soaring*.

The Altostratus I by John Mc-Master was featured in the cover story of the February 1981 *Soaring*. Mc-Master, the technical soaring editor, called it "Technical Fiction," and his purpose was to satirize, through parody, factors in soaring that bothered him, particularly the rapidly spiraling cost of open racers without a corresponding increase in performance, and the increasing emphasis on the "need to win" that takes the fun out of soaring. Jack Olsen's exciting painting of the Altostratus I on the front cover showed what a sailplane of the 21st century might look like.

Dick Butler's 23-meter modification of the ASW-17 was an example of another way to get more performance. Unable to get a Nimbus III in time for the WSC, he modified an ASW-17 by adding a 6-meter center section on a cooperative venture with the Schleicher Co., which made the ASW-17-23 competitive with the Nimbus III.

The Schweizer Sprite (1-36) was type certified and in production. It was designed to fill the void between training and competition sailplanes and to meet the needs of the recreational pilot.

New Womens' Record

The winds on September 28, 1981, were right for flying the Appalachin

The Sprite flies over Harris Hill, with the NSM and the two glider hangars below.
(Schweizer Aircraft Corporation)

Doris Grove, world women's out-and-return record holder, seated in a Nimbus 3 at the Ridge Soaring Gliderport in Pennsylvania.
(Ridge Soaring)

ridges and Doris Grove dispelled any possible doubts about her soaring ability by setting a new world out-and-return record. She flew a Nimbus II sailplane for a distance of 700.7 miles, or 1127.28 kilometers.

The Solar Challenger

In the story of Paul MacCready's Solar Challenger project in December 1981 *Soaring,* there was an editorial "box" that contained the following comments by MacCready:

> Some of us on the Challenger team are exploring and talking about a small, light, self-launching sailplane. . . . One concept is a small "Challenger" using a 6 hp engine, light loading, not requiring an airport, only a little clear space. No ATC problem. Slow speed and low mass means that if you had to, you could land in the trees, or even hit the side of a house and escape injury. Surrounding structure could act as further protection.

We ought to be able to soar like a buzzard. The machine ought to be strong, convenient, controllable, operate in a 20–25 mph range, and in the case of real emergency have an explosively opened chute that could deploy 30–100 feet above the ground. These are things that people should be working on.

Other Happenings during 1981

The Giltner Memorial Trophy Award in memory of Joe Giltner was created by his soaring friends and is to be awarded each year for the fastest task time at the 15-Meter National Championships.

The SSA took over the Kolstad Youth Award during 1981 to make it a national award. It had been awarded 12 times since 1968, and the 1981 winner was Dick Mockler. Jack Lambie told of his latest adventure in the story "In Search of the Condor" in the March 1981 issue of *Soaring*. It covered his delivery flight of a motor glider to Paraguay.

Jim Rhine of the Tulsa Skyhawks

died in January. Jim was known by most competition pilots of that time as the "voice of the startline." He was assisted by his wife Gerry, and he was the mainstay of the Tulsa Skyhawks. Jim Nash-Webber, former chairman of the SSA Technical Board and key soaring person at MIT, also died during 1981. He was the principal organizer of the MIT symposiums.

The 50th Anniversary of SSA, 1982

When I began this history in 1981, I felt that the logical stopping point would be May 11, 1982, exactly 50 years after the SSA was formed. I expected the book to be finished soon after that. It has taken much longer to research and write this history than I thought it would, but I decided to keep the same ending point. However, this chapter will include other 50th anniversary events that occurred after that date.

The January 1982 *Soaring* featured an article entitled "SSA's Golden Anniversary." Various commemorative activities were scheduled for the year, and *Soaring* magazine was to have a feature historical article each month. The May issue was to be a special jumbo-sized golden anniversary edition.

The SSA Anniversary Committee, with Marion Barritt and Dick Schreder as co-chairmen, were planning two *Soaring* Safaris, one in the western half of the United States, ending in Heber City, Utah, and the other in the eastern half, ending at Harris Hill, New York. Pilots would start from their home base and soar to these goals in a series of flights. Special activities were planned at each goal.

A golden anniversary trophy competition would also be held in each re-

Carl Herold, SSA president, during the SSA's 50th anniversary year. He is noted for "Herold's Hearsay" column in *Soaring*, the "CH" handicapping factor, and for being very active in many phases of soaring.

(Don Monroe, SSA files)

gion for the fastest time around a 300-kilometer triangle during the summer of 1982. The trophies were created by Ron Chitwood of Richland, Washington.

President's Report

Comments from President Carl Herold's first editorial follow:

I am honored to be your President during 1982, the year of the Society's 50th Anniversary.

Along with the regular fare of problems to solve, we face the lack of growth of our overall membership . . ., a lack of new two-place training gliders, the continued reduction in the clubs' generation of new glider pilots, and the reduction of viable commercial operations. The reasons for the foregoing are many and varied, but the message is clear. Without an adequate growth in students, the soaring movement and the Society will decline and become a subject for historians to research. In addition, fuel cost, towplane noise, high cost of flight training, low use participation, high property values, high interest rates, and increasing bureaucracy are all negative factors. However, we need to respond with changes in order to achieve the 3–5 percent annual growth rate we have had from WW II to 1979.

Today we are now at a crossroads where the Society needs to play a greater role in its (SSA) future. . . . The Society needs to expend its limited resources in addressing growth, while continuing to maintain membership approval.

Preparations for the 1983 WSC

In order to prepare the U.S. team for the 1983 WSC in Argentina, the SSA sent Karl Striedieck, a potential team pilot, to compete in the 1982 Argentina Nationals in January. His task was to evaluate the soaring and to get answers to a list of questions that the Contest Committee had prepared. After attending, Striedieck wrote an article entitled "Argentina Previsited" for the April 1982 *Soaring*. He said that the Argentina National was really a small international contest since 10 pilots were entered from six other countries: Austria, France, Spain, Switzerland, West Germany, and the United States. Although Striedieck had one "zero day," he finished the contest in third place and won 6 of the 10 contest days. His report confirmed that there were excellent soaring conditions there, and he brought back information for the U.S. team.

11th National Convention, 1982

The Houston Soaring Community sponsored the March 3–7 convention, which was to celebrate the 50th anniversary of the SSA. Two novelties for an SSA convention were a 16-page historical program and a special historical exhibit at the entrance to the Albert Thomas Convention Center.

About 700 delegates were registered and 1,800 others paid to visit the exhibition, which included 20 sailplanes and a large number of booths selling soaring equipment. A full schedule of meetings and technical sessions was spread over three days. The awards banquet had astronaut Story Musgrave as the principal speaker.

Directors' Winter Meeting, 1982

The executive director reported to the directors meeting in Houston on March 6, 1982, that the membership was still on the decline and as of December 31, 1981, was 371 below the level of a year earlier. He noted that the new auditors had recommended some changes in accounting practices that resulted in a less favorable report for 1981. However, no dues increase was considered necessary.

The urgency to relocate the SSA offices had lessened since the City of Santa Monica was involved in legal proceedings with the FAA, as federal funds had been used for the airport.

The Sailplane Homebuilders Association (SHA) was approved as a division of the SSA, pending the submission of necessary documents.

The Training and Safety Board chairman, Gene Hammond, recommended that a new badge, the Bronze "C," be created between the "C" and the Silver "C" badges, to provide for another step in preparing the student for cross-country flying.

Some directors were concerned about SSA's responsibility for the safety of the homebuilt sailplane plans and kits advertised in *Soaring*, and a decision was made to develop procedures for the evaluation of the safety of advertised products.

The Insurance Committee was to look into the availability and cost of professional liability insurance protection for the directors.

The Member Relation Board had grown to 10 committees and the chairman recommended that it be divided into two boards: an Affiliates and Divisions Board and a revised Member Relations Board. The bylaws were changed accordingly.

The name of the Ad Hoc Relocation Committee was changed to the Permanent Headquarters Committee, and it was to develop long-range plans for a permanent headquarters.

Michelle Silver, who had been as-

The SSA Board of Directors at its 50th anniversary directors' meeting in Houston. Top, left to right: Ray A. Young, William Sproull, A. J. Smith, Clifton F. von Kann, Bernald S. Smith, William S. Ivans, James Maupin, Richard N. Hall, Judy Lincoln, Sam A. Francis, Marion I. Barritt, Marion Griffith (seated), E. Gene Hammond, Hal M. Lattimore, Richard E. Schreder, C. Edwin Sessions, Carl D. Herold, A. C. Williams, and Bryan G. Utley. Bottom: W. Woodward, Sterling V. Starr, Floyd J. Sweet, Jon Mead, Donald Knypstra, Paul A. Schweizer, and Ted E. Sharp.

(SSA files)

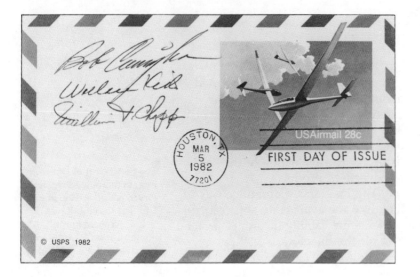

© USPS 1982

The first day of use of the international airmail sailplane postcard was at the SSA 50th Anniversary Convention at Houston.

(NSM Collection)

sistant editor of *Soaring*, was named promotion manager.

The U.S. Soaring Airmail Postcard

There had been three previous unsuccessful attempts to get the U.S. Postal Service to issue a soaring stamp. A new effort was made to get a stamp for the 50th anniversary of the SSA. A Soaring Stamp Proposal Committee was formed: Floyd Sweet was to handle the Washington, D.C., liaison with the U.S. Postal Service, Simine Short of the Elmira Stamp Club the technical details, and Shirley Sliwa of the NSM was to coordinate these efforts. An international airmail postcard was issued at the soaring convention in Houston with an impressive "first day of issue" ceremony on March 5, 1982. At the SSA awards banquet, Simine Short was presented an SSA certificate of appreciation for the important part that she played in getting the soaring postcard.

The NSM has a fine collection of both soaring stamps and first day covers. Maurice Whitney, with the assistance of Dale May and other stamp collectors, assembled a collection of soaring stamps of the world. Simine Short acquired an extensive collection of glider first day covers for the NSM.

The CIVV Meeting

The March 26, 1982, meeting in Paris was attended by Bill Ivans, Bob Buck, and Bernald S. Smith, who had succeeded in getting the committee to change the location of its 1983 spring meeting from Paris to the Reno, Nevada, convention. At the meeting, it was assumed that Argentina would go through with its WSC, and it was decided to hold the WSC for 1985 in Rieti, Italy. Benalla, Australia, was selected for the 20th WSC in 1987.

Clubs in SSA History

Michelle Silver, assistant editor of *Soaring*, who had been writing the "Accent on Clubs" column since August 1979, wrote a comprehensive history of soaring clubs entitled "Clubs in SSA's History." In this piece, she traces the development of clubs through the years and shows how varied they are. She sums up the story:

> Of the 200+ clubs currently operating in the United States, 120 are Chapters of the SSA. Their membership rosters comprise 4,970 SSA members, or just about a third of all SSA members. . . . Nineteen of these Chapters are in California, and New York and Texas have eight each. Illinois, Ohio and Virginia have six Chapters each; Colorado and Pennsylvania five; Massachusetts, Michigan, and New Jersey have four Chapters each.
>
> It has long been this author's opinion that clubs are the backbone of the soaring movement. They bring new pilots into the sport and train them. They generate interest in soaring on a local level and make the sport available to anyone. When one looks at the multitude of activities carried on by clubs throughout the history of the sport, and today in terms of sponsoring local, regional, and national contests, in terms of sponsoring conven-

tions, symposiums, and safety seminars, and in terms of the training support and encouragement for excellence in soaring, it is clear that the development of expansion and health of our sport is due to a great extent to the work of soaring clubs.

The First Anniversary Event

The first event took place on May 11, 1982, exactly 50 years after the formation of the SSA in New York City. This celebration on the brow of Harris Hill dedicated the Memorial Wing Pylon in memory of the soaring pilots who had flown over Harris Hill. As the ceremonies were taking place, a glider mail flight by HHSC member Martin Green, in his 1-26, the *Yellow Canary*, towed by veteran HHSC member Howard Trampenau in a Super-Cub, flew over the pylon and aero-towed to Norwich, New York. There the postmaster and Warren Eaton, Jr., accepted the delivery of the mail.

The Golden Anniversary Edition

The May 1982 issue of *Soaring* magazine was called the golden anniversary edition. Bernald S. Smith had organized an informal meeting during the 1981 convention to discuss the special anniversary issue and to develop a list of soaring people who could contribute to this historical issue. Doug Lamont and his staff put together this special issue while carrying out their normal work. At 116 pages, this turned out to be the largest and most impressive issue of *Soaring* to date and included seven special historic articles by Richard H. Benbough, Howard E. Burr, Lloyd M. Licher, Bertha Ryan, Alcide Santilli, Paul A. Schweizer, and Michelle M. Silver.

The Hall of Fame Weekend

The East Coast safari was to terminate at Harris Hill, the Friday of the Memorial Day weekend, May 28–30, 1982.

The history of soaring is told at the National Soaring Museum. A view of the exhibition hall showing seven of the growing NSM collection of sailplanes.

(Tony Fusare)

The Elmira areas gift to the SSA on its 50th anniversary, a stainless steel sculpture by Ernest Schweizer.

(Daniel Driscoll)

as chairman. At the Hall of Fame banquet, W. Frank Kelsey and Joachim P. Kuettner were inducted into the Hall of Fame and Floyd Sweet was the principal speaker.

Other 50th Anniversary Events

Several anniversary activities occurred at the time of the 15-Meter National Soaring Championships at Harris Hill in July. After the contest awards breakfast, a three-gull stainless steel mobile sculpture by Ernest Schweizer was dedicated by the Community Soaring Committee to the SSA on its 50th anniversary.

A plaque located in the NSM with the name of the founders of the SSA was then dedicated. Following the SSA directors' meeting, the community banquet was held at the Elmira College banquet hall. This event saluted the SSA Founders and SSA's 50th anniversary. The two living founders were present: Capt. Ralph S. Barnaby and Gus Haller. Paul B. MacCready was the principal speaker.

On Saturday morning, the second national soaring landmark was dedicated at the brow of Harris Hill to mark the Rhodes farm, where the SSA conducted its first National Soaring Contest in 1932, and to acknowledge the community support that has kept soaring in the Harris Hill area in the forefront for the past 50 years.

To help celebrate this event, the Elmira Stamp Club had a special cachet made and mail imprinted with this cachet was flown that day from Harris Hill to Hammondsport, "the cradle of aviation," by Juergen Loenholdt in his Grob motorglider.

General Situation on May 11, 1982

The SSA found itself facing a number

However, the weather did not cooperate, so no one made it in by sailplane, although some trailered their sailplanes to Harris Hill. That night the NSM held an open house to mark the opening of the special 50th anniversary exhibit, which included the two most popular sailplanes at the 1932 Nationals, the Franklin and the Baker-McMillen Cadet.

During the balance of the weekend, the Vintage Soaring Association held a regatta at Harris Hill, and the NSM conducted two seminars, one on the early history of American soaring, led by Vic Saudek, and the other on competition flying with Roy McMaster of matters on May 11, 1982, as this history ends. The one of gravest concern was the still declining membership. Steps had to be taken to get the membership growing again.

What the SSA needed was a long-range plan to get it growing again. Sterling Starr of the Development Board was to submit a proposal for "long-range development" to the directors at their forthcoming meeting in Elmira. Michelle Silver had developed a recruitment and promotional plan for 1983 that would also be considered at that meeting.

By this time, Great Britain and Argentina were engaged in their dispute over the Falkland Islands, and the future of the WSC in Argentina in January 1983 was in doubt. John Dezzutti was authorized to determine whether any U.S. sites might be interested in hosting the 1983 International, in case the CIVV reopened the bids.

These items, plus many others, would make the July directors' meeting a busy one.

Chapter 14

The Present and the Future

Where Soaring Is Today and Which Way Should It Go?

Over these 50-plus years of the SSA's history, one factor that stands out most vividly is the enthusiasm and dedication of the many people who have helped gliding and soaring and the SSA grow. Someone has always come forward, ready to pitch in, whenever the need has arisen. Starting from a very modest beginning, soaring in the United States has become one of the leading movements in the soaring world, despite many obstacles and little government help. By 1985, the United States had won five world championships, surpassed only by West Germany, with six, and equaling Great Britain. It has also done well in world records, which, as of November 1983, totaled eight world records, second to West Germany with nine. It was also close to the top in the number of Diamond badges held. Furthermore, the SSA's *Soaring* has been an outstanding publication among flight periodicals throughout the world. In addition, the United States has made many scientific and technical contributions to motorless flight. The SSA is a viable organization and can be proud of what it has accomplished in its first 50 years.

In reliving those years as I wrote this book, it became evident to me that several areas need attention if we are to grow and carry out SSA's purpose of promoting all phases of motorless flight during SSA's second 50 years. I take the liberty here of expressing my own thoughts on possible solutions to some of these problems.

Need for Growth

Soaring during the SSA's first 25 years grew steadily, but only averaged about a gain of 40 members a year. It was difficult to get into soaring in the early years since there were few commercial operators. As a result, almost everyone had to start in a soaring club. However, the typical club at that time had its hands full taking care of its existing members, and often had to limit its membership.

At the start of the second 25-year period, the SSA was put on a more businesslike bases. More commercial operators were starting up around the country, and they made it easier to give soaring a try without having to take out a club membership. Pilot candidates could learn to fly from a CO and could fly his equipment until they joined a club or bought their own sailplane. As more people became involved, publicity increased, and for the next 23 years the SSA grew at an average rate of over 650 members a year, 16 times the rate of the first 25 years.

A sharp reversal of SSA growth

SSA MEMBERSHIP CURVE

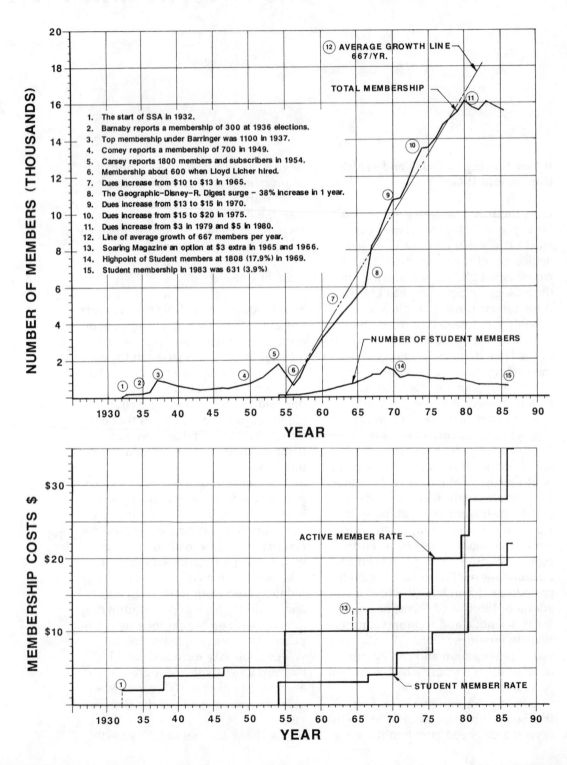

1. The start of SSA in 1932.
2. Barnaby reports a membership of 300 at 1936 elections.
3. Top membership under Barringer was 1100 in 1937.
4. Comey reports a membership of 700 in 1949.
5. Carsey reports 1800 members and subscribers in 1954.
6. Membership about 600 when Lloyd Licher hired.
7. Dues increase from $10 to $13 in 1965.
8. The Geographic–Disney–R. Digest surge – 38% increase in 1 year.
9. Dues increase from $13 to $15 in 1970.
10. Dues increase from $15 to $20 in 1975.
11. Dues increase from $3 in 1979 and $5 in 1980.
12. Line of average growth of 667 members per year.
13. Soaring Magazine an option at $3 extra in 1965 and 1966.
14. Highpoint of Student members at 1808 (17.9%) in 1969.
15. Student membership in 1983 was 631 (3.9%).

occurred in 1980, when the economy worsened and it was necessary to hike membership rates. Thereafter, the SSA stopped growing, and the membership curve still shows no growth at the time that this is being written in 1986. Unfortunately, a number of factors are limiting the growth of soaring: the high cost of sailplanes, tow planes, and flight equipment; the escalating cost of liability insurance; and the increasing air space problems. As a result, the few U.S. sailplane manufacturers have phased out of the business, some COs have closed their doors, and new COs are discouraged from starting. If soaring activity continues to decline, costs will increase further, soaring will soon be limited to the more affluent, and the "little guys," who have traditionally accounted for the majority of SSA memberships, will be discouraged from entering the field.

Some believe that the SSA is in danger of becoming a competition-oriented organization rather than one attuned to all phases of soaring. The real problem is that because of its small size and budget, SSA can only afford to maintain a small staff, which cannot possibly attend to all the many phases of soaring. However, if the SSA could promote all those phases, its growth would surely be renewed and it would be able to support the greater costs involved.

Being a small national organization has its disadvantages. SSA's limited membership is not very impressive when arguing its case for a "place in the sky." If it had double or triple its present membership, the SSA would have more "clout." Consider what the EAA has done. The facts all point to one conclusion: SSA has to grow if it is to carry out its assigned mission.

A related problem is the need to give more attention to soaring enthusiasts who are not active now but want to be kept up to date. They include some past officers, directors, and many others who have contributed much over the years, but who have discontinued their memberships owing to the cost. They are candidates for a lower-priced membership that could be mainly a subscription to *Soaring* magazine. This membership might be priced on the basis of the incremental cost of publishing the extra copies of the magazine required, plus the cost of keeping their names on the SSA computer. Many in this group have done much for soaring and the SSA over the years, and this gesture would be an appropriate expression of thanks.

The Safety Image

The poor safety record of soaring is adversely affecting its growth. Now that the sport has expanded and sailplanes are capable of higher performance, more attention needs to be given to the transition to the more sophisticated sailplanes. In fact, in some cases "the ease and safety" has been oversold.

The safety record has also been affected by the greater emphasis on competitive soaring and racing. Many new pilots are being swept into this phase of soaring before they are ready. They are bypassing the usual training period of several years in moderate performance sailplanes, where they can learn how to fly well while earning their badges without the "crutch" of higher performance. In this way they will have an opportunity to fly in varied conditions and obtain needed experience in off-field landings. Such experiences are required to adequately prepare a pilot for competition in high-performance sailplanes.

There are other areas in which safety can be enhanced—notably, proving the crash resistance and pilot protection of sailplanes, changing the contest rules to minimize "gaggles" and potential midairs, discourage the use of ballast and flying at such high wing loadings, and encourage the use of lighter sailplanes so that soaring can be done during a greater portion of the day and lower kinetic energy landings can be made. The Soaring Safety Foundation has been working to improve the safety and training of glider pilots, without discouraging the newcomers from starting or those who have started from continuing. Better training methods will help to meet the SSF's aims. A three-level system has been suggested: *Level I* would qualify pilots for local flying in training and intermediate sailplanes; *Level II* would qualify pilots for cross-country and badge flying; and *Level III* would qualify pilots for flying in competitions in high-performance sailplanes. Such a plan would enable pilots to work their way up the ladder at their own pace and would allow them to spread the cost over a longer period. This should help to improve safety, and in the long run will also reduce costs and keep more people soaring.

U.S. Sailplanes

U.S. pilots used to have a choice of American-built sailplanes in the 1970s, when four manufacturers were producing high-performance sailplanes and a number of other manufacturers were producing sailplane kits. With the growing economic problems of the early 1980s and the high value of the dollar, the prices of imported sail-

planes became so low that American manufacturers could no longer compete.

Then the dollar began to fall, and a reversal occurred, so that now the prices of imported sailplanes have escalated to where they are very expensive. This would have caused U.S. manufacturers to start up again, except for two factors: the extremely high cost of product liability insurance and the small sailplane market owing to the lack of growth of soaring in the United States. Even if an answer is found to the insurance problem, it is doubtful that any U.S. manufacturer would start up unless soaring begins to grow again. Something is needed to stimulate the market and to appeal to a much broader segment of the public, and to get the costs down so that many more can afford to be involved.

Another way that costs can be reduced is to work toward greater utilization of the existing equipment. The typical Club or CO's equipment is used only a small percentage of the time. By scheduling training and introductory rides before and after the peak soaring activity, and during the week, greater utilization can be made of the equipment, and the costs reduced. This does not give any immediate help to the manufacturers, but will in time as the costs of soaring is reduced and activities grows.

Class Flying and the Iceberg

Peter Bowers compared a properly balanced soaring movement to an iceberg. The base of the iceberg includes introductory rides, training, and local "joy riding," while on the top are the world and national competitions, and record flying with recreational and sport flying in between. As the sport grows, there is little room at the top and the expansion must come in the area between. More class flying is needed to appeal to a broader interest. Before this can happen, the SSA will have to give more "status" to class flying in lower-performance sailplanes. Too often pilots become frustrated at not being able to compete with the "elite" in the top national contests and so drift away. We also often lost those who have moved too quickly into high-performance sailplanes and gotten in "over their heads." If the SSA is to achieve an adequate growth rate, it must expand class flying so that there is a place for every pilot and sailplane, since there is little room at the top!

An important step in this direction was the creation of the Sports Class. With the growing number of sailplanes that are no longer competitive in their original class, efforts are being made to get their owners to fly them in the Sports Class, where sailplanes are handicapped in order to level their performance in contests. In the United States the "CH" factor has proven to be quite fair. Interest in the Sports Class is increasing as more Sports Class regional and national meets are being held and pilots see the fun of competing in handicapped sailplanes.

One-Design Sailplanes

The present international and national contests have become a designer's and manufacturer's contest, since having a top sailplane is an important part of winning. The steady improvements in sailplane performance push up prices and make sailplanes more sophisticated; that limits the number of pilots who can afford to compete.

If this trend continues, soaring will reach the point that sailing did at the turn of the century, when only the wealthy could afford the large sailing yachts that were necessary to be competitive. The one-design sailboat concept was developed to correct this and provided sailing competition at many levels of cost and sophistication. Today, most sailing is done in one-design class sailboats.

It is most unfortunate that World War II prevented the trial of one-design sailplane competition in the 1940 Olympics. The basic concept of having all pilots flying the same type of sailplane is the ultimate in fair competition, and a valid reason why one-design classes should be considered for international competition. Although soaring was accepted for the 1940 Olympics, it was not pushed after the war. The soaring world seemed to feel that the FAI world soaring championships provided ample opportunity for international competition, and there was concern about the "professional pilot" problem and the greater possibility of international politics becoming involved.

As this chapter is being written, the International Olympic Committee announced that, soaring could be one of the Olympic air sports. This would give soaring and the SSA new opportunities for more exposure and growth and perhaps provide an affordable type of sailplane that would encourage more people around the world to become active in soaring.

If soaring is to expand in the United States, there should be a number of one-design classes at different levels of cost, performance, and demand upon the pilot and crew. The 1-26 has shown how successful one-design competition can be in the low-cost, sailplane. Even though it has been around for over 30 years and is at the low limit of performance, its popularity continues. New classes can provide the opportunity to use other types of competition rules to broaden the appeal of soaring.

Affiliates and Divisions

SSA's growth can be boosted by promoting the formation of more affiliates and divisions (A&Ds). In the past, the SSA has done very little of this type of promotion, except for supporting sailplane homebuilders, and encouraging them to form the Sailplane Homebuilders Association (SHA). The SSA needs to assist other potential affiliates and divisions and make available a series of services, at cost, to such groups to encourage them to form and to simplify their operations. These services could include such things as maintaining memberships lists, handling the production and distribution of newsletters, and even doing the membership billing and collecting for these groups. Such services should help existing groups to keep operating and encourage new ones to form. There are a good number of potential affiliates and divisions among business members, college soaring clubs, commercial operators, competition pilots, disabled soaring pilots, motorgliding, national soaring centers, other one-design groups, RC sailplane modelers, Sailplane ACRO Association, scientific and technical groups, youth groups, and the Women Soaring Pilots Association.

A Place to Fly

Places to fly are becoming an increasing problem. There is already a shortage in some areas, and some sites are under pressure from urban and suburban expansion. The expanding air space regulations provide the greatest

threat and there is a growing objection to the tow plane noise. As a result, there is need to assist clubs, commercial operators, and other groups to hold on to their sites and to help any new clubs or COs to get a place to fly. It is often difficult to convince an airport operator, or the neighbors around a proposed site, to agree to a soaring operation. This is even more of a problem when the government or a community is involved, particularly when an individual or small group is making the request. If the SSA, or a nonprofit affiliated national organization, was available to help them, they would have a much better chance of succeeding. In the case of government surplus or standby airports, and national parkland, such help would be a necessity.

Promotion and Advertising

In general the SSA has been an inwardly directed organization, talking mostly to itself instead of to the outside world. There have been few ongoing promotion programs, as evidenced by the three promotion managers who have come and gone over an eight-year period. The past growth has been due mainly to three factors: (1) favorable publicity from newspapers and magazine articles, films, and TV ads; (2) the commercial operators' public relations efforts in advertising and promotion, and the resulting introductory flights; and (3) word of mouth. Several times the COs have had a cooperative advertising program with the SSA, but too much was expected of a one-shot program. A few years ago a CO proposal for another cooperative program was turned down because the available funds were needed for a training manual.

It is felt that a large factor in the steady growth of soaring in the 1960s and 1970s was the cooperative national SAC-dealer advertising and promotion program that evolved during that period. SAC and its dealers spent close to $500,000 in that program, and it generated thousands of inquiries, which in some years totaled 10,000 or more. As the economy slowed down in the early 1980s and soaring began to stagnate, the program was phased out.

Soaring pilots owe a debt of gratitude to the commercial operators, who, in the main, are a dedicated group and work hard to provide a place to fly as well as soaring services. It is a risky business venture, but most COs are in it because they love soaring. Good growth would help many to become successful businesses something most COs deserve.

The SSA will have a difficult time to meet its growth goals unless it reaches out and becomes more visible and carries out an aggressive national advertising program. More effort should be made to encourage the media to give motorless flight greater coverage.

SSA and the Youth

One of the SSA's goals was to establish a national youth glider program, and a number of attempts were made to launch such a program. It is disappointing that none of these became a continuing program, although some gliding is still done by the CAP and Boy Scouts, and in some clubs.

European countries continue to sponsor youth glider programs in order to develop pilots for military, airline, and commercial roles and to prepare young people for living in a world where aviation will play a steadily increasing part. Canada has a very successful glider program known as the Air Cadet League of Canada, which exposes thousands of cadets to gliding. Approximately 400 go to solo status each year. Multiply this by 10 (the U.S.-Canadian population ratio) and you can see the potential of such a program in the United States. Beside motivating young people to consider a flying career and using this program as a screening process, a glider course is a character-building experience, and an opportunity to find out whether or not flying is for them. It is still a worthwhile service for young people, even though many may not choose to continue flying.

An active national youth program should also help to increase SSA membership. SSA would be doing a worthwhile service for young people, which would help to justify FAA support as well as give additional justification for its nonprofit status.

The present SSA youth program consists of a partial subsidization of the student membership, and the administration of the Kolstad Award. Since 1969 there has been a drastic reduction in the number of student members, from a high of 18 percent in 1969 (1,808) to a low of 2.3 percent (504) at the end of 1984. One reason for this marked change has no doubt been the 450 percent increase in the cost of the student membership in SSA, which rose from $4 in 1969 to $18 in 1980. Another factor was the lack of any organized effort to attract young people to soaring. Before 1969 there was much favorable publicity about young people in soaring, such as the TV show "The Boy and the Condors" and the national CAP program.

When the student membership was established, the dues were determined by using the incremental cost of the additional *Soaring* magazine that had to be printed. As student membership rates increased over the next 15 years, from 23 percent to 64 percent of the cost of a full membership, they have been bearing an increased portion of a full membership.

If after 1969 the student membership had grown at the same rate as the total membership, the SSA would have had a total of almost 3,000 student members by 1980. Something must be done to make student membership more appealing. They need to feel part of an organization by having an attractive name, insignia, or other special identification that can be used on jackets or caps. This would help them to feel that they belong.

Perhaps we ought to go back to the incremental way of pricing the student membership, plus the other costs of servicing this type of membership. In addition, we should consider creating a student group membership, wherein four or more students could form a group that would receive only one copy of *Soaring*, although each would receive the other benefits of the student memberships. In this way, the cost of membership could be brought way down without further costs to the SSA.

The SSA took a step ahead in encouraging young people when it took over the Kolstad Award. It now needs to expand its efforts to increase the endowment so that a greater number of scholarships can be given and the dollar amount of each increased. It also needs to increase the visibility of the award through publicity and promotion. Outside help from foundations and groups that support youth programs should be investigated. With the approach of another pilot shortage, a training program like the pre–World War II CPTP is needed. The success of the Air Force Academy Glider Program

should give added support for such a program.

Clubs, Chapters, and Regional Organizations

Chapters are the backbone of the SSA, since they agree that all their members should maintain some type of SSA membership. For those that require all their members to maintain voting membership in SSA, a rebate is given the chapter. Those clubs that are not chapters are urged to join. New clubs are encouraged to form and are urged to become a chapter. The SSA has few additional perks to offer the club except for the chapter rebate.

Getting new clubs to form is easier in areas having regional organizations (RO). The ROs usually coordinate activity in their area and can be a source of help to the new club. The contests, special meetings, and other activities that they sponsor can stimulate interest in new clubs. An increased number of regional organizations around the United States along with a growing number of clubs would be a positive factor in any growth program.

Conclusion

Some time ago the SSA directors recognized the need for a long-range plan of expansion for the SSA. In August of 1983, it announced such a plan. Of the five areas in which it would concentrate at the start, the two given top priority were *membership growth* and *safety and training*, with *self-regulation and certification, air space preservation, and airport retention* following in that order. As the plan proceeds, other areas will be addressed.

The growth plan includes a goal of 10 percent per year, which is about double the growth rate of the period from 1966 to 1980.

Unfortunately, growth has stagnated since 1980. It can be argued that this is similar to what private power flying has experienced. The reasons are generally the same: high costs, greater complexity of flying in today's airspace, safety concerns, and the competition from the many other activities that attract people looking for something interesting and exciting to do outdoors.

Soaring does have a number of unique features that can attract those who fly, or who would like to fly. If these features are aggressively pushed, and some of the other growth factors that I have mentioned are considered, soaring and the SSA could experience good growth during its second 50 years.

List of Abbreviations

AAA	All American Aviation
A & D	Affiliates and Divisions
AFB	Air Force Base
A E S MIT	Aeronautical Engineering Society of MIT
AIAA	American Institute of Aeronautics and Astronautics
AMAC	American Motorless Aviation Corp.
AMS	American Meterology Society
AOPA	Aircraft Owners and Pilots Association
ARSA	Airport Radar Service Area
ASA	American Soaring Association
ASH	*American Soaring Handbook*
ATC	Approved Type Certificate
AYA	Air Youth of America
BGA	British Gliding Association
BM	Business Member
CAA	Civil Aeronautics Authority
CAP	Civil Air Patrol
CAR	Civil Air Regulations
CAT	Clear Air Turbulence
CFI	Chief Flight Instructor
CIVL	FAI Hang Glider Division
CIVV	FAI Soaring Division (after CVSM)
CO	Commercial Operator
COBM	Commercial Operator Business Member
CPTP	Civil Pilot Training Program
CTGC	Carnegie Tech Glider Club
CSA	Collegiate Soaring Association
CVSM	FAI Soaring Division (before CIVV)
EAA	Experimental Aircraft Association
EAC	Elmira Association of Commerce
EASC	Elmira Area Soaring Corporation
EGCA	Evans Glider Club of America
EMGAM	Every Member Get a Member
FAA	Federal Aviation Administration
FAC	Federal Aviation Commission
FAI	Federal Aeronautique International
FAR	Federal Aviation Regulations
FRP	Fiberglass-Reinforced Plastic
FSS	Flight Service Station
GCH	Glider Criteria Handbook
HHSC	Harris Hill Soaring Corporation
HG	Hang Gliding
IAS	Institute of Aeronautical Sciences
ISTUS	International Study Society for Soaring Flight

JAR	Joint Air Regulations	PGC	Philadelphia Glider Council
LFS	German FAA	RAF	Royal Air Force
LK	Laister Kauffman	RO	Regional Organization
LRPC	Long-Range Planning Committee	RC	Radio Control
MGC	Mercury Glider Club	SAC	Schweizer Aircraft Corporation
MIT	Massachusetts Institute of Technology	SCSA	Southern California Soaring Association
MMAC	Mercury Model Airplane Club	SHA	Sailplane Homebuilders Association
MPA	Man-Powered Aircraft	SLS	Self-Launching Sailplane
NAA	National Aeronautics Association	SSA	Soaring Society of America, Inc.
NACA	National Advisory Committee for Aeronautics	SSS	Schweizer Soaring School
		SSF	Soaring Safety Foundation
NASA	National Air and Space Administration	STD-CL	Standard Class
		STEG	Southern Tier Economic Growth
NASM	National Air and Space Museum	STOL	Slow Takeoff and Landing
NGA	National Glider Association	TSA	Texas Soaring Association
NPRM	Notice of Proposed Rule Making	TRSA	Terminal Radar Service Area
NSC	National Soaring Contest		
NSF	National Soaring Foundation	ULT	Ultralight Sailplane
NSM	National Soaring Museum	USAF	United States Air Force
NYU	New York University	UCLA	University of California at Los Angeles
ONR	Office of Naval Research		
OSTIV	International Scientific and Technical Organization	VSA	Vintage Soaring Association
		WSC	World Soaring Championships

Yearly Fact Sheets

Soaring Year 1932

Event of the Year: Organization of the SSA.

Edward S. Evans Trophy for National Champion: J. K. O'Meara.

Officers: W. E. Eaton, President; A. C. Haller, Vice-president; A. L. Lawrence, secretary; A. L. Lawrence, treasurer.

Directors: R. S. Barnaby, E. W. Cleveland, W. E. Eaton, W. Enyart, R. E. Franklin, C. Gale, A. C. Haller, A. Hastings, R. Holderman, F. K. Iszard, W. Klemperer, A. L. Lawrence, E. Southee, S. P. Voorhees, E. P. Warner.

Soaring Year 1933

Event of the Year: SSA joins ISTUS.

Edward S. Evans Trophy: S. W. Smith.

Officers: W. E. Eaton, President; W. Klemperer, vice-president; R. C. du Pont, vice-president; A. L. Lawrence, secretary; A. L. Lawrence, treasurer.

Directors: R. S. Barnaby, H. W. Bowlus, R. C. du Pont, W. E. Eaton, W. Enyart, R. E. Franklin, C. Gale, A. C. Haller, F. K. Iszard, W. Klemperer, K. O. Lange, A. L. Lawrence, M. Schempp, E. Southee, E. P. Warner.

Soaring Year 1934

Event of the Year: R. C. du Pont set world distance record.

Edward S. Evans Trophy: R. C. du Pont.

Officers: W. E. Eaton, president; R. C. du Pont, vice-president; W. Klemperer, vice-president; A. L. Lawrence, secretary; A. L. Lawrence, treasurer.

Directors: All the same as 1933.

Soaring Year 1935

Event of the Year: Navy Glider Program at Pensacola.

Edward S. Evans Trophy: R. C. du Pont.

Officers: R. S. Barnaby, president; R. C. du Pont, vice-president; W. Klemperer, vice-president; L. B. Barringer, secretary; L. B. Barringer, secretary (E. Southee replaced Barringer as secretary-treasurer in July).

Directors: R. S. Barnaby, L. B. Barringer, W. H. Bowlus, R. C. du Pont, W. Enyart, R. E. Franklin, C. Gale, A. C. Haller, D. Hamilton, F. K. Iszard, W. Klemperer, K. O. Lange, A. L. Lawrence, W. McGrath, M. Schempp, A. B. Schultz, E. Southee, E. P. Warner; and C. B. Milliken, director-at-large.

Soaring Year 1936

Events of the Year: du Pont heads Executive Committee.

Edward S. Evans Trophy: C. Decker.

Officers: R. S. Barnaby, president; E. Southee, vice-president; K. O. Lange, vice-president; D. Hamilton, secretary; R. C. du Pont, treasurer.

Directors: R. S. Barnaby, W. H. Bowlus, R. C. du Pont, Mrs. W. E. Eaton, W. Enyart, R. E. Franklin, C. Gale, A. C. Haller, D. Hamilton, F. K. Iszard, W. Klemperer, K. O. Lange, A. L. Lawrence, W. McGrath, Y. Sekella, S. W. Smith, E. Southee, E. P. Warner; and J. K. O'Meara, director-at-large.

Soaring Year 1937

Event of the Year: First issue of *Soaring* magazine appears.

Edward S. Evans Trophy: R. C. du Pont.

Officers: R. C. du Pont, president; R. S. Barnaby, vice-president; W. Klemperer, vice-president; A. L. Lawrence, secretary; P. Pierce, treasurer; Dr. K. O. Lange, chairman of Contest Board.

Directors: R. S. Barnaby, W. H. Bowlus, J. Buxton, Mrs. W. E. Eaton, W. Enyart, R. E. Franklin, D. Hamilton, C. Gale, Dr. K. O. Lange, A. L. Lawrence, Dr. W. Klemperer, P. Pierce, G. Scheurer, Y. Sekella, S. Smith, E. Southee, H. Wightman; and L. Barringer and A. Schultz, directors-at-large.

Soaring Year 1938

Events of the Year: First National Gliding and Soaring Convention.

Edward S. Evans Trophy: E. Lehecka.

Officers: R. C. du Pont, president; C. Gale, vice-president; W. Klemperer, vice-president; A. L. Lawrence, secretary; Mrs. W. E. Eaton, treasurer; and K. O. Lange, chairman of the Contest Board.

Directors: R. S. Barnaby, J. Buxton, W. H. Bowlus, C. Decker, R. C. du Pont, Mrs. W. E. Eaton, W. Enyart, R. E. Franklin, J. Funk, C. Gale, W. Klemperer, K. O. Lange, A. L. Lawrence, G. Scheurer, A. Schultz, Y. Sekella, E. Southee, M. Stoughton; and W. McGrath and E. A. Lehecka, directors-at-large.

Soaring Year 1939

Event of the Year: Change in executive secretary from Barringer to Wightman.

Edward S. Evans Trophy: C. Decker.

Warren E. Eaton Memorial Trophy: R. C. du Pont.

Officers: R. C. du Pont, president; C. Gale, vice-president; W. Klemperer, vice-president; A. L. Lawrence, secretary; Mrs. W. E. Eaton, treasurer; and A. L. Lawrence, chairman of the Contest Board.

Directors: R. S. Barnaby, J. Buxton, C. Decker, R. C. du Pont, Mrs. W. E. Eaton, W. Enyart, R. E. Franklin, J. Funk, C. Gale, W. Klemperer, K. O. Lange, A. L. Lawrence, E. A. Lehecka, W. McGrath, A. Schultz, E. Southee, M. Stoughton.

Soaring Year 1940

Event of Year: Pre-World War II buildup of soaring.

E. S. Evans Trophy: J. Robinson.

W. E. Eaton Memorial Trophy: R. M. Stanley.

Officers: E. Southee (4), R. Stanley (1), R. S. Barnaby (7), president; J. S. Charles, vice-president; R. Stanley, vice-president; F. J. Sweet, secretary; C. Decker, treasurer.

Directors: R. S. Barnaby, J. Buxton, S. Corcoran, C. Decker, R. C. du Pont, W. Enyart, F. Funk, R. E. Franklin, C. Gale, A. L. Lawrence, E. A. Lehecka, G. Lewis, W. McGrath, A. Schultz, E. Southee, R. S. Stanley, M. Stoughton, F. J. Sweet; and L. Barringer and W. Klemperer, directors-at-large.

Soaring Year 1941

Event of the Year: U.S. Military Glider Program starts.

E. S. Evans Trophy: John Robinson.

W. E. Eaton Memorial Trophy: F. J. Sweet.

Officers: P. Leonard, president; D. Hamilton, vice-president; J. Buxton, vice-president; P. Leonard, secretary; A. Schultz, treasurer.

Directors: R. S. Barnaby, J. Buxton, J. S. Charles, S. Corcoran, C. Decker, R. C. du Pont, W. Enyart, R. E. Franklin, C. Gale, W. Klemperer, E. A. Lehecka, P. Leonard, W. McGrath, H. Montgomery, J. Robinson, A. Schultz, R. Stanley, F. J. Sweet; and D. Hamilton and J. Stienhauser, directors-at-large.

Soaring Year 1942 –1945

Event of the Year: Gliders in World War II.

E. S. Evans Trophy: No awards.

W. E. Eaton Memorial Trophy: B. Shupack for 1945.

Officers: P. Leonard, president; D. Hamilton, vice-president; J. Buxton, vice-president; B. Shupack, secretary; A. Schultz, treasurer.

Directors: R. S. Barnaby, L. Barringer, J. S. Charles, S. Corcoran, C. Decker, R. E. Franklin, C. Gale, W. Klemperer, E. A. Lehecka, P. Leonard, H. Montgomery, J. Robinson, V. Saudek, A. Schultz, B. Shupack, R. Stanley, F. J. Sweet; and D. Hamilton and J. Stienhauser, directors-at-large.

Soaring Year 1946

Event of the Year: Soaring became active again.

E. S. Evans Trophy: John Robinson.

W. E. Eaton Memorial Trophy: B. L.
   Wiggin.

Officers: R. S. Barnaby, president;
   B. Shupack, vice-president;
   W. Klemperer, vice-president;
   C. Gale, secretary; E. A. Lehecka,
   treasurer.

Directors: R. S. Barnaby, G. Briegleb,
   S. Corcoran, J. S. Charles,
   A. Dawydoff, C. Gale,
   W. Hammond, P. Leonard, E. A. Le-
   hecka, W. Klemperer, A. Raspet,
   J. Robinson, A. Schultz,
   E. Schweizer, P. A. Schweizer,
   B. Shupack, S. Smith, F. J. Sweet;
   and T. Boyer and J. W. Laister,
   directors-at-large.

Soaring Year 1947   *Event of the Year:* First National in the
   West.

R. C. du Pont Memorial Trophy: R. J.
   Comey.

W. E. Eaton Memorial Trophy: P.
   Tuntland.

Officers: E. Reeves, president; R. Blaine,
   vice-president; R. Stanley, vice-president; P. Schweizer, secretary; J. S.
   Charles, treasurer.

Directors: R. S. Barnaby, T. Boyer,
   G. Briegleb, S. Corcoran, J. S.
   Charles, A. Dawydoff, F. Compton,
   P. Leonard, W. Klemperer,
   A. Raspet, E. J. Reeves, J. Robinson,
   A. Schultz, E. Schweizer, P. A.
   Schweizer, B. Shupack, F. J. Sweet,
   P. Tuntland; and R. Blaine and
   R. Parker, directors-at-large.

Soaring Year 1948   *Events of the Year:* MacCready wins National Championship.

*Warren E. Eaton Memorial Tro-
   phy:* Francis B. Compton.

R. C. du Pont Memorial Trophy: Paul B.
   MacCready, Jr.

Lewin B. Barringer Memorial Trophy: Don
   Pollard.

Officers: E. J. Reeves, president;
   R. Blaine, vice-president; R. Stanley,
   vice-president, P. A. Schweizer, secretary; J. S. Charles, treasurer.

Directors: R. S. Barnaby, T. Boyer,
   G. Briegleb, J. S. Charles, F. B.
   Compton, W. Coverdale,
   A. Dawydoff, P. Leonard,

W. Klemperer, A. Raspet, E. J.
   Reeves, J. Robinson, A. Schultz,
   P. A. Schweizer, B. Shupack,
   R. Stanley, F. J. Sweet, P. Tuntland;
   and J. Spurgeon and R. Parker, direc-
   tors-at-large.

Soaring Year 1949   *Events of the Year:* FAI General Confer-
   ences in Cleveland.

W. E. Eaton Memorial Trophy: Harland
   Ross & Robert F. Symons.

R. C. du Pont Memorial Trophy: Paul B.
   MacCready, Jr.

Officers: E. J. Reeves, president; F. B.
   Compton, vice-president;
   W. Klemperer, vice-president; P. A.
   Schweizer, secretary; J. S. Charles,
   treasurer.

Directors: R. S. Barnaby, T. Boyer,
   G. Briegleb, J. S. Charles, R. Comey,
   W. Coverdale, F. B. Compton,
   A. Dawydoff, W. Klemperer,
   E. Knight, A. Raspet, J. Robinson,
   P. A. Schweizer, B. Shupack,
   R. Stanley, F. J. Sweet, P. Tuntland;
   and T. Nelson and H. Carson, direc-
   tors-at-large.

Soaring Year 1950   *Event of the Year:* W. S. Ivans sets two
   world altitude records.

W. E. Eaton Memorial Trophy: Paul B.
   MacCready, Jr.

*R. C. du Pont Memorial Tro-
   phy:* Richard H. Johnson.

Lilienthal Medal: William S. Ivans.

Officers: E. J. Reeves, president; R. S.
   Barnaby, vice-president;
   W. Klemperer, vice-president; P. A.
   Schweizer, secretary; J. S. Charles,
   treasurer.

Directors: R. S. Barnaby, W. F. Briegleb,
   J. Carsey, H. Carson, J. S. Charles,
   R. Comey, F. B. Compton,
   W. Coverdale, A. Dawydoff,
   W. Klemperer, A. Raspet, E. J.
   Reeves, J. Robinson, E. Knight, P. A.
   Schweizer, B. Shupack, R. Stanley,
   F. J. Sweet; and T. Nelson and
   E. Yerian, directors-at-large.

Soaring Year 1951   *Event of the Year:* Johnson breaks the
   world distance record.

W. E. Eaton Memorial Trophy: William S.
   Ivans.

R. C. du Pont Memorial Trophy: Richard H. Johnson.

Lewin B. Barringer Memorial Trophy: William C. Beuby.

Officers: J. Carsey, president; R. S. Barnaby, vice-president; W. Klemperer, vice-president; P. A. Schweizer, secretary; B. Shupack, treasurer.

Directors: R. S. Barnaby, J. Carsey, H. Carson, J. S. Charles, R. Comey, W. Coverdale, A. Dawydoff, W. S. Ivans, W. Klemperer, T. Nelson, A. Raspet, E. J. Reeves, J. Robinson, H. Ross, P. A. Schweizer, B. Shupack, F. J. Sweet, E. Yerian; and P. Mulloy and F. B. Compton, directors-at-large.

Soaring Year 1952 *Event of the Year:* The United States sends a full team to World Soaring Championships in Spain.

W. E. Eaton Memorial Trophy: Jon D. Carsey.

R. C. du Pont Memorial Trophy: Richard H. Johnson.

L. B. Barringer Memorial Trophy: Paul F. Bikle.

Paul E. Tuntland Memorial Award: Dr. August Raspet.

Officers: J. Carsey, president; R. S. Barnaby, vice-president; T. Nelson, vice-president; P. A. Schweizer, secretary; B. Shupack, treasurer.

Directors: R. S. Barnaby, W. G. Briegleb, J. Carsey, H. Carson, J. S. Charles, F. B. Compton, W. Coverdale, A. Dawydoff, W. S. Ivans, W. Klemperer, A. Raspet, E. J. Reeves, J. Robinson, H. Ross, P. A. Schweizer, B. Shupack, F. J. Sweet, E. Yerian; and H. Entz, P. Mulloy, G. Stillwagon, and J. Simmons, directors-at-large.

Soaring Year 1953 *Event of the Year:* Three sailplanes fly to Idlewild Airport, New York, during National at Harris Hill.

W. E. Eaton Memorial Trophy: Ernest and Paul A. Schweizer.

R. C. du Pont Memorial Trophy: Paul B. MacCready, Jr.

L. B. Barringer Memorial Trophy: Paul F. Bikle.

P. E. Tuntland Memorial Award: Dr. Joachim Kuettner.

Officers: J. Carsey, president; R. S. Barnaby, vice-president; T. Nelson, vice-president; P. A. Schweizer, secretary; E. J. Reeves, treasurer.

Directors: R. S. Barnaby, W. G. Briegleb, H. Burr, J. Carsey, F. B. Compton, W. Coverdale, L. Gehrlein, W. S. Ivans, K. Klemperer, P. B. MacCready, Sr., A. Raspet, E. J. Reeves, H. Ross, P. A. Schweizer, B. Shupack, F. J. Sweet, E. Yerian; and H. Entz, P. Mulloy, L. Dagget, and J. S. Charles, directors-at-large.

Soaring Year 1954 *Event of the Year:* Soaring Hall of Fame established.

W. E. Eaton Memorial Trophy: Ted Nelson.

R. C. du Pont Memorial Trophy: Richard H. Johnson.

L. B. Barringer Memorial Trophy: Paul F. Bikle.

Paul Tissandier Diploma: Ralph S. Barnaby.

P. E. Tuntland Memorial Award: Harold E. Klieforth.

Hall of Fame: W. Hawley Bowlus, Richard C. du Pont, Warren E. Eaton, Wolfgang Klemperer, Paul B. MacCready, Jr., John Robinson.

Officers: F. J. Sweet, president; R. S. Barnaby, vice-president; T. Nelson, vice-president; P. A. Schweizer, secretary; E. J. Reeves, treasurer.

Directors: R. S. Barnaby, P. F. Bikle, W. G. Briegleb, H. Burr, J. Carsey, F. B. Compton, W. Coverdale, L. Gehrlein, W. S. Ivans, W. Klemperer, P. B. MacCready, Sr., P. B. MacCready, Jr., T. Nelson, A. Raspet, E. J. Reeves, P. A. Schweizer, B. Shupack, F. J. Sweet, and P. Bowers, P. Mulloy, A. Schultz; and R. Symons, directors-at-large.

Soaring Year 1955 *Event of the Year:* The Jet-Stream Project.

W. E. Eaton Memorial Trophy: Earl R. Southee.

R. C. du Pont Memorial Trophy: Kempes Trager.

L. B. Barringer Memorial Trophy: Paul F. Bikle.

P. E. Tuntland Memorial Award: Joachim Kuettner.

The Larissa Stroukoff Memorial Trophy: Stephen J. Bennis.

Hall of Fame: R. S. Barnaby, L. Barringer, E. and P. Schweizer, P. E. Tuntland, W. and O. Wright.

Officers: F. J. Sweet, president; R. S. Barnaby, vice-president; T. Nelson, vice president; P. A. Schweizer, secretary; E. J. Reeves, treasurer.

Directors: R. S. Barnaby, P. F. Bikle, H. Burr, W. Coverdale, L. Gehrlein, W. S. Ivans, R. H. Johnson, W. Klemperer, P. B. MacCready, Sr., P. B. MacCready, Jr., T. Nelson, A. Raspet, E. J. Reeves, E. and P. Schweizer, S. Smith, F. J. Sweet; and L. Bryan, W. Eaton, Jr., W. Emuart, and B. Shupack, directors-at-large.

Soaring Year 1956

Event of the Year: P. B. MacCready, Jr. wins World Soaring Championship.

Lilienthal Medal: Paul B. MacCready, Jr.

W. E. Eaton Memorial Trophy: R. E. Franklin.

R. C. du Pont Memorial Trophy: Lyle A. Maxey.

L. B. Barringer Memorial Trophy: Paul F. Bikle.

P. E. Tuntland Memorial Award: Paul B. MacCready, Jr.

The Larissa Stroukoff Memorial Trophy: Lyle A. Maxey.

Hall of Fame: J. Buxton, R. H. Johnson, J. K. O'Meara, A. Raspet.

Officers: (July 1956-June 1957): F. J. Sweet, president; B. F. Bikle, vice-president; S. Smith, vice-president; P. A. Schweizer, secretary; E. J. Reeves, treasurer.

Directors: R. S. Barnaby, H. Burr, J. Carsey, P. F. Bikle, W. G. Briegleb, W. Coverdale, L. Gehrlein, W. S. Ivans, W. Klemperer, R. S. Johnson, P. B. MacCready, Jr., T. Nelson, A. Raspet, E. and P. Schweizer, S. Smith, F. J. Sweet, K. Trager; and J. Randall, W. Fuchs, E. Knight, J. Robertson, and H. Selvidge, directors-at-large.

Soaring Year 1957

Event of the Year: SSA hired an Executive Secretary.

W. E. Eaton Memorial Trophy: Anne and Gus Briegleb.

R. C. du Pont Memorial Trophy: Stanley W. Smith.

L. B. Barringer Memorial Trophy: Sterling Starr.

The Larissa Stroukoff Memorial Trophy: Paul A. Schweizer.

P. E. Tuntland Memorial Award: Stanley W. Smith.

Hall of Fame: A. B. Schultz, S. W. Smith, R. E. Franklin.

Officers: (July 1957-December 1957): P. A. Schweizer, president; W. S. Ivans, vice-president; S. W. Smith, vice-president; W. Fuchs, secretary; H. Selvidge, treasurer.

Directors: R. S. Barnaby, H. Burr, J. Carsey, P. F. Bikle, W. G. Briegleb, W. Coverdale, L. Gehrlein, W. S. Ivans, W. Klemperer, R. S. Johnson, P. B. MacCready, Jr., T. Nelson, A. Raspet, E. and P. Schweizer, S. Smith, F. J. Sweet, K. Trager; and F. B. Compton, W. Fuchs, J. Nowak, J. Robertson, and H. Selvidge, directors-at-large.

Soaring Year 1958

Event of the Year: First regional directors take office.

W. E. Eaton Memorial Trophy: No award.

R. C. du Pont Memorial Trophy: Richard E. Schreder.

L. B. Barringer Memorial Trophy: Julien J. Audette.

Paul Tissandier Diploma: P. A. Schweizer.

The Larissa Stroukoff Memorial Trophy: Richard E. Schreder.

P. E. Tuntland Memorial Award: No award.

Hall of Fame: W. F. Briegleb, R. F. Symons.

Officers: P. A. Schweizer, president; W. S. Ivans, vice-president; S. W. Smith, vice-president; W. Fuchs, secretary; H. Selvidge, treasurer.

Directors: J. Anthony, S. J. Bennis, P. Bikle, W. G. Briegleb, H. Burr, J. Carsey, W. Coverdale, K. Flaglor,

L. Gehrlein, W. S. Ivans, R. H. Johnson, J. Lincoln, T. Mahony, R. Moore, T. Nelson, P. B. Mac-Cready, Jr., P. A. Schweizer, R. B. Smith, F. J. Sweet, K. Trager; and F. B. Compton, W. Fuchs, J. Nowak, J. M. Robertson, and H. Selvidge, directors-at-large.

Soaring Year 1959

Event of the Year: Bylaw change establishes chapter rebate.

W. E. Eaton Memorial Trophy: Erwin J. Reeves.

Lilienthal Medal: Richard E. Schreder.

R. C. du Pont Memorial Trophy: Richard H. Johnson.

L. B. Barringer Memorial Trophy: Harland Ross.

P. E. Tuntland Memorial Award: Dewey J. Mancusco.

The Larissa Stroukoff Memorial Trophy: Richard E. Schreder.

Hall of Fame: Harland C. Ross.

Officers: H. Selvidge, president; P. A. Schweizer, vice-president; J. Lincoln, vice-president; J. Robertson, secretary; T. E. Sharp, treasurer.

Directors: J. Anthony, S. J. Bennis, P. F. Bikle, W. G. Briegleb, B. Cohen, F. B. Compton, W. Coverdale, K. Flaglor, W. S. Ivans, R. H. Johnson, J. Lincoln, T. Mahoney, R. Moore, T. Nelson, J. Nowak, P. B. MacCready, Jr., H. Ross, P. A. Schweizer, E. Seymour, R. B. Smith; W. R. Fuchs, J. M. Robertson, H. Selvidge, T. E. Sharp, and F. J. Sweet, directors-at-large; and R. S. Barnaby and Wolfgang Klemperer, honorary directors.

Soaring Year 1960

Event of the Year: Dick Schreder lands in East Germany.

W. E. Eaton Memorial Trophy: Capt. Ralph S. Barnaby.

R. C. du Pont Memorial Trophy: Richard E. Schreder.

L. B. Barringer Memorial Trophy: Joseph C. Lincoln.

P. E. Tuntland Memorial Award: Harland C. Ross.

The Larissa Stroukoff Memorial Trophy: Richard E. Schreder.

Hall of Fame: Paul F. Bikle, J. Shelly Charles.

Officers: H. Selvidge, president; P. A. Schweizer, vice-president; J. C. Lincoln, vice-president; J. M. Robertson, secretary; B. M. Ryan, treasurer; Capt. R. S. Barnaby, and Dr. Wolfgang B. Klemperer, honorary vice-president; L. Licher, executive secretary; D. Matlin, general counsel.

Directors: J. Anthony, L. B. Bachtell, S. J. Bennis, P. F. Bikle, W. G. Briegleb, B. Cohen, F. B. Compton, W. Coverdale, Jr., K. E. Flaglor, C. F. Henderson, W. S. Ivans, R. H. Johnson, J. C. Lincoln, R. L. Moore, J. Nowak, H. C. Ross, E. D. Seymour, R. B. Smith, S. V. Starr; and J. M. Robertson, B. M. Ryan, P. A. Schweizer, H. Selvidge, and F. J. Sweet, directors-at-large.

Soaring Year 1961

Event of the Year: Paul Bikle sets two world altitude records.

W. E. Eaton Memorial Trophy: Dr. Harner Selvidge.

R. C. du Pont Memorial Trophy: A. J. Smith.

L. B. Barringer Memorial Trophy: J. D. Ryan.

P. E. Tuntland Memorial Award: No award.

Paul Tissandier Diploma: Ernest Schweizer.

The Larisssa Stroukoff Memorial Trophy: Richard E. Schreder.

Hall of Fame: Jon D. Carsey, Joseph C. Lincoln.

Officers: P. F. Bikle, president; Maj. L. B. Bachtell, vice-president; W. S. Ivans, vice-president; J. M. Robertson, secretary; B. M. Ryan, treasurer; R. S. Barnaby and Dr. W. B. Klemperer, honorary vice-president; L. Licher, executive secretary; D. A. Matlin, general counsel.

Directors: J. Anthony, L. Arnold, L. B. Bachtell, P. F. Bikle, W. G. Briegleb, B. Cohen, F. B. Compton, W. Coverdale, C. F. Henderson, W. S. Ivans, R. L. Moore, J. Nowak, T. Page, E. J. Reeves, H. C. Ross, J. D. Ryan, E. D. Seymour, R. B.

Smith, S. Starr, O. Zauner, and J. M. Robertson, B. M. Ryan, P. A. Schweizer, H. Selvidge, and F. J. Sweet, directors-at-large.

Soaring Year 1962

Event of the Year: Dedication of Gold "C" and Diamond Award Plaque at Smithsonian.

W. E. Eaton Memorial Trophy: Richard E. Schreder.

R. C. du Pont Memorial Trophy: John D. Ryan.

L. B. Barringer Memorial Trophy: Harold W. Jensen.

P. E. Tuntland Memorial Award: No award.

The Larissa Stroukoff Memorial Trophy: C. M. Mears, Jr.

Hall of Fame: William S. Ivans, Richard E. Schreder.

Officers: P. F. Bikle, president; T. Page, vice-president; J. D. Ryan, vice-president; J. Robertson, secretary; B. M. Ryan, treasurer; R. S. Barnaby and W. B. Klemperer, honorary vice-president; L. Licher, executive director, D. A. Matlin, general counsel.

Directors: J. Anthony, L. Arnold, L. B. Bachtell, P. F. Bikle, R. E. Brown, W. Coverdale, W. S. Ivans, N. MacLeod, D. S. May, R. L. Moore, T. Page, W. F. Placek, E. J. Reeves, H. C. Ross, J. D. Ryan, R. E. Schreder, P. A. Schweizer, R. B. Smith, S. Starr, O. Zauner; and K. P. McNaughton, J. J. Randall, J. M. Robertson, B. M. Ryan, H. Selvidge, and F. J. Sweet, directors-at-large.

Soaring Year 1963

Event of the Year: Symon Wave Memorial Awards are established.

W. E. Eaton Memorial Trophy: Dr. Wolfgang B. Klemperer.

R. C. du Pont Memorial Trophy: Richard E. Schreder.

L. B. Barringer Memorial Trophy: Alvin H. Parker.

P. E. Tuntland Memorial Award: Paul F. Bikle.

The Larissa Stroukoff Memorial Trophy: Richard E. Schreder.

Hall of Fame: F. J. Sweet, G. Moffat.

Officers: W. S. Ivans, president; N. MacLeod, vice-president; J. D. Ryan, vice-president; J. Robertson and M. Coverdale, secretary; T. E. Sharp, treasurer; R. S. Barnaby and W. B. Klemperer, honorary vice-president; L. Licher, executive secretary; D. A. Matlin, general counsel.

Directors: L. Arnold, P. F. Bikle, R. E. Brown, M. Coverdale, W. Coverdale, S. du Pont, W. S. Ivans, N. MacLeod, D. S. May, R. L. Moore, T. Page, W. F. Placek, E. J. Reeves, H. C. Ross, J. D. Ryan, R. E. Schreder, P. A. Schweizer, B. S. Smith, S. Starr, O. Zauner; and T. E. Sharp, M. Claybourn, F. J. Sweet, J. Robertson, H. Selvidge, and A. Boyd, directors-at-large.

Soaring Year 1964

Event of the Year: First 1,000-kilometer flight.

Lilienthal Medal: Alvin H. Parker.

W. E. Eaton Memorial Trophy: Paul F. Bikle.

R. C. du Pont Memorial Trophy: Richard H. Johnson.

L. B. Barringer Memorial Trophy: Alvin H. Parker.

P. E. Tuntland Memorial Award: Hans Zacher.

The Larissa Stroukoff Memorial Trophy: J. D. Ryan.

Hall of Fame: Raymond H. Parker, Irving O. Prue.

Officers: W. S. Ivans, president; Otto Zauner, vice-president; J. D. Ryan, vice-president; M. Coverdale, secretary; T. E. Sharp, treasurer; W. B. Klemperer and R. S. Barnaby, honorary vice-president; L. Licher, executive secretary; D. A. Matlin, general counsel.

Directors: L. Arnold, P. F. Bikle, M. Coverdale, W. Coverdale, S. du Pont, B. Greene, W. S. Ivans, D. McNay, D. S. May, R. L. Moore, W. F. Placek, E. J. Reeves, H. C. Ross, J. D. Ryan, R. E. Schreder, P. A. Schweizer, F. Sebek, B. S. Smith, S. V. Starr, O. Zauner; and M. Claybourn, T. Page, H. Selvidge, T. E. Sharp, F. J. Sweet, and J. Tolson, directors-at-large.

Soaring Year 1965

Event of the Year: Fiberglass sailplanes are introduced.

W. E. Eaton Memorial Trophy: J. D. Ryan.

R. C. du Pont Memorial Trophy: Dean Svec.

L. B. Barringer Memorial Trophy: Alvin H. Parker.

The Larissa Stroukoff Memorial Trophy: Richard E. Schreder.

Hall of Fame: Alvin H. Parker, Wallace A. Scott.

SSA Exceptional Service Award: Walter B. Hausler, William S. Ivans, Donald Mosher.

Officers: J. D. Ryan, president; B. W. Greene, vice-president; R. L. Moore, vice-president; T. Page, secretary; T. E. Sharp, treasurer; L. Licher, executive secretary; D. A. Matlin, general counsel.

Directors: L. Arnold, P. F. Bikle, F. B. Compton, M. Coverdale, W. Coverdale, S. du Pont, B. W. Greene, W. S. Ivans, D. May, D. McNay, R. L. Moore, E. J. Reeves, J. D. Ryan, R. E. Schreder, P. A. Schweizer, B. S. Smith, R. B. Smith, S. V. Starr, J. C. Wright, O. Zauner; and M. Claybourn, T. Page, H. Selvidge, T. E. Sharp and F. J. Sweet, directors-at-large.

Soaring Year 1966

Event of the Year: Wave flying spreads out around the United States.

W. E. Eaton Memorial Trophy: Irving O. Prue.

R. C. du Pont Memorial Trophy: Richard E. Schreder.

L. B. Barringer Memorial Trophy: Mike Berger.

The Larissa Stroukoff Memorial Trophy: George B. Moffat, Jr.

Hall of Fame: John D. Ryan, Harvey Stephens.

Exceptional Service Award: Charles F. Abel, Paul A. Schweizer.

Exceptional Achievement Award: George B. Moffat, Jr.

Officers: J. D. Ryan, president; B. Greene, vice-president; S. V. Starr, vice-president; T. Page, secretary;

T. E. Sharp, treasurer; R. S. Barnaby, honorary president; L. Licher, executive secretary; D. A. Matlin, general counsel.

Directors: P. F. Bikle, F. B. Compton, M. Coverdale, W. Coverdale, S. du Pont, B. Greene, W. S. Ivans, R. L. Klemmedson, D. May, D. McNay, C. M. Mears, R. L. Moore, E. J. Reeves, J. D. Ryan, R. E. Schreder, P. A. Schweizer, B. S. Smith, R. B. Smith, J. C. Wright, O. Zauner; and B. Allen, T. Page, H. Selvidge, T. E., Sharp, S. V. Starr, and F. J. Sweet, directors-at-large.

Soaring Year 1967

Event of the Year: The explosion of interest in soaring.

W. E. Eaton Memorial Trophy: Richard H. Johnson.

R. C. du Pont Memorial Trophy: Andrew J. Smith.

L. B. Barringer Memorial Trophy: Wallace A. Scott.

P. E. Tuntland Memorial Award: Alan C. Bemis.

The Larissa Stroukoff Memorial Trophy: A. J. Smith.

Paul Tissandier Diploma: William S. Ivans.

Hall of Fame: Alexis Dawydoff, Elizabeth Woodward.

Exceptional Service: S. A. Aldott, Lloyd Licher, H. M. Claybourn, Bertha Ryan.

Officers: S. V. Starr, president; M. Coverdale, vice-president; J. C. Wright, vice-president; T. Page, secretary; T. E. Sharp, treasurer; R. S. Barnaby, honorary vice-president; L. Licher, executive secretary; D. A. Matlin, general counsel.

Directors: P. F. Bikle, E. H. Butts, H. M. Claybourn, F. D. Compton, M. Coverdale, W. Coverdale, S. du Pont, F. Harris, W. S. Ivans, R. Johnson, R. L. Klemmedson, D. May, C. M. Mears, W. Mullen, R. E. Schreder, P. A. Schweizer, B. S. Smith, R. B. Smith, F. J. Sweet, J. C. Wright; and B. Allen, T. Page, H. Selvidge, T. E. Sharp, S. Starr, and G. Voltz, directors-at-large.

Soaring Year 1968
Event of the Year: Karl Striedieck sets world out-and-return record.

W. E. Eaton Memorial Trophy: Leslie Arnold.

R. C. du Pont Memorial Trophy: Ben Greene.

L. B. Barringer Memorial Trophy: Wallace A. Scott.

P. E. Tuntland Memorial Award: Pat Beaty and Fritz Johl.

The Larissa Stroukoff Memorial Trophy: Glen Derijinsky, Jr.

Paul Tissandier Diploma: P. F. Bikle.

Hall of Fame: A. J. Smith, Helen R. Dick.

Kolstad Youth Scholarship Award: Michael Opitz.

Exceptional Achievements: Jean Doty.

Officers: S. V. Starr, president; M. Coverdale, vice-president; H. M. Claybourn, vice-president; T. Page, secretary; T. E. Sharp, treasurer; Capt. R. S. Barnaby and E. J. Reeves, honorary vice-president; L. Licher, executive secretary; M. Goldman, general counsel.

Directors: P. F. Bikle, H. M. Claybourn, F. B. Compton, M. Coverdale, W. Coverdale, S. du Pont, F. Harris, L. Hull, W. S. Ivans, D. Johnson, R. H. Johnson, R. L. Klemmedson, D. May, C. M. Mears, W. Mullen, P. A. Schweizer, A. J. Smith, B. S. Smith, F. J. Sweet; and B. Allen, T. Page, J. Ryan, H. Selvidge, T. E. Sharp, and S. V. Starr, directors-at-large.

Soaring Year 1969
Event of the Year: SSA adds a Standard Class National.

W. E. Eaton Memorial Trophy: H. Marshall Claybourn.

R. C. du Pont Memorial Trophy: George B. Moffat, Jr.

L. B. Barringer Memorial Trophy: W. A. Scott.

P. E. Tuntland Memorial Award: No award.

The Larissa Stroukoff Memorial Trophy: Wallace A. Scott.

Hall of Fame: H. M. Claybourn, Jack Laister.

Officers: B. S. Smith, president; M. Coverdale, vice-president; H. M. Claybourn, vice-president; L. Hull, secretary; T. E. Sharp, treasurer; R. S. Barnaby and E. J. Reeves, honorary vice-president; L. Licher, executive secretary; M. L. Goodman, general counsel.

Directors: P. F. Bikle, R. Chase, H. M. Claybourn, F. B. Compton, M. Coverdale, W. Coverdale, S. du Pont, F. Harris, L. Hull, W. S. Ivans, D. Johnson, R. H. Johnson, D. May, W. Mullen, J. M. Robertson, P. A. Schweizer, E. Seagers, A. J. Smith, B. S. Smith, F. J. Sweet; and B. Allen, R. B. Buck, J. Ryan, R. E. Schreder, H. Selvidge, and T. E. Sharp, directors-at-large.

Soaring Year 1970
Event of the Year: First U.S.-conducted World Soaring Championship.

W. E. Eaton Memorial Trophy: Lloyd and Rose Marie Licher.

R. C. du Pont Memorial Trophy: Ross Briegleb.

L. B. Barringer Memorial Trophy: Ben Greene and Wallace Scott.

P. E. Tuntland Memorial Award: Paul F. Bikle.

The Larissa Stroukoff Memorial Trophy: James G. Smiley.

Standard Class Trophy: George B. Moffat, Jr.

Hall of Fame: Ben W. Greene, E. J. Reeves.

SSA Special Service Award: M. Coverdale, W. S. Ivans, Catherine Jones, Bonnett Rogers, Theodore E. Sharp, B. S. Smith, S. V. Starr.

SSA Special Achievements: E. H. Butts, C. C. Conway, B. W. Greene, Fritz Kahl, George B. Moffat, Jr., Wallace A. Scott, A. J. Smith, J. Williams, and the Southern California Competition Club.

Officers: B. S. Smith, president; M. Coverdale, vice-president; J. Cohen, vice-president; L. Hull, secretary; T. E. Sharp, treasurer; R. S. Barnaby and E. J. Reeves, honorary vice-president; L. Licher, executive secretary; M. Goldman, general counsel.

Directors: P. F. Bikle, T. Chase, F. B. Compton, M. Coverdale, W. Coverdale, S. du Pont, H. Higgins, L. Hull, W. S. Ivans, H. Lattimore, R. H. Johnson, D. May, T. Page, J. D. Ryan, P. A. Schweizer, E. Seagers, A. J. Smith, B. S. Smith, F. J. Sweet, J. Williams; and B. Allen, J. Conn, M. Griffith, R. E. Schreder, H. Selvidge, and T. E. Sharp, directors-at-large.

Soaring Year 1971 *Event of the Year:* The Hang Glider Position Paper.

W. E. Eaton Memorial Trophy: Florence and Walter Hausler.

R. C. du Pont Memorial Trophy: A. J. Smith.

L. B. Barringer Memorial Trophy: Wallace A. Scott.

P. E. Tuntland Memorial Award: P. F. Bikle.

The Larissa Stroukoff Memorial Trophy: A. J. Smith.

Paul Tissandier Diploma: F. J. Sweet.

Standard Class Trophy: Rudy Allemann.

Hall of Fame: Laurence E. Edgar, Virginia M. Schweizer.

Officers: B. S. Smith, president; M. Coverdale, vice-president; L. Cohen, vice-president; L. Hull, secretary; T. E. Sharp, treasurer; R. S. Barnaby and E. J. Reeves, honorary vice-president; L. Licher, executive secretary; Charles D. Glattly, general counsel.

Directors: P. F. Bikle, R. A. Chase, M. Coverdale, W. Coverdale, S. du Pont, H. Higgins, A. E. Hurst, W. S. Ivans, J. M. Karlovich, H. Lattimore, T. Page, H. Meline, J. D. Ryan, P. A. Schweizer, E. Seagers, A. J. Smith, B. S. Smith, F. J. Sweet, J. Williams, L. Wood; and B. Allen, J. Conn, L. Hull, M. Griffith, R. E. Schreder, and T. E. Sharp, directors-at-large.

Soaring Year 1972 *Events of the Year:* The First Soaring Convention.

W. E. Eaton Memorial Trophy: Helen R. Dick.

R. C. du Pont Memorial Trophy: Raymond Gimmey.

L. B. Barringer Memorial Trophy: Wallace A. Scott.

P. E. Tuntland Memorial Award: Alcide Santilli.

The Larissa Stroukoff Memorial Trophy: Robert Chase.

Standard Class Championship Trophy: Tom Beltz.

Hall of Fame: Francis B. Compton, Bertha M. Ryan.

SSA Exceptional Service Award: Alice Fuchs, William R. Fuchs, T. Page, Harner Selvidge.

SSA Exceptional Achievement Award: Helen R. Dick, Betsy Howell, Karl Striedieck.

Kolstad Youth Scholarship: William Fenton.

Officers: Miles Coverdale, president; Marion Griffith, vice-president; John W. Williams, vice-president; Lewin Hull, secretary; Theodore E. Sharp, treasurer; R. S. Barnaby and E. J. Reeves, honorary vice-president; L. Licher, executive secretary; Charles D. Glattly, general counsel.

Directors: P. F. Bikle, M. Coverdale, Samuel Francis, H. Higgins, A. E. Hurst, W. S. Ivans, J. M. Karlovich, H. Lattimore, H. R. Meline, T. Page, J. D. Ryan, R. E. Schreder, P. A. Schweizer, R. Semans, A. J. Smith, B. S. Smith, F. J. Sweet, G. Tweed, J. W. Williams, L. Wood; and B. Allen, J. Conn, M. Griffith, L. Hull, R. Lecrone, and T. E. Sharp, directors-at-large.

Soaring Year 1973 *Event of the Year:* The Standard Class "flap" continues.

W. E. Eaton Memorial Trophy: Thomas Page.

R. C. du Pont Memorial Trophy: George B. Moffat, Jr.

L. B. Barringer Memorial Trophy: Wallace A. Scott.

The Larissa Stroukoff Memorial Trophy: Thomas Brandies.

Standard Class Championship Trophy: Karl Striedieck.

Hall of Fame: Albert Hastings—Parker Leonard.

SSA Exceptional Service Award: E. H. Butts, George Uveges.

SSA Exceptional Achievement Award: William Holbrook, George B. Moffat, Jr.

Kolstad Youth Scholarship: John Carver.

Officers: Marion Griffith, president; A. E. Hurst, vice-president; L. Wood, vice-president; R. Semans, secretary; T. E. Sharp, treasurer; R. S. Barnaby and E. J. Reeves, honorary vice-president; L. Licher, executive secretary; C. D. Glattly, general counsel.

Directors: R. Allemann, P. F. Bikle, J. Brittingham, M. Coverdale, S. Francis, A. E. Hurst, W. S. Ivans, J. M. Karlovich, H. Lattimore, H. R. Meline, J. D. Ryan, R. E. Schreder, P. A. Schweizer, R. Semans, A. J. Smith, B. S. Smith, F. J. Sweet, G. Tweed, J. W. Williams, L. Wood; and B. A. Allen, J. Conn, M. Griffith, L. Hull, T. Page, and T. E. Sharp, directors-at-large.

Soaring Year 1974

Event of the Year: The energy crunch affects Soaring.

W. E. Eaton Memorial Trophy: Sterling V. Starr.

R. C. du Pont Memorial Trophy: Ben W. Greene.

L. B. Barringer Memorial Trophy: J. S. Trowbridge.

P. E. Tuntland Memorial Award: Robert T. Lamson.

The Larissa Stroukoff Memorial Trophy: Victor L. Peres.

Standard Class Championship Trophy: R. H. Johnson.

Hall of Fame: Stanley A. Hall, W. C. Holbrook.

Exceptional Service: J. S. Herman, Edward Byars, W. C. Holbrook, M. Griffith, C. Herold.

Exceptional Achievements: W. E. Schuemann.

Kolstad Youth Scholarship: Betsy Shannon.

Officers: Marion Griffith, president; A. E. Hurst, vice-president; L. Wood, vice-president; R. E. Schreder, secretary; T. E. Sharp, treasurer; R. S. Barnaby and E. J. Reeves, honorary vice-pres-

ident; L. Licher, executive secretary; C. D. Glattly, general counsel.

Directors: R. Allemann, J. Brittingham, M. Coverdale, G. Christiansen, W. Cleary, S. Francis, W. S. Ivans, H. Lattimore, T. Page, F. Robinson, J. D. Ryan, R. E. Schreder, P. A. Schweizer, R. Semans, A. J. Smith, B. S. Smith, F. J. Sweet, G. Tweed, B. Utley, J. W. Williams; and B. Allen, J. Conn, M. Griffith, A. E. Hurst, T. E. Sharp, and L. Wood, directors-at-large.

Soaring Year 1975

Event of the Year: SSA reaches 10,000 active members.

W. E. Eaton Memorial Trophy: Joseph C. Lincoln.

R. C. du Pont Memorial Trophy: Richard H. Johnson.

L. B. Barringer Memorial Trophy: Wallace A. Scott.

The Larissa Stroukoff Memorial Trophy: Richard H. Johnson.

Standard Class Championship Trophy: Ross S. Briegleb.

Hall of Fame: Thomas Page, Gustav Scheurer.

Exceptional Service Award: Douglas Lamont, Bernald S. Smith.

Exceptional Achievement Award: Richard H. Ball, Jack W. Laister, Babs Nutt, Hanna Duncan, Edward Minghelli, John R. Gravance, Ernest and Leslie Schweizer.

Kolstad Youth Scholarship: Steve Foreman.

Officers: L. Wood, president; S. Francis, vice-president; R. Semans, vice-president, R. E. Schreder, secretary; T. E. Sharp, treasurer; R. S. Barnaby and E. J. Reeves, honorary vice-president; L. Licher, executive secretary; C. D. Glattly, general counsel.

Directors: R. Allemann, J. Bennis, J. Brittingham, G. Christianson, W. Cleary, D. Culpepper, K. Danielson, Helen Dick, S. Francis, W. S. Ivans, H. Lattimore, T. Page, F. Robinson, J. D. Ryan, R. E. Schreder, P. A. Schweizer, A. J. Smith, B. S. Smith, F. J. Sweet, J. Williams; and B. Allen, W. Coverdale, R. Semans, T. E.

Sharp, B. Utley, and L. Wood, directors-at-large.

Soaring Year 1976 *Event of the Year:* Lloyd Licher resigns.

W. E. Eaton Memorial Trophy: John W.
Williams.

R. C. du Pont Memorial Trophy: Al Leffler.

*L. B. Barringer Memorial Tro-
phy:* Wallace A. Scott.

P. E. Tuntland Memorial Award: Oran
Nicks.

*The Larissa Stroukoff Memorial Tro-
phy:* Andrew J. Smith.

Paul Tissandier Diploma: Richard H.
Johnson.

*Standard Class Championship Tro-
phy:* Raymond Gimmey.

Hall of Fame: H. Selvidge, Robert M.
Stanley.

Exceptional Service Award: Jim and Gerry
Rhine, Raymond L. Shamblen.

*Exceptional Achievement
Award:* Charles W. Shaw.

Officers: L. Wood, president; S. F. Francis, vice-president; R. Semans, vice-
president; R. E. Schreder, secretary;
T. E. Sharp, treasurer; R. S. Barnaby
and E. J. Reeves, honorary vice-president; L. Licher, executive secretary;
C. D. Glattly, general counsel.

Directors: R. Allemann, J. Bennis,
J. Brittingham, D. Culpepper,
G. Christiansen, W. Clarey,
K. Danielson, H. Dick, S. Francis,
M. Griffith, W. S. Ivans, T. Page,
F. Robinson, J. D. Ryan, R. E.
Schreder, P. A. Schweizer,
D. Slotten, A. J. Smith, B. S. Smith,
F. J. Sweet; and B. Allen,
H. Lattimore, R. Semans, T. E.
Sharp, S. V. Starr, and B. Utley, di-
rectors-at-large.

Soaring Year 1977 *Event of the Year:* World's first 1,000-mile
flight.

W. E. Eaton Memorial Trophy: Bernald S.
Smith.

R. C. du Pont Memorial Trophy: Richard
Butler.

*L. B. Barringer Memorial Tro-
phy:* Wallace A. Scott.

*P. E. Tuntland Memorial
Award:* Richard H. Johnson.

*The Larissa Stroukoff Memorial Tro-
phy:* Richard Butler.

Paul Tissandier Diploma: Paul B. Mac-
Cready, Jr.

*Standard Class Championship Tro-
phy:* Eric H. Mozer.

Schreder 15-Meter Class Trophy: Karl
Striedieck.

Hall of Fame: Stephen J. Bennis,
Bernard L. Wiggin.

*SSA Exceptional Achievement
Award:* Paul B. MacCready and
Gossamer Condor Team, Karl H.
Striedieck, Col. Joe Engle, USAF, and
the Enterprise Team.

Kolstad Youth Scholarship: Kim McEligot.

Officers: W. Cleary, president; B. Utley,
vice-president; S. Francis, vice-president; R. E. Schreder, secretary; T. E.
Sharp, treasurer; R. S. Barnaby and
E. J. Reeves, honorary vice-president; F. W. Blossom, executive secretary; C. D. Glattly and D. S. Kirbach,
general counsel.

Directors: R. Allemann, J. Bennis,
J. Brittingham, G. Christiansen,
K. Danielson, H. Dick, S. Fly,
S. Francis, M. Griffith, W. S. Ivans,
T. Page, J. D. Ryan, T. E. Schreder,
P. A. Schweizer, D. Slotten, A. J.
Smith, B. S. Smith, F. J. Sweet,
G. Voltz, W. Woodward; and
W. Cleary, V. Powell, T. E. Sharp,
S. V. Starr, and B. Utley, directors-at-
large.

Soaring Year 1978 *Event of the Year:* Washington Convention
aids FAA exposure.

*W. E. Eaton Memorial Tro-
phy:* Theodore E. Sharp.

*R. C. du Pont Memorial Tro-
phy:* Andrew J. Smith.

*L. B. Barringer Memorial Tro-
phy:* Wallace A. Scott.

P. E. Tuntland Memorial Award: NASA-
FAA-SSA Team.

*The Larissa Stroukoff Memorial Tro-
phy:* Andrew J. Smith.

Paul Tissandier Diploma: Gustav Scheurer.

Standard Class Championship Trophy: Laszlo Horvath.

Schreder 15-Meter Class Trophy: George B. Moffat, Jr.

Hall of Fame: William H. Coverdale, Chester J. Decker.

Exceptional Service Awards: William B. Cleary, Charles T. McKinnie.

Exceptional Achievement Award: William D. English, Jr.

Kolstad Youth Scholarship: Jeffrey Ohmart, Todd Tracey.

Officers: W. Cleary, president; B. Utley, vice president; S. Francis, vice president; R. E. Schreder, secretary; T. E. Sharp, treasurer; R. S. Barnaby, and E. J. Reeves, honorary vice-president; F. B. Blossom, executive secretary; D. Kirbach, general counsel.

Directors: R. Allemann, J. Bennis, J. Brittingham, G. Christiansen, S. Fly, S. Francis, M. Griffith, W. S. Ivans, R. Kramer, D. Knypstra, T. Page, J. D. Ryan, R. E. Schreder, P. A. Schweizer, D. Slotten; A. J. Smith, B. S. Smith, F. J. Sweet, G. Voltz, W. Woodward; and W. Cleary, V. Powell, T. E. Sharp, S. V. Starr, B. Utley, and L. Wood, directors-at-large.

Soaring Year 1979 Event of the Year: The FAA airspace problem.

W. E. Eaton Memorial Trophy: William B. Cleary.

R. C. du Pont Memorial Trophy: Richard B. Butler.

L. B. Barringer Memorial Trophy: Wallace A. Scott.

P. E. Tuntland Memorial Award: Richard H. Johnson.

The Larissa Stroukoff Memorial Trophy: Richard W. Butler.

Standard Class Championship Trophy: Dave Culpepper.

Schreder-15 Meter Class Trophy: Eric H. Mozer.

Hall of Fame: Alcide Santilli, Sterling V. Starr.

Exceptional Service Awards: J. V. Doty, C. V. Lindsay, T. Page.

Exceptional Achievement Award: Stanley W. Smith.

Kolstad Youth Scholarship: None.

Officers: B. G. Utley, president; W. Woodward, vice-president; C. D. Herold, vice-president; R. E. Schreder, secretary; T. E. Sharp, treasurer; R. S. Barnaby and E. J. Reeves, honorary vice-president; F. Blossom, executive secretary; D. Kirbach, general counsel.

Directors: J. Bennis, J. M. Brittingham, S. E. Fly, S. A. Francis, R. N. Hall, E. G. Hammond, C. D. Herold, W. S. Ivans, D. Knypstra, R. T. Lamson, H. M. Lattimore, T. Page, R. E. Schreder, P. A. Schweizer, D. R. Slotten, A. J. Smith, B. S. Smith, F. J. Sweet, W. Woodward, R. A. Young; and B. Allen, W. B. Cleary, R. K. Ferguson, T. E. Sharp, S. V. Starr, and B. G. Utley, directors-at-large.

Soaring Year 1980 Event of the Year: 50th Anniversary of the First National.

W. E. Eaton Memorial Trophy: Douglas and Lianna Lamont.

R. C. du Pont Memorial Trophy: Richard W. Butler.

L. B. Barringer Memorial Trophy: Wallace A. Scott.

P. E. Tuntland Memorial Award: David J. Marsden.

The Larissa Stroukoff Memorial Trophy: Richard W. Butler.

Standard Class Championship Trophy: Karl H. Striedieck.

Schreder-15 Meter Class Trophy: Karl H. Striedieck.

Hall of Fame: Karl H. Striedieck; Victor M. Saudek.

Exceptional Service Awards: Stanley A. Hall, Hal M. Lattimore, E. J. Reeves, Bertha M. Ryan, Charlie Spratt.

Exceptional Achievement Award: Nelson Shapter.

Kolstad Youth Scholarship: Alice Goodlette, John Mills.

Officers: B. G. Utley, president; W. Woodward, vice-president; C. D. Herold, vice-president; R. E. Schreder, secretary; T. E. Sharp, treasurer; R. S. Barnaby and E. J. Reeves, honorary vice-president; John Dezzutti, executive secretary; D. Kirbach, general counsel.

Directors: J. Bennis, J. M. Brittingham, S. A. Francis, R. N. Hall, E. G. Hammond, C. D. Herold, W. S. Ivans, D. Knypstra, R. T. Lamson, H. M. Lattimore, R. E. Schreder, P. A. Schweizer, C. E. Sessions, D. R. Slotten, A. J. Smith, B. S. Smith, F. J. Sweet, B. G. Utley, A. C. Williams, R. A. Young; and B. Allen, W. B. Cleary, R. K. Ferguson, T. E. Sharp, S. V. Starr, and W. Woodward, directors-at-large.

Soaring Year 1981

Event of the Year: SSA's growth stops.

W. E. Eaton Memorial Trophy: Brian G. Utley.

R. C. du Pont Memorial Trophy: Richard H. Johnson.

L. B. Barringer Memorial Trophy: Marion S. Griffith, Jr.

The Larissa Stroukoff Memorial Trophy: Richard H. Johnson.

Standard Class Championship Trophy: Karl Striedieck.

Schreder 15-Meter Class Trophy: Raymond H. Gimmey.

Hall of Fame: William Frank Kelsey, Joachim P. Kuettner.

Exceptional Service Awards: Emil Kissel, John M. Brittingham.

Exceptional Achievement Award: Doris F. Grove, Bernard H. Paiewonsky, Rudolf W. Mozer.

Kolstad Youth Scholarship: David Mockler.

Officers: B. G. Utley, president; C. D. Herold, vice-president; A. C. Williams, vice-president; R. E. Schreder, secretary; T. E. Sharp, treasurer; R. S. Barnaby and E. J. Reeves, honorary vice-president; John P. Dezzutti, executive secretary; D. Kirbach, general counsel.

Directors: J. Bennis, J. M. Brittingham, S. A. Francis, R. N. Hall, E. G. Hammond, C. D. Herold, W. S. Ivans, D. Knypstra, R. T. Lamson, H. M. Lattimore, R. E. Schreder, P. A. Schweizer, C. E. Sessions, D. R. Slotten, A. J. Smith, B. S. Smith, F. J. Sweet, B. G. Utley, A. C. Williams, R. A. Young, and M. I. Barritt, E. W. Langworthy, J. Mead, T. E. Sharp, S. V. Starr, and W. Woodward, directors-at-large.

Soaring Year 1982

Event of the Year: 50th anniversary of SSA.

W. E. Eaton Memorial Trophy: Gustav Scheurer.

R. C. du Pont Memorial Trophy: George B. Moffat, Jr.

L. B. Barringer Memorial Trophy: Wallace A. Scott.

P. E. Tuntland Memorial Award: George J. Vakkur.

The Larissa Stroukoff Memorial Trophy: George B. Moffat, Jr.

Paul Tissandier Diploma: William G. Briegleb.

Standard Class Championship Trophy: Eric H. Mozer.

Schreder 15-Meter Class Trophy: Douglas L. Jacobs.

Hall of Fame: Emil A. Lehecka, Lloyd M. Licher.

Exceptional Service Awards: Richard H. Johnson, Bernald S. Smith.

Exceptional Achievement Awards: Marion I. Barritt, Elbert L. Rutan, Shirley Sliwa.

Officers: C. D. Herold, president; C. E. Sessions, vice-president; A. C. Williams, vice-president; R. E. Schreder, secretary; T. E. Sharp, treasurer; R. S. Barnaby and E. J. Reeves, honorary vice-president; John P. Dezzutti, executive secretary; D. Kirbach, general counsel.

Directors: J. Bennis, S. A. Francis, M. I. Barritt, R. N. Hall, E. G. Hammond, C. D. Herold, W. S. Ivans, D. Knypstra, J. R. Lincoln, H. M. Lattimore, J. Maupin, R. E. Schreder, P. A. Schweizer, C. E. Sessions, A. J. Smith, B. S. Smith, F. J. Sweet, B. G. Utley, A. C. Williams, R. A. Young; and M. S. Griffith, Jr., E. W. Langworthy, J. Mead, T. E. Sharp, S. V. Starr, and W. Woodward, directors-at-large.

Index

Names

Page numbers in italics refer to figure captions

Subjects